SHONEN JUMP MANGA

PIECE

Vol. 87
BITTERSWEET

STORY AND ART BY
EIICHIRO ODA

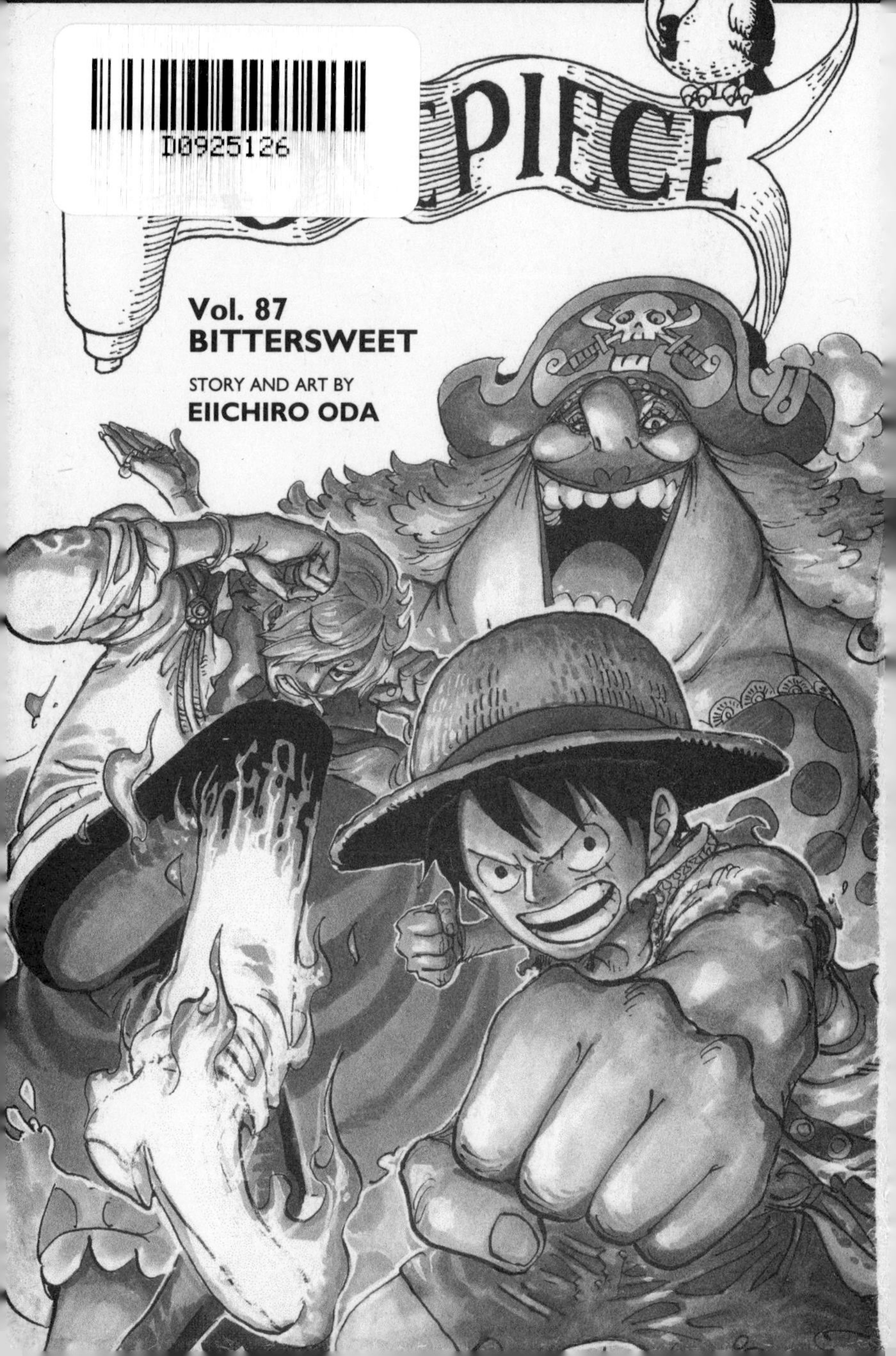

尾田栄一郎

There! I did it! Enjoy volume 87!!

-Eiichiro Oda, 2018

Eiichiro Oda began his manga career at the age of 17, when his one-shot cowboy manga **Wanted!** won second place in the coveted Tezuka manga awards. Oda went on to work as an assistant to some of the biggest manga artists in the industry, including Nobuhiro Watsuki, before winning the Hop Step Award for new artists. His pirate adventure **One Piece**, which debuted in **Weekly Shonen Jump** in 1997, quickly became one of the most popular manga in Japan.

Characters

The Straw Hat Crew

Monkey D. Luffy

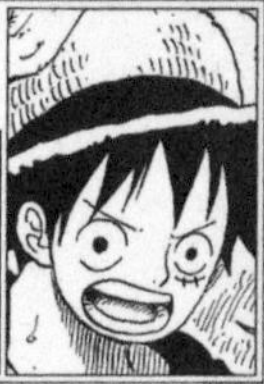

A young man who dreams of becoming the Pirate King. After training with Rayleigh, he and his crew head for the New World!

Captain, Bounty: 500 million berries

Roronoa Zolo

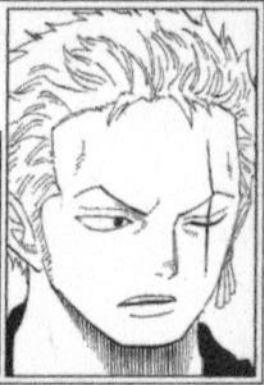

He swallowed his pride and asked to be trained by Mihawk on Gloom Island before reuniting with the rest of the crew.

Fighter, Bounty: 320 million berries

Nami

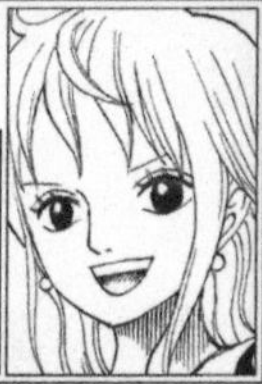

She studied the weather of the New World on the small Sky Island Weatheria, a place where weather is studied as a science.

Navigator, Bounty: 66 million berries

Usopp

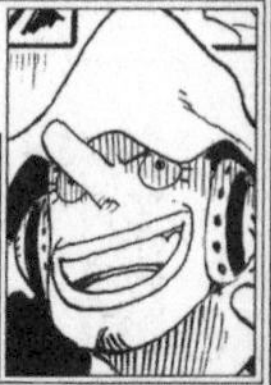

He trained under Heracles at the Bowin Islands to become the King of Snipers.

Sniper, Bounty: 200 million berries

Sanji

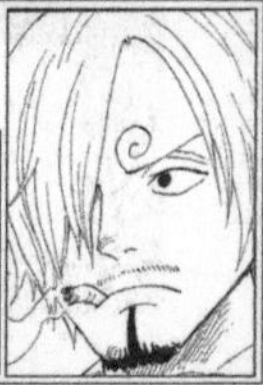

After fighting the New Kama Karate masters in the Kamabakka Kingdom, he returned to the crew.

Cook, Bounty: 177 million berries

Tony Tony Chopper

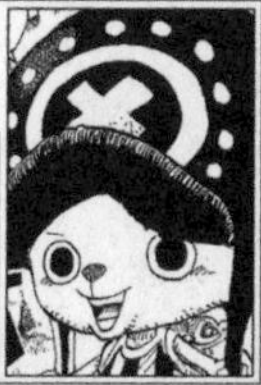

After researching powerful medicine in Birdie Kingdom, he reunited with the rest of the crew.

Ship's Doctor, Bounty: 100 berries

Nico Robin

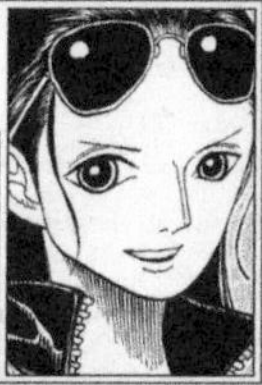

She spent her time in Baltigo with the leader of the Revolutionary Army: Luffy's father, Dragon.

Archeologist, Bounty: 130 million berries

Franky

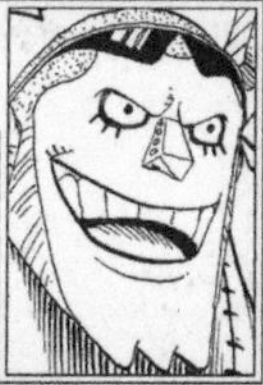

He modified himself in Future Land Baldimore and turned himself into Armored Franky before reuniting with the rest of the crew.

Shipwright, Bounty: 94 million berries

Brook

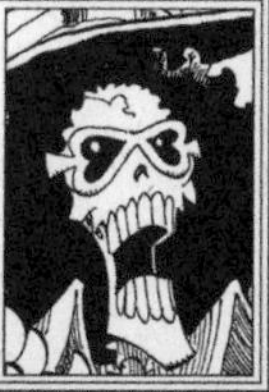

After being captured and used as a freak show by the Longarm Tribe, he became a famous rock star called "Soul King" Brook.

Musician, Bounty: 83 million berries

Shanks

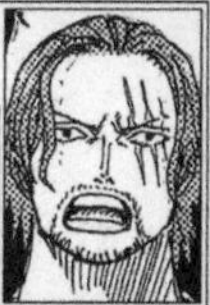

One of the Four Emperors. Waits for Luffy in the "New World," the second half of the Grand Line.

Captain of the Red-Haired Pirates

Big Mom Pirates

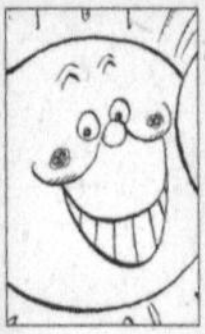
Prometheus the Sun

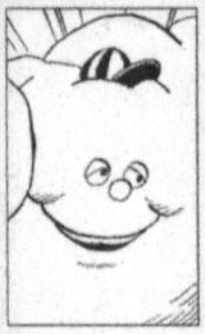
Zeus the Storm Cloud

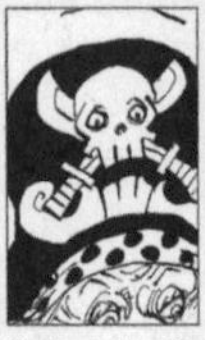
Napoleon the Bicorn Hat

Charlotte Linlin

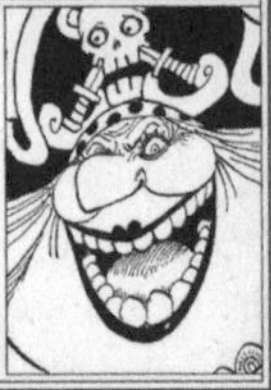

One of the Four Emperors. Known as Big Mom. Uses the Soul-Soul Fruit powers to pull life span from people.

Captain, Big Mom Pirates

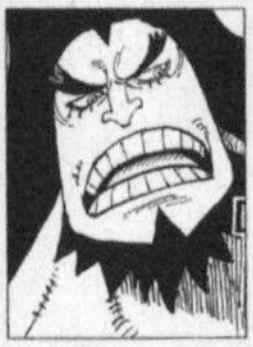
C. Oven

4th Son of Charlotte

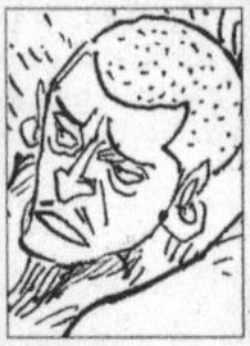
C. Daifuku

3rd Son of Charlotte

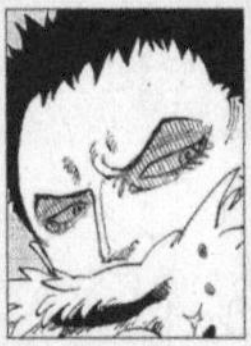
C. Katakuri (Sweet 3)

2nd Son of Charlotte

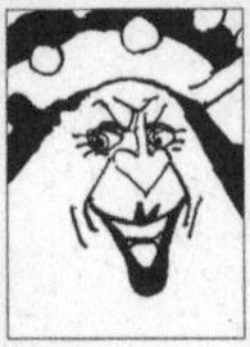
C. Compote

1st Daughter of Charlotte

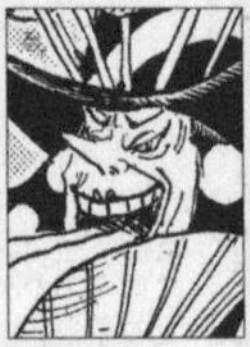
C. Perospero

1st Son of Charlotte

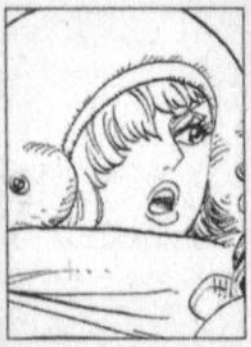
C. Smoothie (Sweet 3)

14th Daughter of Charlotte

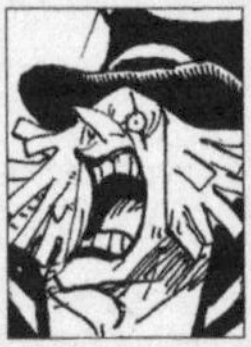
C. Montd'or

19th Son of Charlotte

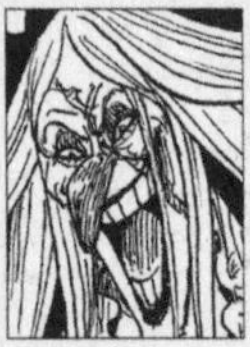
C. Brulee

8th Daughter of Charlotte

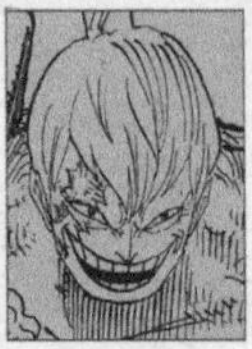
C. Cracker (Sweet 3)

10th Son of Charlotte

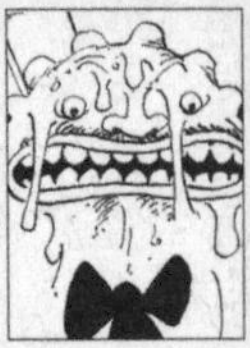
C. Opera

5th Son of Charlotte

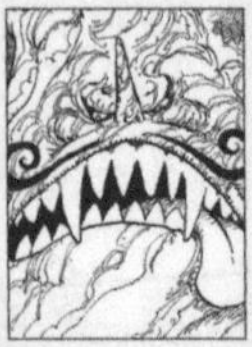
Kingbaum

Master of the Seducing Woods

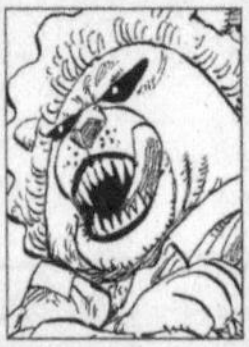
Pekoms

Fighter, Big Mom Pirates

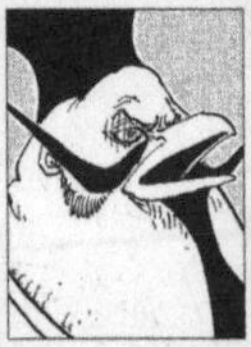
Count Niwatori

Fighter, Big Mom Pirates

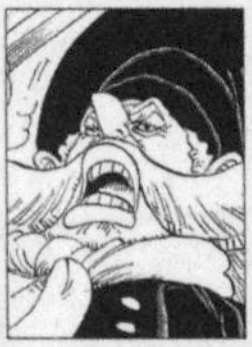
"Gourmet Knight" Streusen

Head Chef, Big Mom Pirates

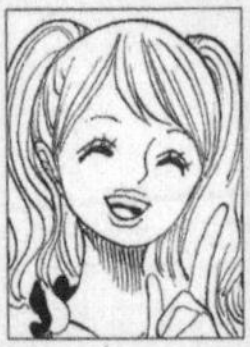
Charlotte Pudding

35th Daughter of Charlotte

As a mere cog of secret plots from both Big Mom and his own family, Sanji is trapped in a bad situation with no apparent way out. When Luffy comes to get him back, Sanji clashes with his former captain, unable to speak his true feelings. Eventually, he breaks down and admits that he wants to return to the *Sunny*. But in order to do that, he needs to prevent Big Mom's true goal—the slaughter of his family! Jimbei's suggestion to tackle this tremendous challenge is to join forces with Bege, but the plan fails spectacularly! Bege then turns into a castle to protect them for a time, but on the outside, the crew is surrounded by deadly foes...

The story of ONE PIECE 1»87

Germa 66

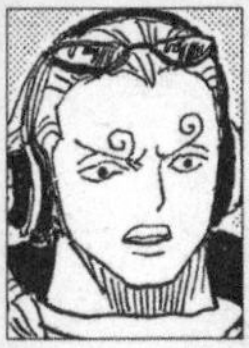
Yonji
Fourth Son of Vinsmoke

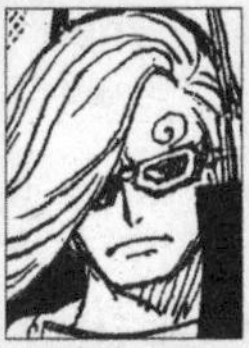
Niji
Second Son of Vinsmoke

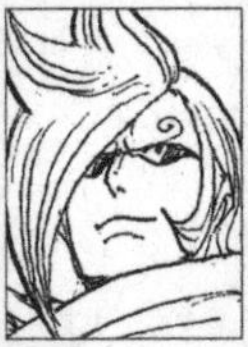
Ichiji
Eldest Son of Vinsmoke

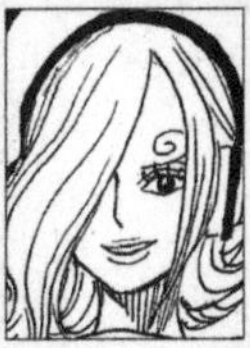
Reiju
Eldest Daughter of Vinsmoke

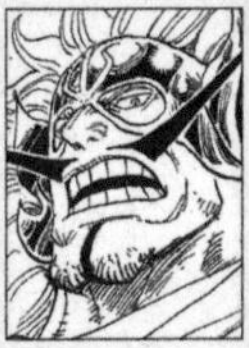
Vinsmoke Judge
King of Germa Kingdom

Firetank Pirates

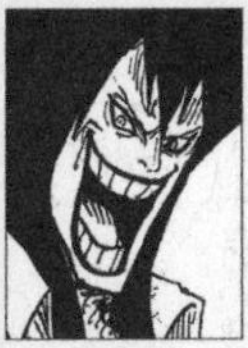
"Gangster" Gastino
Evil Scientist

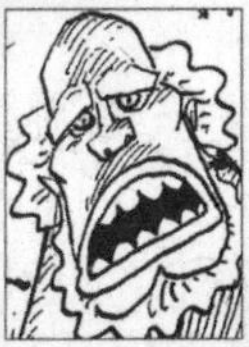
Gotti
Assassin, Firetank Pirates

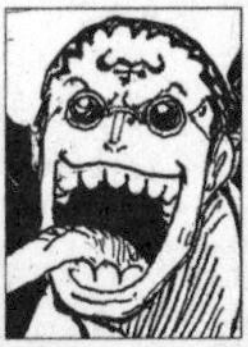
Vito
Consultant, Firetank Pirates

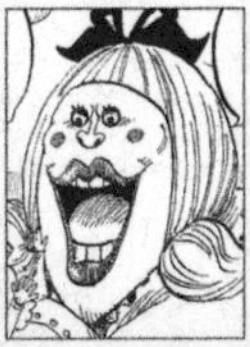
C. Chiffon (Bege's Wife)
22nd Daughter of Charlotte

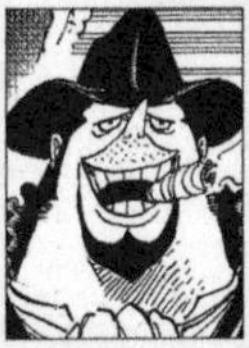
Capone "Gang" Bege
Captain of the Firetank Pirates

Minks

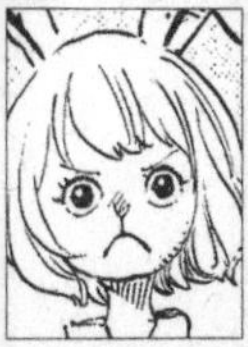
Carrot (Bunny Mink)
Battlebeast Tribe, Kingsbird

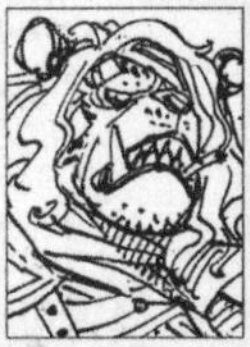
Treetop Pedro (Jaguar Mink)
Leader of the Guardians

Sun Pirates

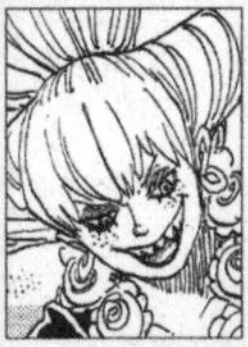
C. Praline (Aladdin's Wife)
21st Daughter of Charlotte

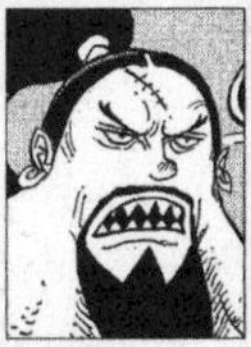
Aladdin
First Mate, Sun Pirates

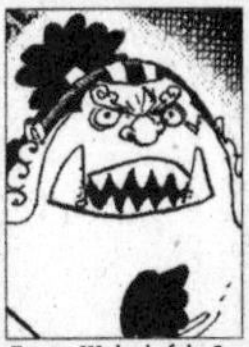
Former Warlord of the Sea
Jimbei
Captain of the Sun Pirates

Story

After two years of hard training, the Straw Hat pirates are back together, first at the Sabaody Archipelago and then through Fish-Man Island to their next stage: the New World!!

After defeating Doflamingo, Luffy and crew's next goal is to topple Kaido, an Emperor of the Sea. But a wrench is thrown into the works when Sanji leaves the crew because he's part of a political marriage to Big Mom's daughter.

Vol. 87
BITTERSWEET

CONTENTS

Chapter 870:
PARTING

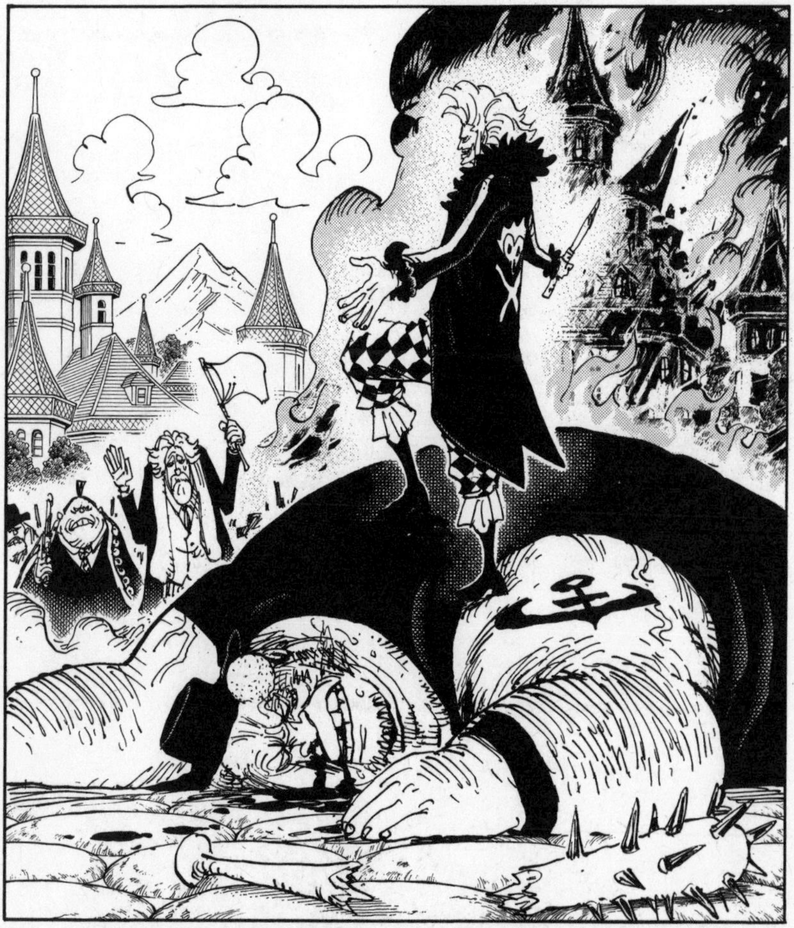

THE SAGA OF THE SELF-PROCLAIMED STRAW HAT FLEET VOL. 7, BARTOLOMEO: "I FIND AND CRUSH THE BADDEST GUY IN PORT"

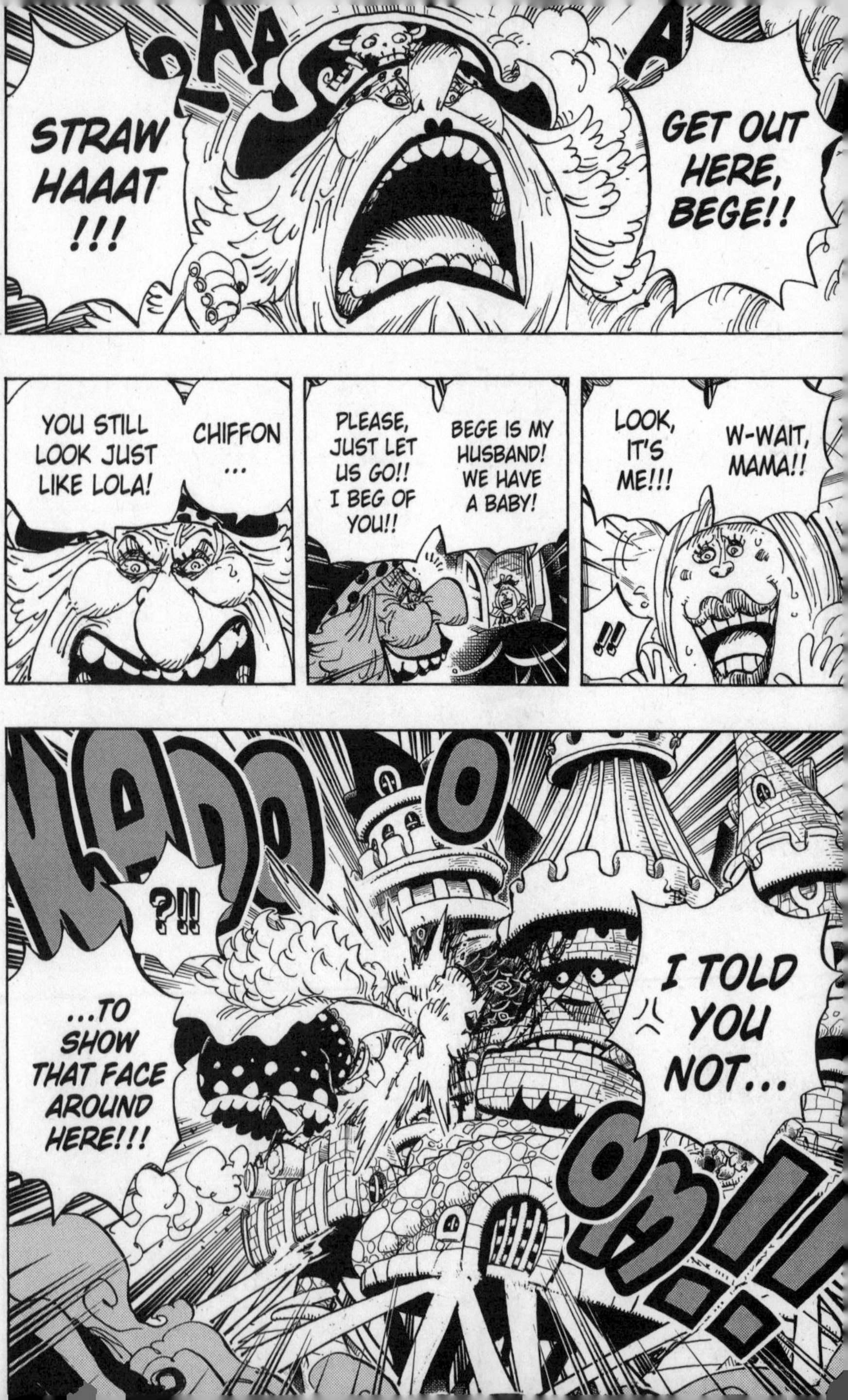
GET OUT HERE, BEGE!!
STRAW HAAAT!!!
W-WAIT, MAMA!!
LOOK, IT'S ME!!!
!!
BEGE IS MY HUSBAND! WE HAVE A BABY!
PLEASE, JUST LET US GO!! I BEG OF YOU!!
CHIFFON ...
YOU STILL LOOK JUST LIKE LOLA!
I TOLD YOU NOT...
?!!
...TO SHOW THAT FACE AROUND HERE!!!

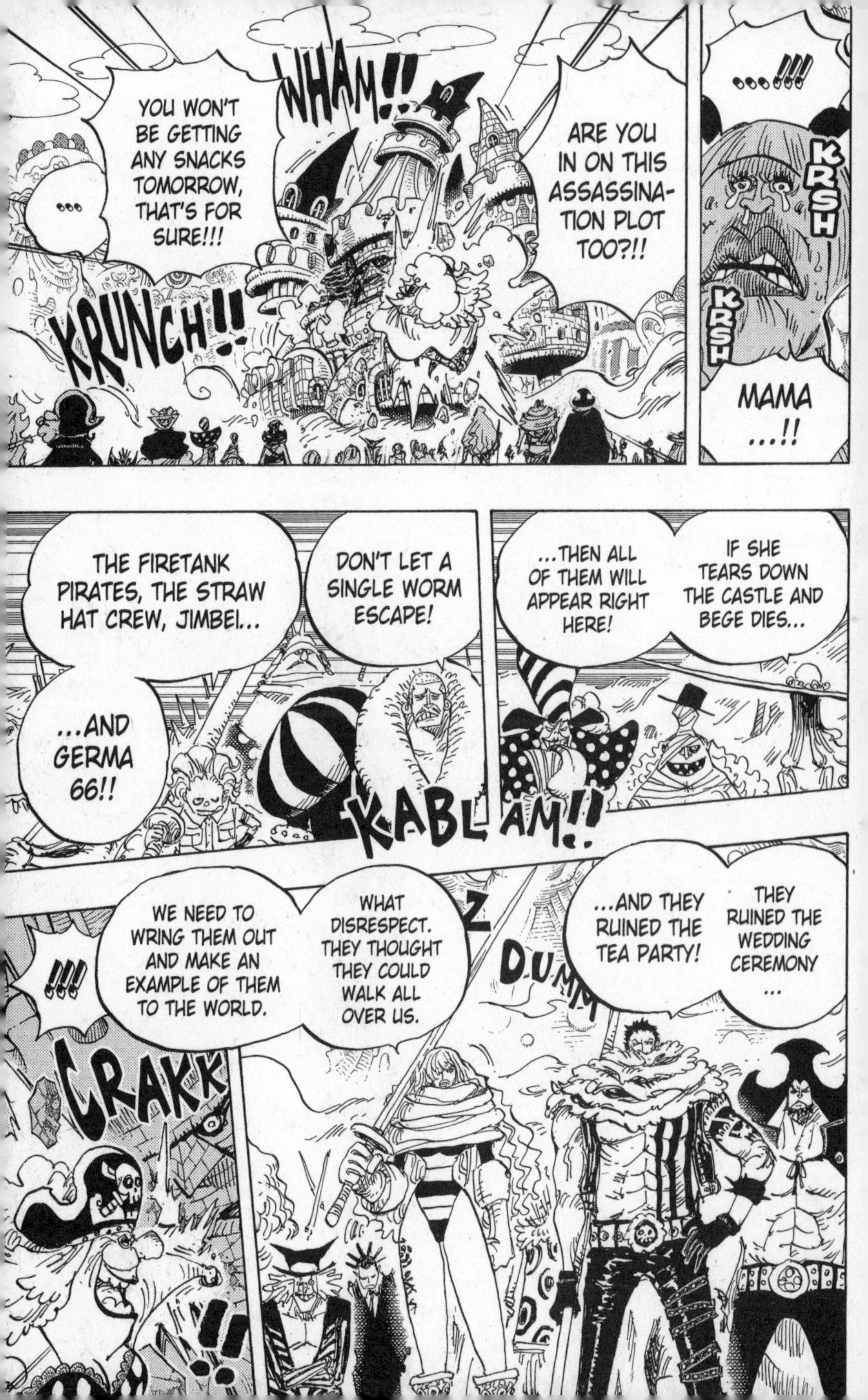
...!!!
KRSH
KRSH
MAMA ...!!
ARE YOU IN ON THIS ASSASSINATION PLOT TOO?!!
WHAM!!
YOU WON'T BE GETTING ANY SNACKS TOMORROW, THAT'S FOR SURE!!!
...
KRUNCH!!
IF SHE TEARS DOWN THE CASTLE AND BEGE DIES...
...THEN ALL OF THEM WILL APPEAR RIGHT HERE!
DON'T LET A SINGLE WORM ESCAPE!
THE FIRETANK PIRATES, THE STRAW HAT CREW, JIMBEI...
...AND GERMA 66!!
KABLAM!!
THEY RUINED THE WEDDING CEREMONY ...
...AND THEY RUINED THE TEA PARTY!
Z
DUMM
WHAT DISRESPECT. THEY THOUGHT THEY COULD WALK ALL OVER US.
WE NEED TO WRING THEM OUT AND MAKE AN EXAMPLE OF THEM TO THE WORLD.
!!!
CRAKK
!!

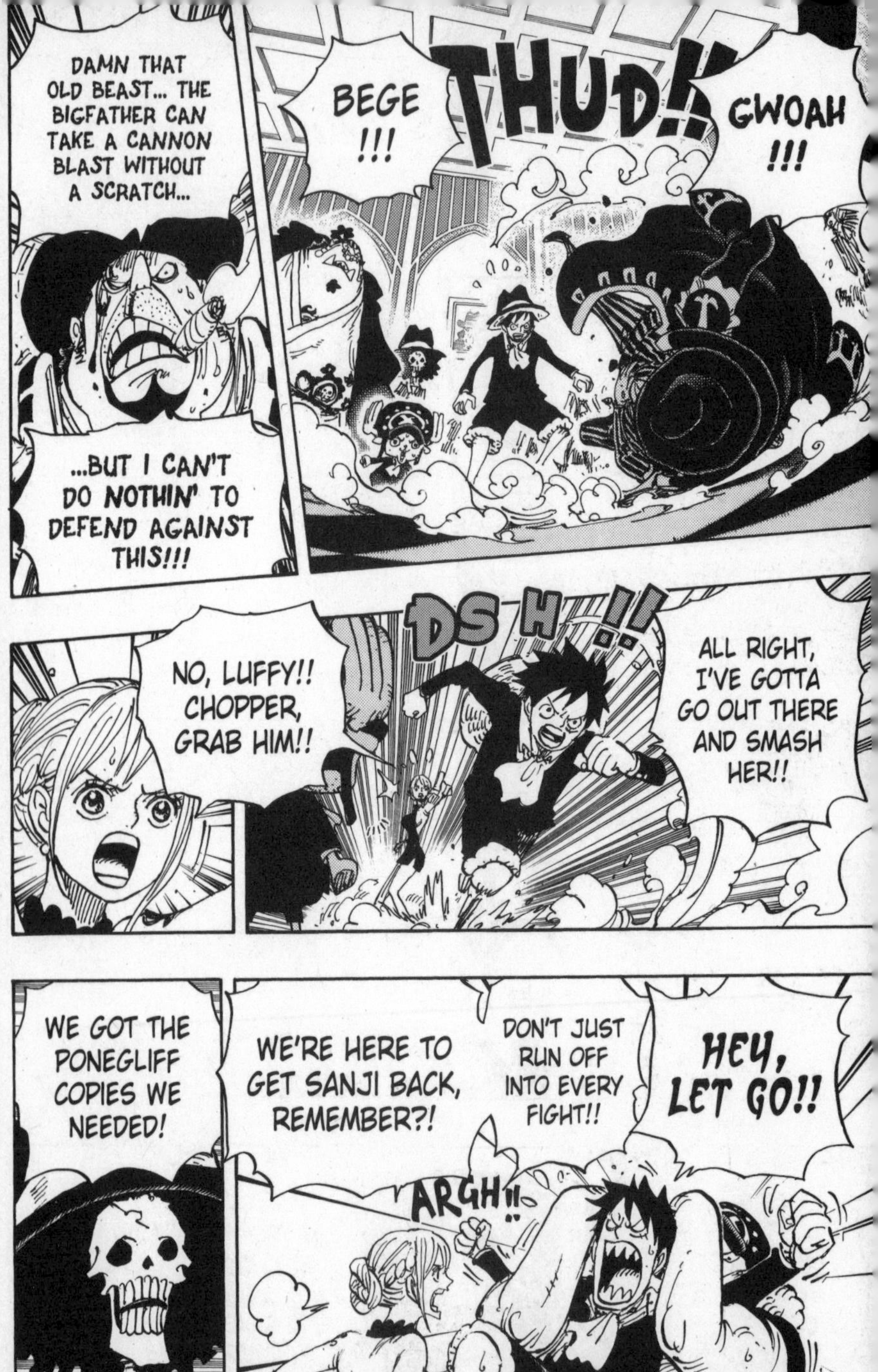
GWOAH !!!
THUD!!
BEGE !!!
DAMN THAT OLD BEAST... THE BIGFATHER CAN TAKE A CANNON BLAST WITHOUT A SCRATCH...
...BUT I CAN'T DO NOTHIN' TO DEFEND AGAINST THIS!!!
ALL RIGHT, I'VE GOTTA GO OUT THERE AND SMASH HER!!
DSH!!
NO, LUFFY!! CHOPPER, GRAB HIM!!
HEY, LET GO!!
DON'T JUST RUN OFF INTO EVERY FIGHT!!
WE'RE HERE TO GET SANJI BACK, REMEMBER?!
ARGH!!
WE GOT THE PONEGLIFF COPIES WE NEEDED!

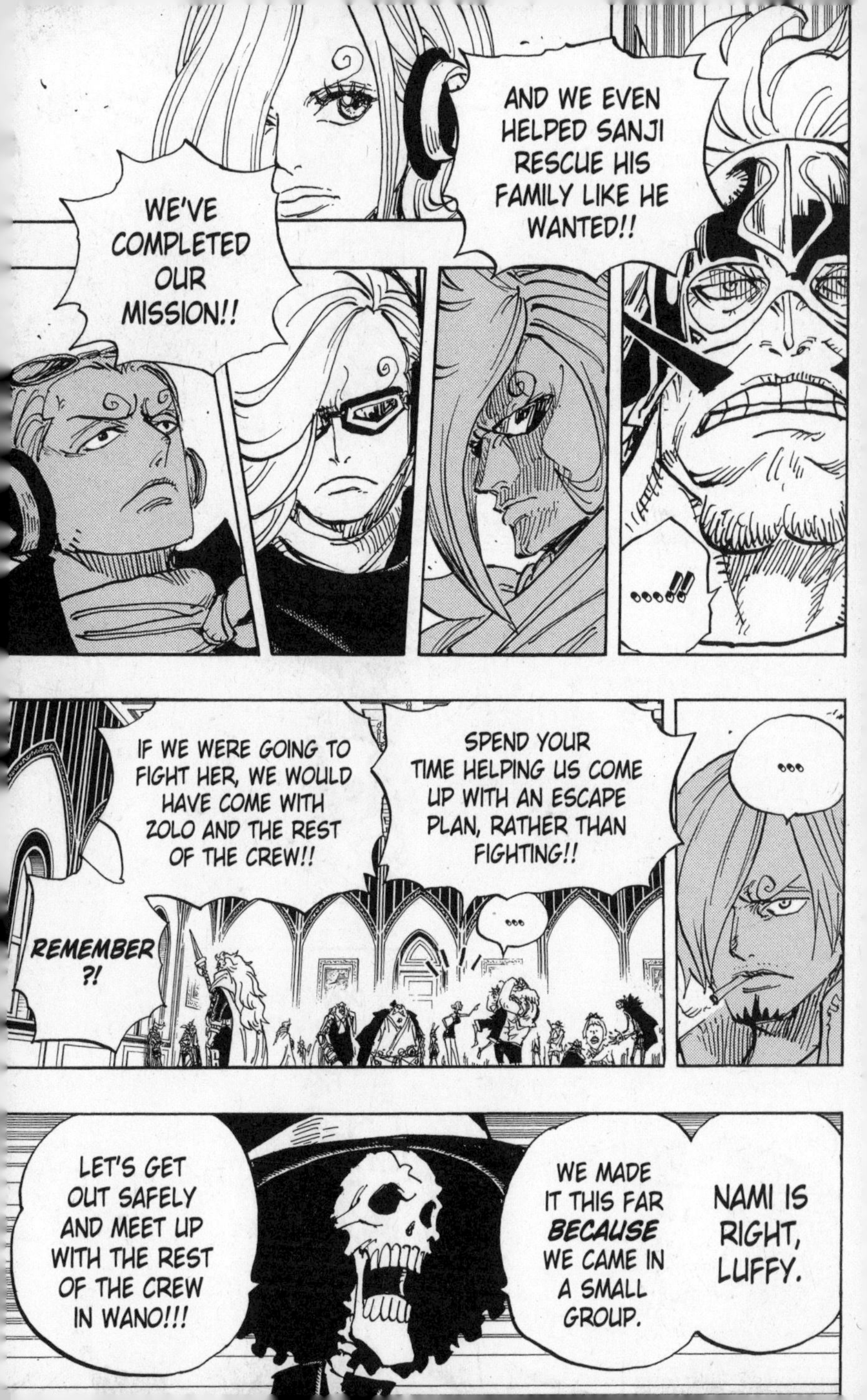
AND WE EVEN HELPED SANJI RESCUE HIS FAMILY LIKE HE WANTED!!
WE'VE COMPLETED OUR MISSION!!
...!!
...
SPEND YOUR TIME HELPING US COME UP WITH AN ESCAPE PLAN, RATHER THAN FIGHTING!!
IF WE WERE GOING TO FIGHT HER, WE WOULD HAVE COME WITH ZOLO AND THE REST OF THE CREW!!
...
REMEMBER ?!
NAMI IS RIGHT, LUFFY.
WE MADE IT THIS FAR BECAUSE WE CAME IN A SMALL GROUP.
LET'S GET OUT SAFELY AND MEET UP WITH THE REST OF THE CREW IN WANO!!!

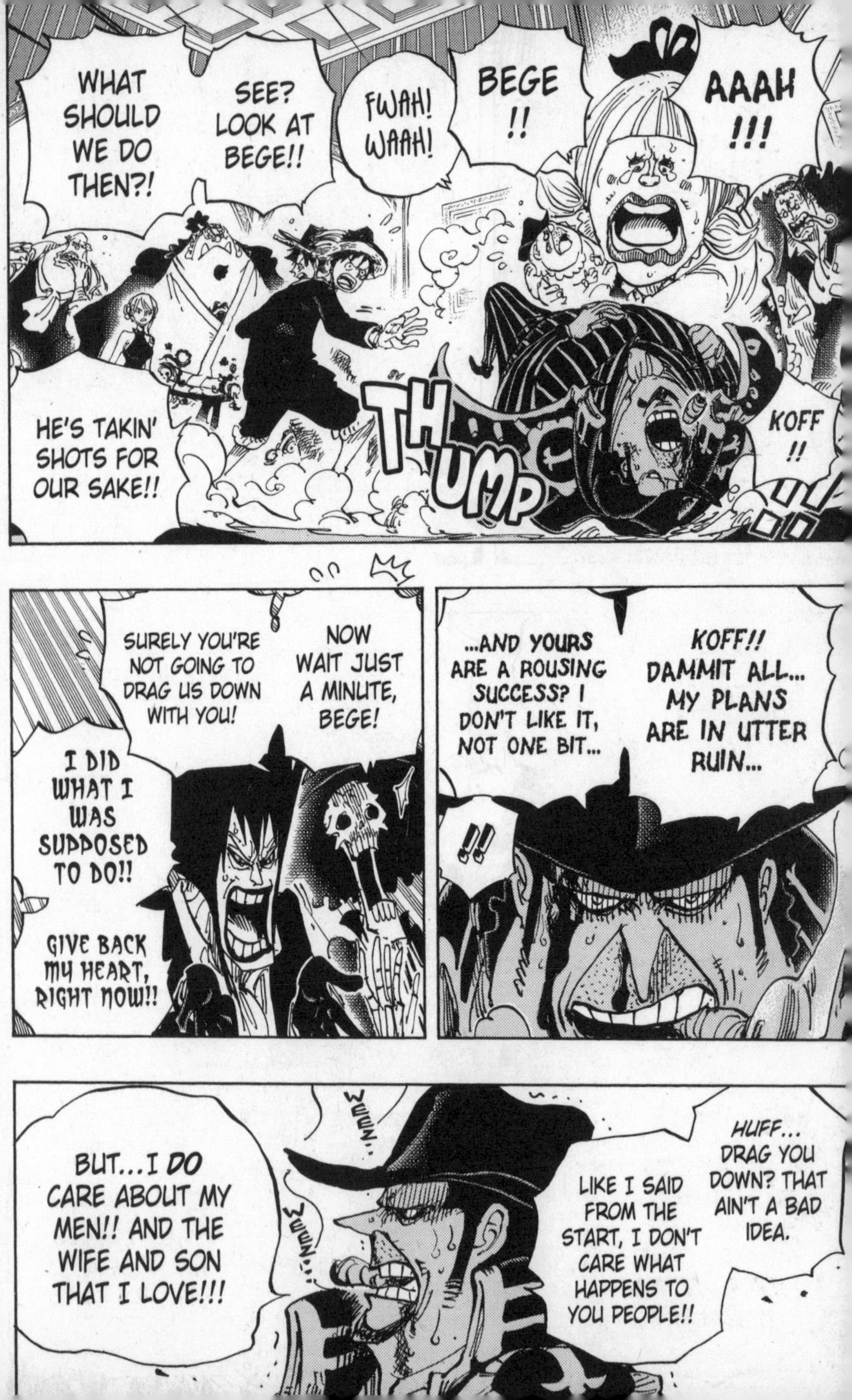

AAAH!!!
BEGE!!
FWAH! WAAH!
SEE? LOOK AT BEGE!!
WHAT SHOULD WE DO THEN?!
KOFF!!
THUMP
HE'S TAKIN' SHOTS FOR OUR SAKE!!
KOFF!! DAMMIT ALL... MY PLANS ARE IN UTTER RUIN...
...AND YOURS ARE A ROUSING SUCCESS? I DON'T LIKE IT, NOT ONE BIT...
!!
NOW WAIT JUST A MINUTE, BEGE!
SURELY YOU'RE NOT GOING TO DRAG US DOWN WITH YOU!
I DID WHAT I WAS SUPPOSED TO DO!!
GIVE BACK MY HEART, RIGHT NOW!!
HUFF... DRAG YOU DOWN? THAT AIN'T A BAD IDEA.
LIKE I SAID FROM THE START, I DON'T CARE WHAT HAPPENS TO YOU PEOPLE!!
WEEZ
WEEZ
BUT...I DO CARE ABOUT MY MEN!! AND THE WIFE AND SON THAT I LOVE!!!

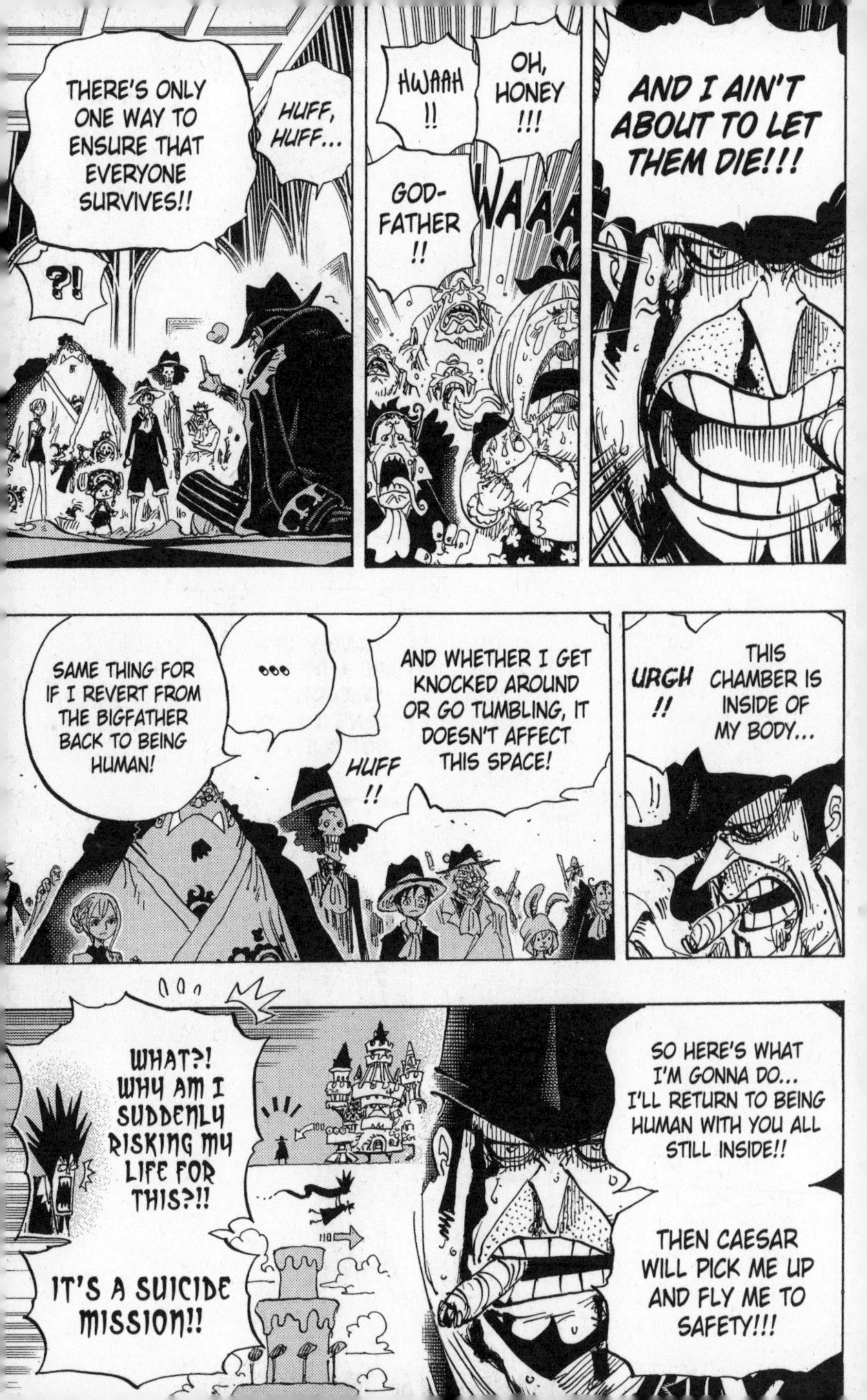
AND I AIN'T ABOUT TO LET THEM DIE!!!
OH, HONEY !!!
HWAAH !!
WAAA
GOD-FATHER !!
HUFF, HUFF...
THERE'S ONLY ONE WAY TO ENSURE THAT EVERYONE SURVIVES!!
?!
THIS CHAMBER IS INSIDE OF MY BODY...
URGH !!
AND WHETHER I GET KNOCKED AROUND OR GO TUMBLING, IT DOESN'T AFFECT THIS SPACE!
HUFF !!
...
SAME THING FOR IF I REVERT FROM THE BIGFATHER BACK TO BEING HUMAN!
SO HERE'S WHAT I'M GONNA DO... I'LL RETURN TO BEING HUMAN WITH YOU ALL STILL INSIDE!!
THEN CAESAR WILL PICK ME UP AND FLY ME TO SAFETY!!!
WHAT?! WHY AM I SUDDENLY RISKING MY LIFE FOR THIS?!!
IT'S A SUICIDE MISSION!!

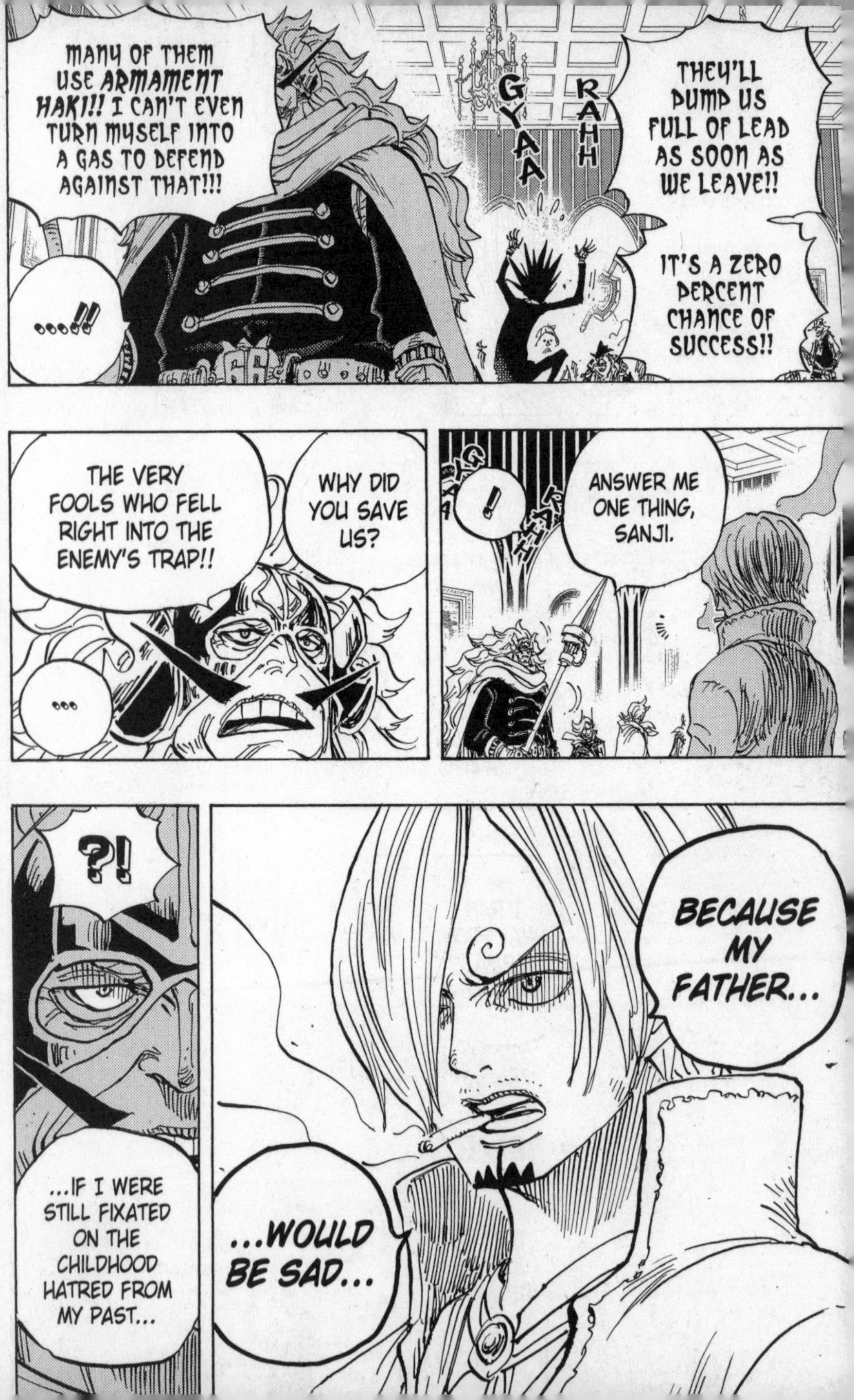
THEY'LL DUMP US FULL OF LEAD AS SOON AS WE LEAVE!!
IT'S A ZERO PERCENT CHANCE OF SUCCESS!!
RAHH
GYAA
MANY OF THEM USE ARMAMENT HAKI!! I CAN'T EVEN TURN MYSELF INTO A GAS TO DEFEND AGAINST THAT!!!
...!!
ANSWER ME ONE THING, SANJI.
!
WHY DID YOU SAVE US?
THE VERY FOOLS WHO FELL RIGHT INTO THE ENEMY'S TRAP!!
...
BECAUSE MY FATHER...
...WOULD BE SAD...
?!
...IF I WERE STILL FIXATED ON THE CHILDHOOD HATRED FROM MY PAST...

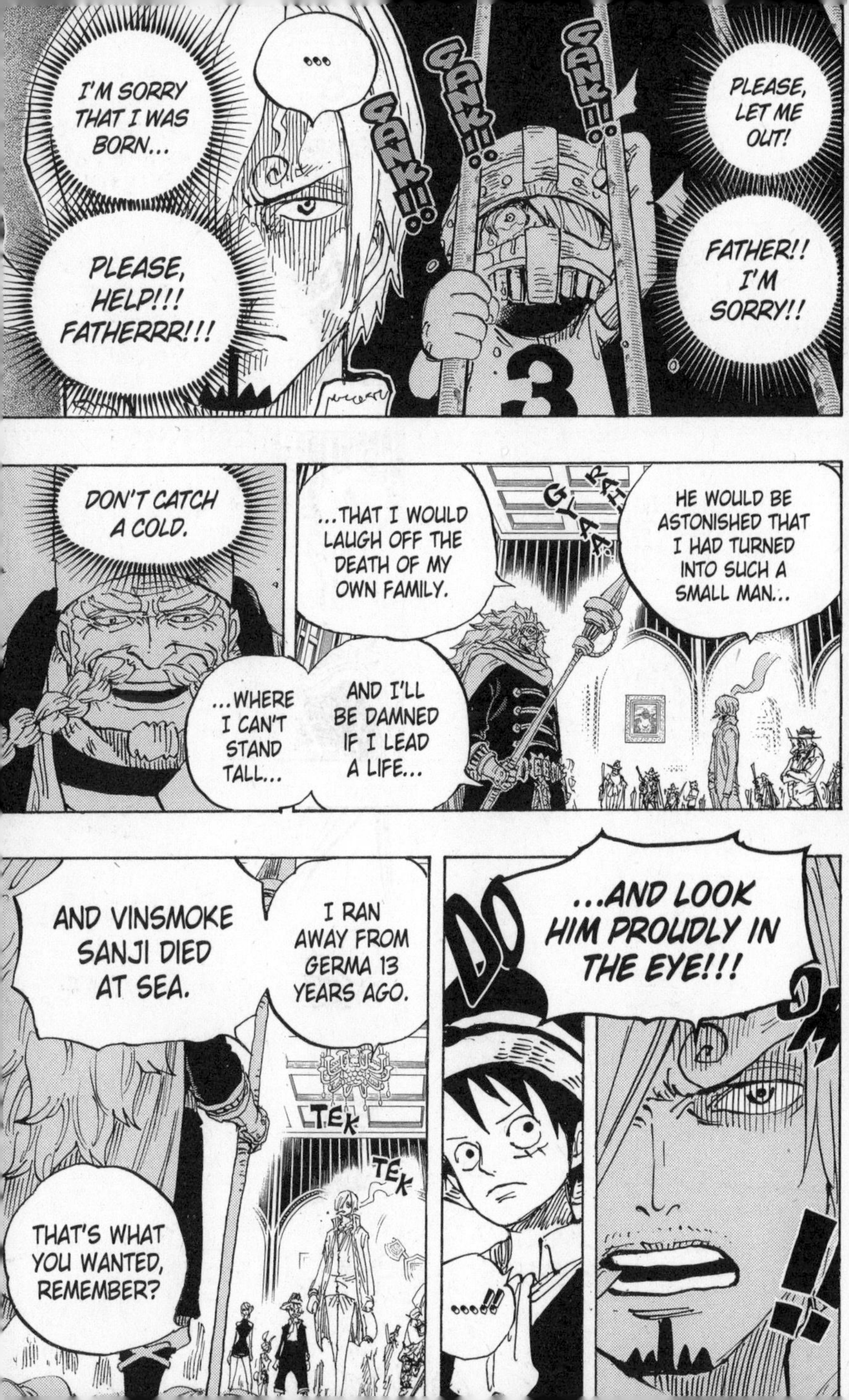
PLEASE, LET ME OUT!
GANK!!
GANK!!
GANK!!
...
I'M SORRY THAT I WAS BORN...
FATHER!! I'M SORRY!!
PLEASE, HELP!!! FATHERRR!!!
HE WOULD BE ASTONISHED THAT I HAD TURNED INTO SUCH A SMALL MAN...
GYAAAH
...THAT I WOULD LAUGH OFF THE DEATH OF MY OWN FAMILY.
AND I'LL BE DAMNED IF I LEAD A LIFE...
...WHERE I CAN'T STAND TALL...
DON'T CATCH A COLD.
...AND LOOK HIM PROUDLY IN THE EYE!!!
DO
...!!
I RAN AWAY FROM GERMA 13 YEARS AGO.
AND VINSMOKE SANJI DIED AT SEA.
TEK
TEK
THAT'S WHAT YOU WANTED, REMEMBER?

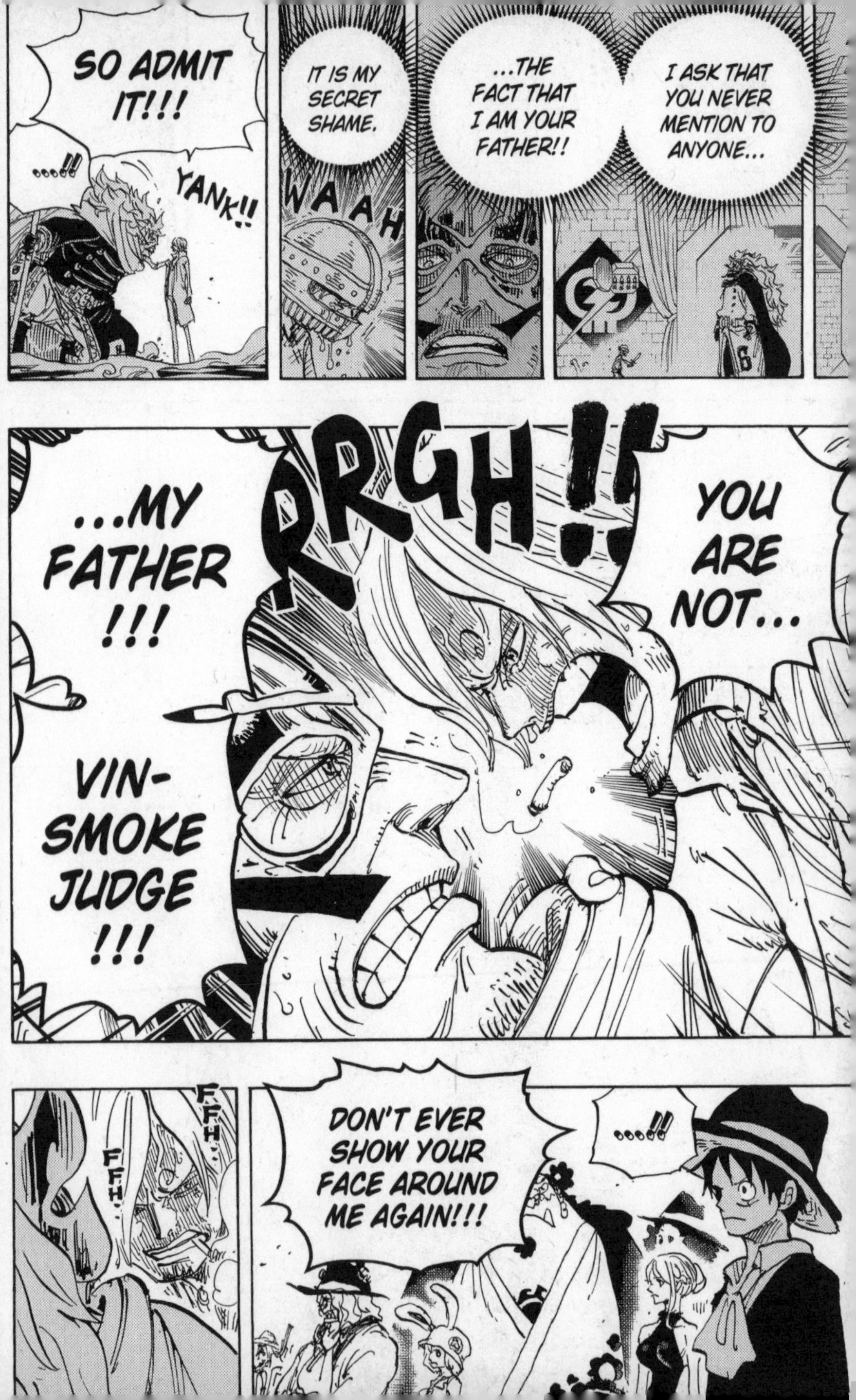
I ASK THAT YOU NEVER MENTION TO ANYONE...
...THE FACT THAT I AM YOUR FATHER!!
IT IS MY SECRET SHAME.
WAAAH
SO ADMIT IT!!!
YANK!!
...!!
YOU ARE NOT...
RGH!!
...MY FATHER!!!
VIN-SMOKE JUDGE!!!
...!!
DON'T EVER SHOW YOUR FACE AROUND ME AGAIN!!!
FFH
FFH

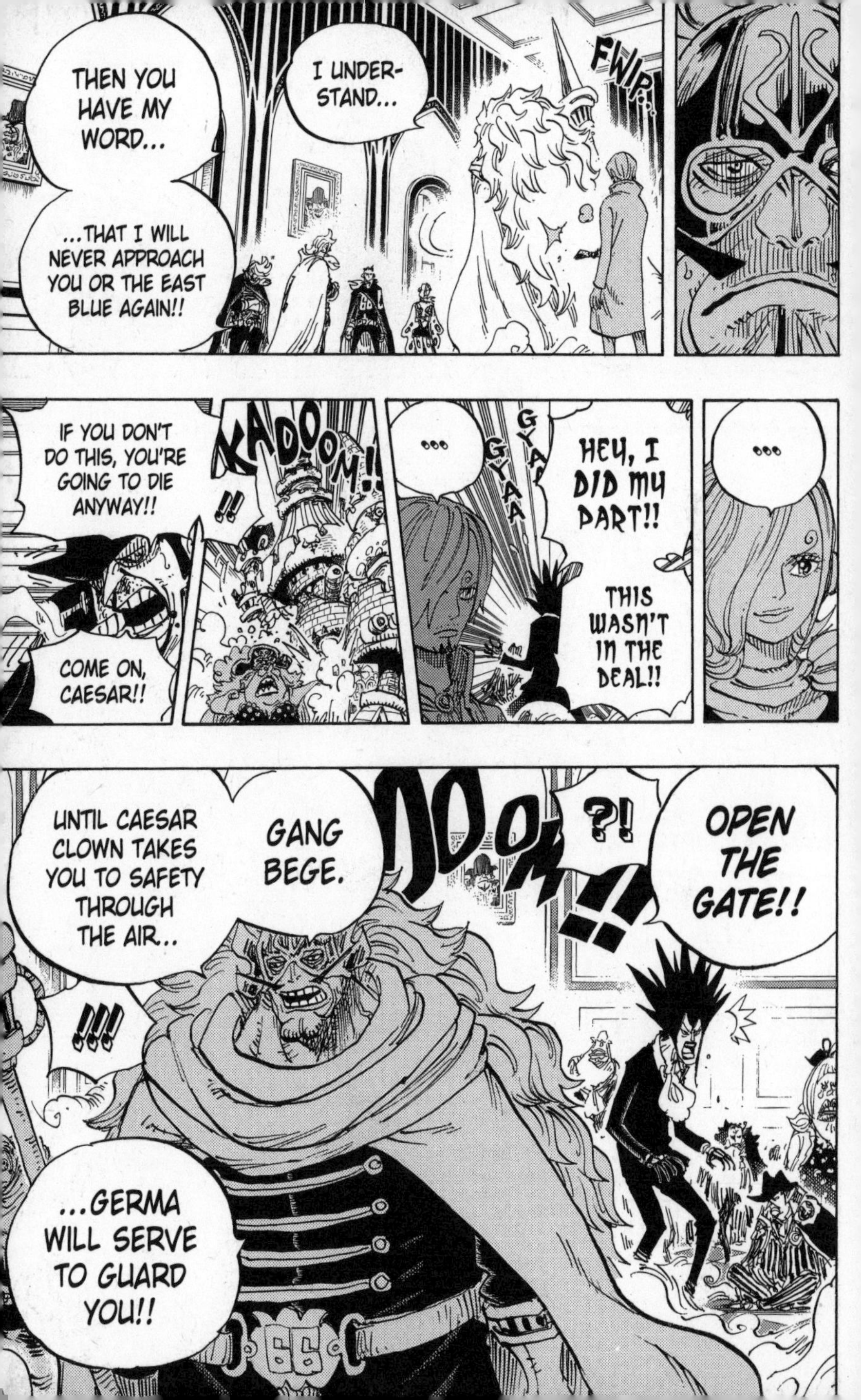
FWIP...
I UNDER-STAND...
THEN YOU HAVE MY WORD...
...THAT I WILL NEVER APPROACH YOU OR THE EAST BLUE AGAIN!!
...
HEY, I DID MY PART!!
GYAA GYAA
...
THIS WASN'T IN THE DEAL!!
KADOOM!!
!!
IF YOU DON'T DO THIS, YOU'RE GOING TO DIE ANYWAY!!
COME ON, CAESAR!!
OPEN THE GATE!!
?!
DOOM!!
GANG BEGE.
UNTIL CAESAR CLOWN TAKES YOU TO SAFETY THROUGH THE AIR..
!!!
...GERMA WILL SERVE TO GUARD YOU!!

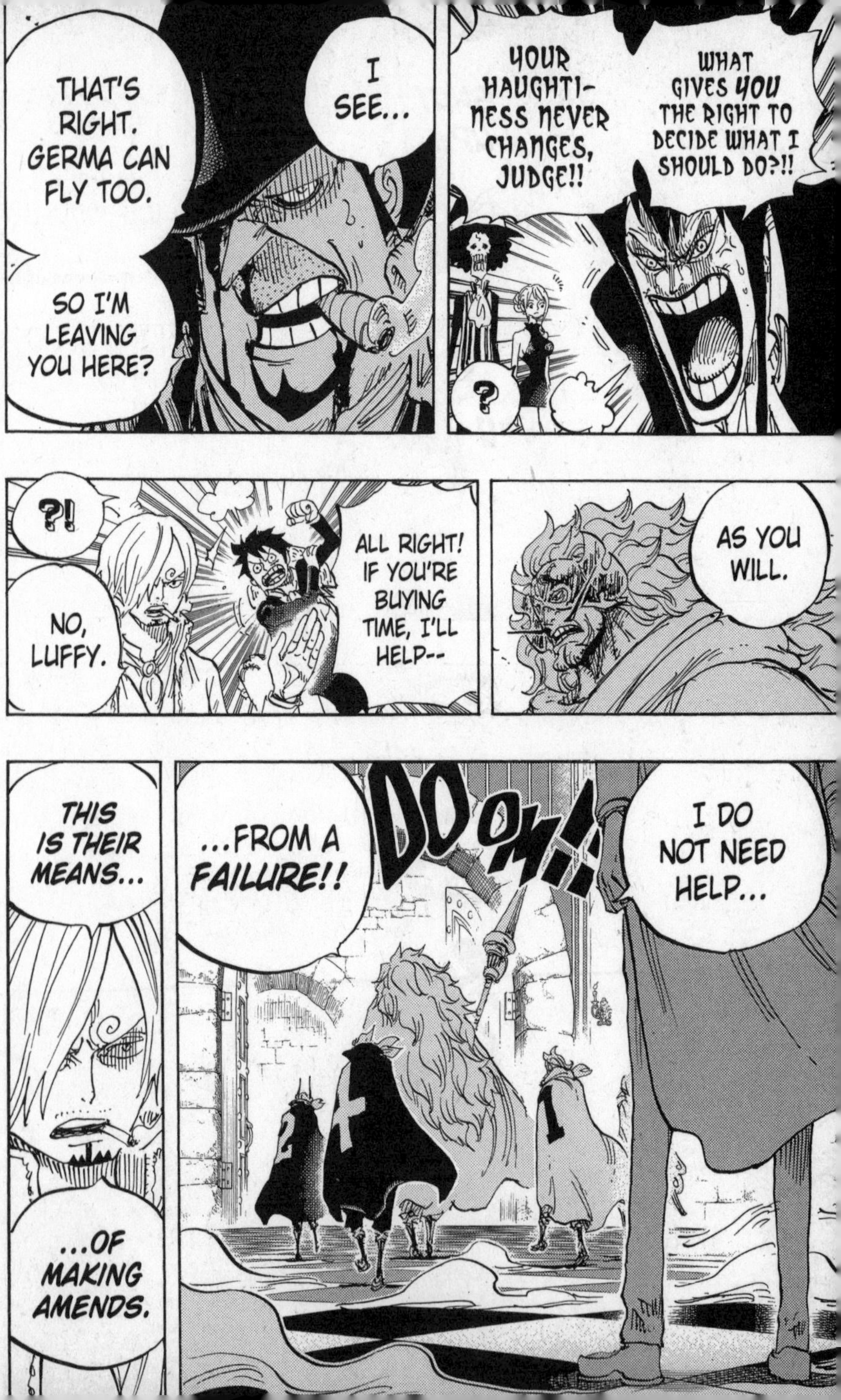
WHAT GIVES YOU THE RIGHT TO DECIDE WHAT I SHOULD DO?!!
YOUR HAUGHTI-NESS NEVER CHANGES, JUDGE!!
?
I SEE...
THAT'S RIGHT. GERMA CAN FLY TOO.
SO I'M LEAVING YOU HERE?
AS YOU WILL.
ALL RIGHT! IF YOU'RE BUYING TIME, I'LL HELP--
?!
NO, LUFFY.
I DO NOT NEED HELP...
DOOM!!
...FROM A FAILURE!!
THIS IS THEIR MEANS...
...OF MAKING AMENDS.

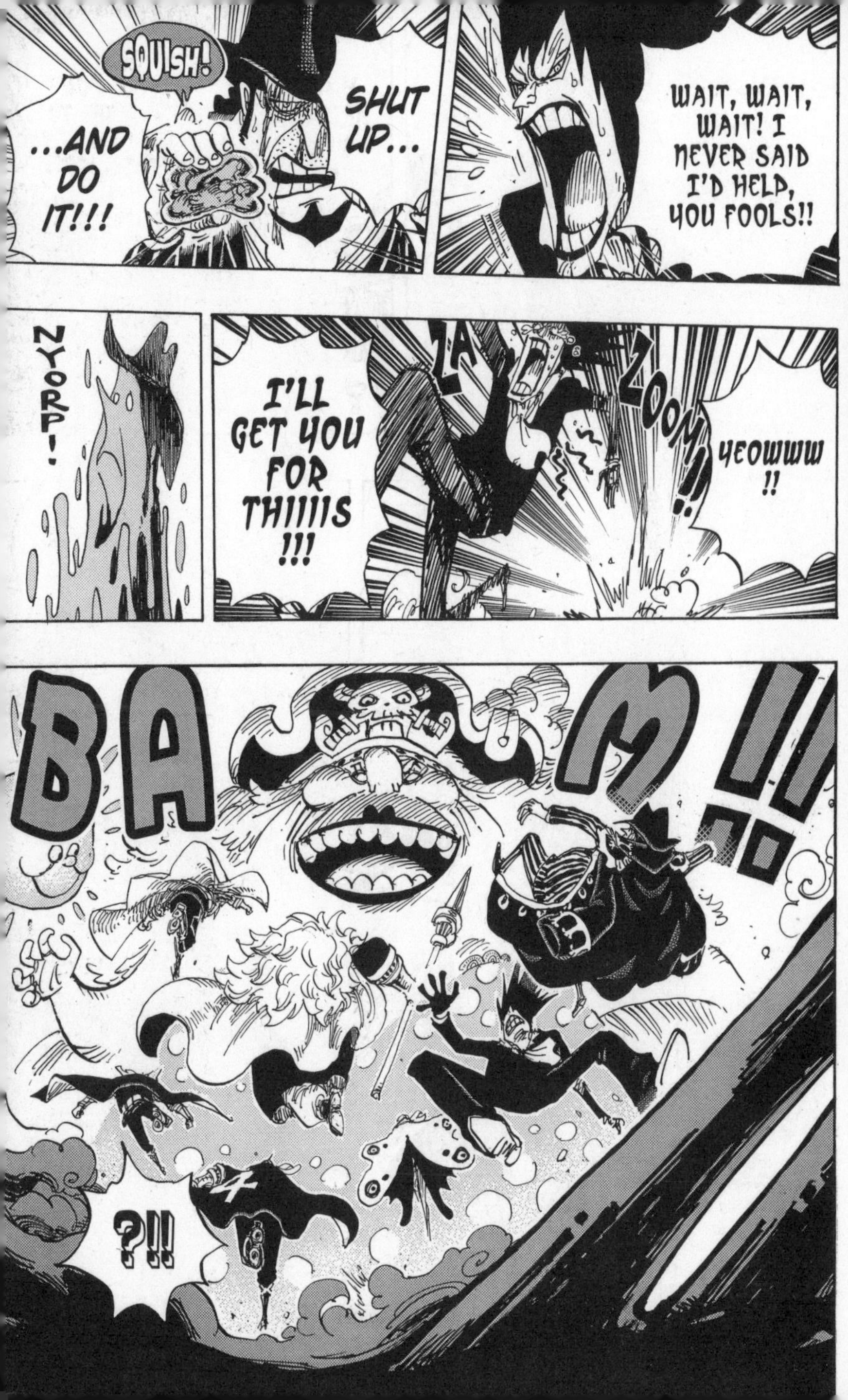
WAIT, WAIT, WAIT! I NEVER SAID I'D HELP, YOU FOOLS!!
SHUT UP...
SQUISH!
...AND DO IT!!!
YEOWWW!!
ZOOM!!
I'LL GET YOU FOR THIIIIS!!!
NYORP!
BAM!!
?!!

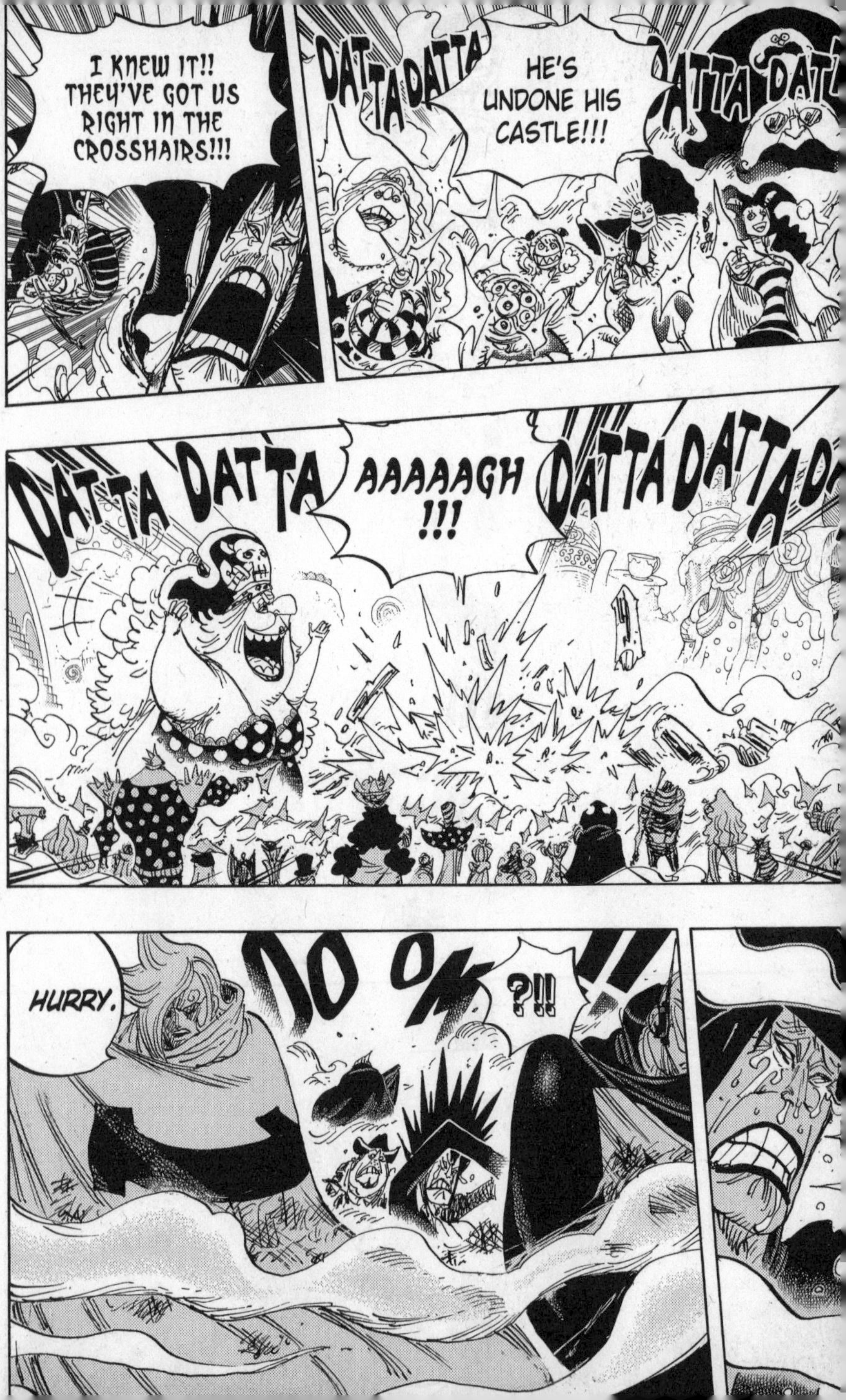
DATTA DATTA
HE'S UNDONE HIS CASTLE!!!
DATTA DATTA
I KNEW IT!! THEY'VE GOT US RIGHT IN THE CROSSHAIRS!!!
DATTA DATTA
AAAAAGH !!!
DATTA DATTA
?!!
HURRY.

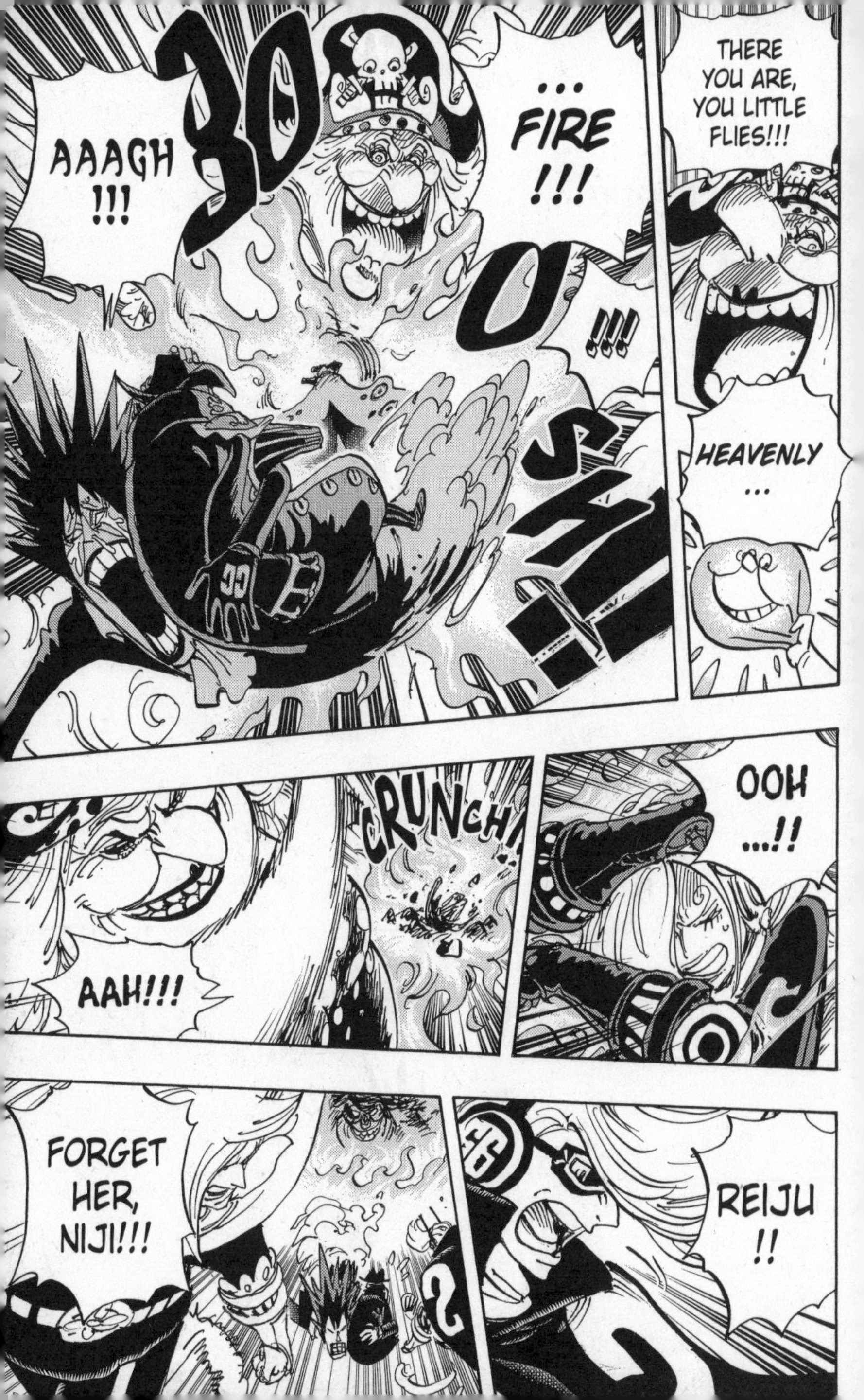
THERE YOU ARE, YOU LITTLE FLIES!!!
HEAVENLY ...
... FIRE !!!
BOOSH!!!
AAAGH !!!
OOH ...!!
CRUNCH!
AAH!!!
REIJU !!
FORGET HER, NIJI!!!

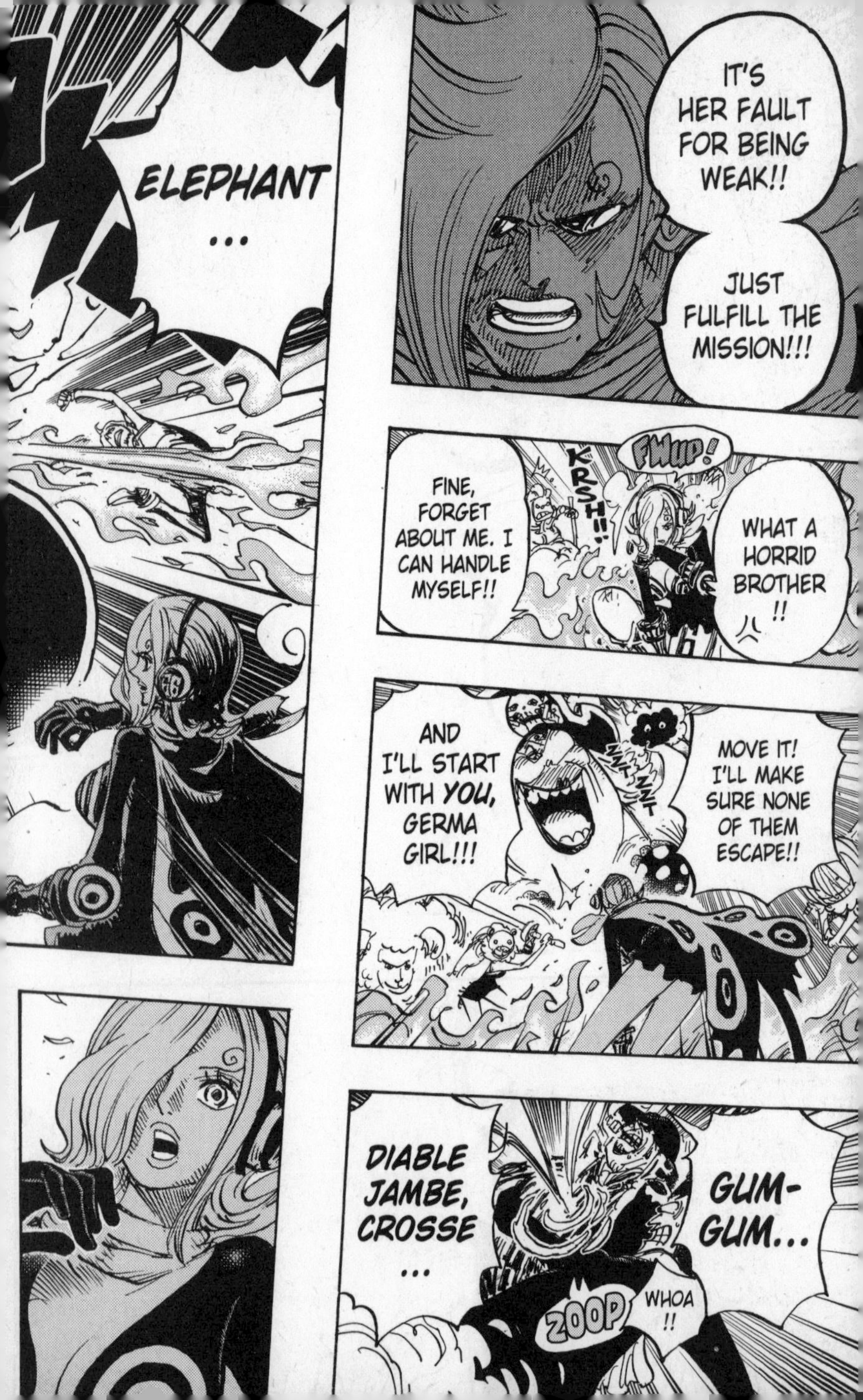
IT'S HER FAULT FOR BEING WEAK!!
JUST FULFILL THE MISSION!!!
ELEPHANT ...
FWUP!
KRSH!!
WHAT A HORRID BROTHER!!
FINE, FORGET ABOUT ME. I CAN HANDLE MYSELF!!
MOVE IT! I'LL MAKE SURE NONE OF THEM ESCAPE!!
ZZT ZZT
AND I'LL START WITH YOU, GERMA GIRL!!!
GUM-GUM...
DIABLE JAMBE, CROSSE ...
WHOA!!
ZOOP

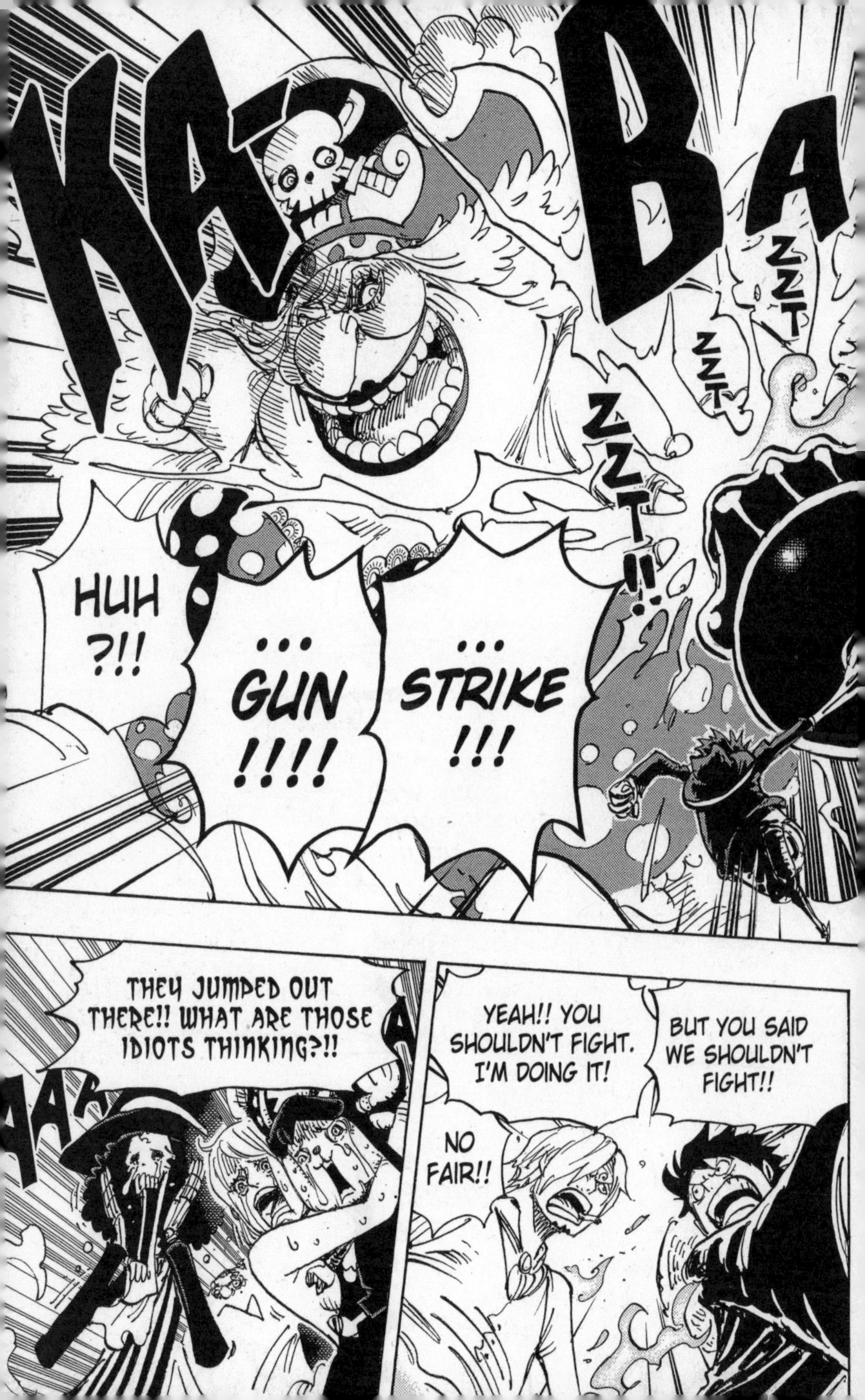
KABA
ZZZT
ZZZT
ZZZT!!
...STRIKE!!!
...GUN!!!!
HUH?!!
BUT YOU SAID WE SHOULDN'T FIGHT!!
YEAH!! YOU SHOULDN'T FIGHT. I'M DOING IT!
NO FAIR!!
THEY JUMPED OUT THERE!! WHAT ARE THOSE IDIOTS THINKING?!!

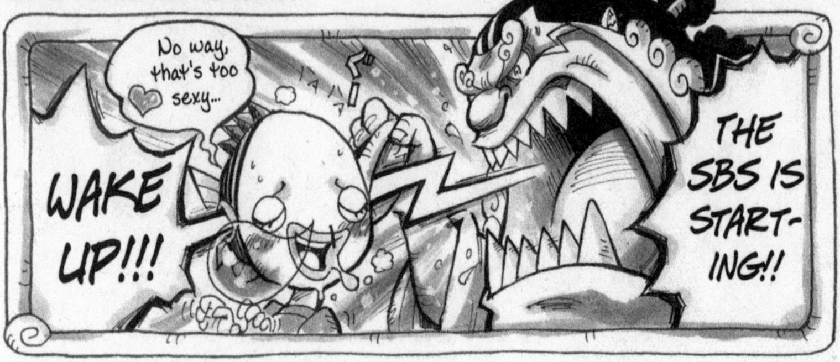
No way, that's too sexy...
WAKE UP!!!
THE SBS IS START-ING!!

(Hippo Iron, Saitama)

Q: I've always been an animal lover, so I was super excited when the minks showed up! As a sign of my gratitude, I have a message from my pet cat…

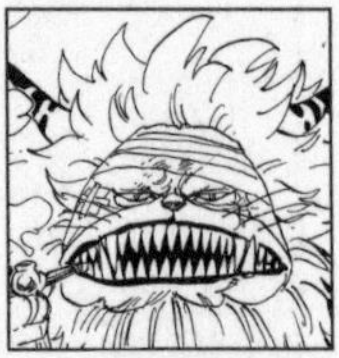

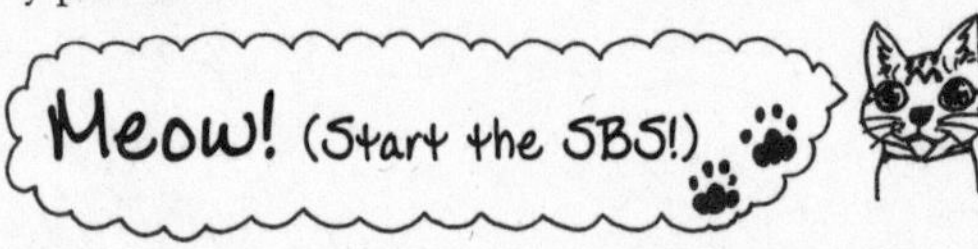
Meow! (Start the SBS!)

--Y, born in the year of the arabesque-patterned rabbit

A: I can't believe this!! Even a cat is starting this segment before me!!

Q: Hi there, Odacchi!!! Bege's kid sure looks a lot like him, and he's even got what looks like stubble above his lip. Is that baby already shaving? And what does this mean for his, uh...body hair? If he's got, um…you know…then does Chiffon get really grossed out when she changes his diapers?

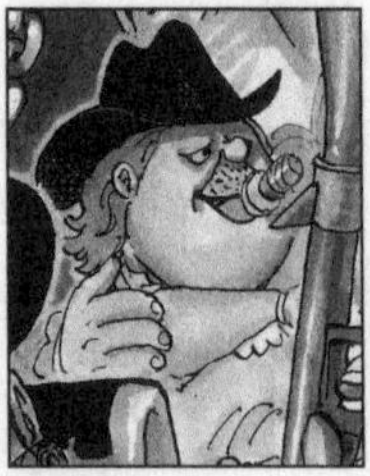

--Portgaz D. Ayana

A: First of all, Chiffon is not going to have any problem with it. She's his mother! Now, as for Pez's little triangle under his nose... Well, the most natural answer is probably...a tortilla chip? It certainly looks like a mustache. As for your question, the answer is...drum roll please! *Drrrr-he's-rrrr-got-rrrr-facial-rrrr-and-rrrrr-pubichair-rrrrrrr...*

I'm not telling you the answer!!

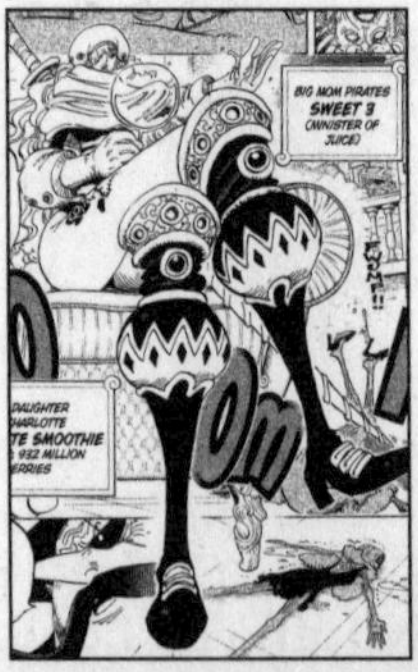
BIG MOM PIRATES
SWEET 3
(MINISTER OF JUICE)
DAUGHTER
CHARLOTTE

Q: Can I lick Smoothie's legs? That's what Chamoro Shimizu asked me to say.

--Match and Takeshi

A: That sick bastard!!

Q: Draw more fanservice!! *Growr!!* That's what Chamoro Shimizu asked me to say.

--Match and Takeshi

A: That sick bastard!!

Chapter 871:
YOU CAN DO IT, CAESAR!!

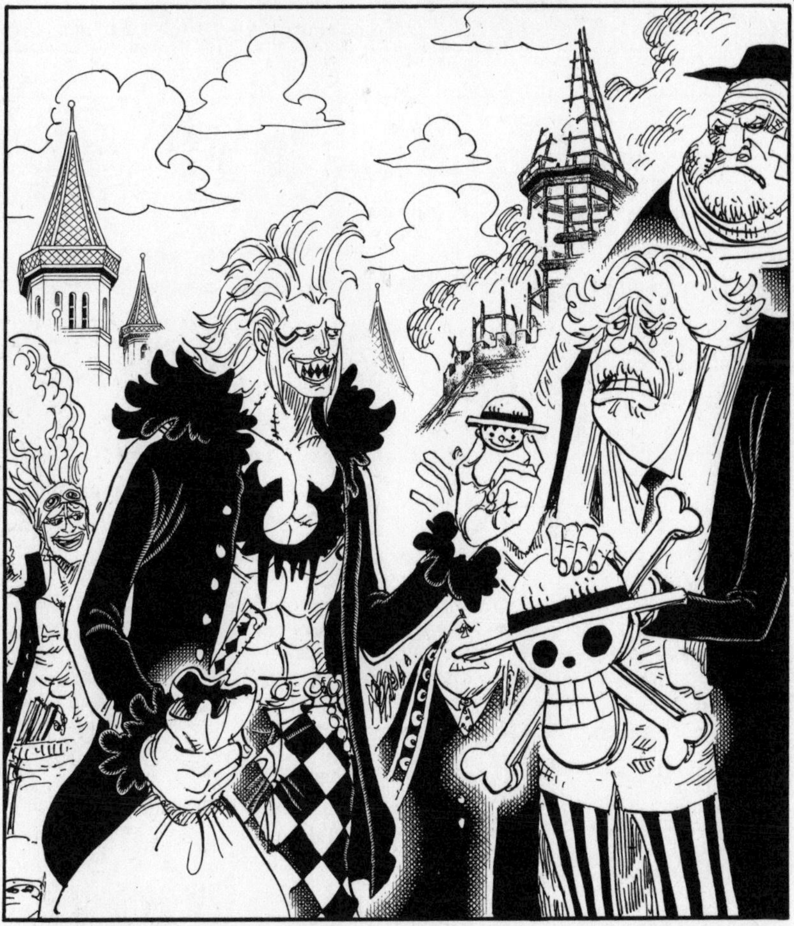

THE SAGA OF THE SELF-PROCLAIMED STRAW HAT FLEET
VOL. 8, BARTOLOMEO: "PASSING OFF STRAW HAT CREW STICKERS AND MISTER LUFFY PINS TO THE HOOLIGANS ON THE CHEAP"

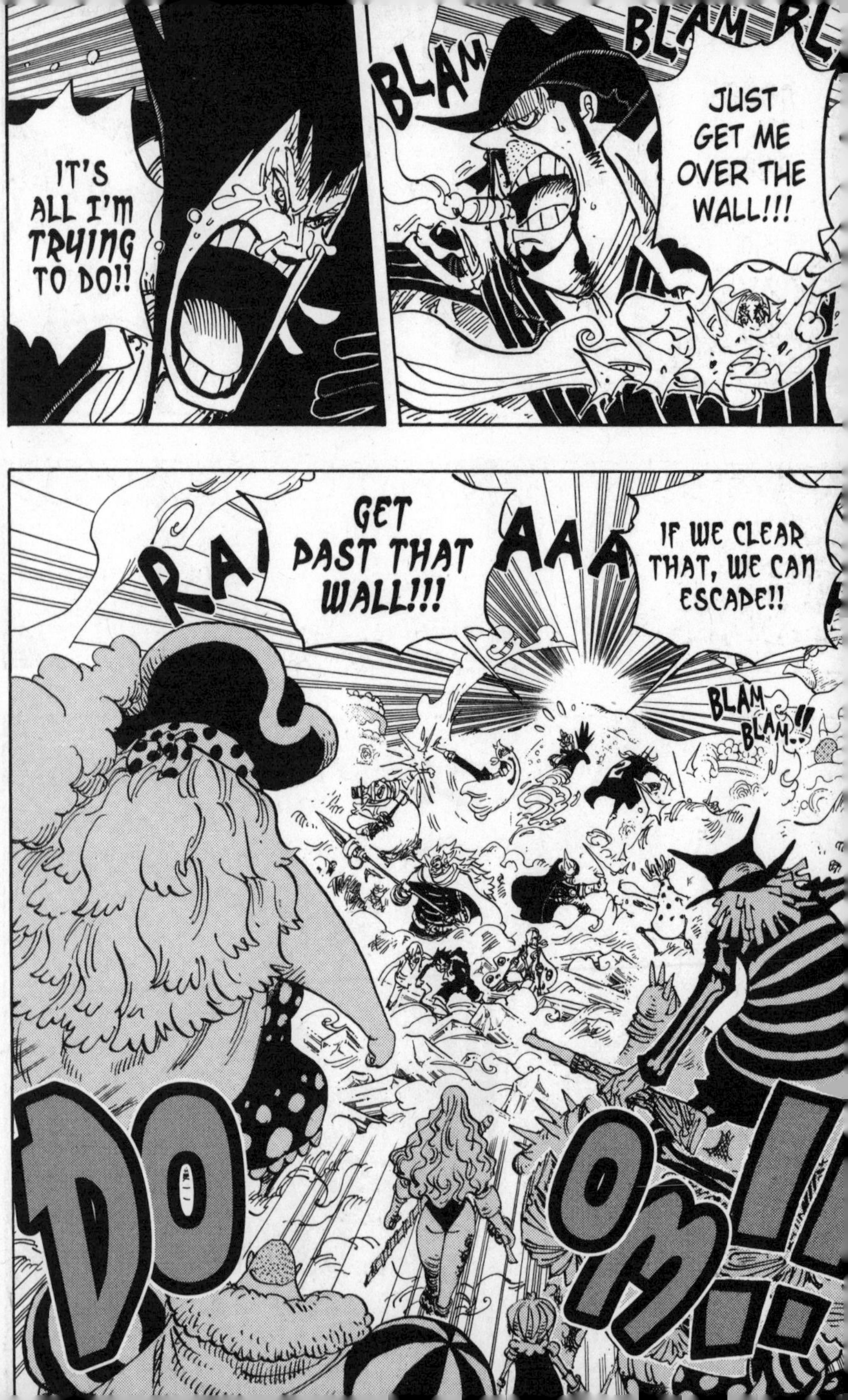
BLAM
BLAM BL
JUST GET ME OVER THE WALL!!!
IT'S ALL I'M TRYING TO DO!!
IF WE CLEAR THAT, WE CAN ESCAPE!!
AAA
GET PAST THAT WALL!!!
RA
BLAM BLAM!!
DOOM!!

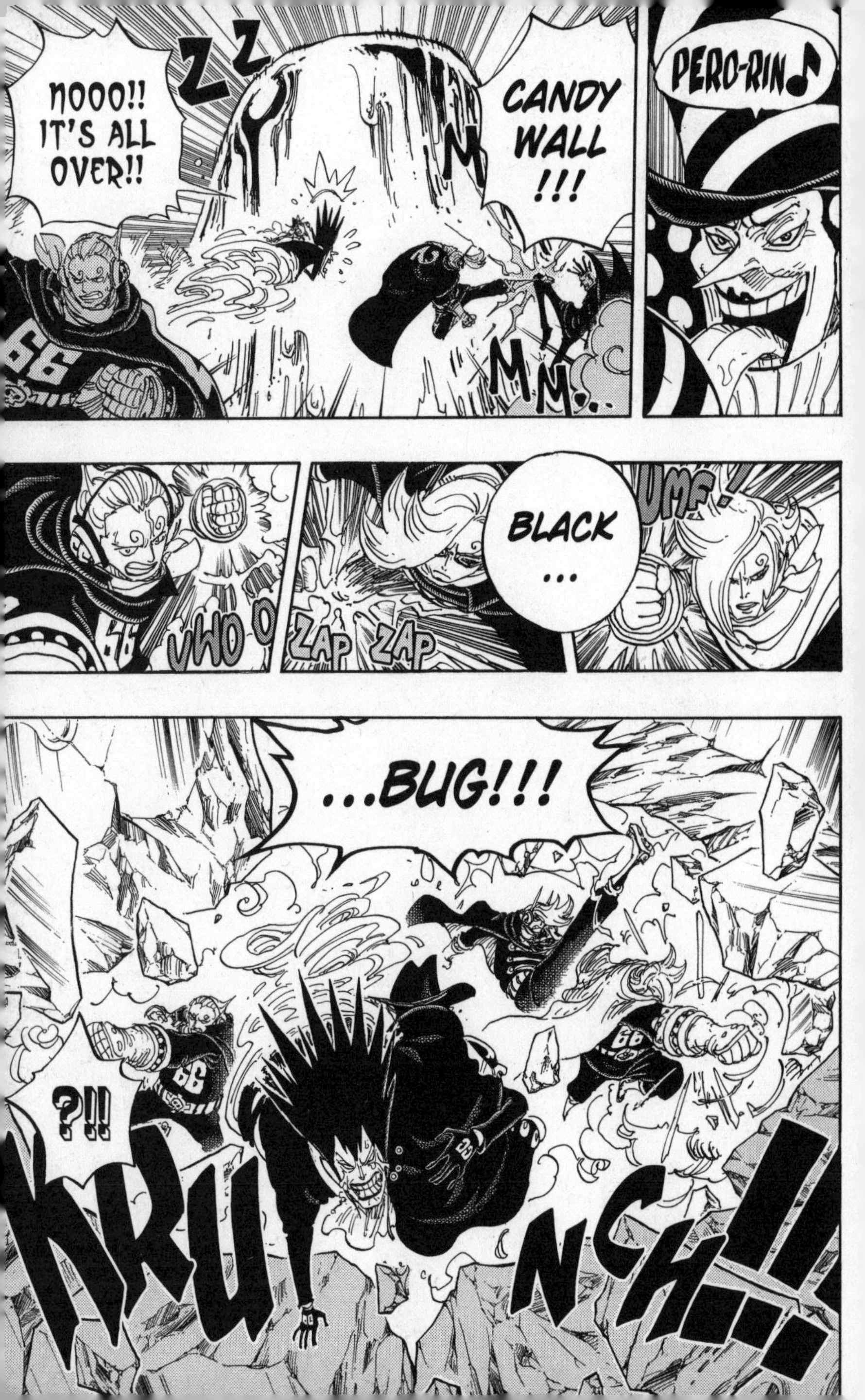
PERO-RIN♪
CANDY WALL!!!
ZZ
M
MM..
NOOO!! IT'S ALL OVER!!
UMF!
BLACK ...
ZAP ZAP
VWOO
...BUG!!!
?!!
KRUNCH!!

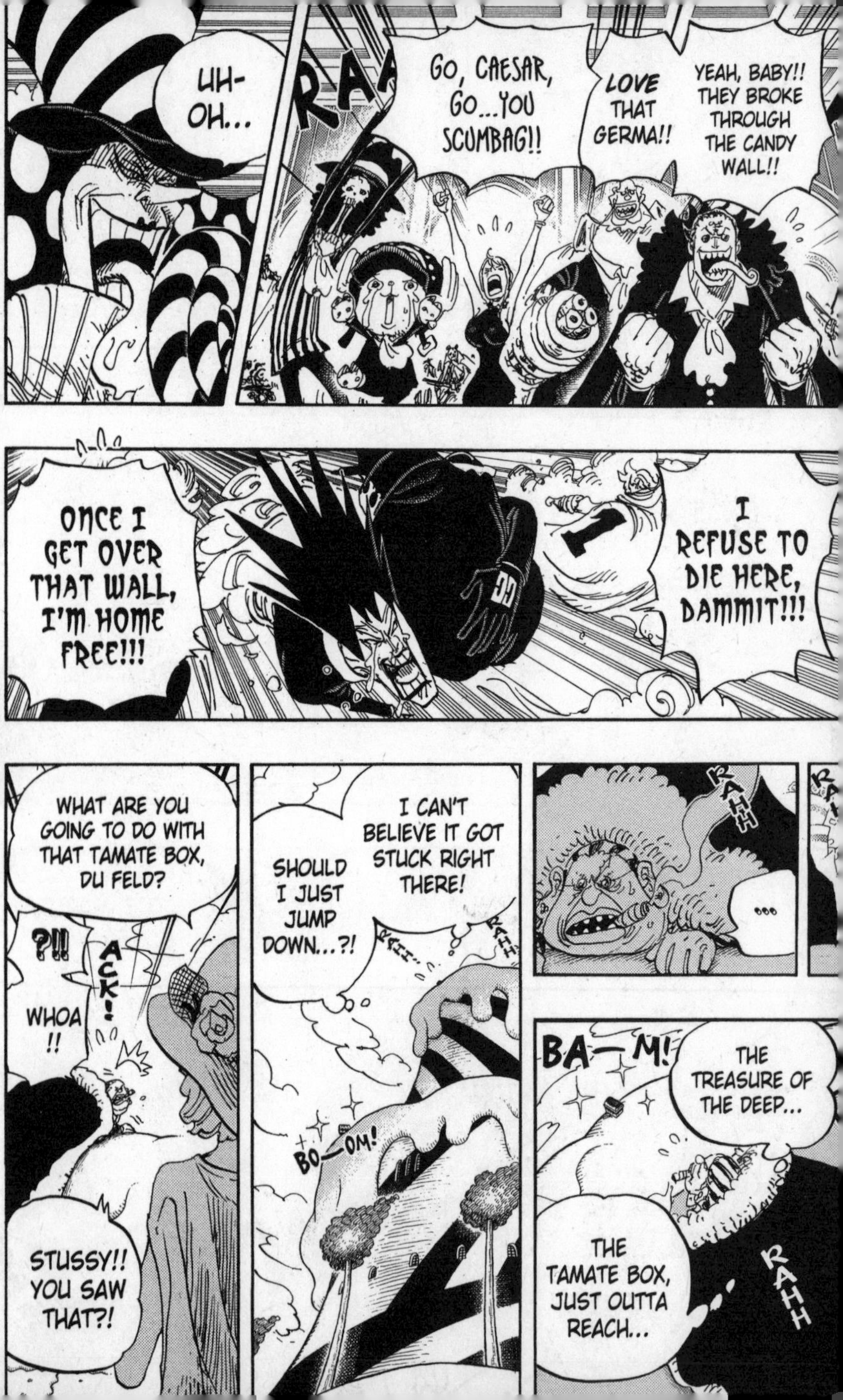
YEAH, BABY!! THEY BROKE THROUGH THE CANDY WALL!!
LOVE THAT GERMA!!
GO, CAESAR, GO...YOU SCUMBAG!!
RAA
UH-OH...
I REFUSE TO DIE HERE, DAMMIT!!!
ONCE I GET OVER THAT WALL, I'M HOME FREE!!!
RAHH
...
BA-M!
THE TREASURE OF THE DEEP...
THE TAMATE BOX, JUST OUTTA REACH...
RAHH
I CAN'T BELIEVE IT GOT STUCK RIGHT THERE!
SHOULD I JUST JUMP DOWN...?!
RAHH
BO-OM!
WHAT ARE YOU GOING TO DO WITH THAT TAMATE BOX, DU FELD?
?!!
ACK!
WHOA!!
STUSSY!! YOU SAW THAT?!

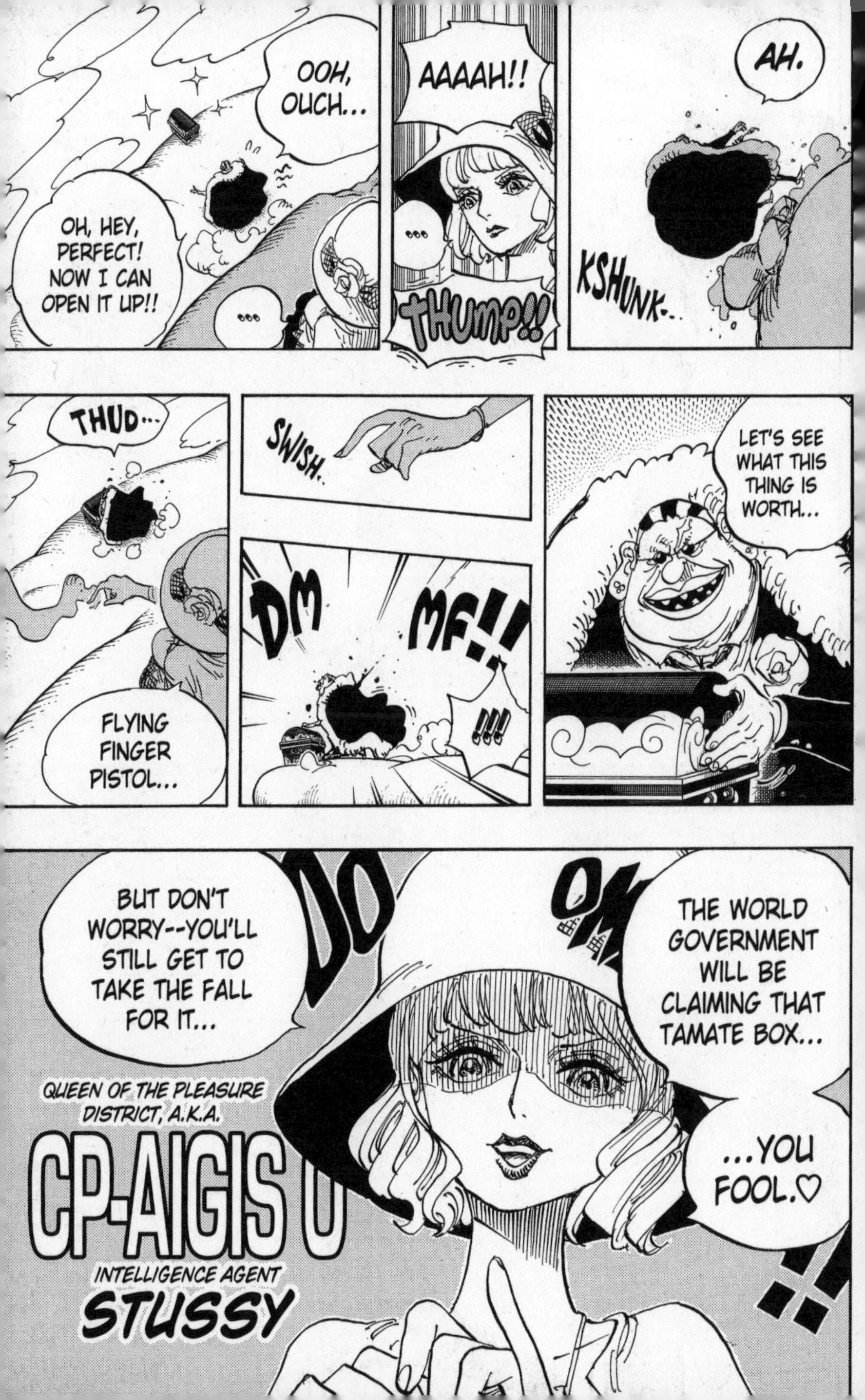
AH.
KSHUNK...
AAAAH!!
...
THUMP!!
OOH, OUCH...
OH, HEY, PERFECT! NOW I CAN OPEN IT UP!!
...
LET'S SEE WHAT THIS THING IS WORTH...
SWISH.
DMMF!!
!!!
THUD...
FLYING FINGER PISTOL...
THE WORLD GOVERNMENT WILL BE CLAIMING THAT TAMATE BOX...
DOOM!!
BUT DON'T WORRY--YOU'LL STILL GET TO TAKE THE FALL FOR IT...
...YOU FOOL.♡
QUEEN OF THE PLEASURE DISTRICT, A.K.A.
CP-AIGIS 0
INTELLIGENCE AGENT
STUSSY

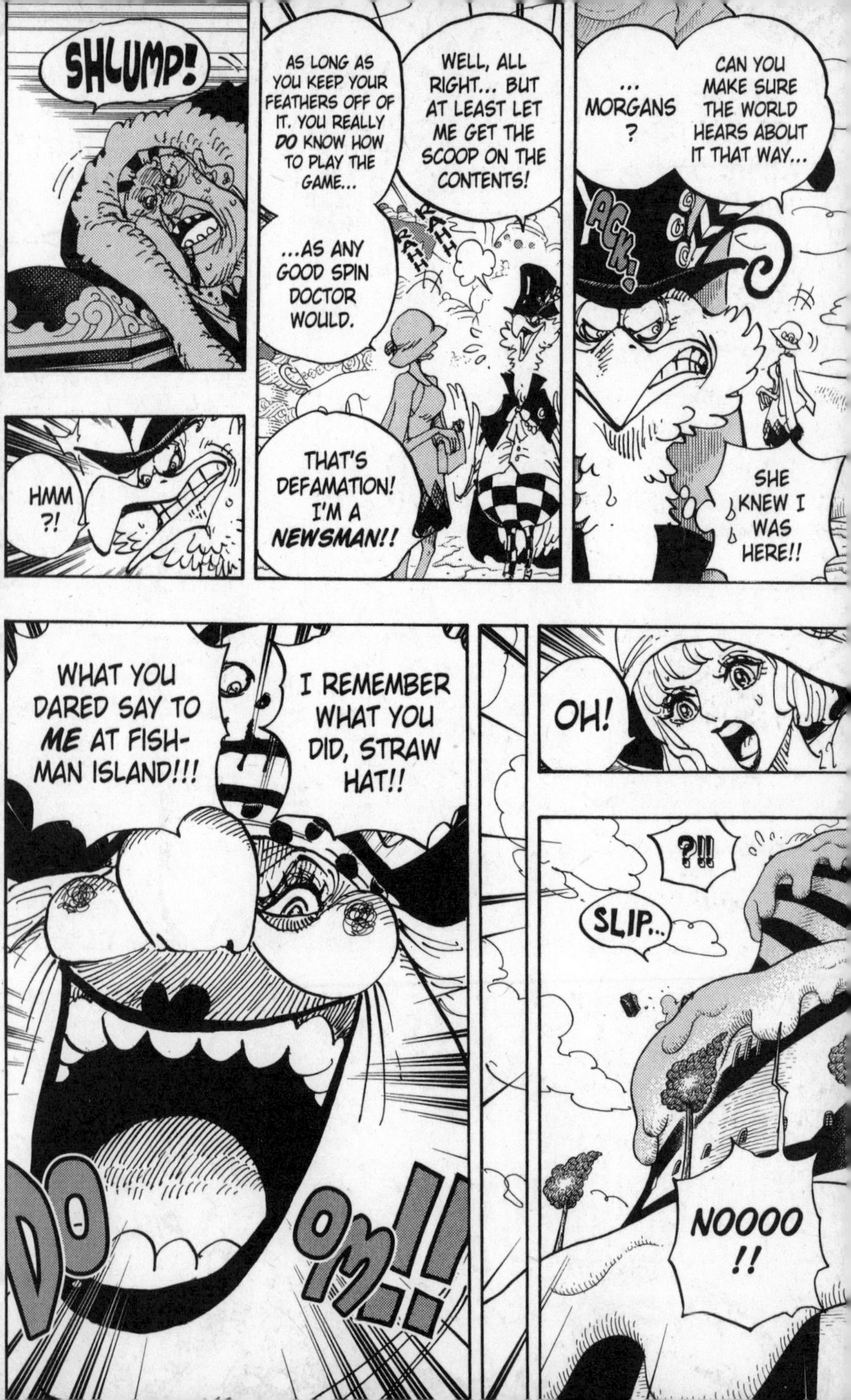
CAN YOU MAKE SURE THE WORLD HEARS ABOUT IT THAT WAY...
ACK!
... MORGANS ?
SHE KNEW I WAS HERE!!
WELL, ALL RIGHT... BUT AT LEAST LET ME GET THE SCOOP ON THE CONTENTS!
AS LONG AS YOU KEEP YOUR FEATHERS OFF OF IT. YOU REALLY DO KNOW HOW TO PLAY THE GAME...
RAHH RAHH
...AS ANY GOOD SPIN DOCTOR WOULD.
THAT'S DEFAMATION! I'M A NEWSMAN!!
SHLUMP!
HMM ?!
OH!
?!!
SLIP...
NOOOO !!
I REMEMBER WHAT YOU DID, STRAW HAT!!
WHAT YOU DARED SAY TO ME AT FISH-MAN ISLAND!!!
DOOM!!

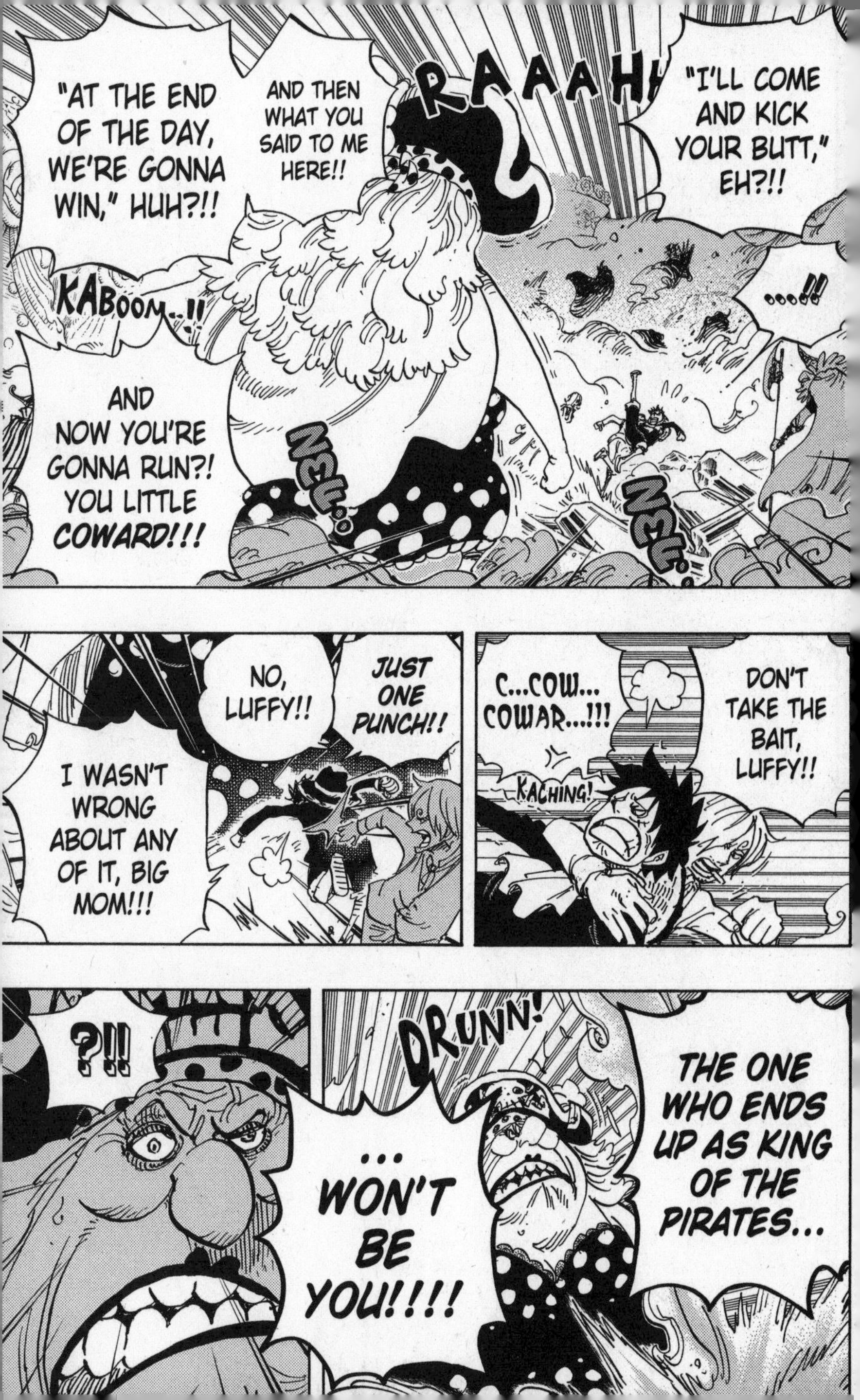
"I'LL COME AND KICK YOUR BUTT," EH?!!
RAAAH!
AND THEN WHAT YOU SAID TO ME HERE!!
"AT THE END OF THE DAY, WE'RE GONNA WIN," HUH?!!
....!!
KABOOM..!!
AND NOW YOU'RE GONNA RUN?! YOU LITTLE COWARD!!!
NGG..
NGG..
DON'T TAKE THE BAIT, LUFFY!!
C...COW... COWAR...!!!
KACHING!
JUST ONE PUNCH!!
NO, LUFFY!!
I WASN'T WRONG ABOUT ANY OF IT, BIG MOM!!!
DRUNN!
THE ONE WHO ENDS UP AS KING OF THE PIRATES...
...WON'T BE YOU!!!!
?!!

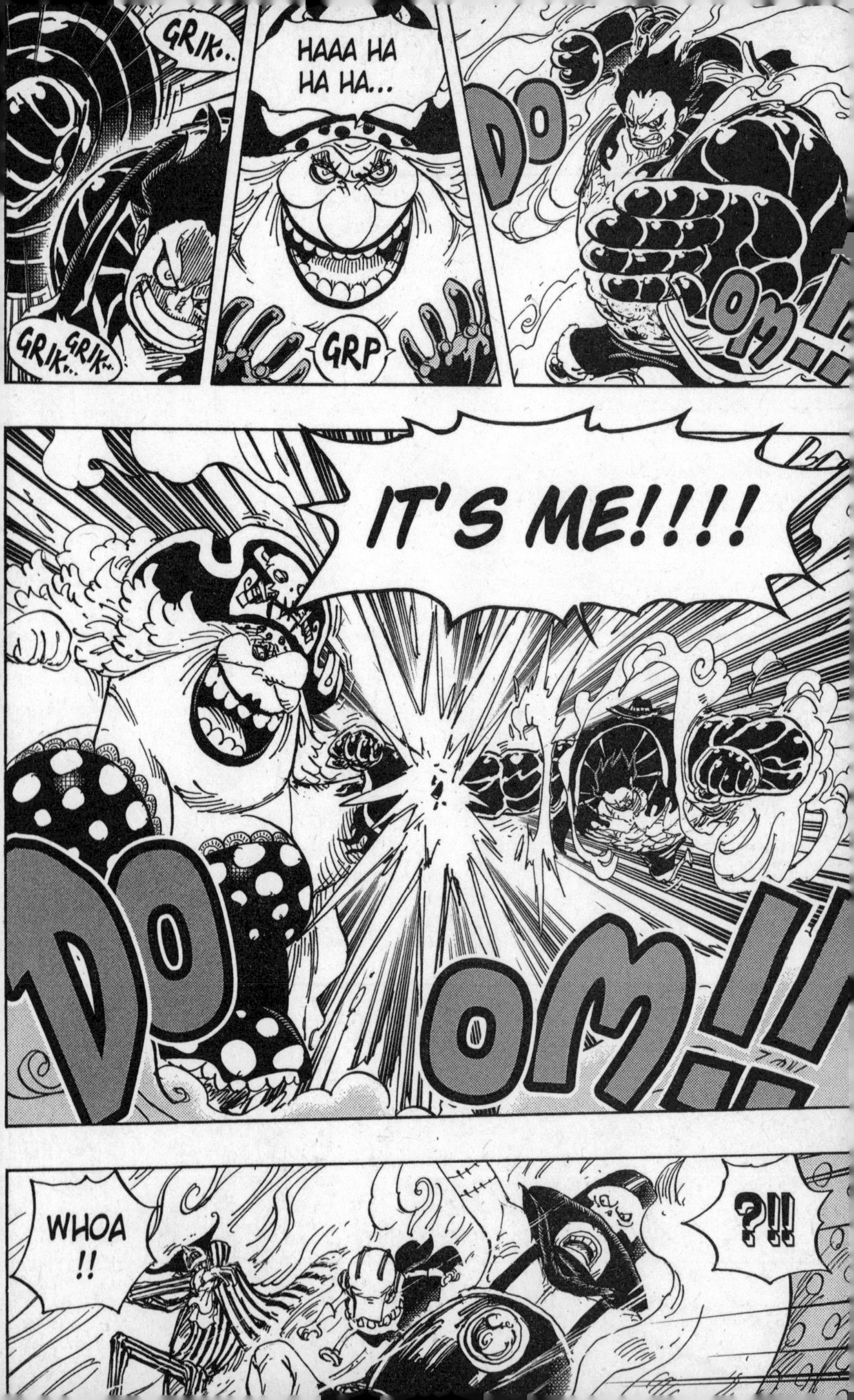
DOOM!!
HAAA HA HA HA...
GRP
GRIK...
GRIK... GRIK...
IT'S ME!!!!
DOOM!!
?!!
WHOA !!

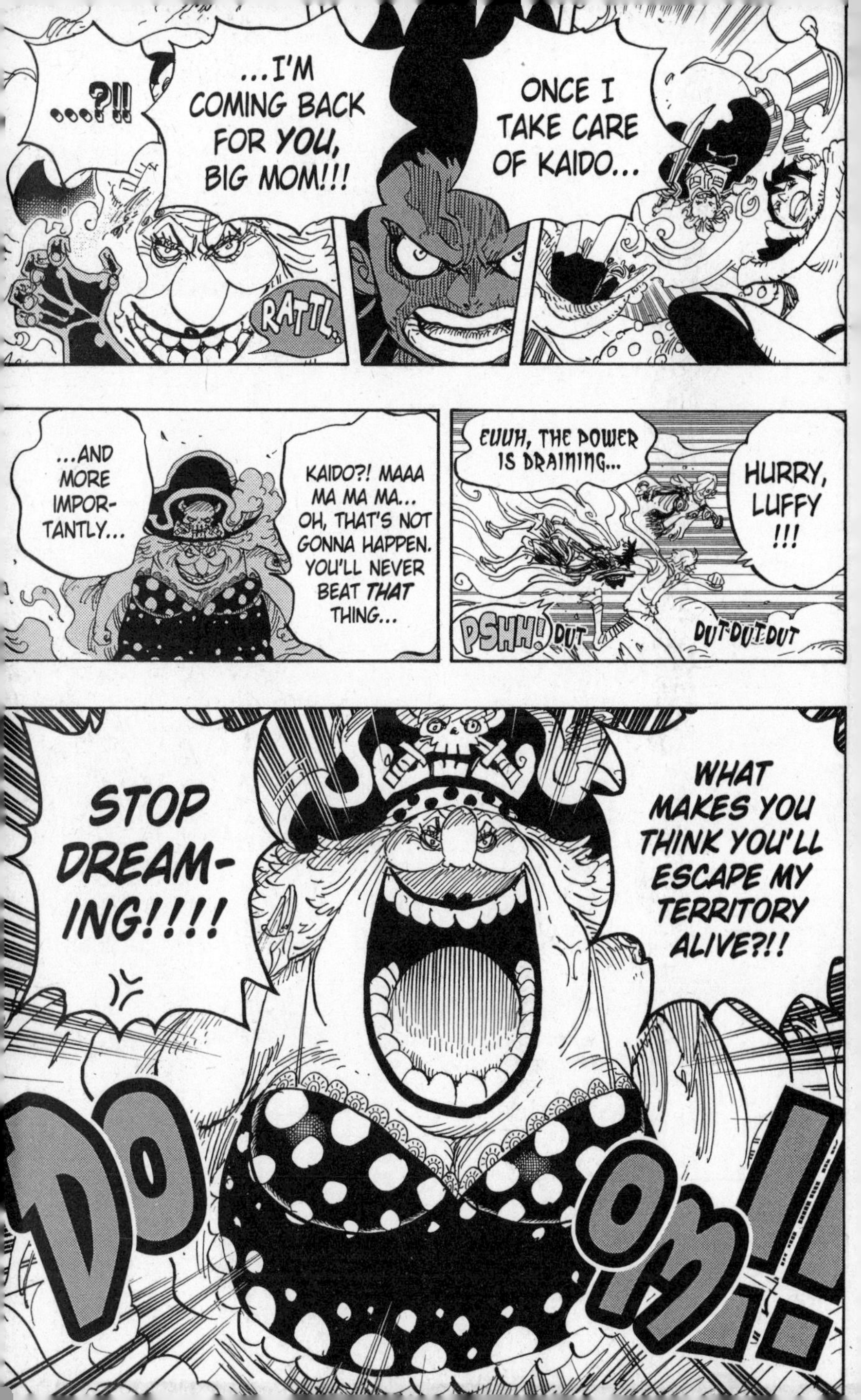
ONCE I TAKE CARE OF KAIDO...
...I'M COMING BACK FOR YOU, BIG MOM!!!
...?!!
RATTL
HURRY, LUFFY!!!
EUUH, THE POWER IS DRAINING...
PSHH!
DUT
DUT-DUT-DUT
KAIDO?! MAAA MA MA MA... OH, THAT'S NOT GONNA HAPPEN. YOU'LL NEVER BEAT THAT THING...
...AND MORE IMPOR-TANTLY...
WHAT MAKES YOU THINK YOU'LL ESCAPE MY TERRITORY ALIVE?!!
STOP DREAM-ING!!!!
DOOM!!

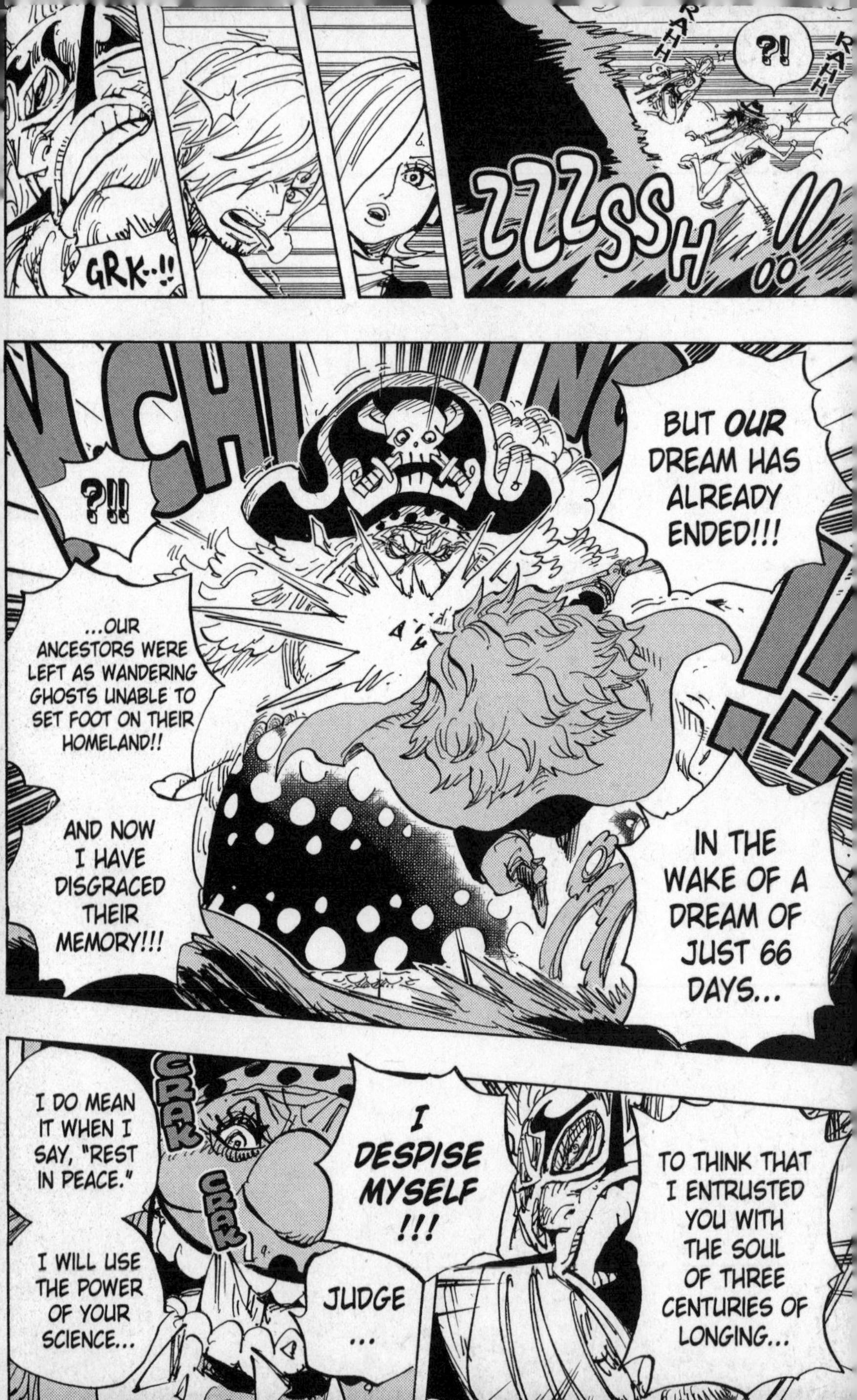
RAHH
?!
RAHH
ZZZSSH!!
GRK..!!
BUT OUR DREAM HAS ALREADY ENDED!!!
?!!
IN THE WAKE OF A DREAM OF JUST 66 DAYS...
...OUR ANCESTORS WERE LEFT AS WANDERING GHOSTS UNABLE TO SET FOOT ON THEIR HOMELAND!!
AND NOW I HAVE DISGRACED THEIR MEMORY!!!
TO THINK THAT I ENTRUSTED YOU WITH THE SOUL OF THREE CENTURIES OF LONGING...
I DESPISE MYSELF!!!
JUDGE...
CRAK
CRAK
I DO MEAN IT WHEN I SAY, "REST IN PEACE."
I WILL USE THE POWER OF YOUR SCIENCE...

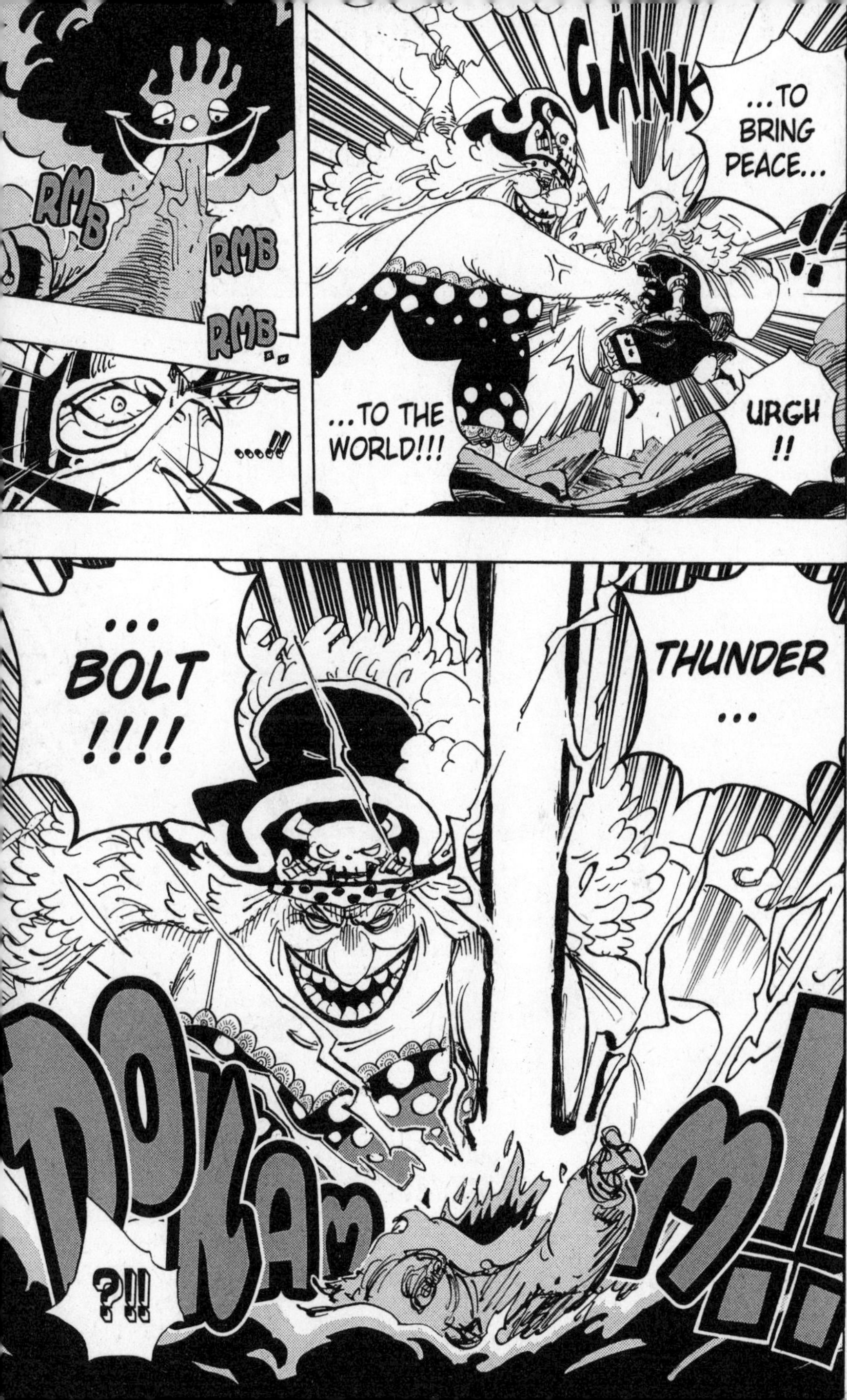
GANK
...TO BRING PEACE...
!!
URGH !!
...TO THE WORLD!!!
RMB
RMB
RMB
....!!
THUNDER ...
... BOLT !!!!
DOKAMM!!
?!!

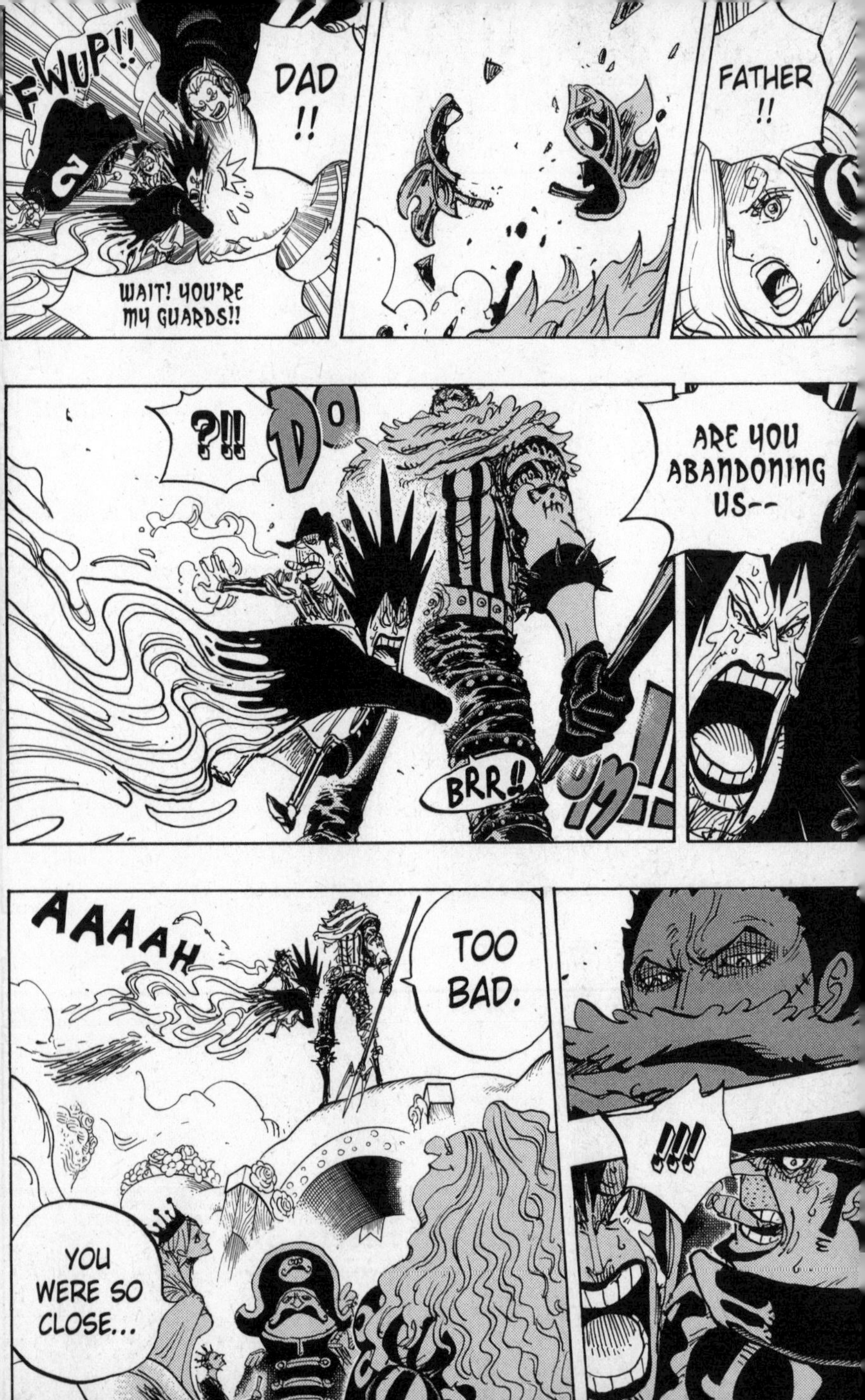

FATHER !!
DAD !!
FWUP!!
WAIT! YOU'RE MY GUARDS!!
ARE YOU ABANDONING US--
DO
?!!
OM
BRR!!
!!!
TOO BAD.
AAAAH
YOU WERE SO CLOSE...

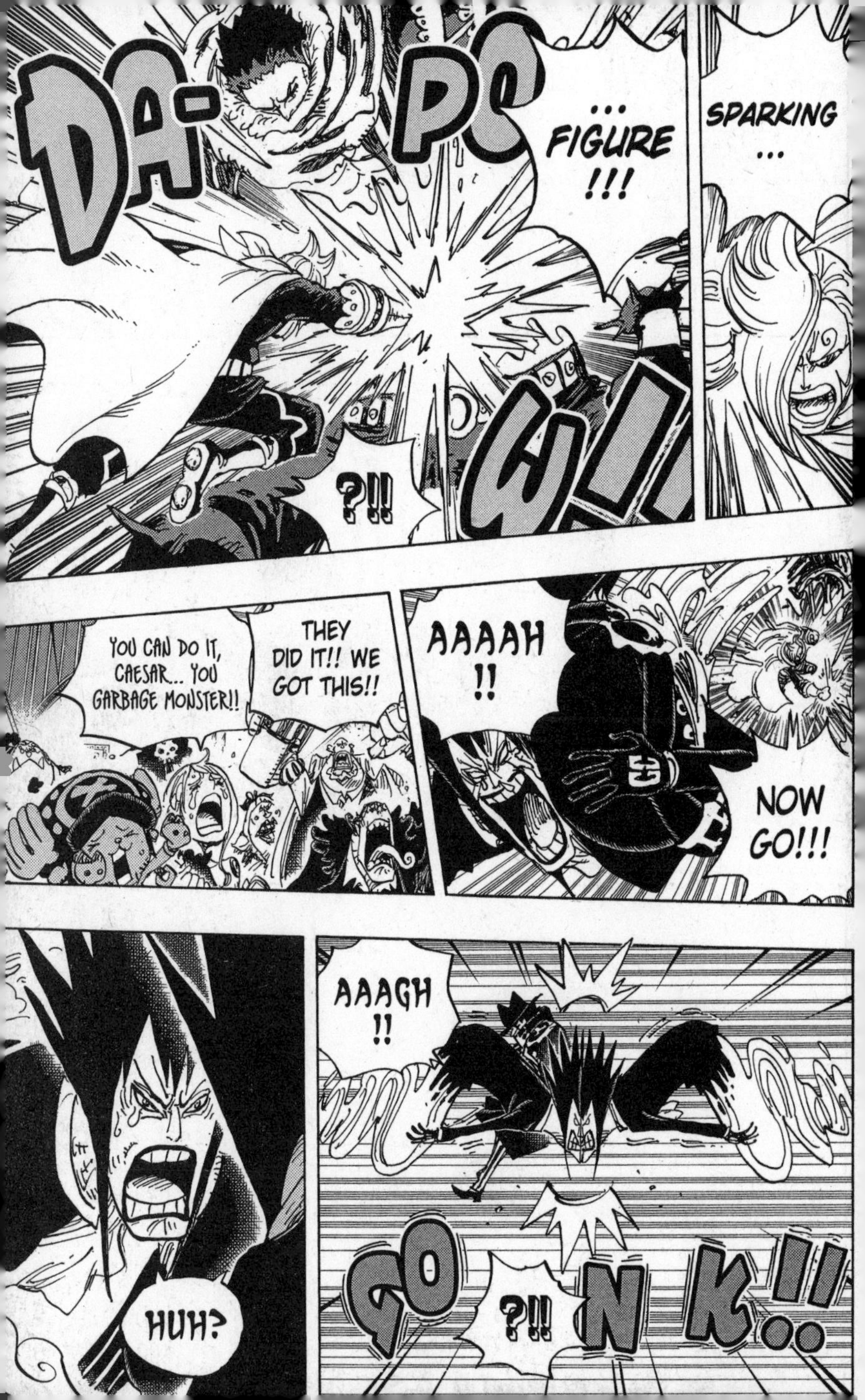

SPARKING ...
... FIGURE !!!
DA-
PO
?!!
NOW GO!!!
AAAAH !!
THEY DID IT!! WE GOT THIS!!
YOU CAN DO IT, CAESAR... YOU GARBAGE MONSTER!!
AAAGH !!
GONK!!
?!!
HUH?

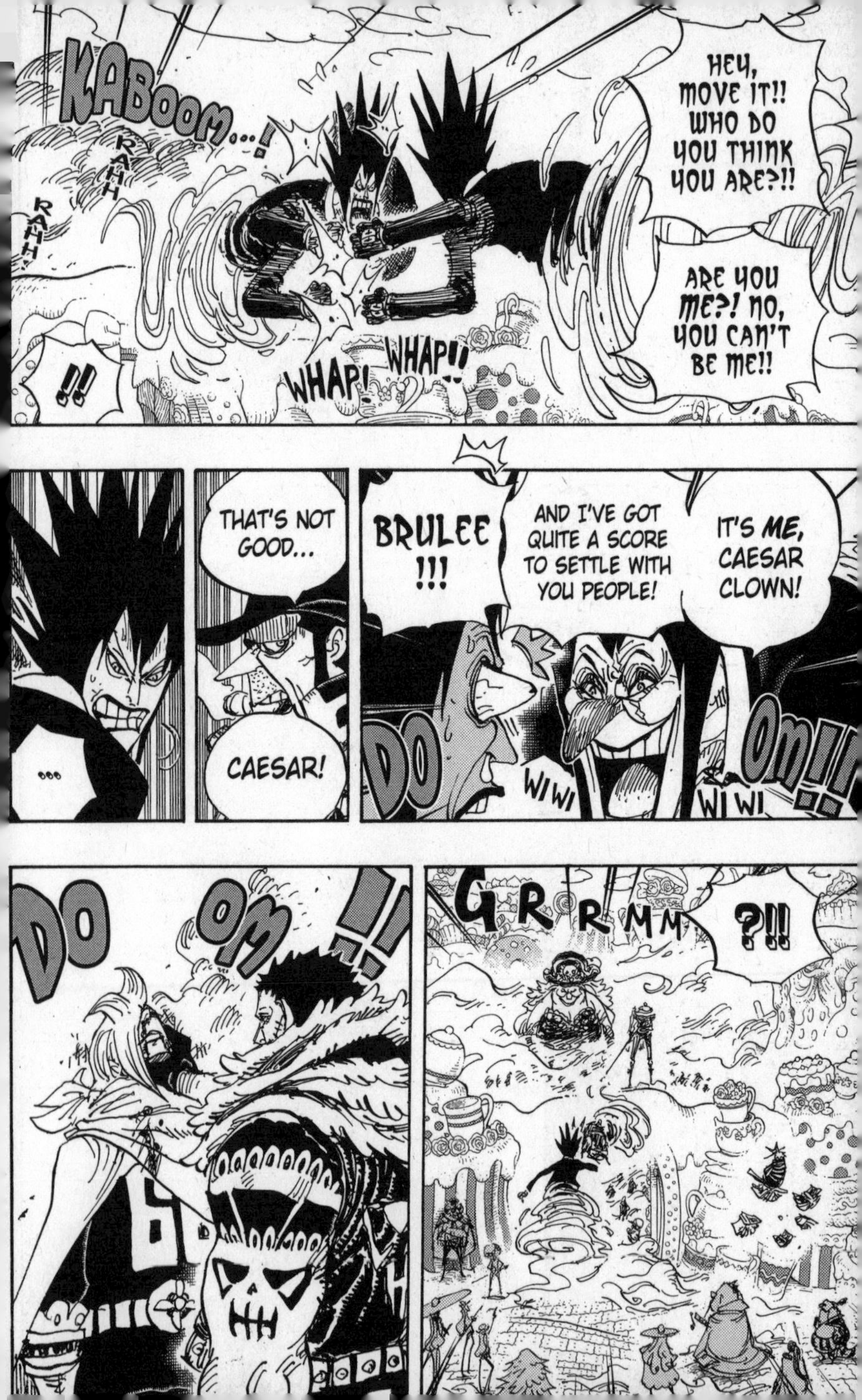
HEY, MOVE IT!! WHO DO YOU THINK YOU ARE?!!
ARE YOU ME?! NO, YOU CAN'T BE ME!!
KABOOM...!
RAHH
RAHH!
WHAP!!
WHAP!
!!
IT'S ME, CAESAR CLOWN!
AND I'VE GOT QUITE A SCORE TO SETTLE WITH YOU PEOPLE!
WI WI
WI WI
DOOM!!
BRULEE!!!
THAT'S NOT GOOD...
CAESAR!
...
?!!
GRRRMM
DOOM!!

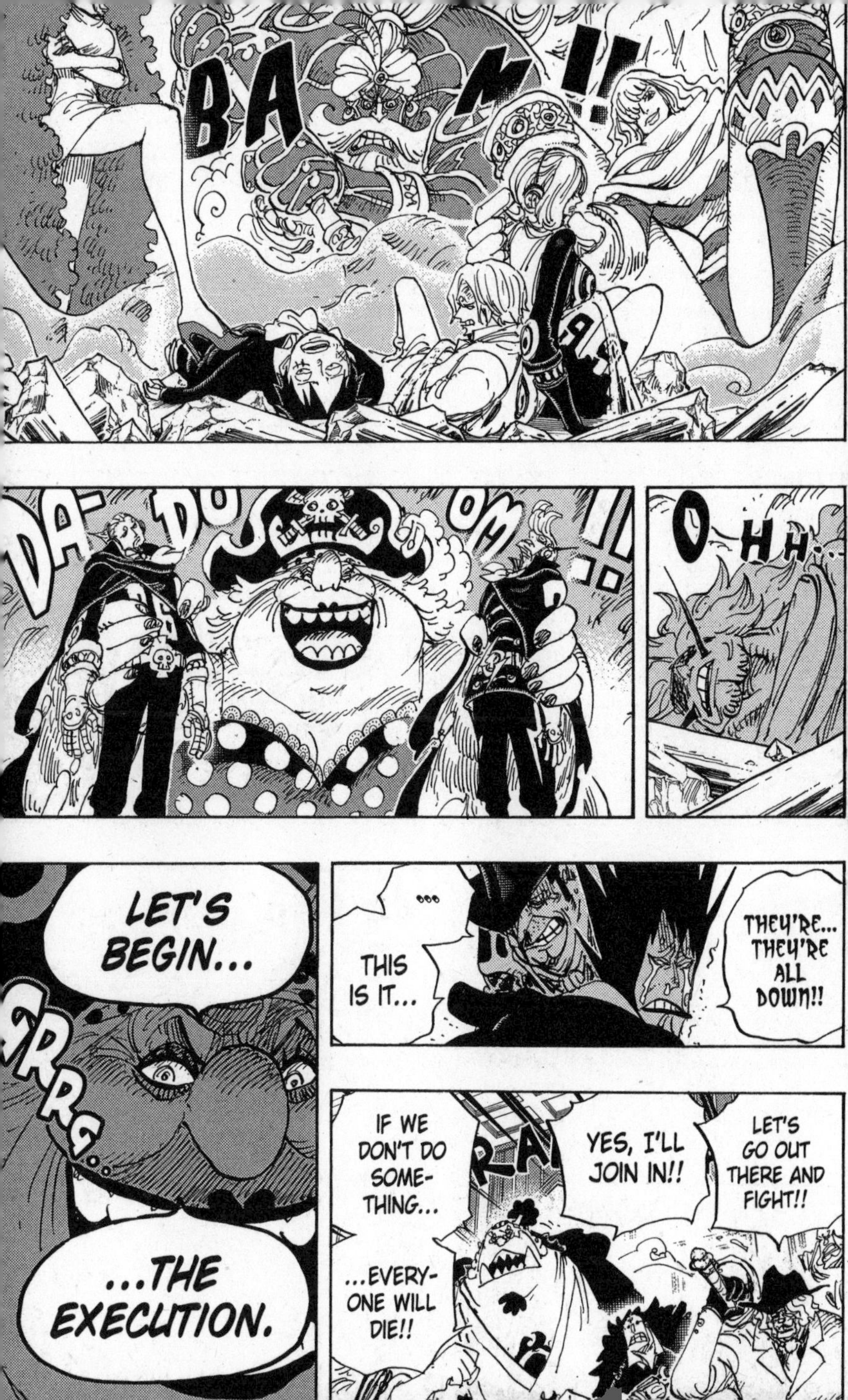
BAM!!
OHH...
DA-DOOM!!
THEY'RE... THEY'RE ALL DOWN!!
...
THIS IS IT...
LET'S GO OUT THERE AND FIGHT!!
YES, I'LL JOIN IN!!
RA
IF WE DON'T DO SOME-THING...
...EVERY-ONE WILL DIE!!
LET'S BEGIN...
GRRG...
...THE EXECUTION.

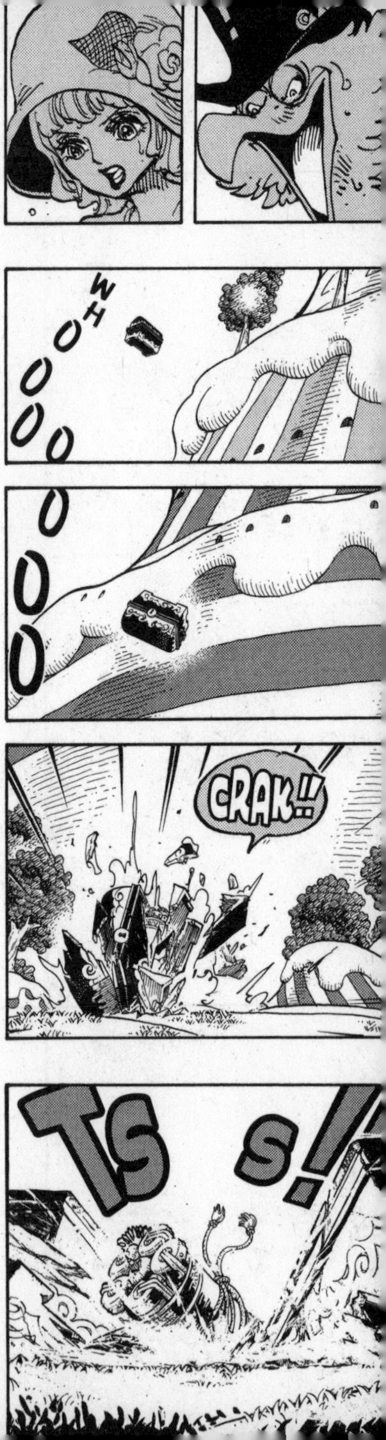
WHOOOOOOOOOOO
CRAK!!
TS S!!
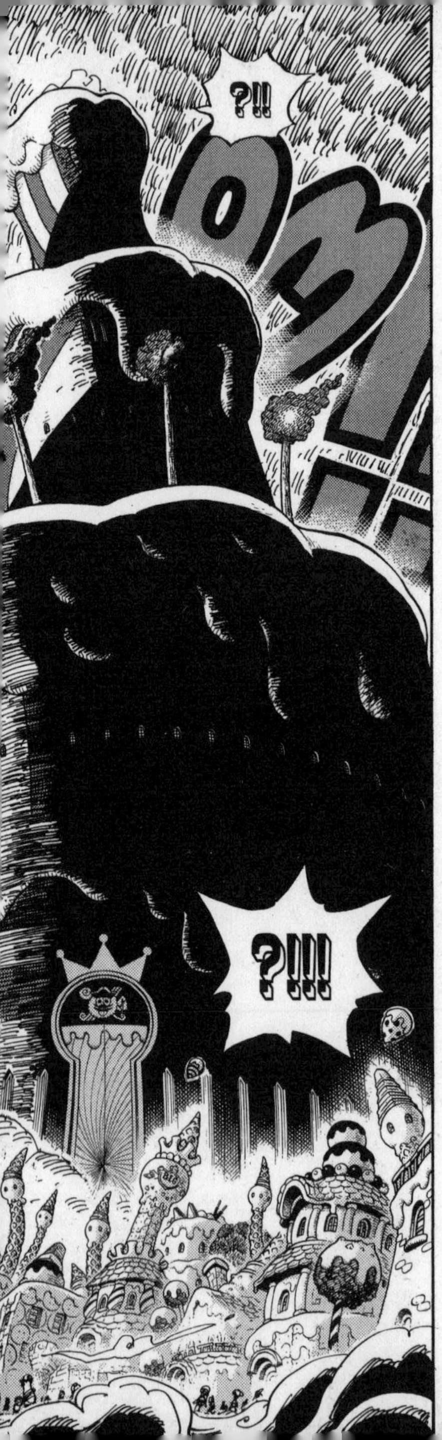
?!!
?!!!

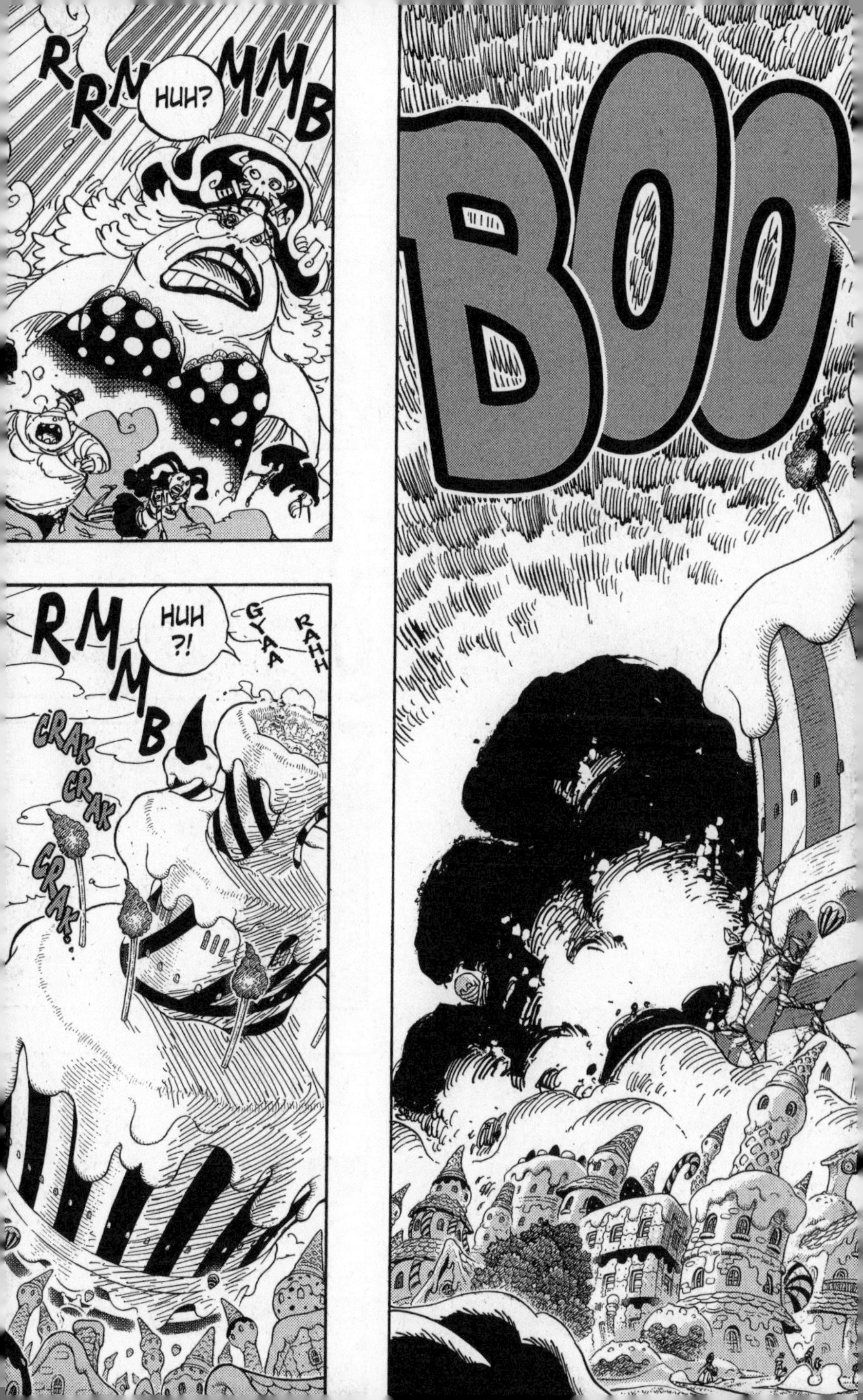
BOOO
RRN
HUH?
MMB
RMMMB
HUH ?!
GYAA
RAHH
CRAK
CRAK
CRAK

Chapter 872: THICK AND FLUFFY

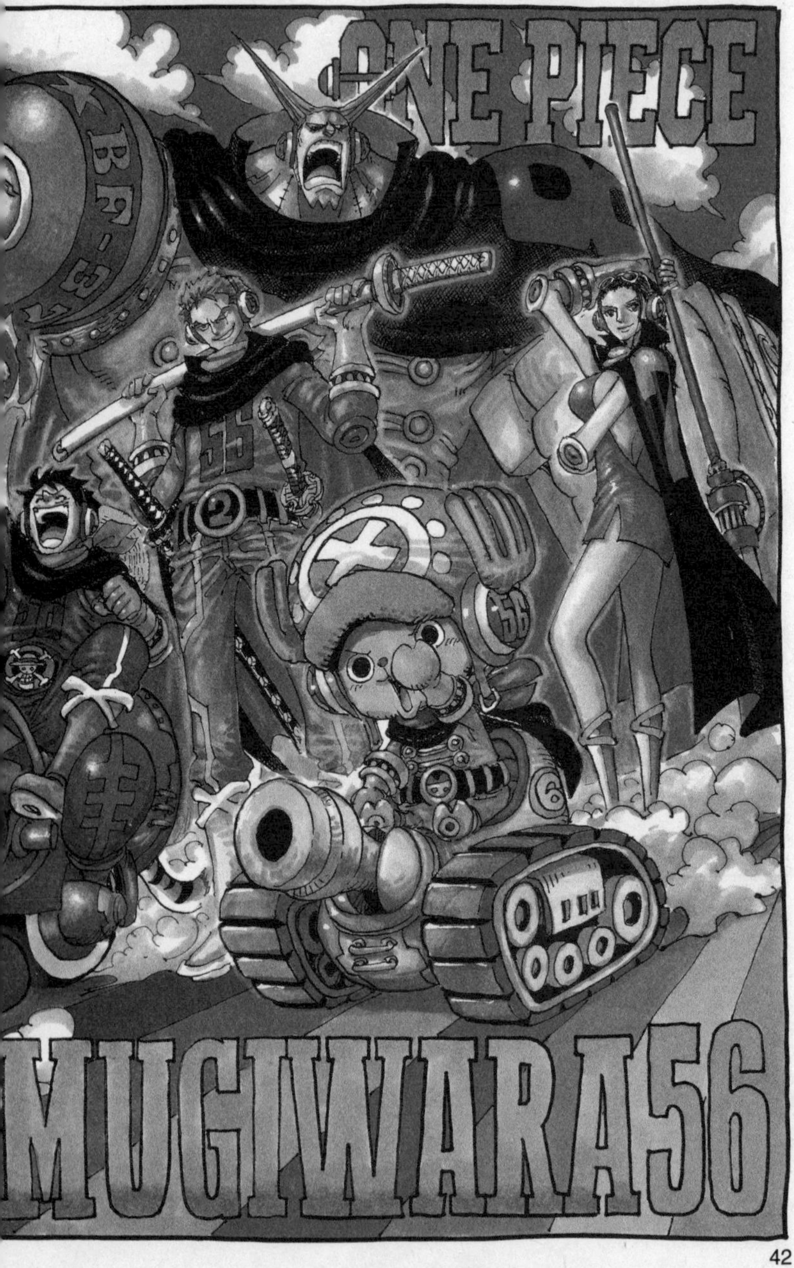
ONE PIECE
BF-3
MUGIWARA56

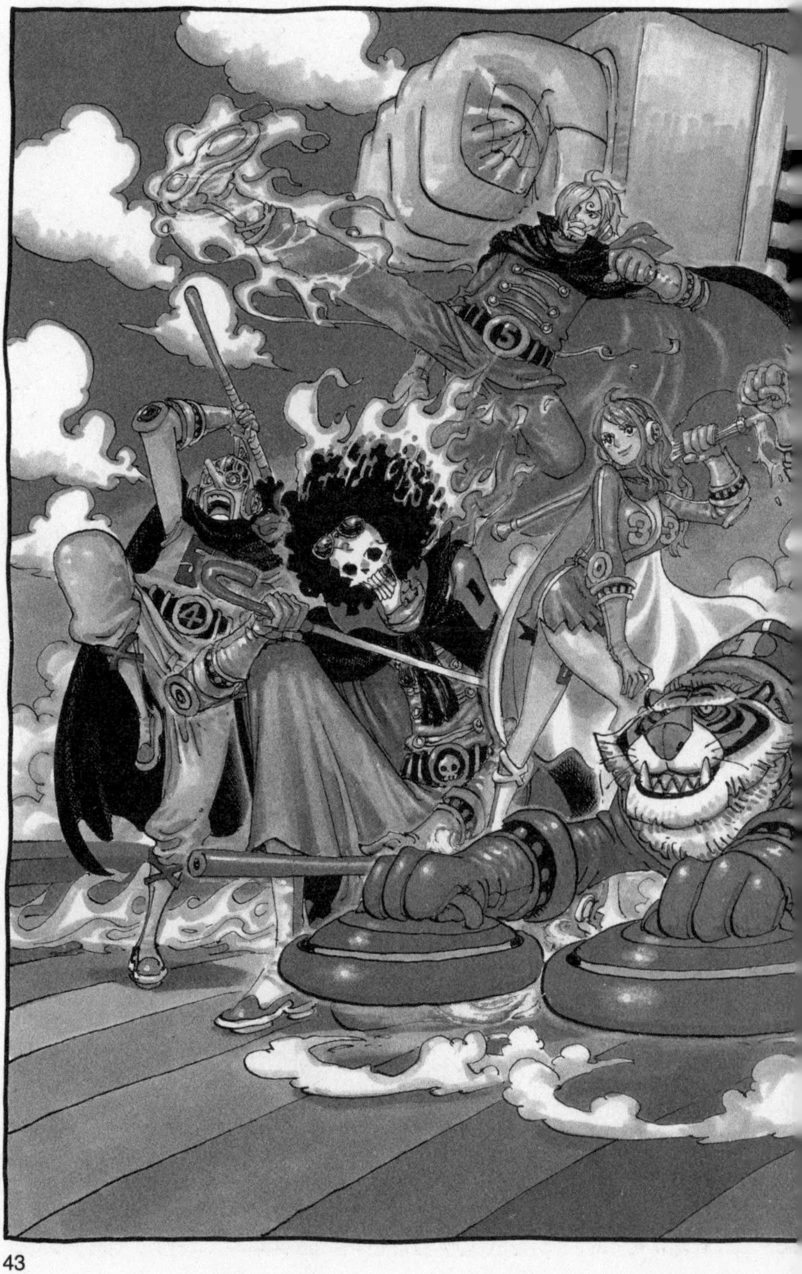

vol.87

ONE PIECE

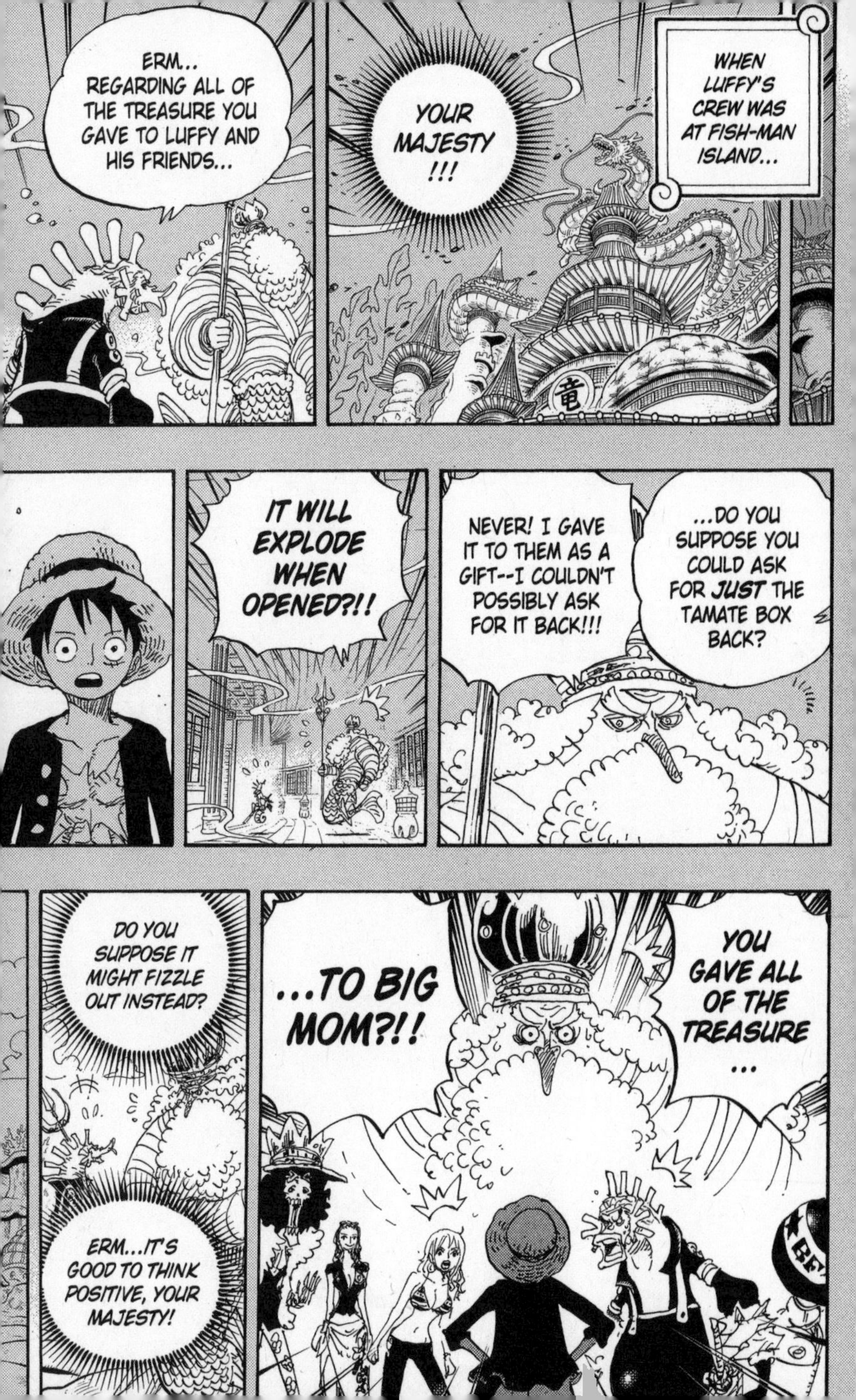
WHEN LUFFY'S CREW WAS AT FISH-MAN ISLAND...
YOUR MAJESTY!!!
ERM... REGARDING ALL OF THE TREASURE YOU GAVE TO LUFFY AND HIS FRIENDS...
...DO YOU SUPPOSE YOU COULD ASK FOR JUST THE TAMATE BOX BACK?
NEVER! I GAVE IT TO THEM AS A GIFT--I COULDN'T POSSIBLY ASK FOR IT BACK!!!
IT WILL EXPLODE WHEN OPENED?!!
YOU GAVE ALL OF THE TREASURE...
...TO BIG MOM?!!
DO YOU SUPPOSE IT MIGHT FIZZLE OUT INSTEAD?
ERM...IT'S GOOD TO THINK POSITIVE, YOUR MAJESTY!

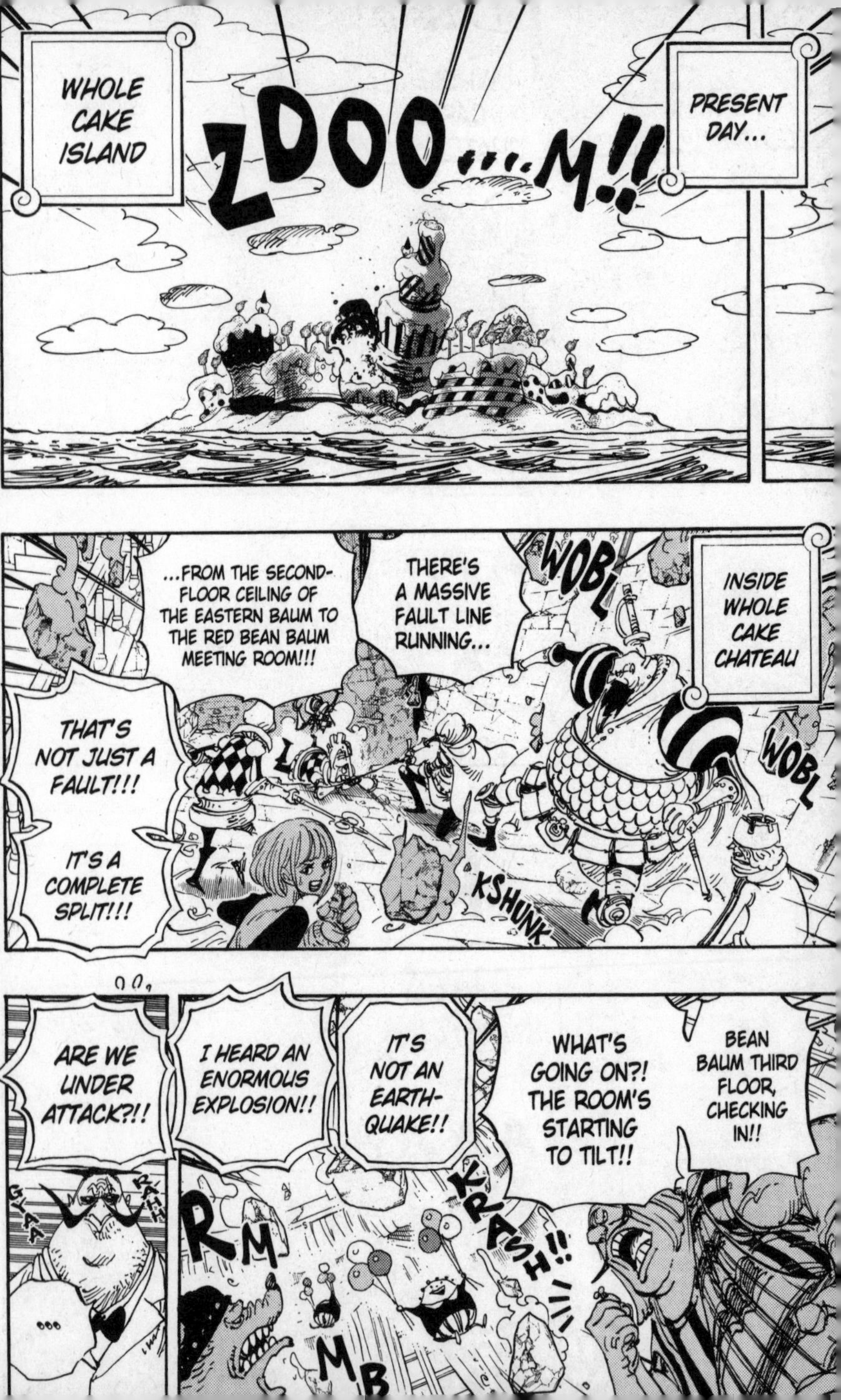
PRESENT DAY...
ZDOOO...M!!
WHOLE CAKE ISLAND
INSIDE WHOLE CAKE CHATEAU
WOBL
THERE'S A MASSIVE FAULT LINE RUNNING...
...FROM THE SECOND-FLOOR CEILING OF THE EASTERN BAUM TO THE RED BEAN BAUM MEETING ROOM!!!
WOBL
KSHUNK
THAT'S NOT JUST A FAULT!!!
IT'S A COMPLETE SPLIT!!!
BEAN BAUM THIRD FLOOR, CHECKING IN!!
WHAT'S GOING ON?! THE ROOM'S STARTING TO TILT!!
IT'S NOT AN EARTH-QUAKE!!
KRASH!!
I HEARD AN ENORMOUS EXPLOSION!!
RMMB
ARE WE UNDER ATTACK?!!
RAHH
GYAA
...

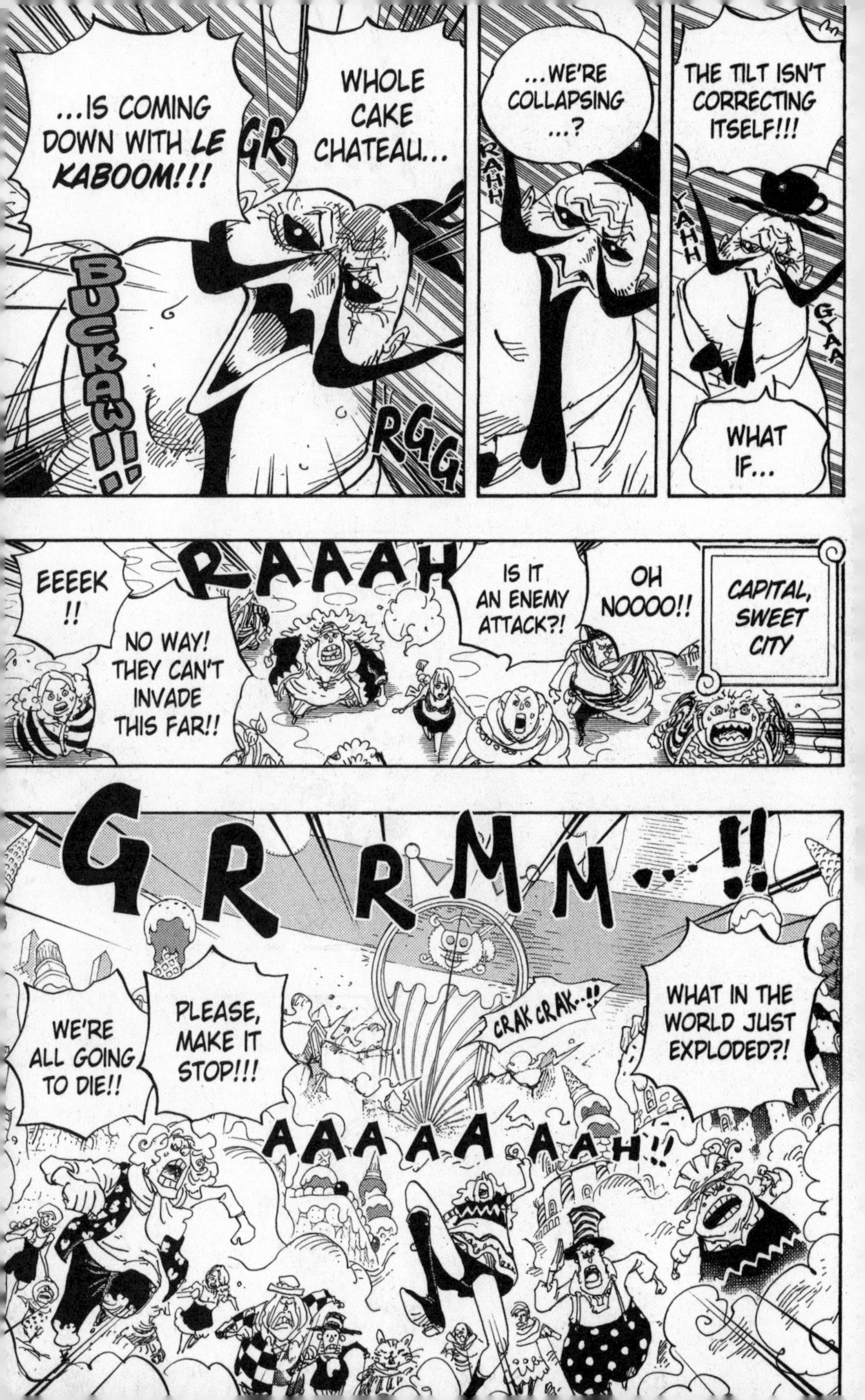
THE TILT ISN'T CORRECTING ITSELF!!!
YAHH
GYAA
WHAT IF...
...WE'RE COLLAPSING ...?
RAHH
WHOLE CAKE CHATEAU...
GR
...IS COMING DOWN WITH LE KABOOM!!!
RGG
BUCKAW!!
CAPITAL, SWEET CITY
OH NOOOO!!
IS IT AN ENEMY ATTACK?!
RAAAH
NO WAY! THEY CAN'T INVADE THIS FAR!!
EEEEK!!
GRRMM..!!
WHAT IN THE WORLD JUST EXPLODED?!
CRAK CRAK..!!
PLEASE, MAKE IT STOP!!!
WE'RE ALL GOING TO DIE!!
AAAAAAAH!!

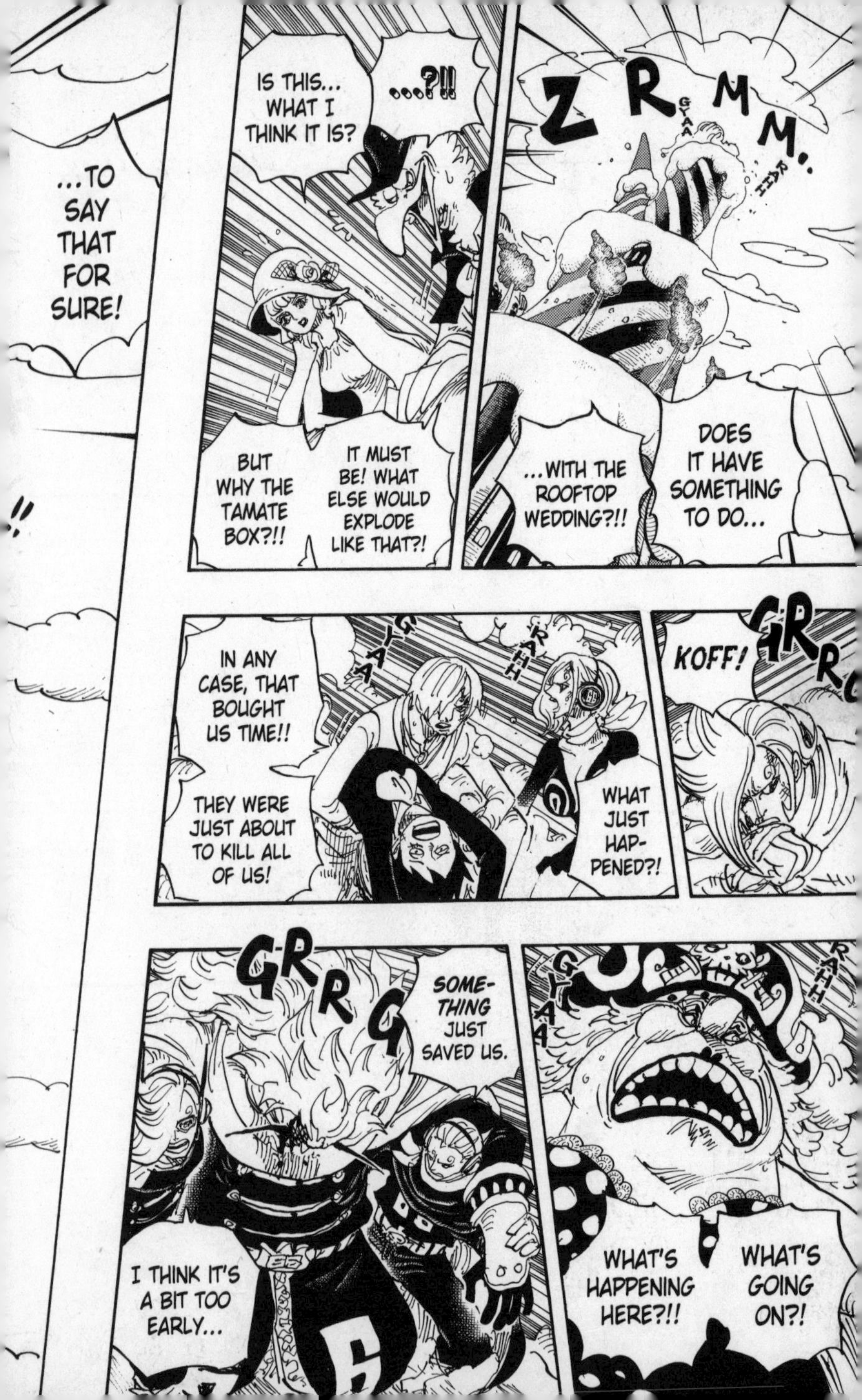
ZRMM..
GYAA
RAHH
DOES IT HAVE SOMETHING TO DO...
...WITH THE ROOFTOP WEDDING?!!
...?!!
IS THIS... WHAT I THINK IT IS?
IT MUST BE! WHAT ELSE WOULD EXPLODE LIKE THAT?!
BUT WHY THE TAMATE BOX?!!
...TO SAY THAT FOR SURE!
!!
GRRG
KOFF!
RAHH
WHAT JUST HAP-PENED?!
GYAA
IN ANY CASE, THAT BOUGHT US TIME!!
THEY WERE JUST ABOUT TO KILL ALL OF US!
RAHH
GYAA
WHAT'S GOING ON?!
WHAT'S HAPPENING HERE?!!
SOME-THING JUST SAVED US.
GRRG
I THINK IT'S A BIT TOO EARLY...

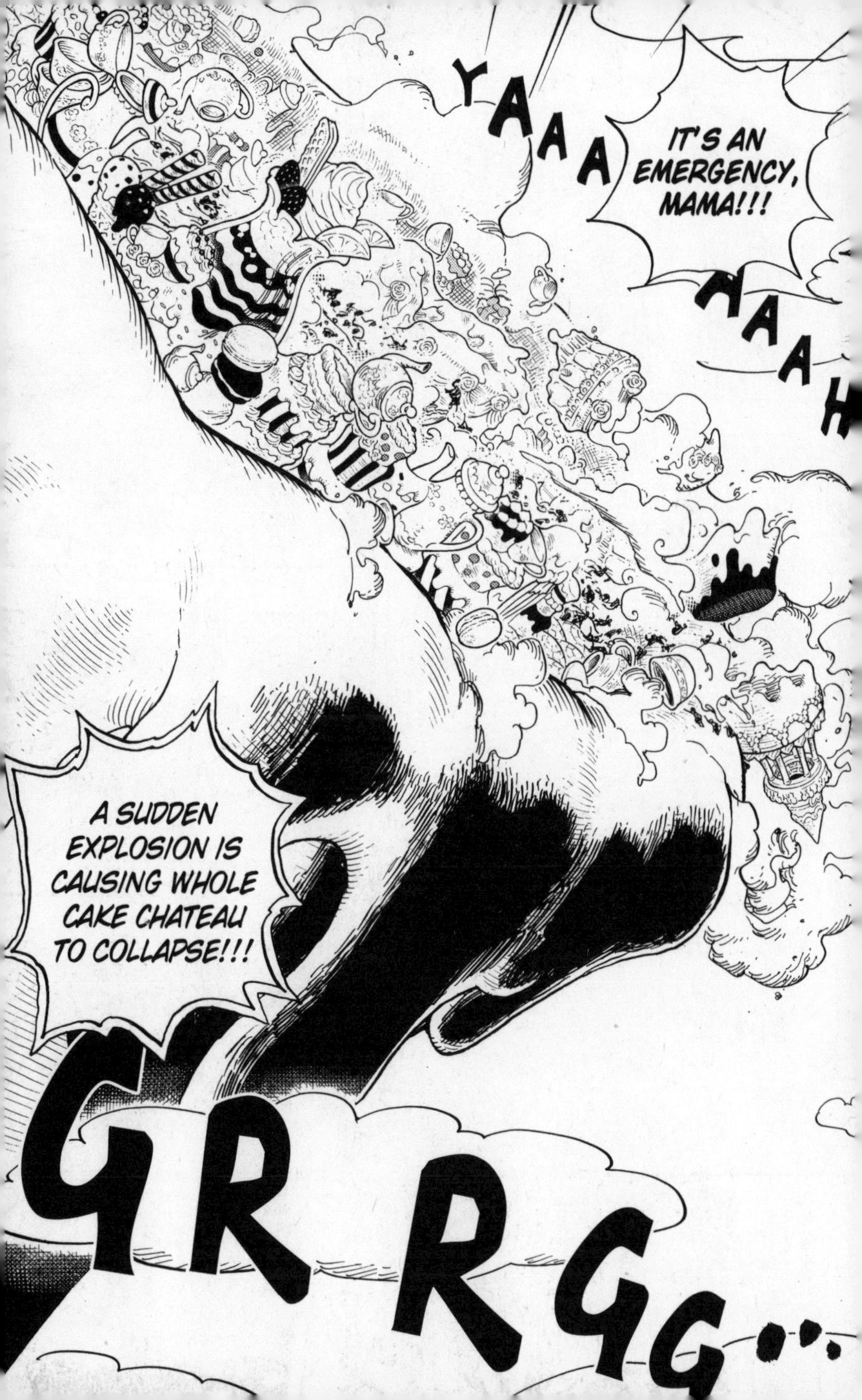
YAAAAAAAH
IT'S AN EMERGENCY, MAMA!!!
A SUDDEN EXPLOSION IS CAUSING WHOLE CAKE CHATEAU TO COLLAPSE!!!
GRRGG...

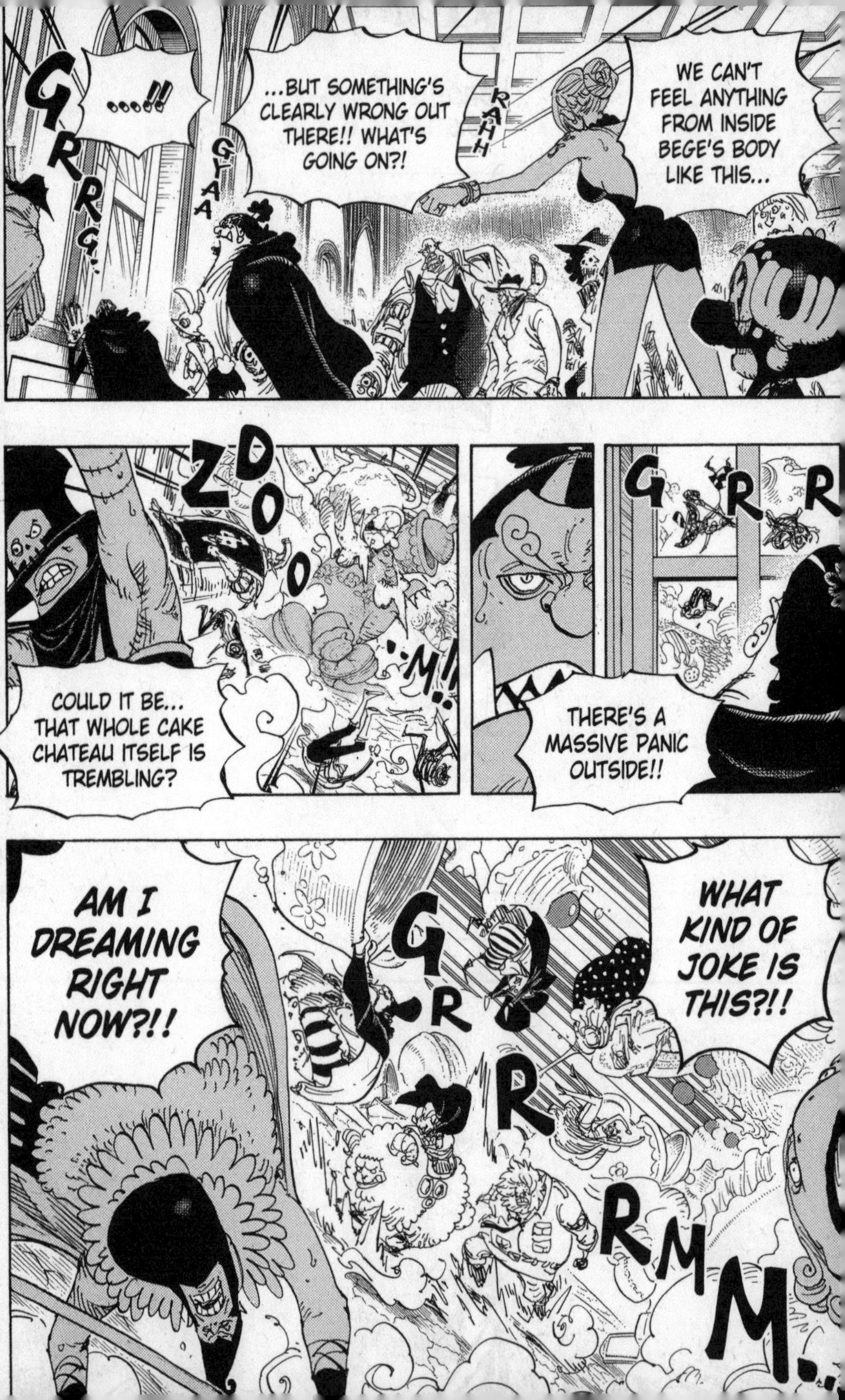
WE CAN'T FEEL ANYTHING FROM INSIDE BEGE'S BODY LIKE THIS...
RAHH
...BUT SOMETHING'S CLEARLY WRONG OUT THERE!! WHAT'S GOING ON?!
GYAA
.....!!
GRRRG!
GRR
THERE'S A MASSIVE PANIC OUTSIDE!!
ZDOOOM!!
COULD IT BE... THAT WHOLE CAKE CHATEAU ITSELF IS TREMBLING?
WHAT KIND OF JOKE IS THIS?!!
GRRRRMM..
AM I DREAMING RIGHT NOW?!!

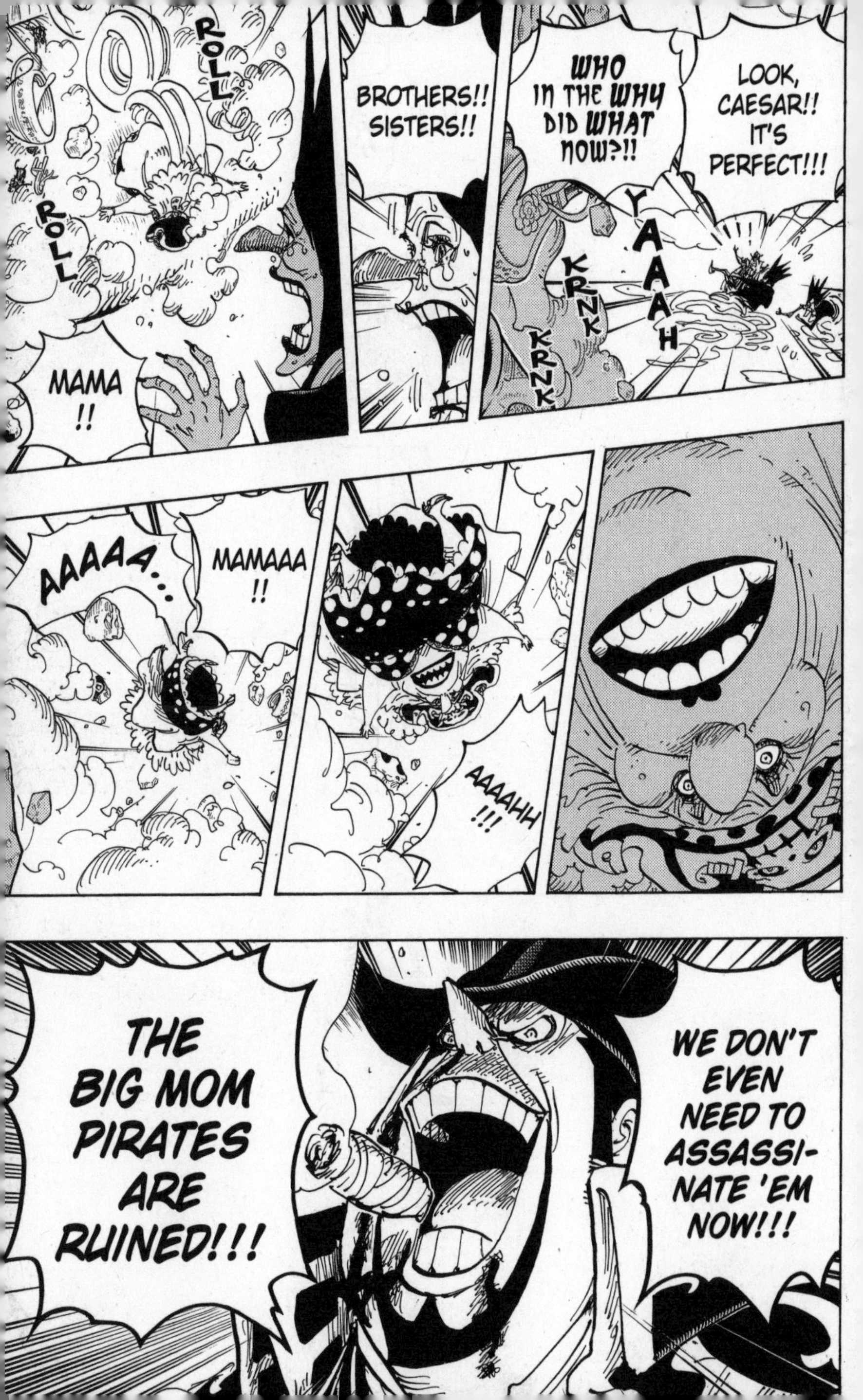
LOOK, CAESAR!! IT'S PERFECT!!!
YAAAH
WHO IN THE WHY DID WHAT NOW?!!
KRNK KRNK
BROTHERS!! SISTERS!!
MAMA !!
ROLL
ROLL
AAAAHH !!!
MAMAAA !!
AAAAA...
WE DON'T EVEN NEED TO ASSASSI- NATE 'EM NOW!!!
THE BIG MOM PIRATES ARE RUINED!!!

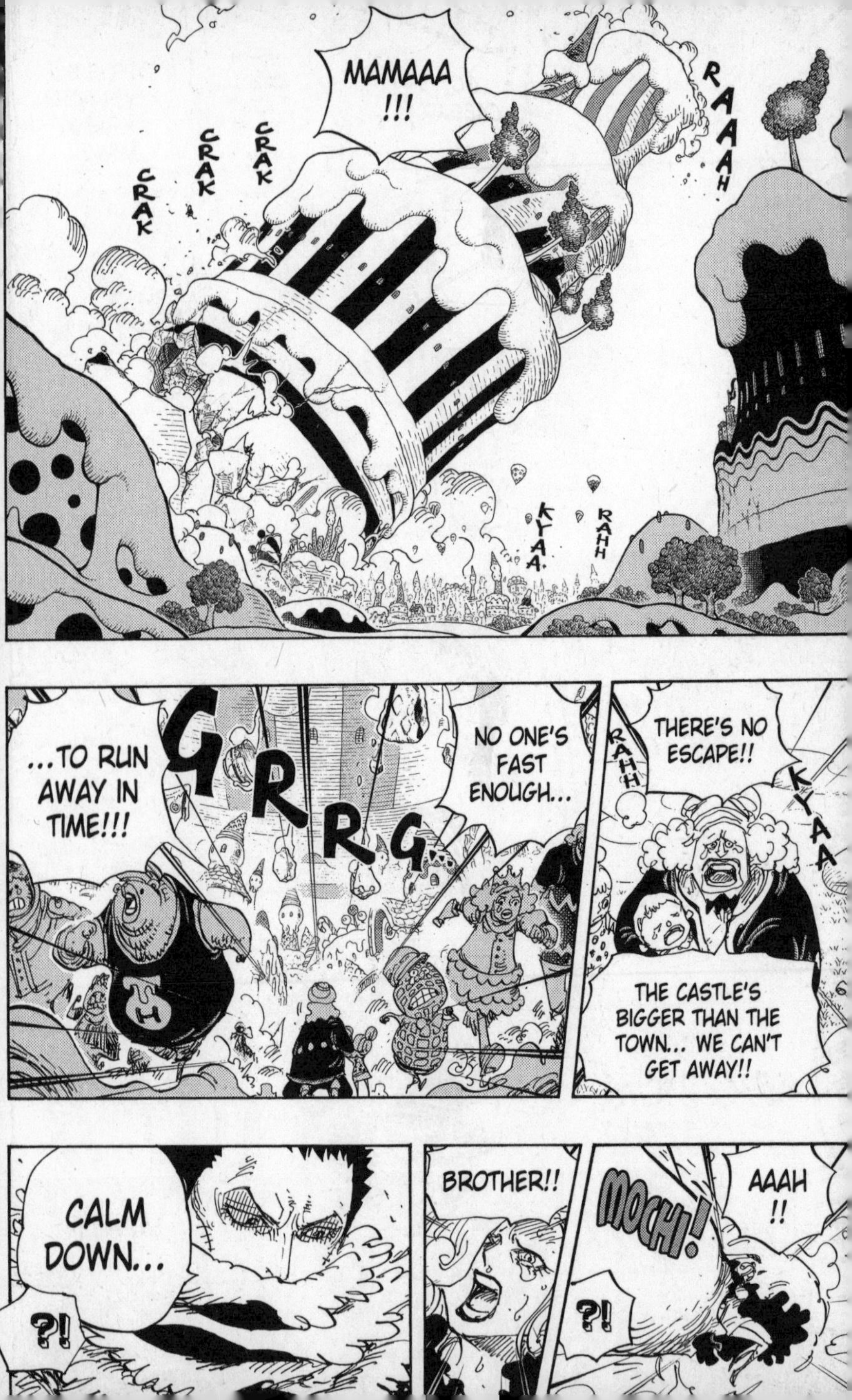
RAAAAH
MAMAAA !!!
CRAK
CRAK
CRAK
RAHH
KYAA
THERE'S NO ESCAPE!!
RAHH
KYAA
THE CASTLE'S BIGGER THAN THE TOWN... WE CAN'T GET AWAY!!
NO ONE'S FAST ENOUGH...
GRRRG
...TO RUN AWAY IN TIME!!!
AAAH !!
MOCHI!
?!
BROTHER!!
CALM DOWN...
?!

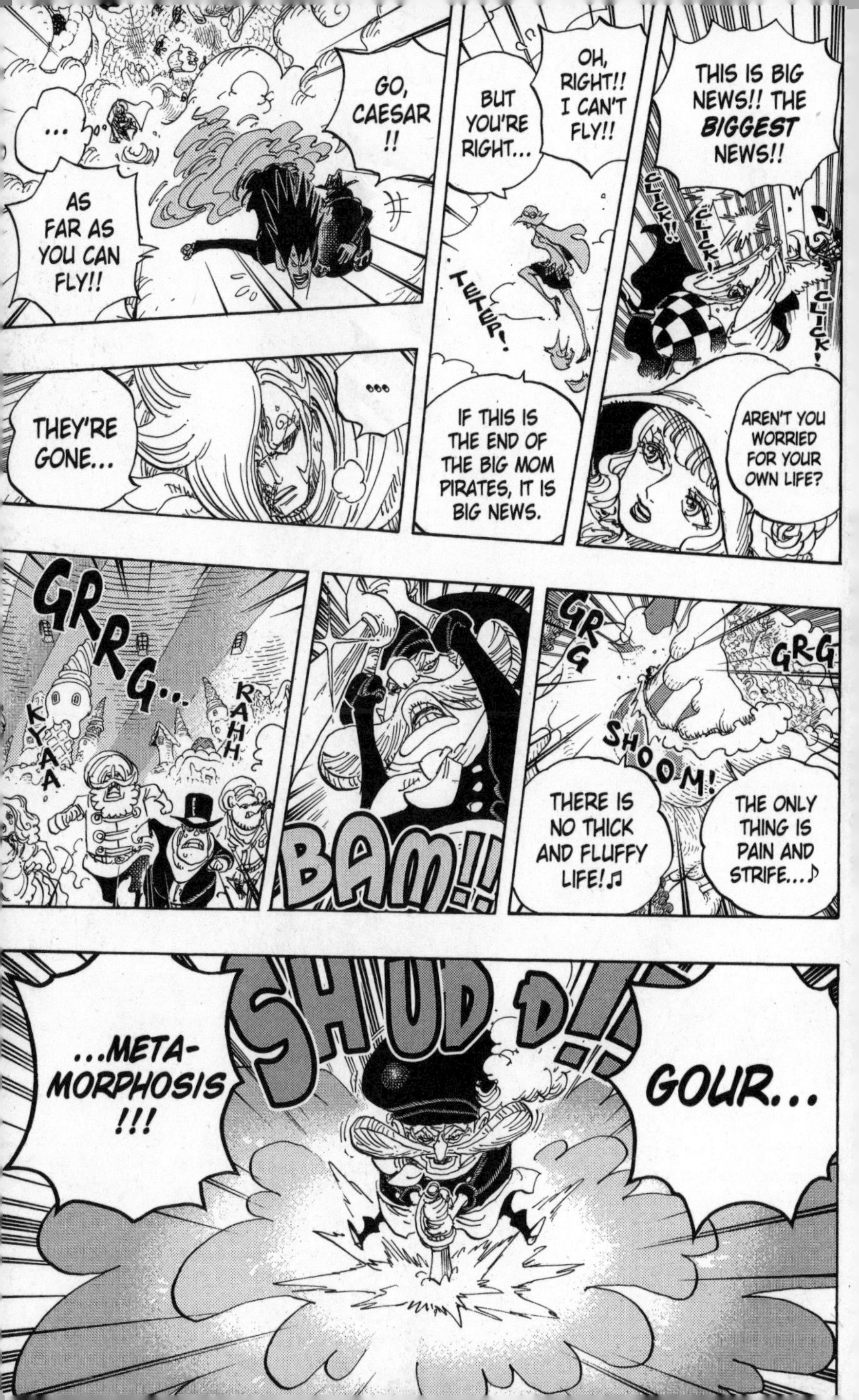
THIS IS BIG NEWS!! THE BIGGEST NEWS!!
CLICK!!
CLICK!
CLICK!
AREN'T YOU WORRIED FOR YOUR OWN LIFE?
OH, RIGHT!! I CAN'T FLY!!
BUT YOU'RE RIGHT...
TETEP!
IF THIS IS THE END OF THE BIG MOM PIRATES, IT IS BIG NEWS.
GO, CAESAR!!
...
AS FAR AS YOU CAN FLY!!
...
THEY'RE GONE...
GR-G
GRG
SHOOM!
THERE IS NO THICK AND FLUFFY LIFE!♫
THE ONLY THING IS PAIN AND STRIFE...♪
BAM!!
GRRRG...
RAHH
KYAA
GOUR...
SHUD D!!
...META-MORPHOSIS!!!

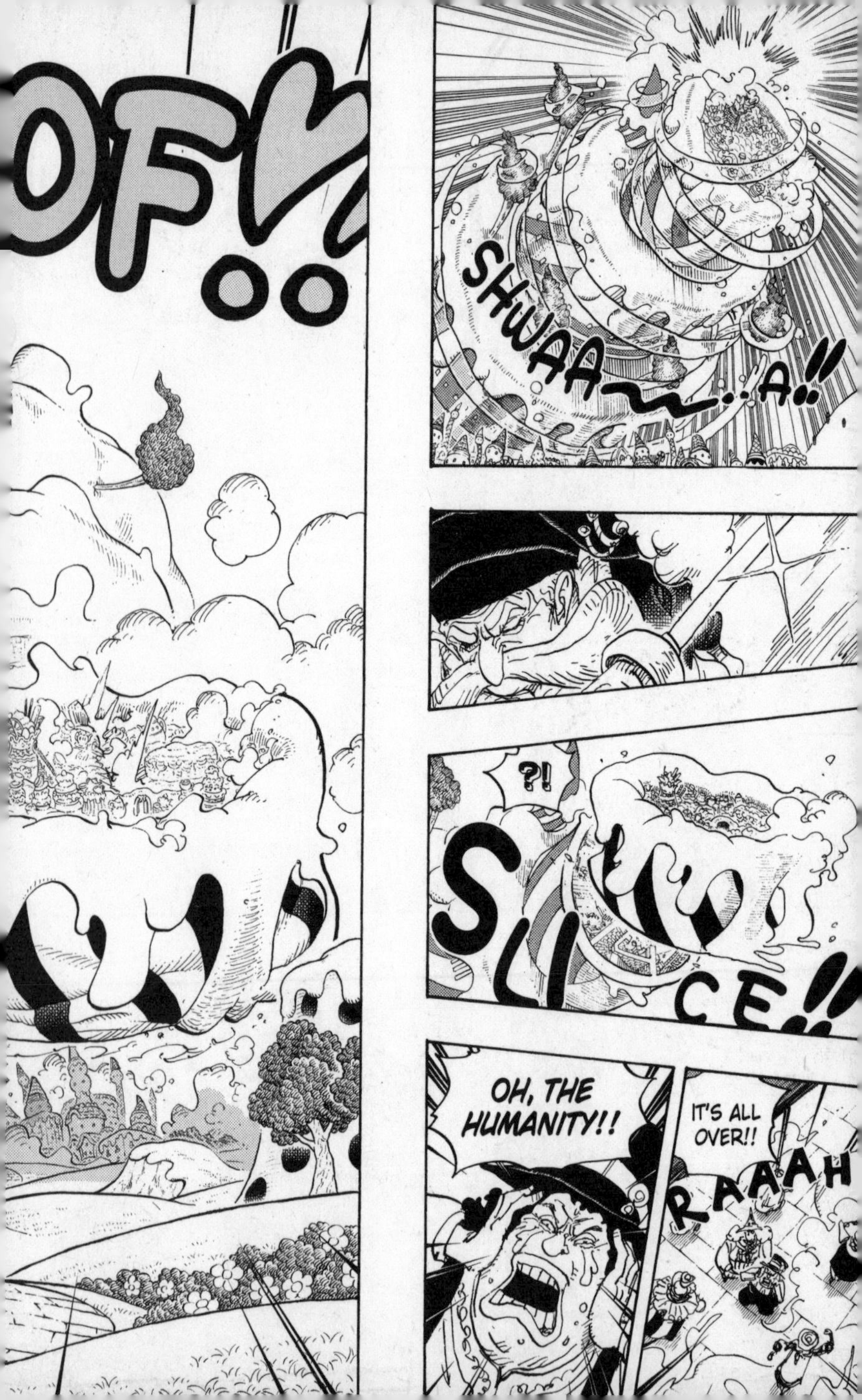
SHWAA~~A!!
?!
SLICE!!
IT'S ALL OVER!!
RAAAH
OH, THE HUMANITY!!
OF!!..

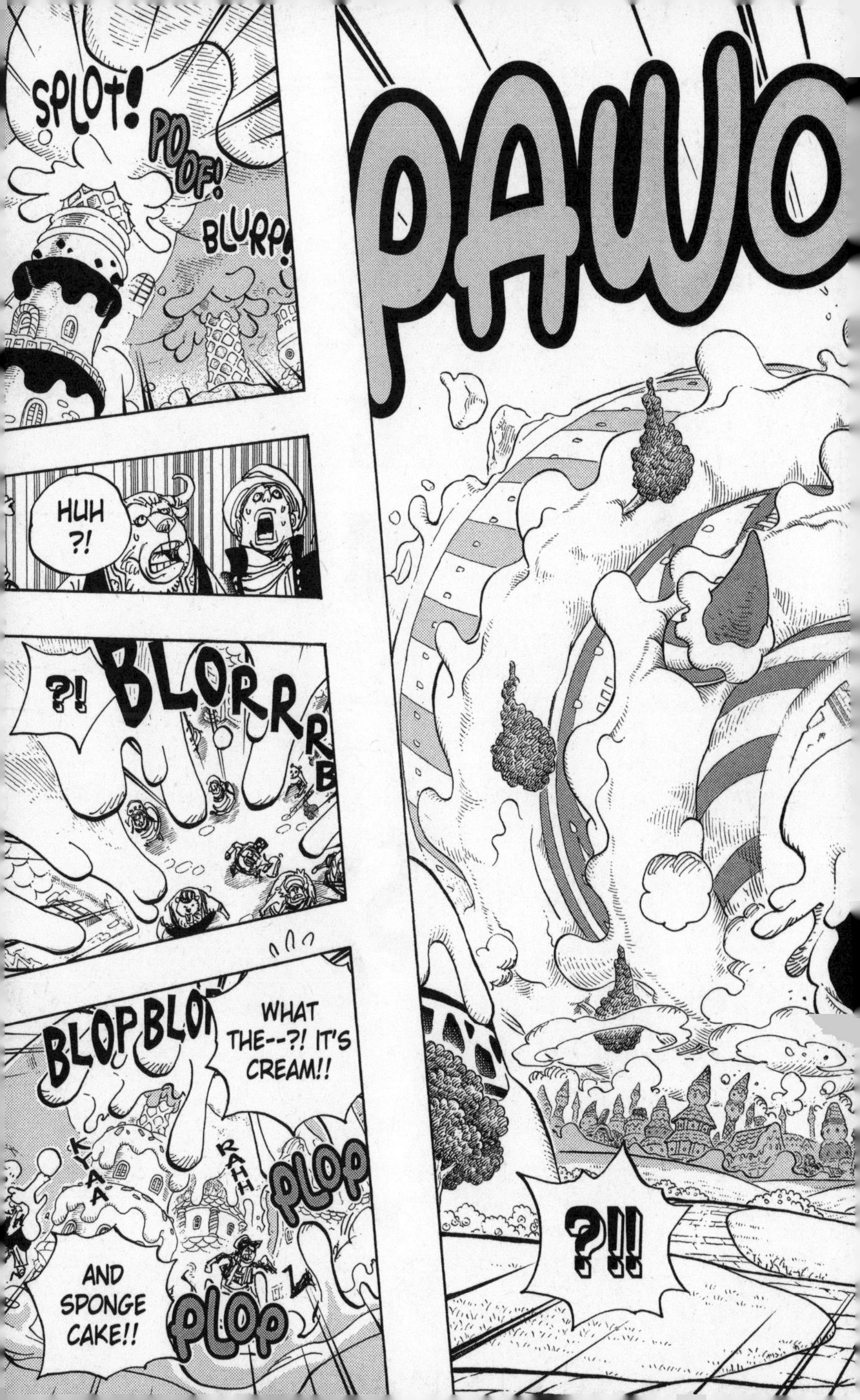
PAWO
?!!
SPLOT!
POOF!
BLURP!
HUH ?!
?!
BLORRRRB
WHAT THE--?! IT'S CREAM!!
BLOP BLO
RAHH
PLOP
KYAA
AND SPONGE CAKE!!
PLOP

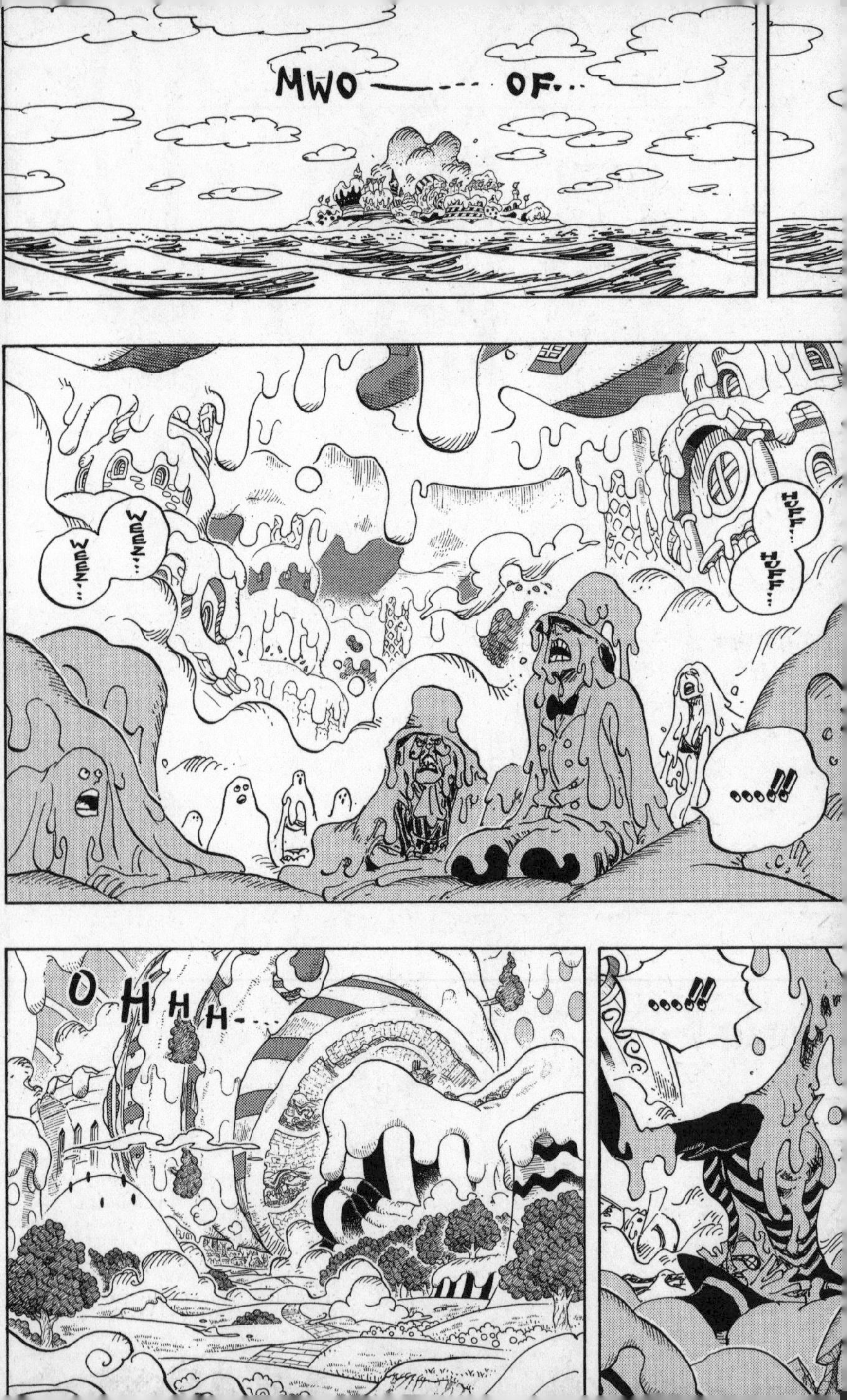
MWO—---- OF...
HUFF... HUFF...
WEEZ... WEEZ...
....!!
....!!
OHHH-...

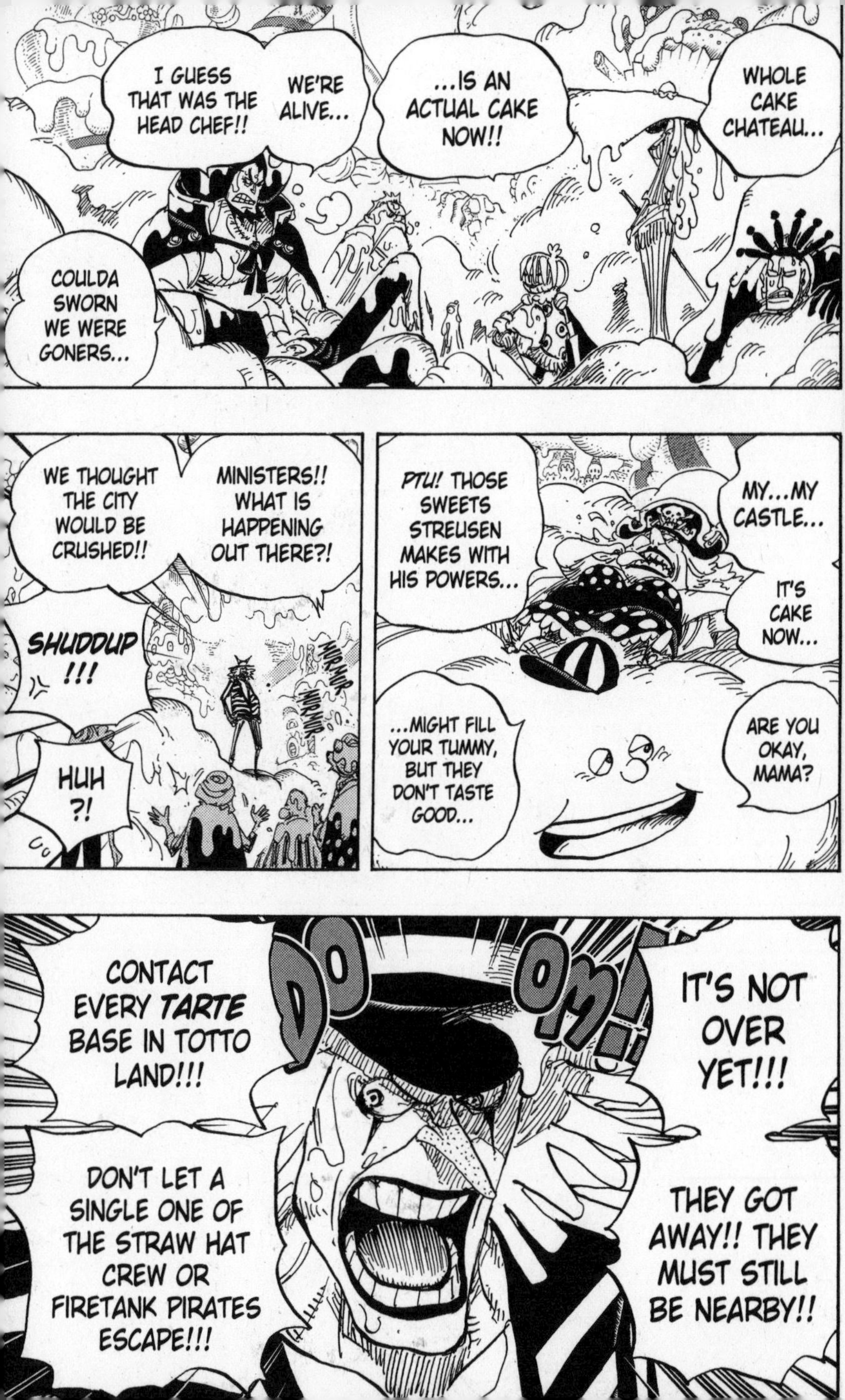
WHOLE CAKE CHATEAU...
...IS AN ACTUAL CAKE NOW!!
WE'RE ALIVE...
I GUESS THAT WAS THE HEAD CHEF!!
COULDA SWORN WE WERE GONERS...
MY...MY CASTLE...
IT'S CAKE NOW...
PTU! THOSE SWEETS STREUSEN MAKES WITH HIS POWERS...
ARE YOU OKAY, MAMA?
...MIGHT FILL YOUR TUMMY, BUT THEY DON'T TASTE GOOD...
MINISTERS!! WHAT IS HAPPENING OUT THERE?!
WE THOUGHT THE CITY WOULD BE CRUSHED!!
MUR MUR
MUR MUR
SHUDDUP!!!
HUH?!
IT'S NOT OVER YET!!!
DOOM
CONTACT EVERY TARTE BASE IN TOTTO LAND!!!
THEY GOT AWAY!! THEY MUST STILL BE NEARBY!!
DON'T LET A SINGLE ONE OF THE STRAW HAT CREW OR FIRETANK PIRATES ESCAPE!!!

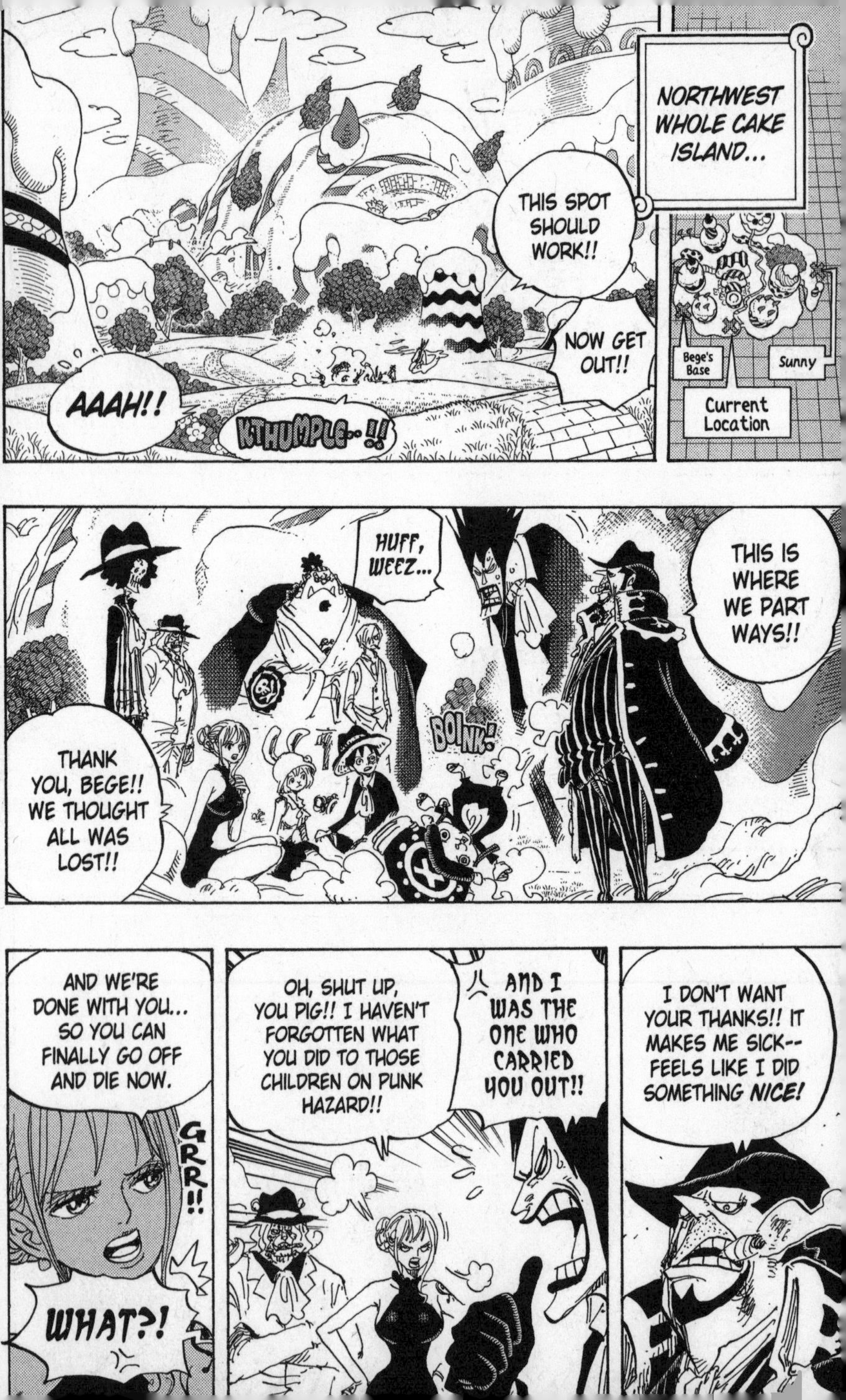
NORTHWEST WHOLE CAKE ISLAND...
Bege's Base
Sunny
Current Location
THIS SPOT SHOULD WORK!!
NOW GET OUT!!
K'THUMPLE..!!
AAAH!!
THIS IS WHERE WE PART WAYS!!
HUFF, WEEZ...
BOINK!
THANK YOU, BEGE!! WE THOUGHT ALL WAS LOST!!
I DON'T WANT YOUR THANKS!! IT MAKES ME SICK--FEELS LIKE I DID SOMETHING NICE!
AND I WAS THE ONE WHO CARRIED YOU OUT!!
OH, SHUT UP, YOU PIG!! I HAVEN'T FORGOTTEN WHAT YOU DID TO THOSE CHILDREN ON PUNK HAZARD!!
AND WE'RE DONE WITH YOU... SO YOU CAN FINALLY GO OFF AND DIE NOW.
GRR!!
WHAT?!

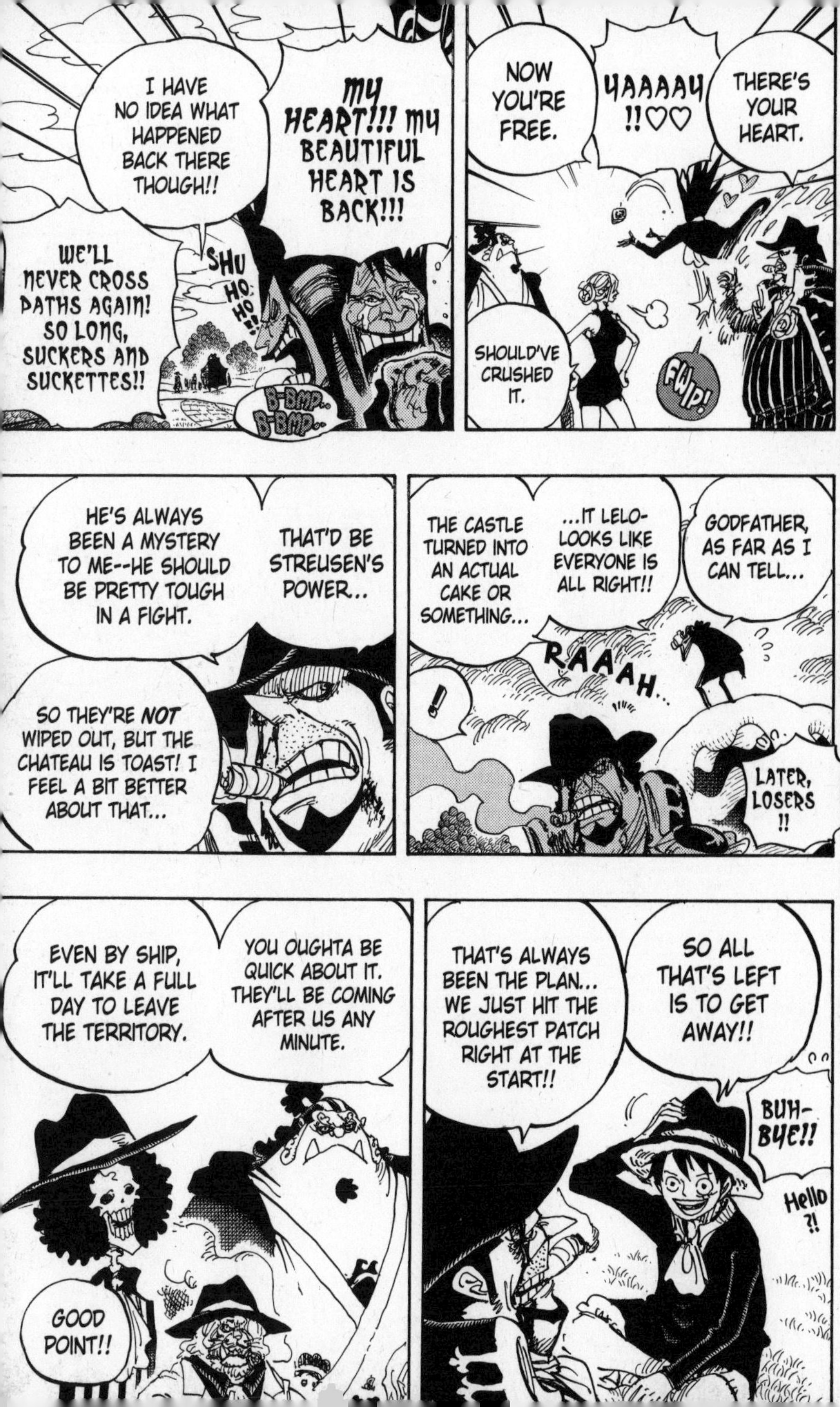
THERE'S YOUR HEART.
YAAAAY !!♡♡
NOW YOU'RE FREE.
FWIP!
SHOULD'VE CRUSHED IT.
MY HEART!!! MY BEAUTIFUL HEART IS BACK!!!
I HAVE NO IDEA WHAT HAPPENED BACK THERE THOUGH!!
B-BMP.. B-BMP..
SHU HO HO!!
WE'LL NEVER CROSS PATHS AGAIN! SO LONG, SUCKERS AND SUCKETTES!!
GODFATHER, AS FAR AS I CAN TELL...
...IT LELO- LOOKS LIKE EVERYONE IS ALL RIGHT!!
THE CASTLE TURNED INTO AN ACTUAL CAKE OR SOMETHING...
RAAAH...
!
LATER, LOSERS !!
THAT'D BE STREUSEN'S POWER..
HE'S ALWAYS BEEN A MYSTERY TO ME--HE SHOULD BE PRETTY TOUGH IN A FIGHT.
SO THEY'RE *NOT* WIPED OUT, BUT THE CHATEAU IS TOAST! I FEEL A BIT BETTER ABOUT THAT...
SO ALL THAT'S LEFT IS TO GET AWAY!!
THAT'S ALWAYS BEEN THE PLAN... WE JUST HIT THE ROUGHEST PATCH RIGHT AT THE START!!
BUH-BYE!!
Hello ?!
YOU OUGHTA BE QUICK ABOUT IT. THEY'LL BE COMING AFTER US ANY MINUTE.
EVEN BY SHIP, IT'LL TAKE A FULL DAY TO LEAVE THE TERRITORY.
GOOD POINT!!

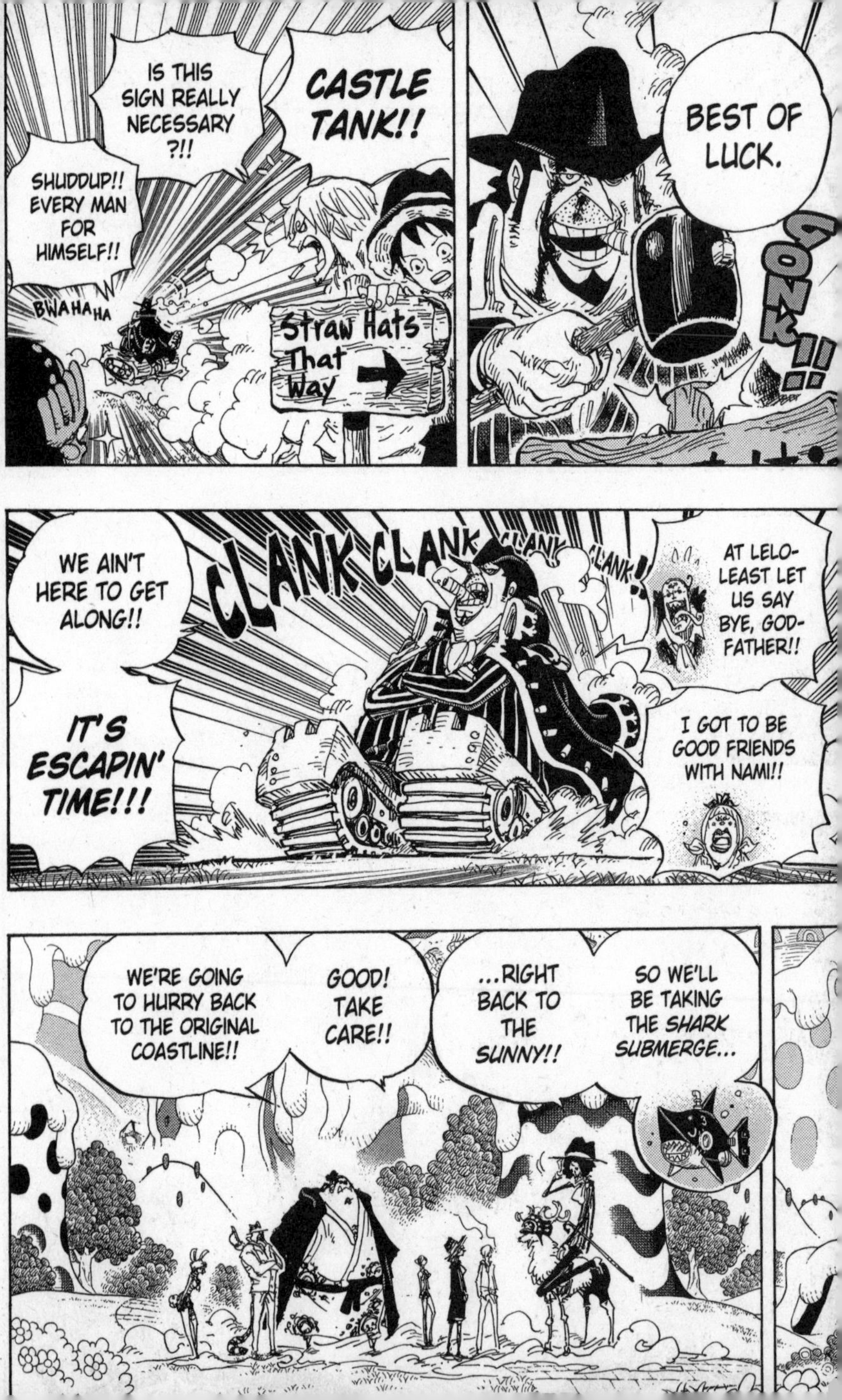
BEST OF LUCK.
GONK!!!!
CASTLE TANK!!
IS THIS SIGN REALLY NECESSARY?!!
SHUDDUP!! EVERY MAN FOR HIMSELF!!
BWAHAHA
Straw Hats That Way
AT LELO-LEAST LET US SAY BYE, GOD-FATHER!!
I GOT TO BE GOOD FRIENDS WITH NAMI!!
CLANK CLANK CLANK CLANK!!
WE AIN'T HERE TO GET ALONG!!
IT'S ESCAPIN' TIME!!!
SO WE'LL BE TAKING THE SHARK SUBMERGE...
...RIGHT BACK TO THE SUNNY!!
GOOD! TAKE CARE!!
WE'RE GOING TO HURRY BACK TO THE ORIGINAL COASTLINE!!

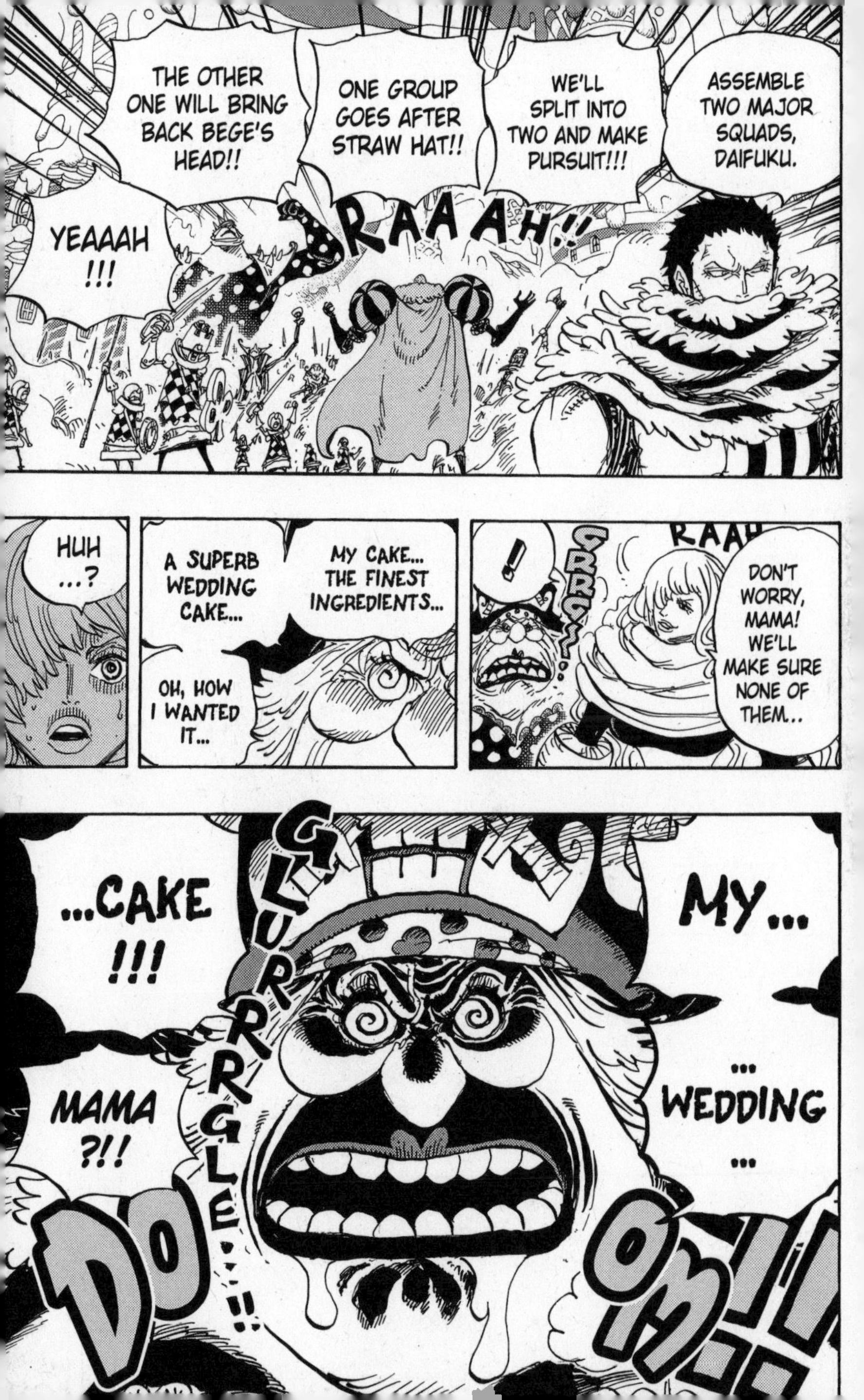

ASSEMBLE TWO MAJOR SQUADS, DAIFUKU.
WE'LL SPLIT INTO TWO AND MAKE PURSUIT!!!
ONE GROUP GOES AFTER STRAW HAT!!
THE OTHER ONE WILL BRING BACK BEGE'S HEAD!!
RAAAH!!
YEAAAH!!!
RAAH
!
GRRG
DON'T WORRY, MAMA! WE'LL MAKE SURE NONE OF THEM..
MY CAKE... THE FINEST INGREDIENTS...
A SUPERB WEDDING CAKE...
OH, HOW I WANTED IT...
HUH ...?
MY...
...WEDDING...
...CAKE!!!
GLURRRRGLE..!!
MAMA ?!!
DOOM!!

SBS Question Corner

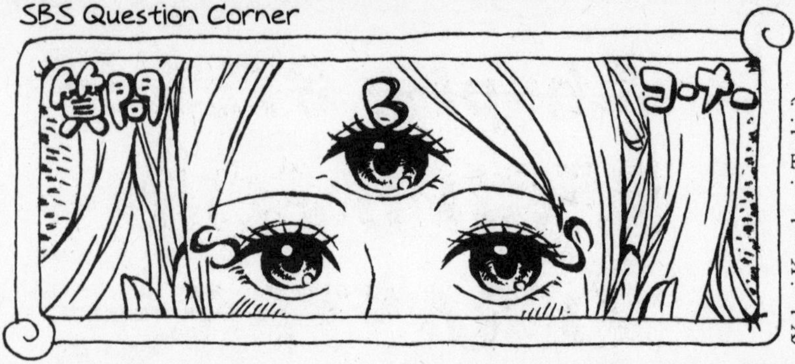
質問
コーナー

(Yukari Kawakami, Tochigi)

Q: Hiya, Odacchi! After that scene in Chapter 858 when Luffy and Brook fixed their teeth by drinking milk, I was wondering: do **all** of the Straw Hats repair their teeth with milk?

--Makizo

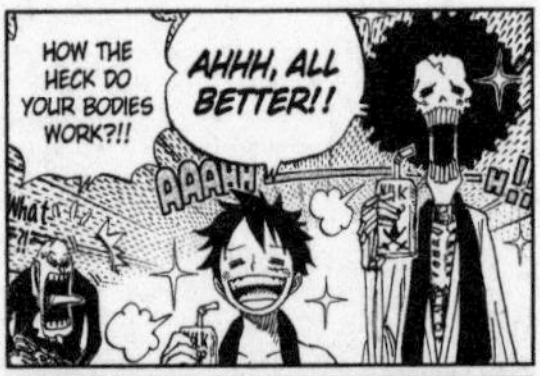
AHHH, ALL BETTER!!
HOW THE HECK DO YOUR BODIES WORK?!!
AAAHH

A: They sure do.
*Please visit the dentist, boys and girls. Luffy and his friends are weird.

Q: What is the name of Red-Haired Shanks's sword?

--Kooshi

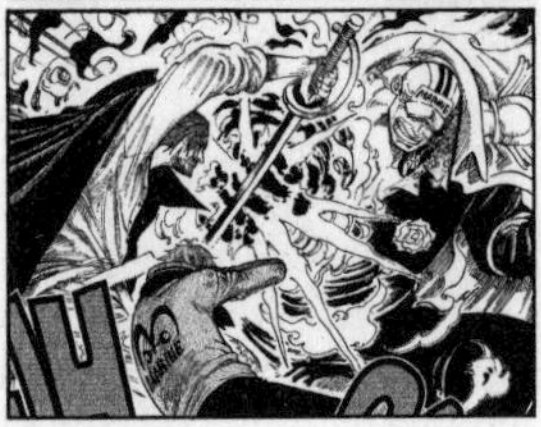

A: Apparently it's called "Griffon." We've known Shanks ever since the very first chapter, but how does he actually fight?

Q: Hello, Mr. Oda!! Vinsmoke Judge and Sanji both have blond hair. So does that mean the other four Vinsmoke children dyed their hair when they were young? Or is it a "bloodline elements" thing?

--Kunlun Pretzel

A: This question came from overseas. It's strange that the siblings all have different-colored hair, isn't it? But it seems you already figured out the answer. This was due to the bloodline element manipulation. Because it didn't work on Sanji, he was the one who ended up with the same hair as his parents.

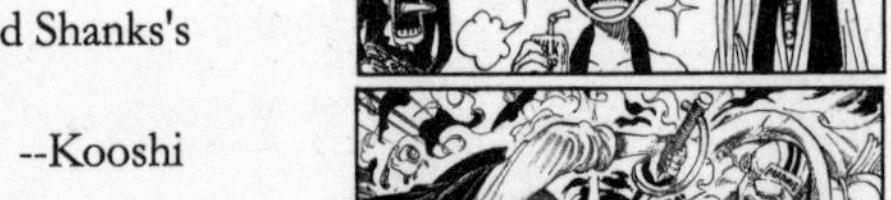

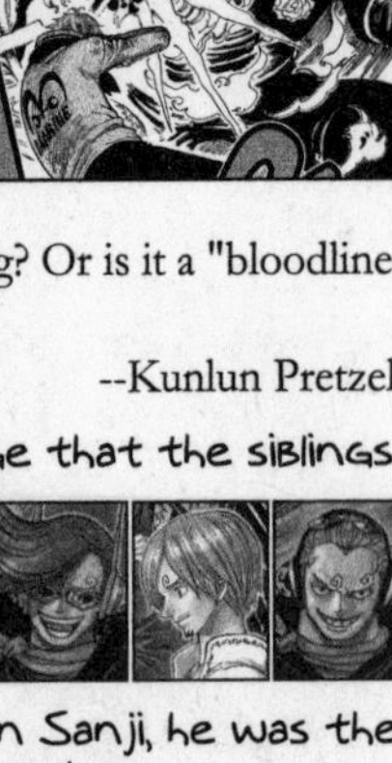
AHA HA HA!! YOU'V GOT TO B DREAMING!
ME, MARRY THA STUPID THUG?!!
B AM!!

Q: I still love Pudding, even after I found out about her true nature.

--Cuteness Is Everything

A: So you've chosen the path of thorns. Witness the tragic fate of man.

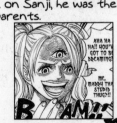

Chapter 873:

RECIPE FOR DISASTER

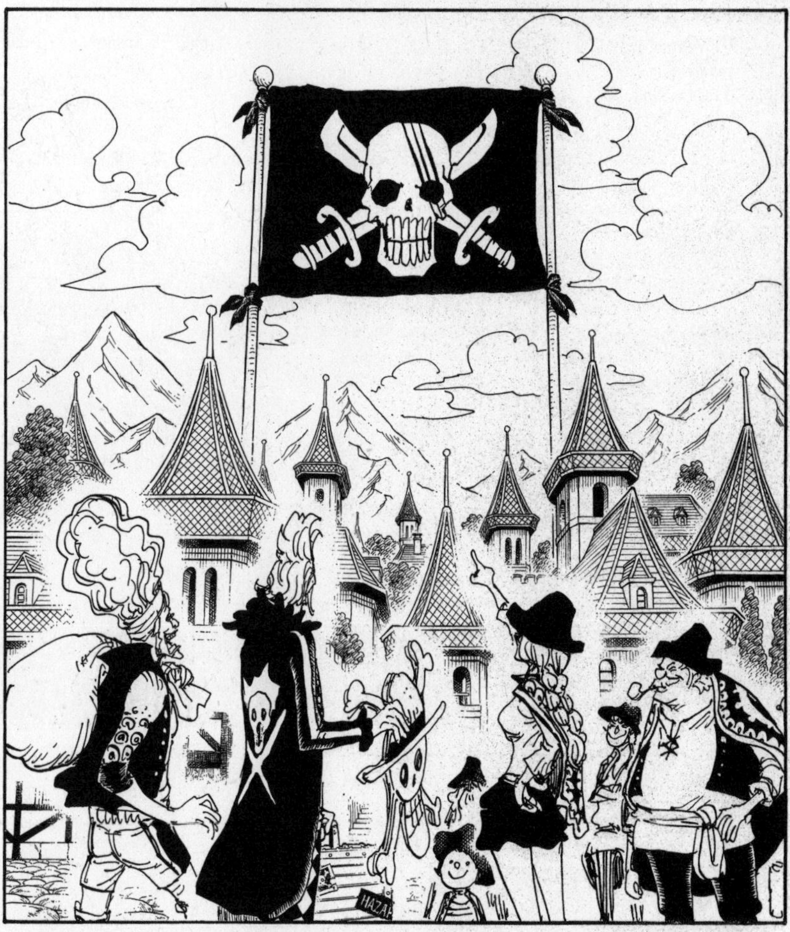

THE SAGA OF THE SELF-PROCLAIMED STRAW HAT FLEET, VOL. 9, BARTOLOMEO: "WE'RE OFFERING ALL CITIZENS A HALF-OFF SALE ON STICKERS, SO ACT NOW AND…WHAT…?"

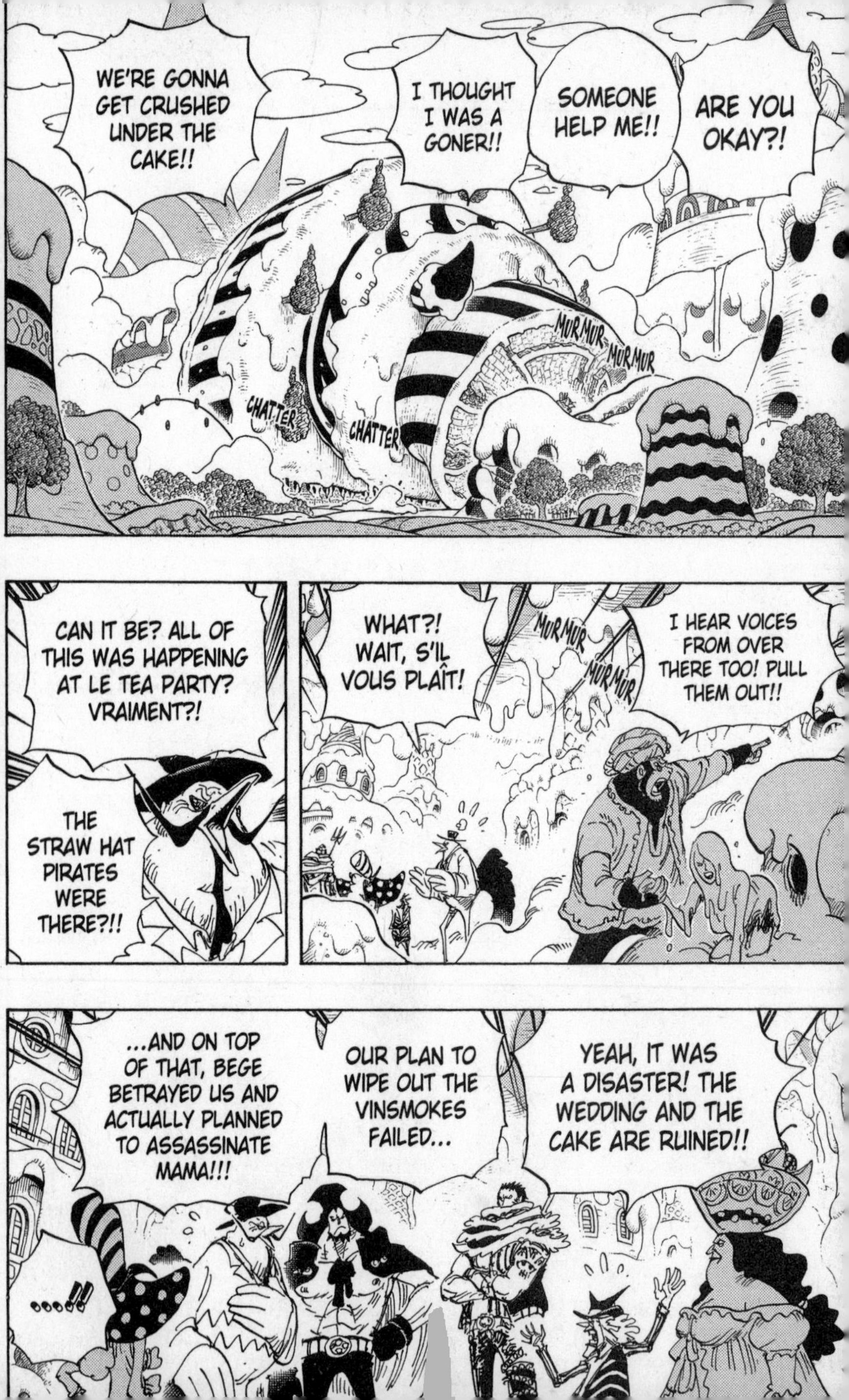
ARE YOU OKAY?!
SOMEONE HELP ME!!
I THOUGHT I WAS A GONER!!
WE'RE GONNA GET CRUSHED UNDER THE CAKE!!
MURMUR MURMUR
CHATTER CHATTER
I HEAR VOICES FROM OVER THERE TOO! PULL THEM OUT!!
MURMUR MURMUR
WHAT?! WAIT, S'IL VOUS PLAÎT!
CAN IT BE? ALL OF THIS WAS HAPPENING AT LE TEA PARTY? VRAIMENT?!
THE STRAW HAT PIRATES WERE THERE?!!
YEAH, IT WAS A DISASTER! THE WEDDING AND THE CAKE ARE RUINED!!
OUR PLAN TO WIPE OUT THE VINSMOKES FAILED...
...AND ON TOP OF THAT, BEGE BETRAYED US AND ACTUALLY PLANNED TO ASSASSINATE MAMA!!!
....!!

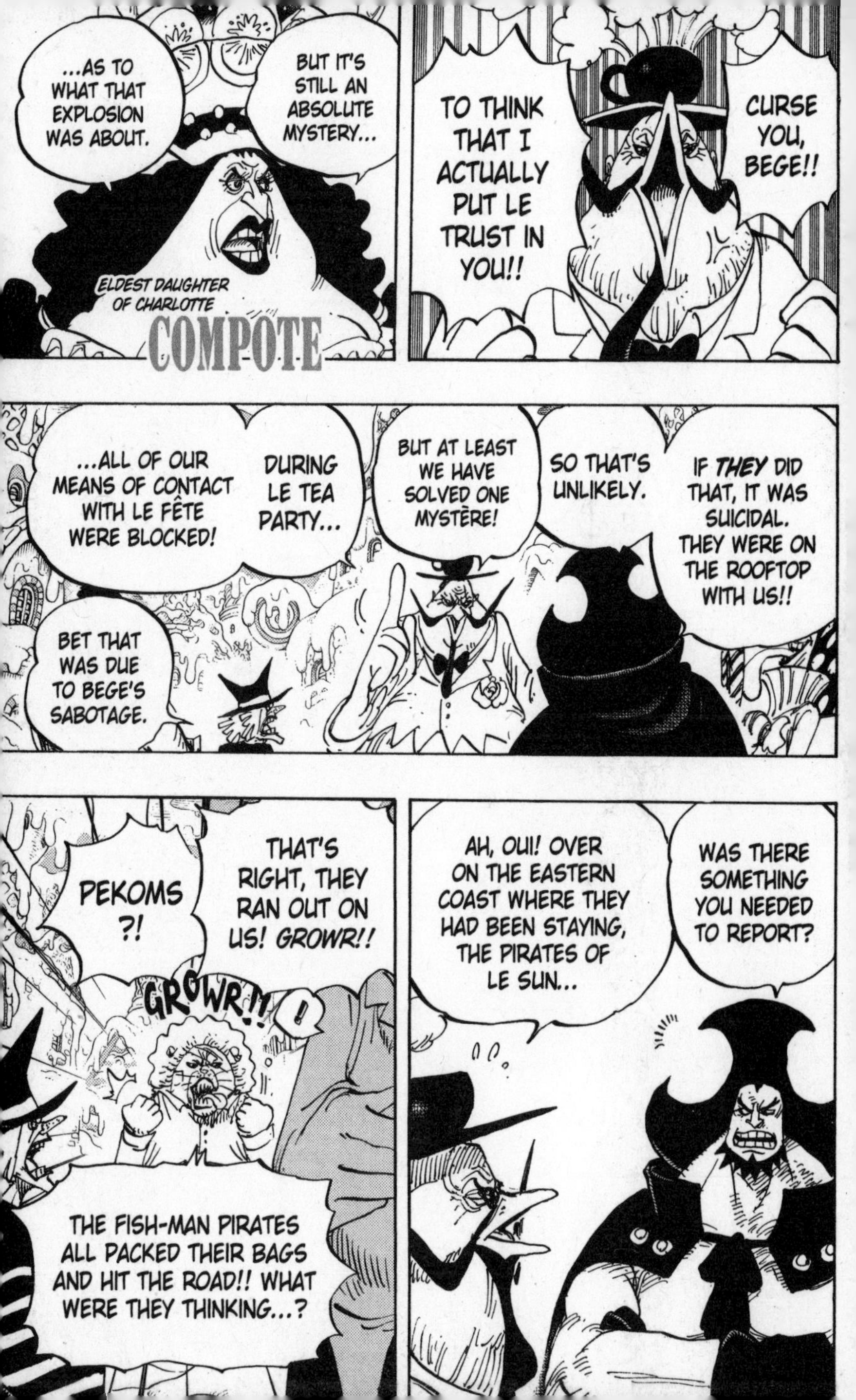
CURSE YOU, BEGE!!
TO THINK THAT I ACTUALLY PUT LE TRUST IN YOU!!
BUT IT'S STILL AN ABSOLUTE MYSTERY...
...AS TO WHAT THAT EXPLOSION WAS ABOUT.
ELDEST DAUGHTER OF CHARLOTTE
COMPOTE
IF *THEY* DID THAT, IT WAS SUICIDAL. THEY WERE ON THE ROOFTOP WITH US!!
SO THAT'S UNLIKELY.
BUT AT LEAST WE HAVE SOLVED ONE MYSTÈRE!
DURING LE TEA PARTY...
...ALL OF OUR MEANS OF CONTACT WITH LE FÊTE WERE BLOCKED!
BET THAT WAS DUE TO BEGE'S SABOTAGE.
WAS THERE SOMETHING YOU NEEDED TO REPORT?
AH, OUI! OVER ON THE EASTERN COAST WHERE THEY HAD BEEN STAYING, THE PIRATES OF LE SUN...
THAT'S RIGHT, THEY RAN OUT ON US! *GROWR!!*
PEKOMS ?!
GROWR!!
!
THE FISH-MAN PIRATES ALL PACKED THEIR BAGS AND HIT THE ROAD!! WHAT WERE THEY THINKING...?

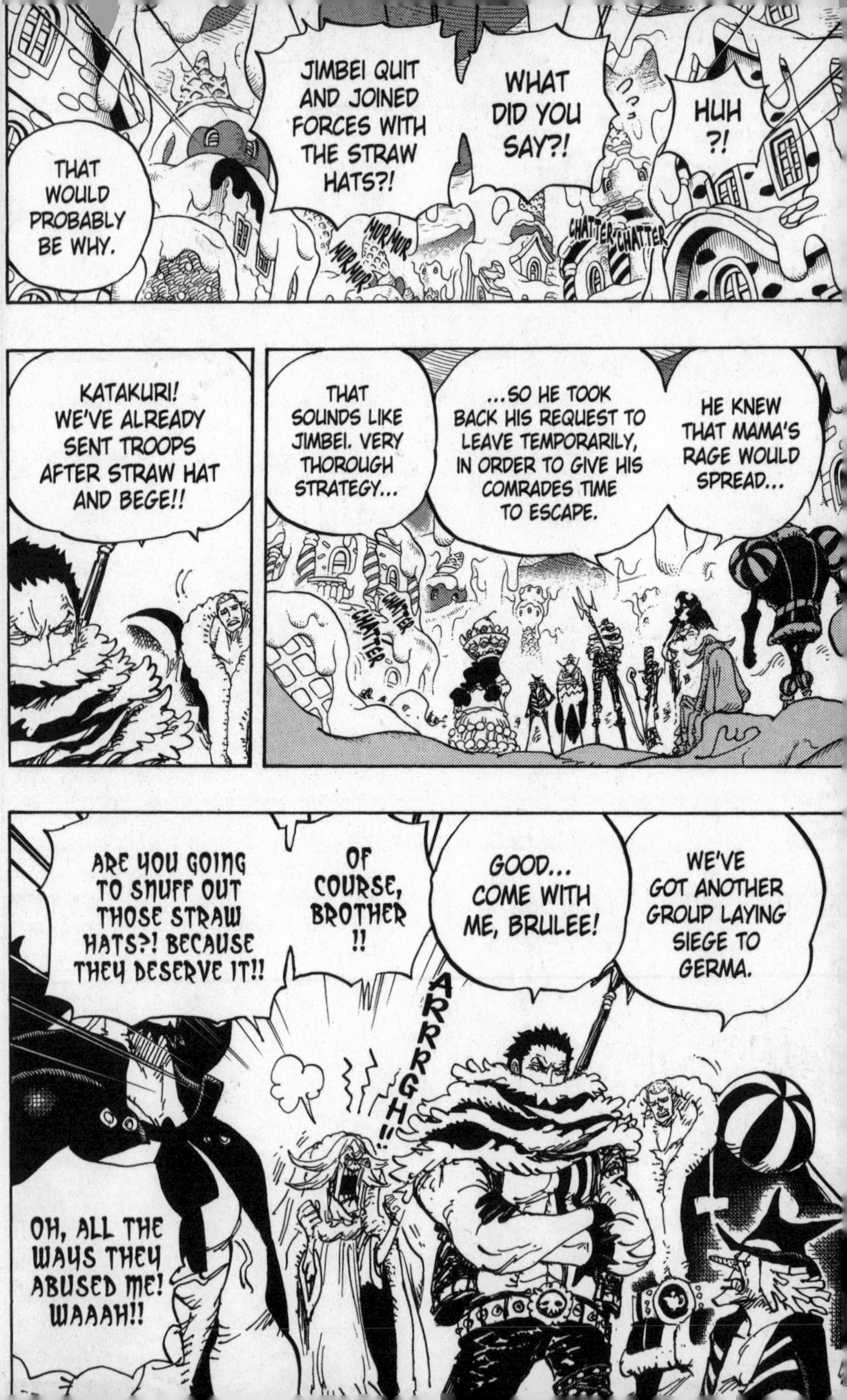
HUH ?!
WHAT DID YOU SAY?!
JIMBEI QUIT AND JOINED FORCES WITH THE STRAW HATS?!
CHATTER CHATTER
MURMUR MURMUR
THAT WOULD PROBABLY BE WHY.
HE KNEW THAT MAMA'S RAGE WOULD SPREAD...
...SO HE TOOK BACK HIS REQUEST TO LEAVE TEMPORARILY, IN ORDER TO GIVE HIS COMRADES TIME TO ESCAPE.
THAT SOUNDS LIKE JIMBEI. VERY THOROUGH STRATEGY...
CHATTER CHATTER
KATAKURI! WE'VE ALREADY SENT TROOPS AFTER STRAW HAT AND BEGE!!
WE'VE GOT ANOTHER GROUP LAYING SIEGE TO GERMA.
GOOD... COME WITH ME, BRULEE!
OF COURSE, BROTHER !!
ARE YOU GOING TO SNUFF OUT THOSE STRAW HATS?! BECAUSE THEY DESERVE IT!!
ARRRGH!!
OH, ALL THE WAYS THEY ABUSED ME! WAAAH!!

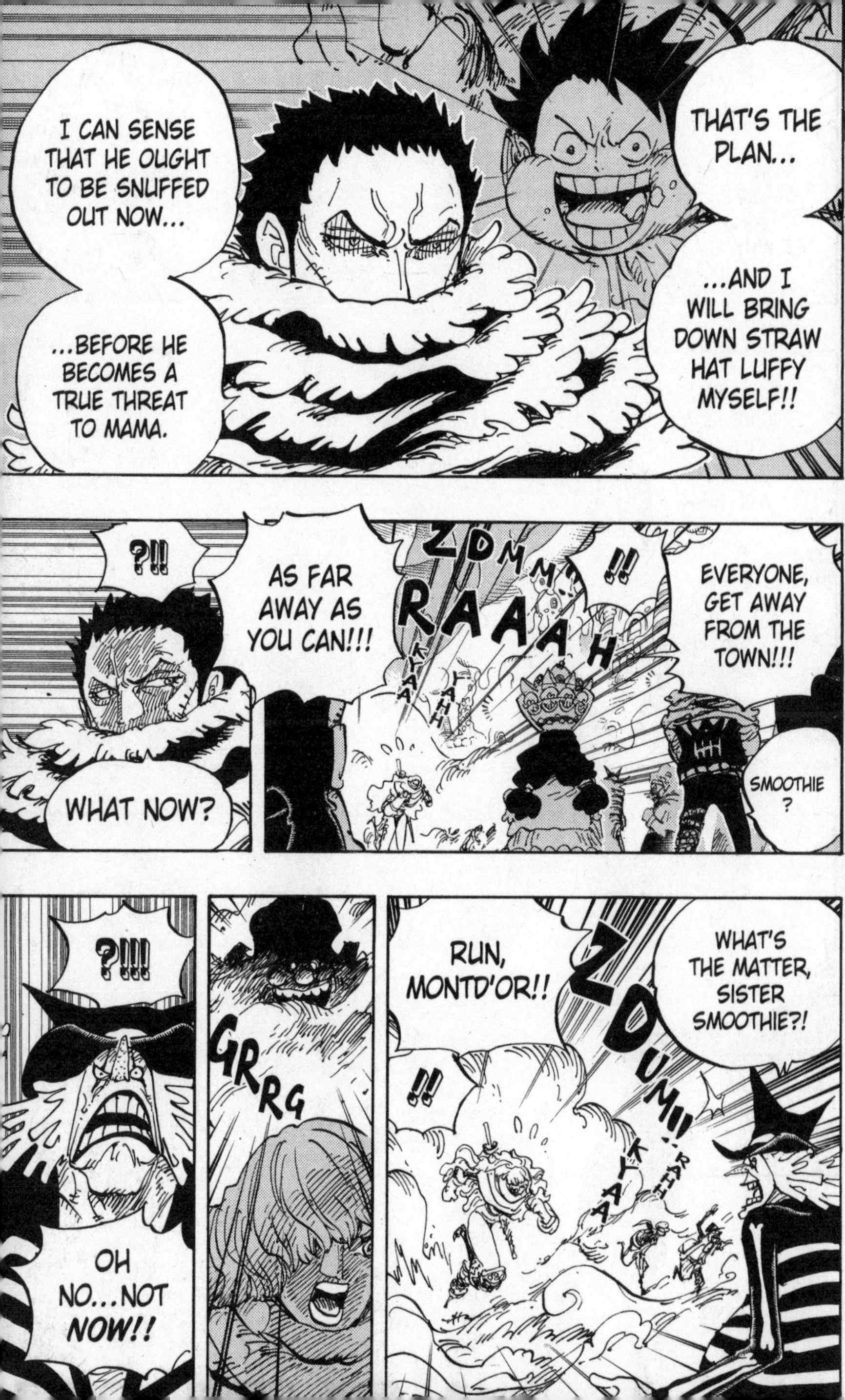

THAT'S THE PLAN...
...AND I WILL BRING DOWN STRAW HAT LUFFY MYSELF!!
I CAN SENSE THAT HE OUGHT TO BE SNUFFED OUT NOW...
...BEFORE HE BECOMES A TRUE THREAT TO MAMA.
EVERYONE, GET AWAY FROM THE TOWN!!!
!!
ZDMMM
RAAAAH
AS FAR AWAY AS YOU CAN!!!
KYAA
YAHH
SMOOTHIE ?
?!!
WHAT NOW?
WHAT'S THE MATTER, SISTER SMOOTHIE?!
ZDUM!!
RUN, MONTD'OR!!
!!
KYAA
RAHH
GRRRG
?!!!
OH NO...NOT NOW!!

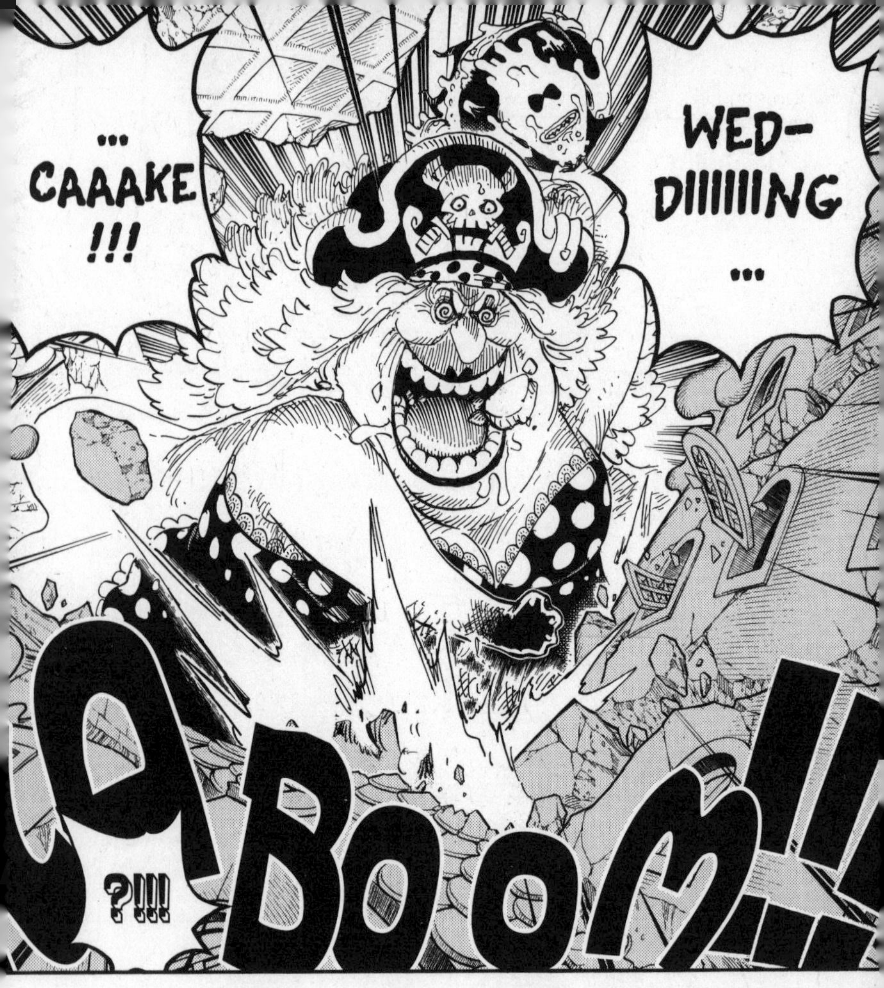
WED-
DIIIIIING
...
... CAAAKE
!!!
BOOM!!!
?!!!
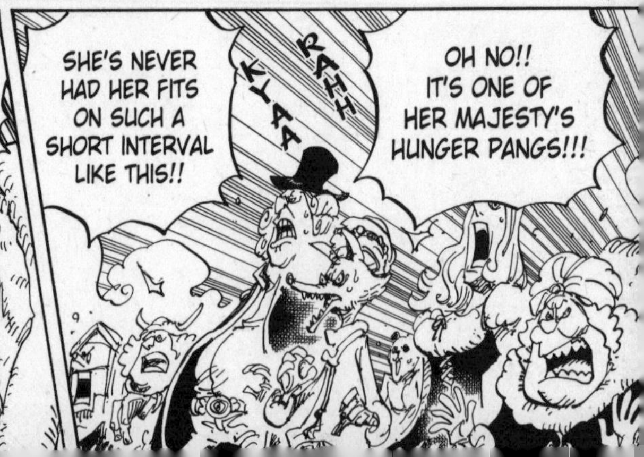
OH NO!!
IT'S ONE OF
HER MAJESTY'S
HUNGER PANGS!!!
RAHH
KYAA
SHE'S NEVER
HAD HER FITS
ON SUCH A
SHORT INTERVAL
LIKE THIS!!
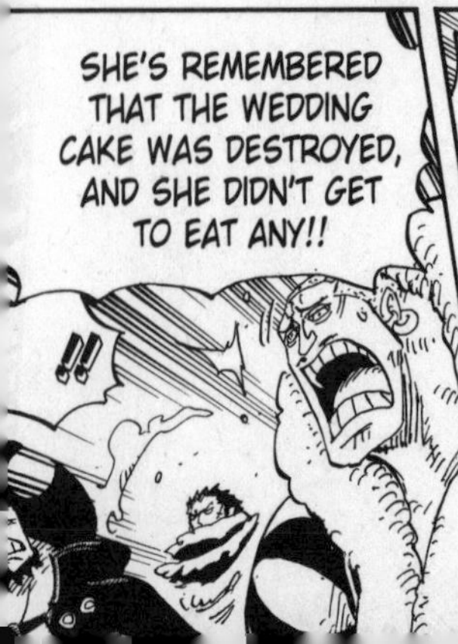
SHE'S REMEMBERED
THAT THE WEDDING
CAKE WAS DESTROYED,
AND SHE DIDN'T GET
TO EAT ANY!!
!!

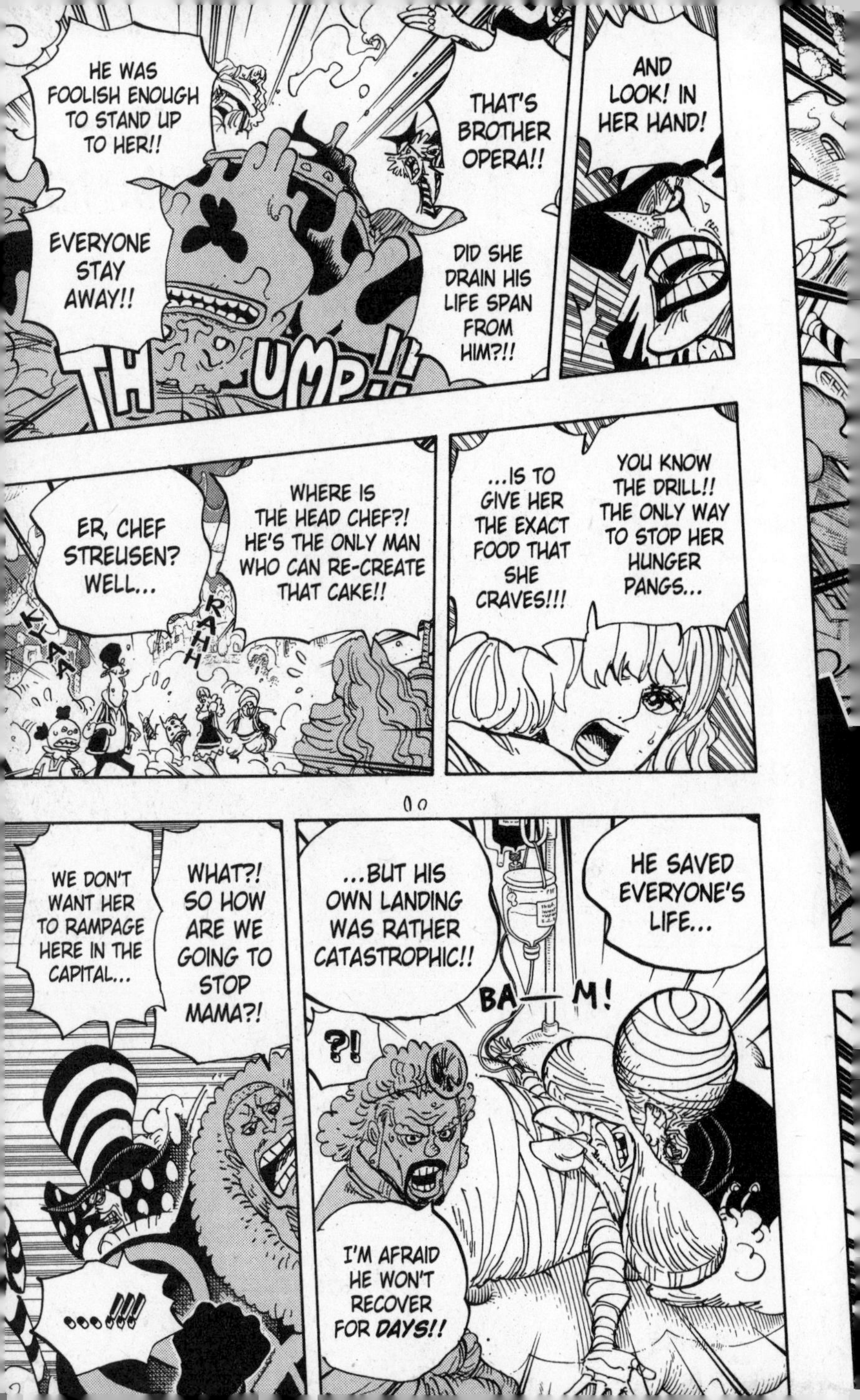
AND LOOK! IN HER HAND!
THAT'S BROTHER OPERA!!
HE WAS FOOLISH ENOUGH TO STAND UP TO HER!!
DID SHE DRAIN HIS LIFE SPAN FROM HIM?!!
EVERYONE STAY AWAY!!
TH UMP!!
YOU KNOW THE DRILL!! THE ONLY WAY TO STOP HER HUNGER PANGS...
...IS TO GIVE HER THE EXACT FOOD THAT SHE CRAVES!!!
WHERE IS THE HEAD CHEF?! HE'S THE ONLY MAN WHO CAN RE-CREATE THAT CAKE!!
ER, CHEF STREUSEN? WELL...
RAHHH
KYAA
HE SAVED EVERYONE'S LIFE...
...BUT HIS OWN LANDING WAS RATHER CATASTROPHIC!!
BA—M!
?!
I'M AFRAID HE WON'T RECOVER FOR DAYS!!
WHAT?! SO HOW ARE WE GOING TO STOP MAMA?!
WE DON'T WANT HER TO RAMPAGE HERE IN THE CAPITAL...
...!!!

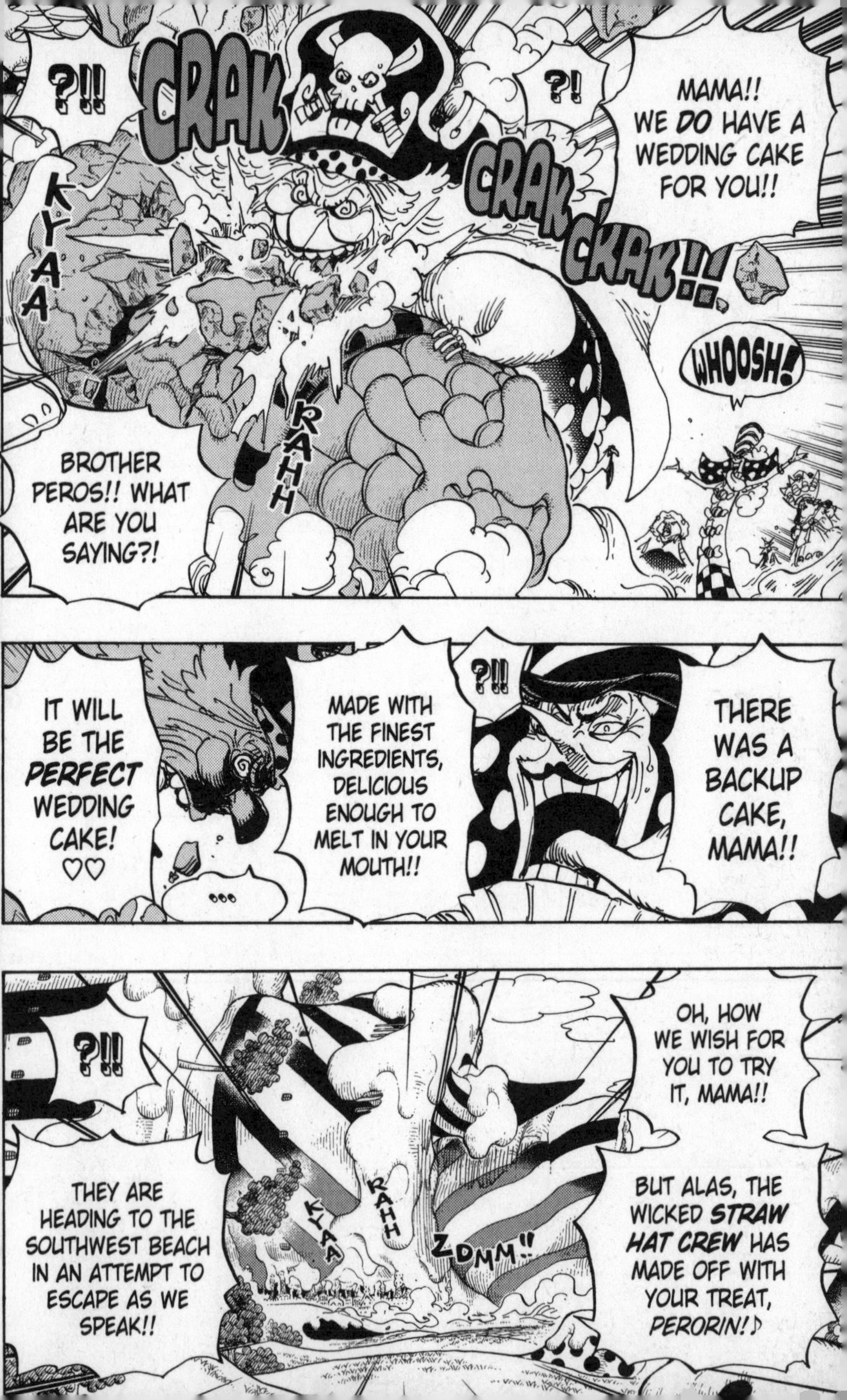
MAMA!! WE DO HAVE A WEDDING CAKE FOR YOU!!
?!
CRAK
CRAK CRAK!!
?!!
KYAA
WHOOSH!
RAHH
BROTHER PEROS!! WHAT ARE YOU SAYING?!
THERE WAS A BACKUP CAKE, MAMA!!
?!!
MADE WITH THE FINEST INGREDIENTS, DELICIOUS ENOUGH TO MELT IN YOUR MOUTH!!
IT WILL BE THE PERFECT WEDDING CAKE! ♡♡
...
OH, HOW WE WISH FOR YOU TO TRY IT, MAMA!!
BUT ALAS, THE WICKED STRAW HAT CREW HAS MADE OFF WITH YOUR TREAT, PERORIN!♪
ZDMM!!
RAHH
KYAA
?!!
THEY ARE HEADING TO THE SOUTHWEST BEACH IN AN ATTEMPT TO ESCAPE AS WE SPEAK!!

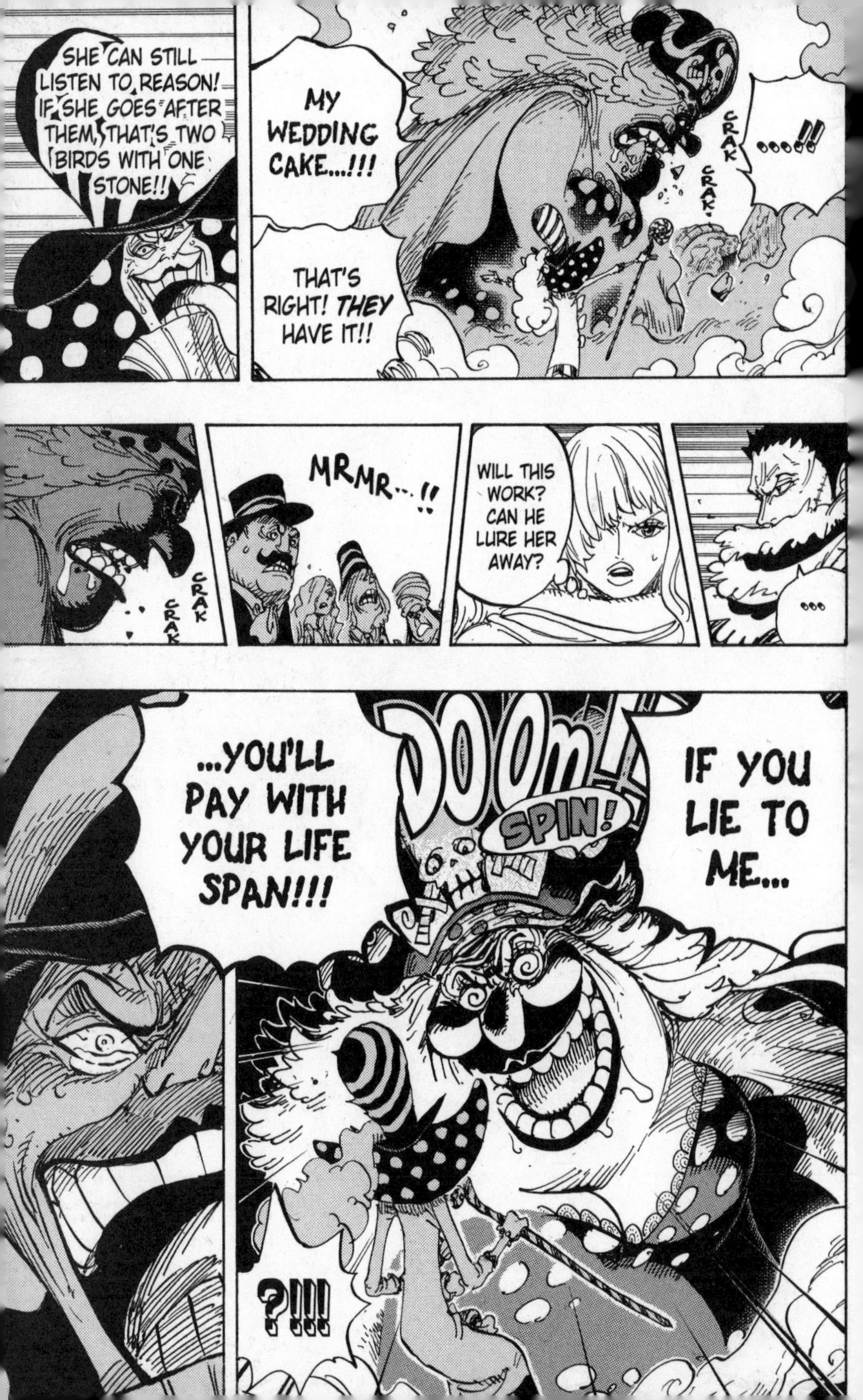

......!!
CRAK
CRAK
MY WEDDING CAKE...!!!
THAT'S RIGHT! THEY HAVE IT!!
SHE CAN STILL LISTEN TO REASON! IF SHE GOES AFTER THEM, THAT'S TWO BIRDS WITH ONE STONE!!
...
WILL THIS WORK? CAN HE LURE HER AWAY?
MRMR...!!
CRAK
CRAK
IF YOU LIE TO ME...
DOOM!
SPIN!
...YOU'LL PAY WITH YOUR LIFE SPAN!!!
?!!!

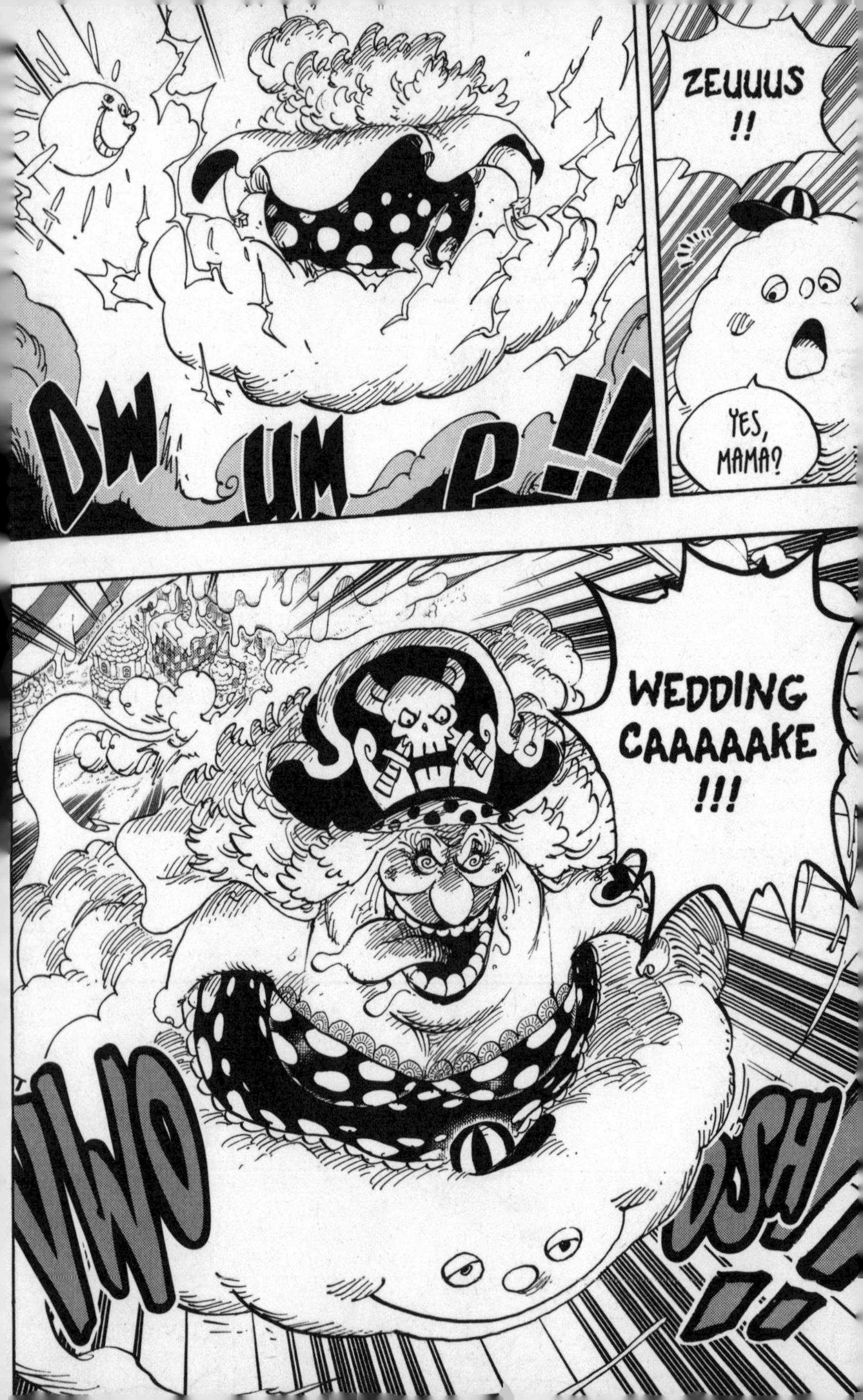
ZEUUUS!!
YES, MAMA?
DWUMP!!
WEDDING CAAAAAKE!!!

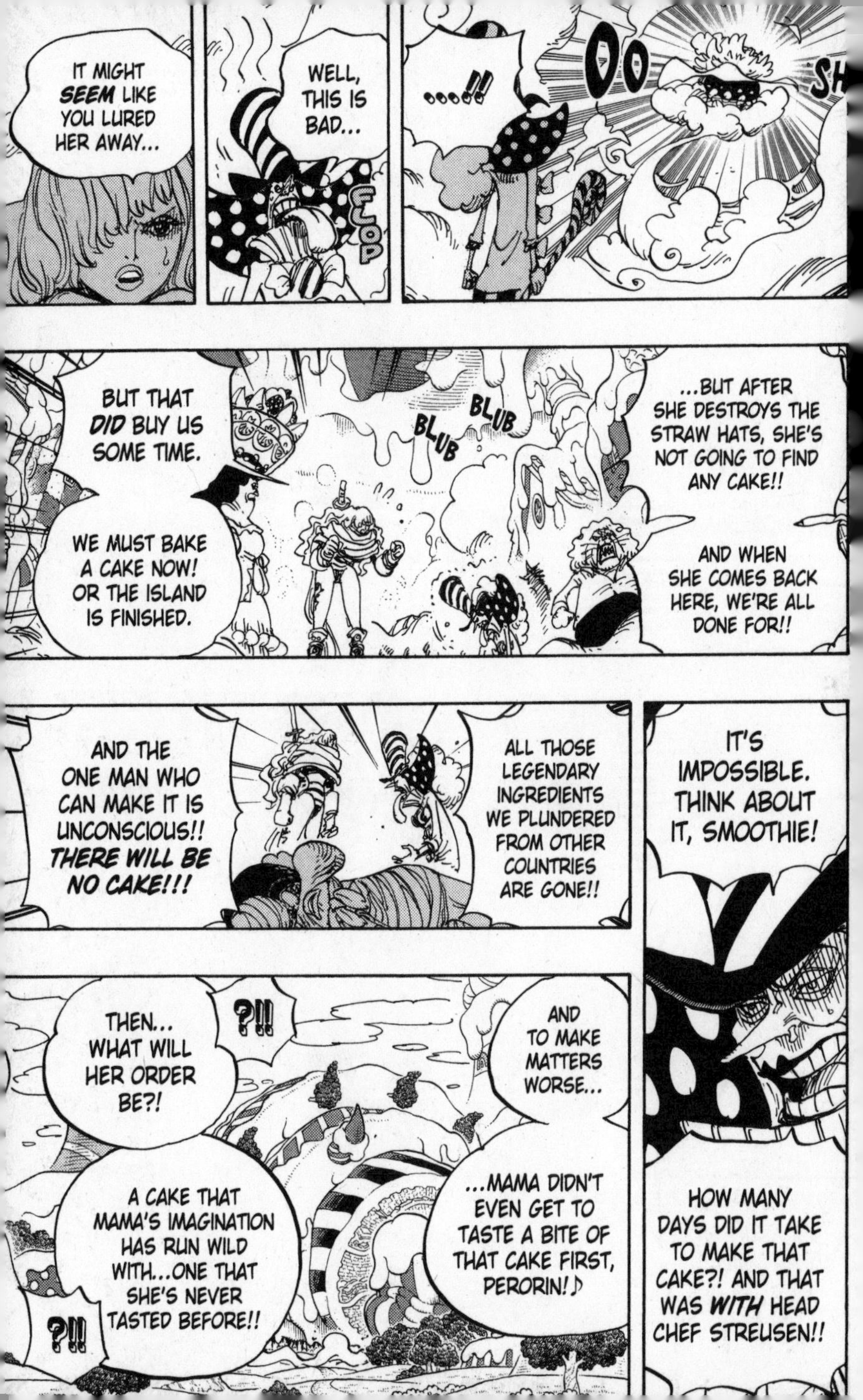
OO
SH
....!!
WELL, THIS IS BAD...
FLOP
IT MIGHT SEEM LIKE YOU LURED HER AWAY...
...BUT AFTER SHE DESTROYS THE STRAW HATS, SHE'S NOT GOING TO FIND ANY CAKE!!
AND WHEN SHE COMES BACK HERE, WE'RE ALL DONE FOR!!
BLUB
BLUB
BUT THAT DID BUY US SOME TIME.
WE MUST BAKE A CAKE NOW! OR THE ISLAND IS FINISHED.
IT'S IMPOSSIBLE. THINK ABOUT IT, SMOOTHIE!
HOW MANY DAYS DID IT TAKE TO MAKE THAT CAKE?! AND THAT WAS WITH HEAD CHEF STREUSEN!!
ALL THOSE LEGENDARY INGREDIENTS WE PLUNDERED FROM OTHER COUNTRIES ARE GONE!!
AND THE ONE MAN WHO CAN MAKE IT IS UNCONSCIOUS!! THERE WILL BE NO CAKE!!!
AND TO MAKE MATTERS WORSE...
...MAMA DIDN'T EVEN GET TO TASTE A BITE OF THAT CAKE FIRST, PERORIN!♪
?!!
THEN... WHAT WILL HER ORDER BE?!
A CAKE THAT MAMA'S IMAGINATION HAS RUN WILD WITH...ONE THAT SHE'S NEVER TASTED BEFORE!!
?!!

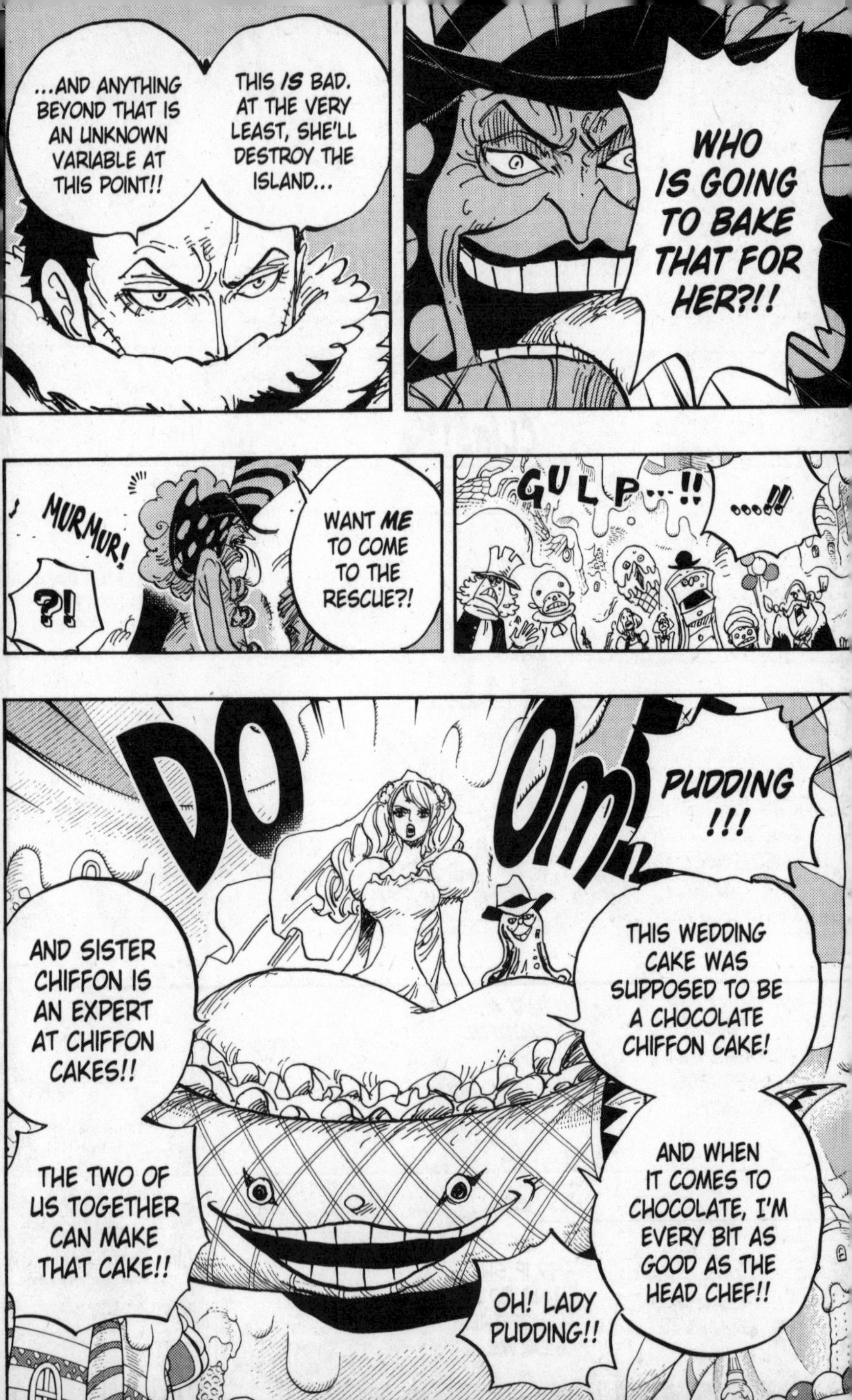
WHO IS GOING TO BAKE THAT FOR HER?!!
THIS IS BAD. AT THE VERY LEAST, SHE'LL DESTROY THE ISLAND...
...AND ANYTHING BEYOND THAT IS AN UNKNOWN VARIABLE AT THIS POINT!!
GULP...!!
...!!
WANT ME TO COME TO THE RESCUE?!
MURMUR!
?!
DOOM
PUDDING!!!
THIS WEDDING CAKE WAS SUPPOSED TO BE A CHOCOLATE CHIFFON CAKE!
AND SISTER CHIFFON IS AN EXPERT AT CHIFFON CAKES!!
AND WHEN IT COMES TO CHOCOLATE, I'M EVERY BIT AS GOOD AS THE HEAD CHEF!!
THE TWO OF US TOGETHER CAN MAKE THAT CAKE!!
OH! LADY PUDDING!!

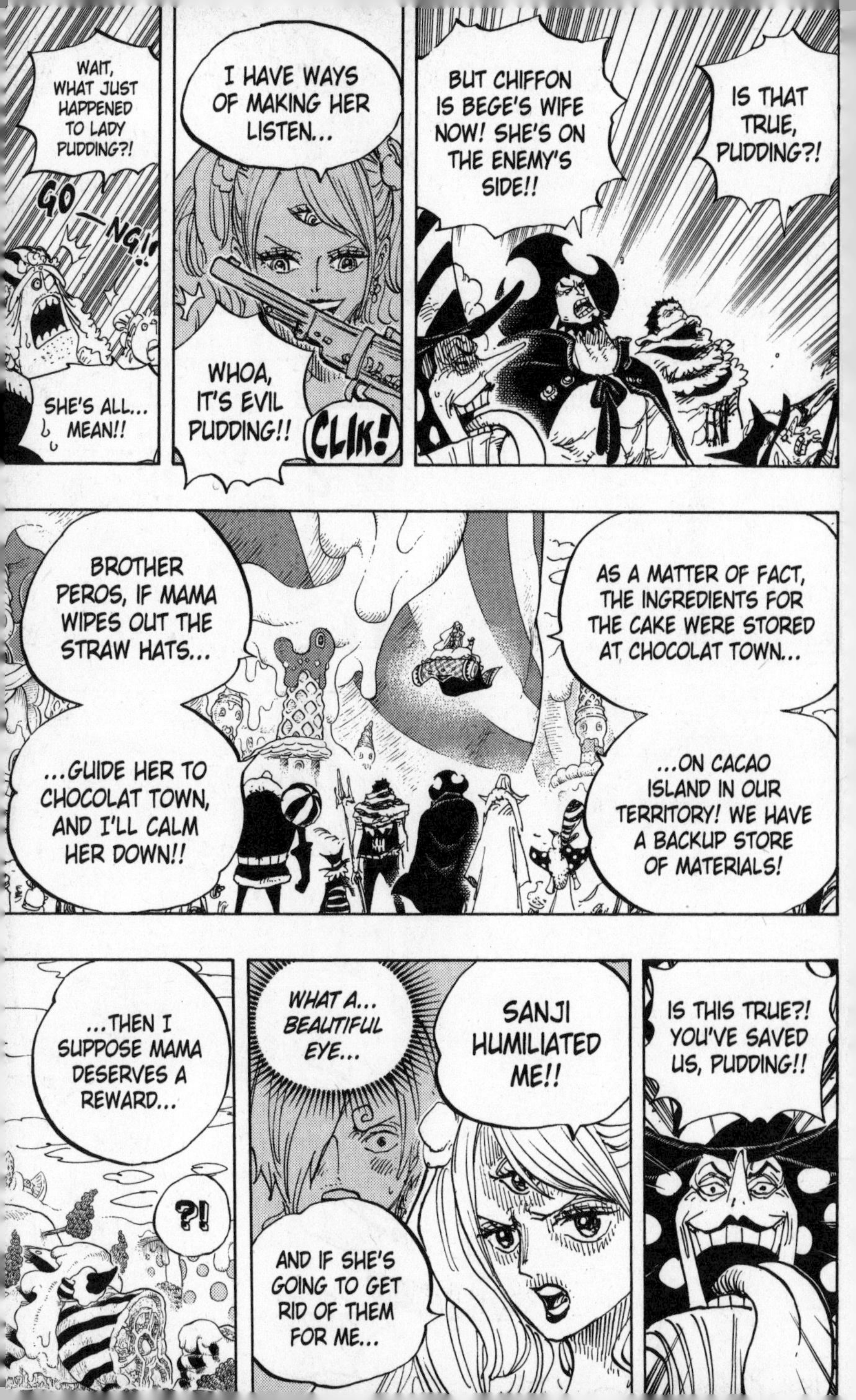
IS THAT TRUE, PUDDING?!
BUT CHIFFON IS BEGE'S WIFE NOW! SHE'S ON THE ENEMY'S SIDE!!
I HAVE WAYS OF MAKING HER LISTEN...
WHOA, IT'S EVIL PUDDING!!
CLIK!
WAIT, WHAT JUST HAPPENED TO LADY PUDDING?!
GO—NG!!
SHE'S ALL... MEAN!!
AS A MATTER OF FACT, THE INGREDIENTS FOR THE CAKE WERE STORED AT CHOCOLAT TOWN...
...ON CACAO ISLAND IN OUR TERRITORY! WE HAVE A BACKUP STORE OF MATERIALS!
BROTHER PEROS, IF MAMA WIPES OUT THE STRAW HATS...
...GUIDE HER TO CHOCOLAT TOWN, AND I'LL CALM HER DOWN!!
IS THIS TRUE?! YOU'VE SAVED US, PUDDING!!
SANJI HUMILIATED ME!!
WHAT A... BEAUTIFUL EYE...
AND IF SHE'S GOING TO GET RID OF THEM FOR ME...
...THEN I SUPPOSE MAMA DESERVES A REWARD...
?!

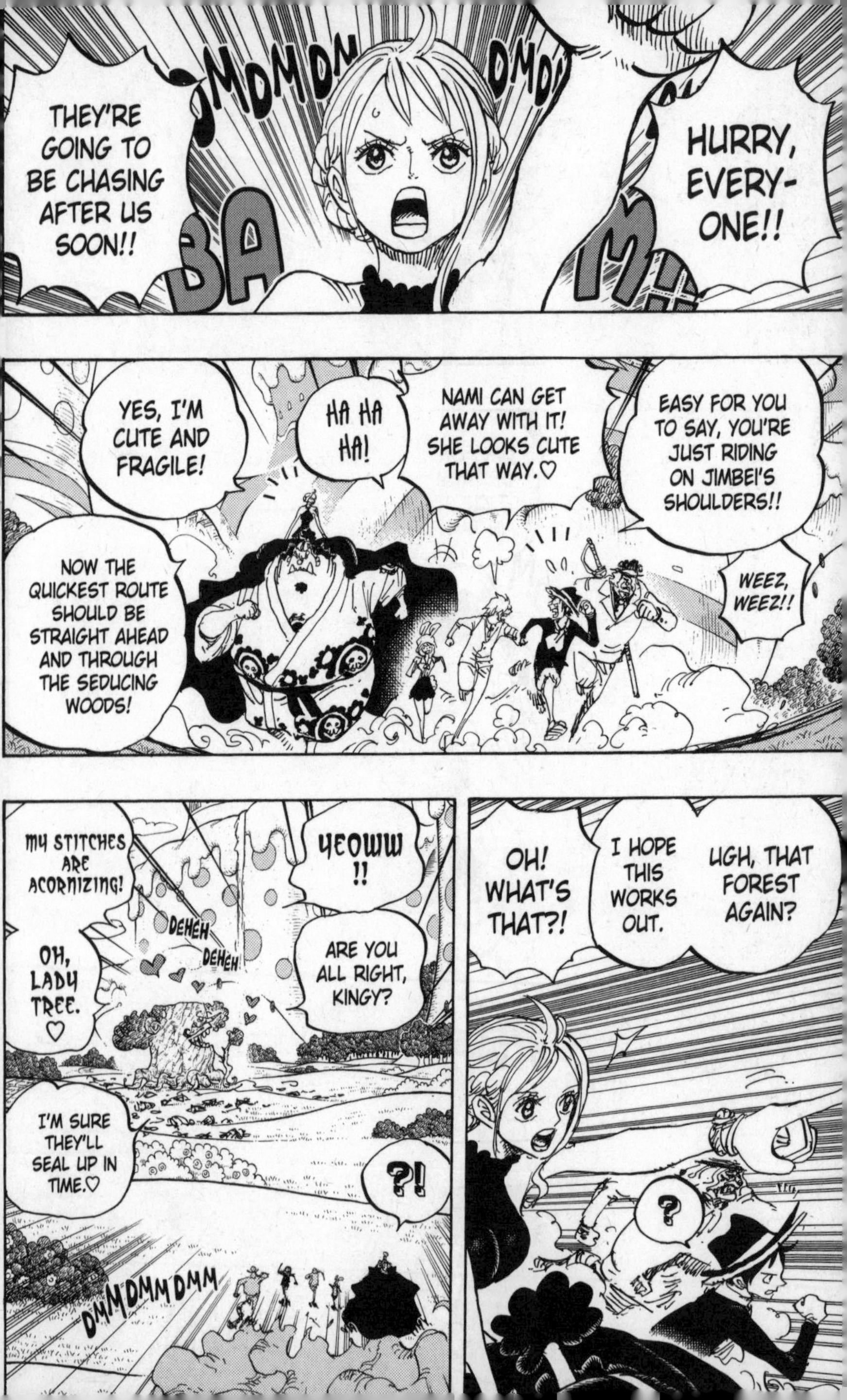
HURRY, EVERYONE!!
THEY'RE GOING TO BE CHASING AFTER US SOON!!
EASY FOR YOU TO SAY, YOU'RE JUST RIDING ON JIMBEI'S SHOULDERS!!
NAMI CAN GET AWAY WITH IT! SHE LOOKS CUTE THAT WAY.♡
HA HA HA!
YES, I'M CUTE AND FRAGILE!
WEEZ, WEEZ!!
NOW THE QUICKEST ROUTE SHOULD BE STRAIGHT AHEAD AND THROUGH THE SEDUCING WOODS!
UGH, THAT FOREST AGAIN?
I HOPE THIS WORKS OUT.
OH! WHAT'S THAT?!
?
YEOWW !!
MY STITCHES ARE ACORNIZING!
DEHEH
DEHEH
ARE YOU ALL RIGHT, KINGY?
OH, LADY TREE. ♡
I'M SURE THEY'LL SEAL UP IN TIME.♡
?!
DMMDMMDMM

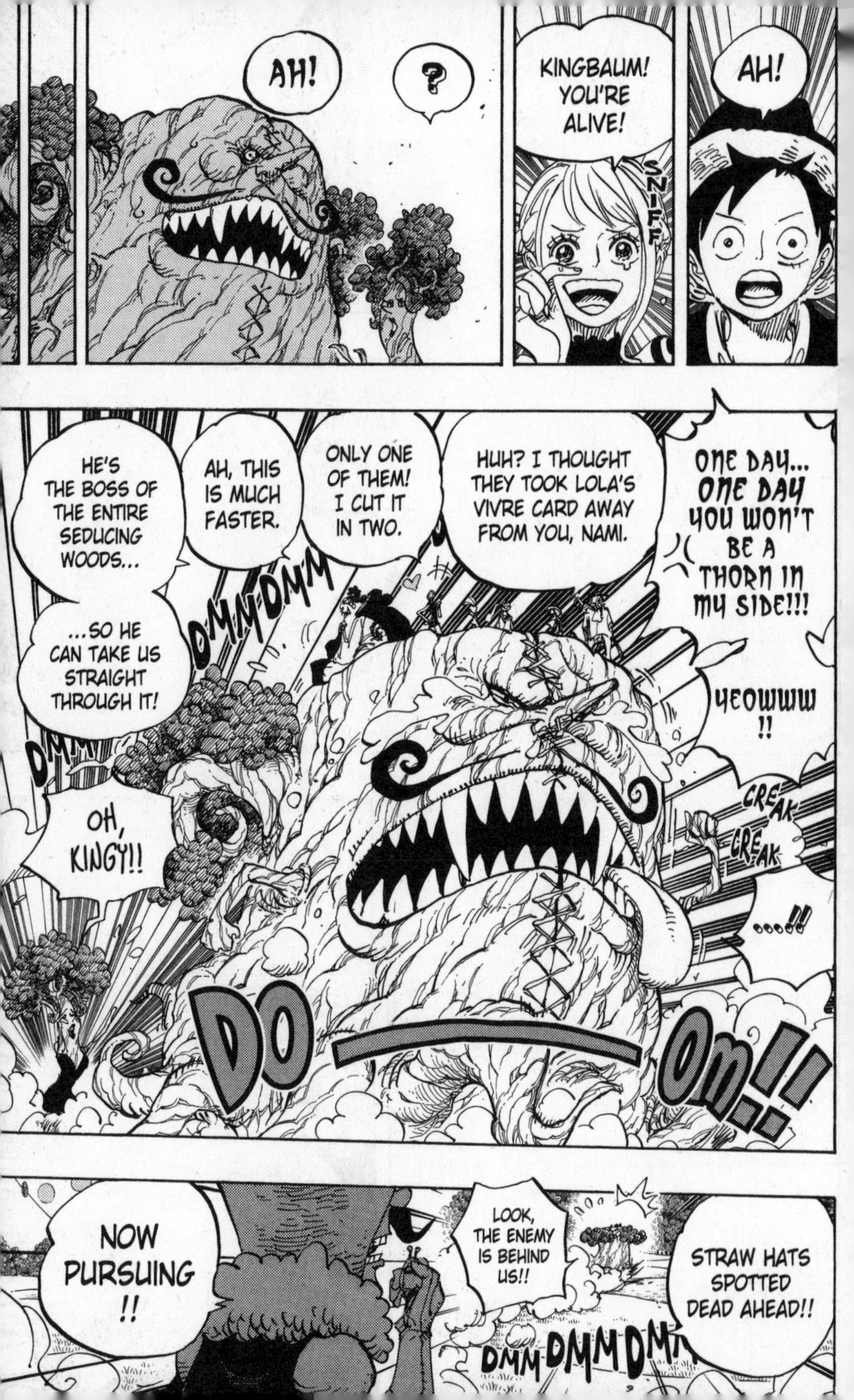
AH!
KINGBAUM! YOU'RE ALIVE!
SNIFF
?
AH!
ONE DAY... ONE DAY YOU WON'T BE A THORN IN MY SIDE!!!
HUH? I THOUGHT THEY TOOK LOLA'S VIVRE CARD AWAY FROM YOU, NAMI.
ONLY ONE OF THEM! I CUT IT IN TWO.
AH, THIS IS MUCH FASTER.
HE'S THE BOSS OF THE ENTIRE SEDUCING WOODS...
DMM DMM
...SO HE CAN TAKE US STRAIGHT THROUGH IT!
YEOWWW!!
CREAK
CREAK
....!!
DMM
OH, KINGY!!
DO—OM!!
STRAW HATS SPOTTED DEAD AHEAD!!
LOOK, THE ENEMY IS BEHIND US!!
NOW PURSUING!!
DMM DMM DMM

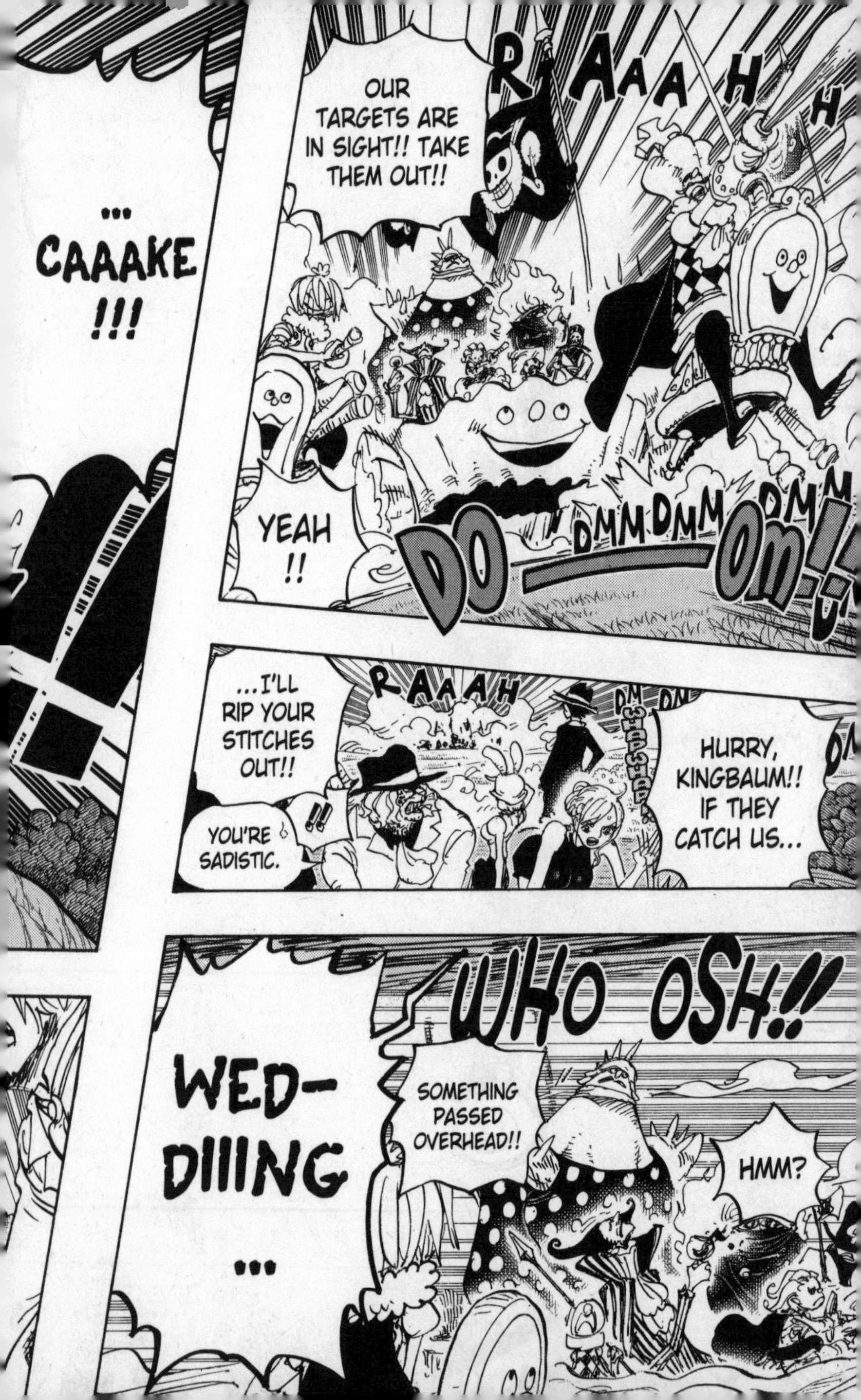
RAAAHH
OUR TARGETS ARE IN SIGHT!! TAKE THEM OUT!!
YEAH!!
DMM DMM DMM
DOOOM!!
HURRY, KINGBAUM!! IF THEY CATCH US...
RAAAH
...I'LL RIP YOUR STITCHES OUT!!
!!
YOU'RE SADISTIC.
...CAAAKE!!!
WHOOSH!!
HMM?
SOMETHING PASSED OVERHEAD!!
WED-DIIING...

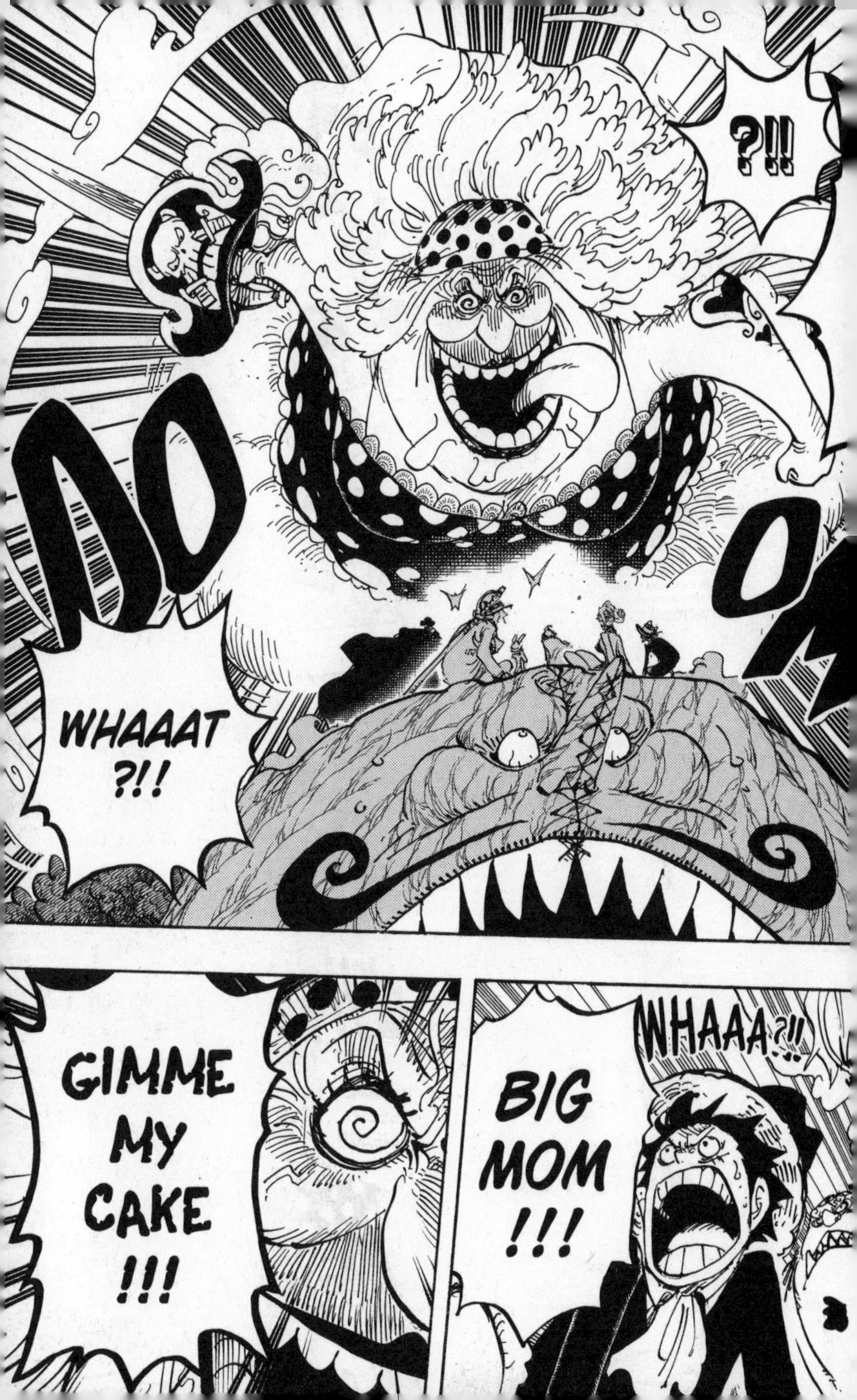
?!!
DO
WHAAAT ?!!
WHAAA?!!
BIG MOM !!!
GIMME MY CAKE !!!

Chapter 874: BE MY SERVANT

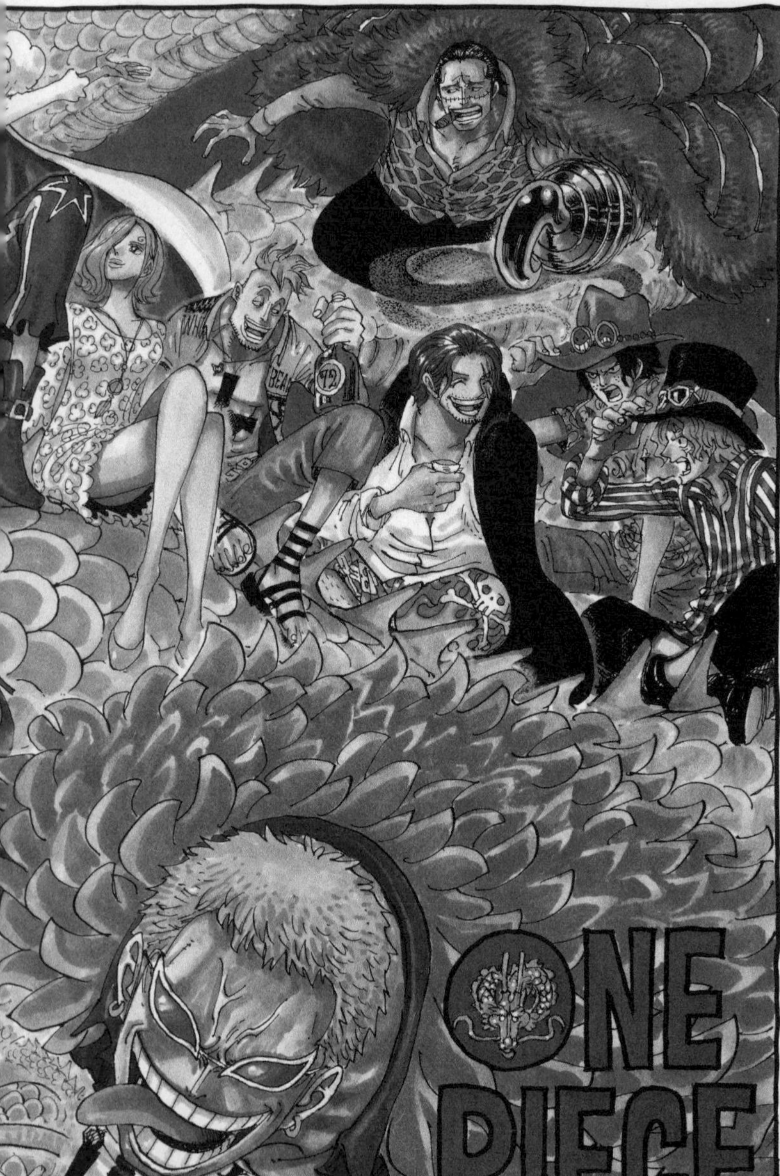
ONE PIECE

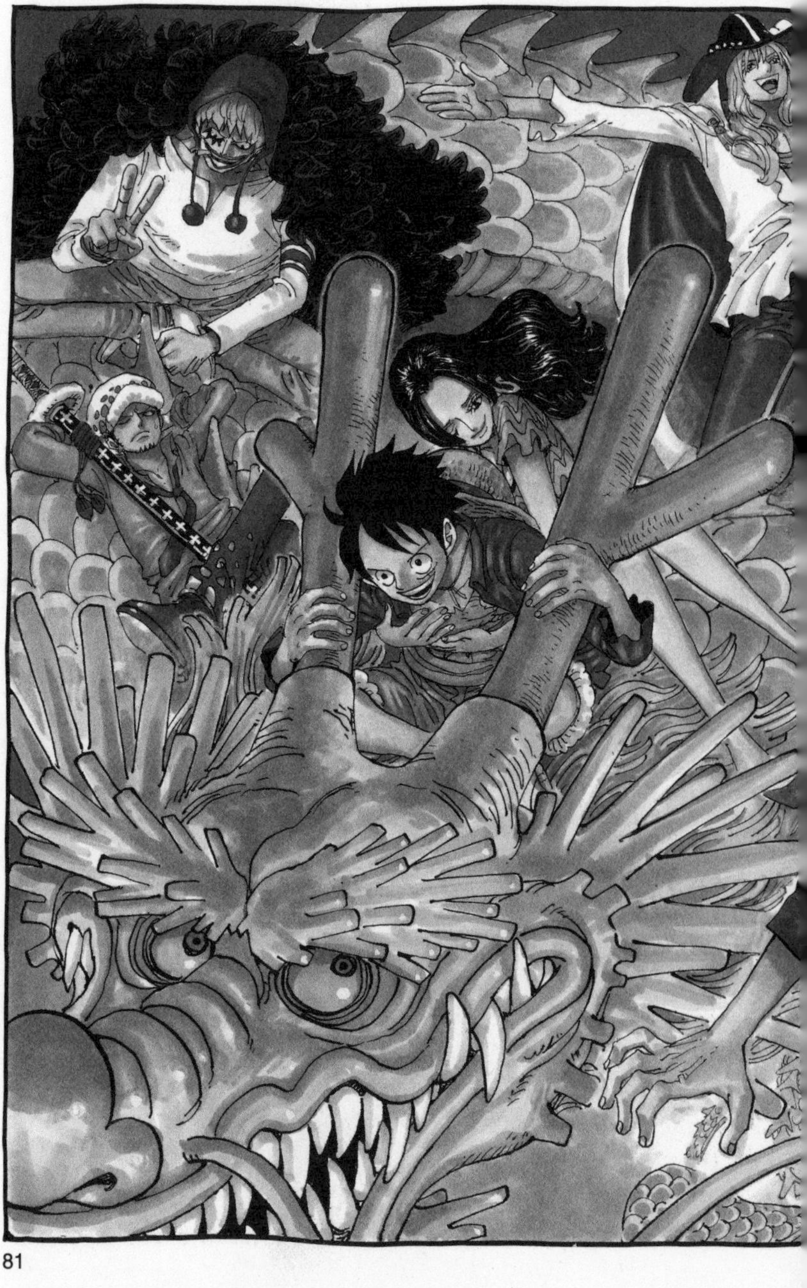

ONE PIECE vol.87

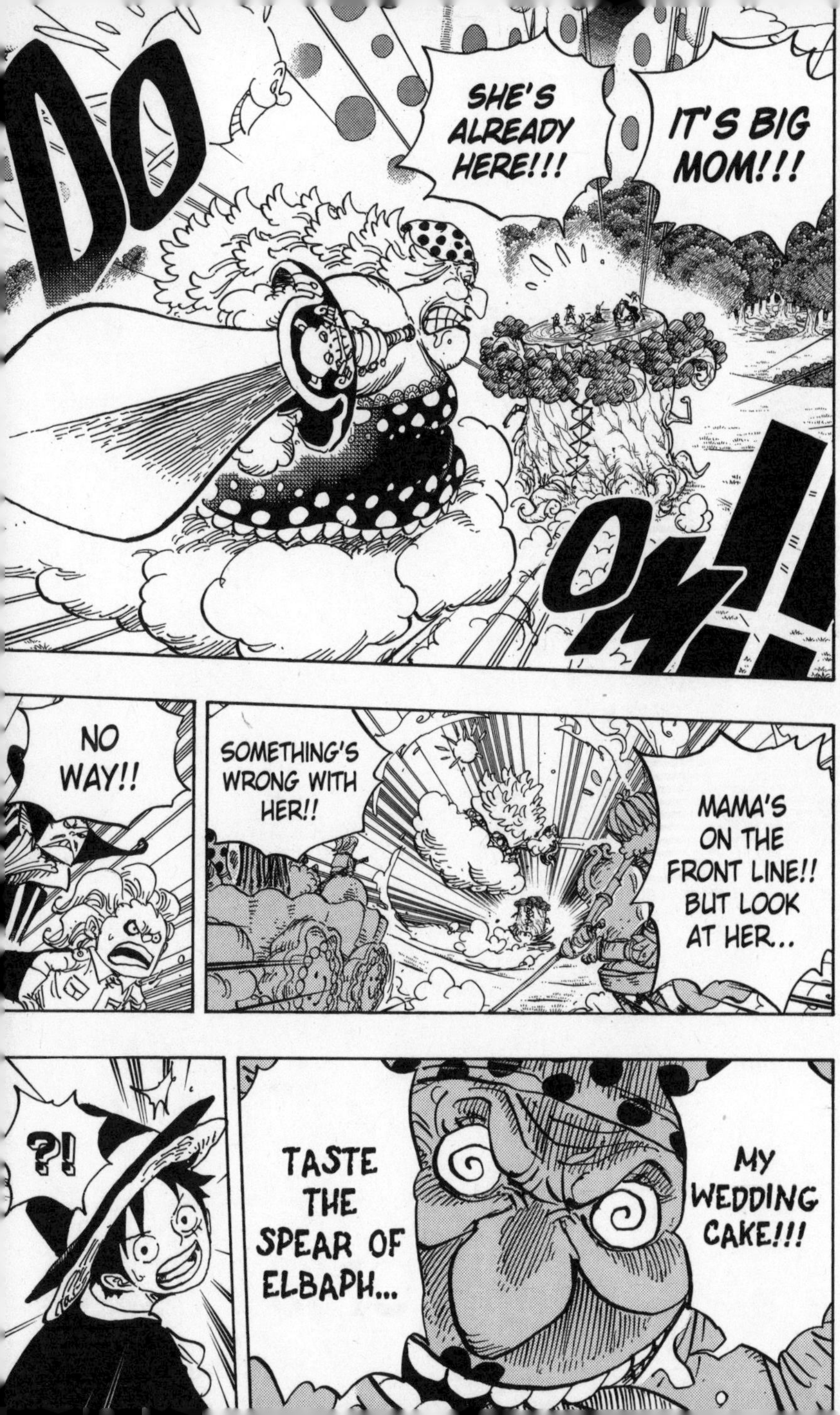
IT'S BIG MOM!!!
SHE'S ALREADY HERE!!!
DO
OM!!
MAMA'S ON THE FRONT LINE!! BUT LOOK AT HER...
SOMETHING'S WRONG WITH HER!!
NO WAY!!
MY WEDDING CAKE!!!
TASTE THE SPEAR OF ELBAPH...
?!

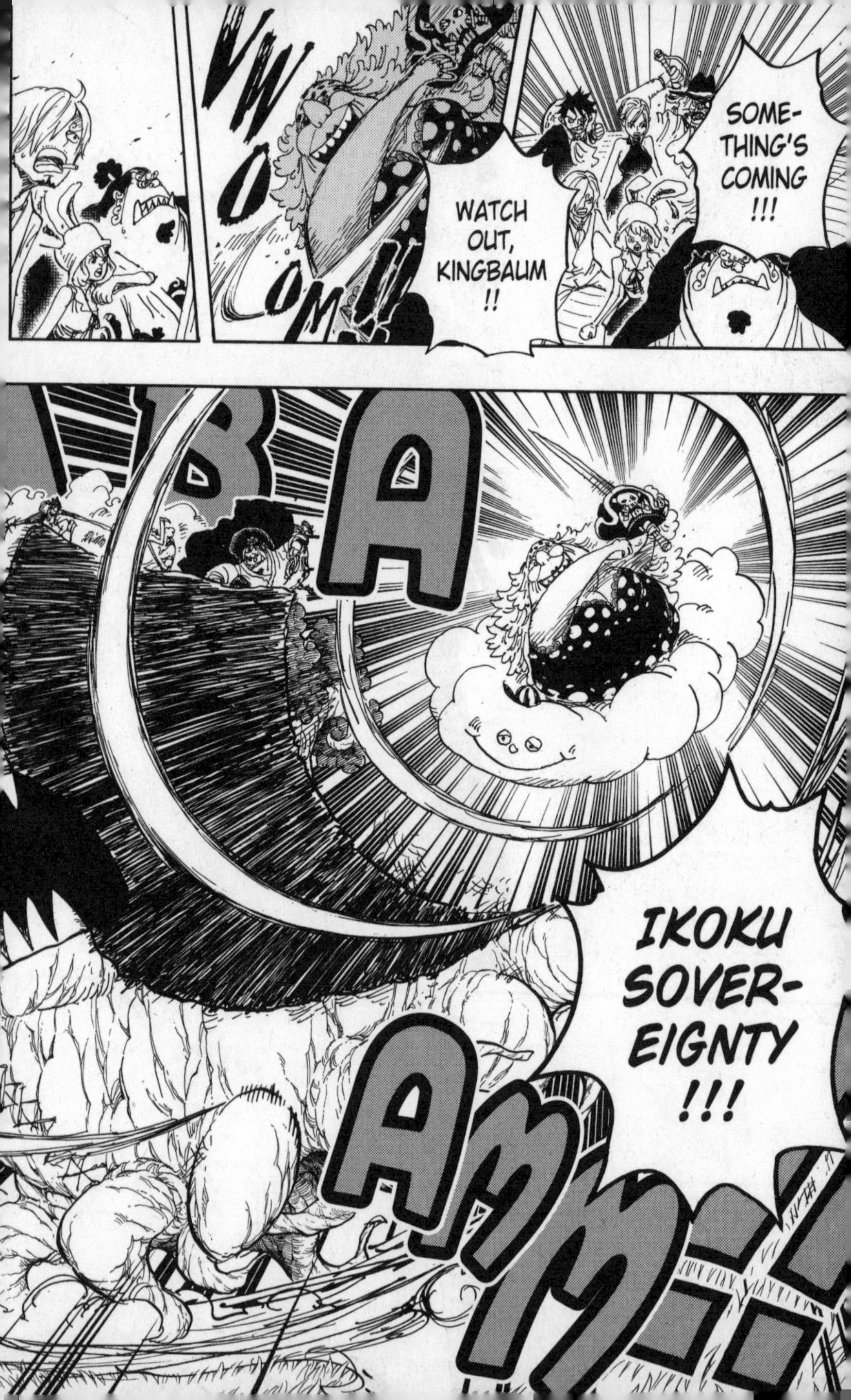

SOME-THING'S COMING!!!
WATCH OUT, KINGBAUM!!
VWOOM
BA
IKOKU SOVER-EIGNTY!!!
AM

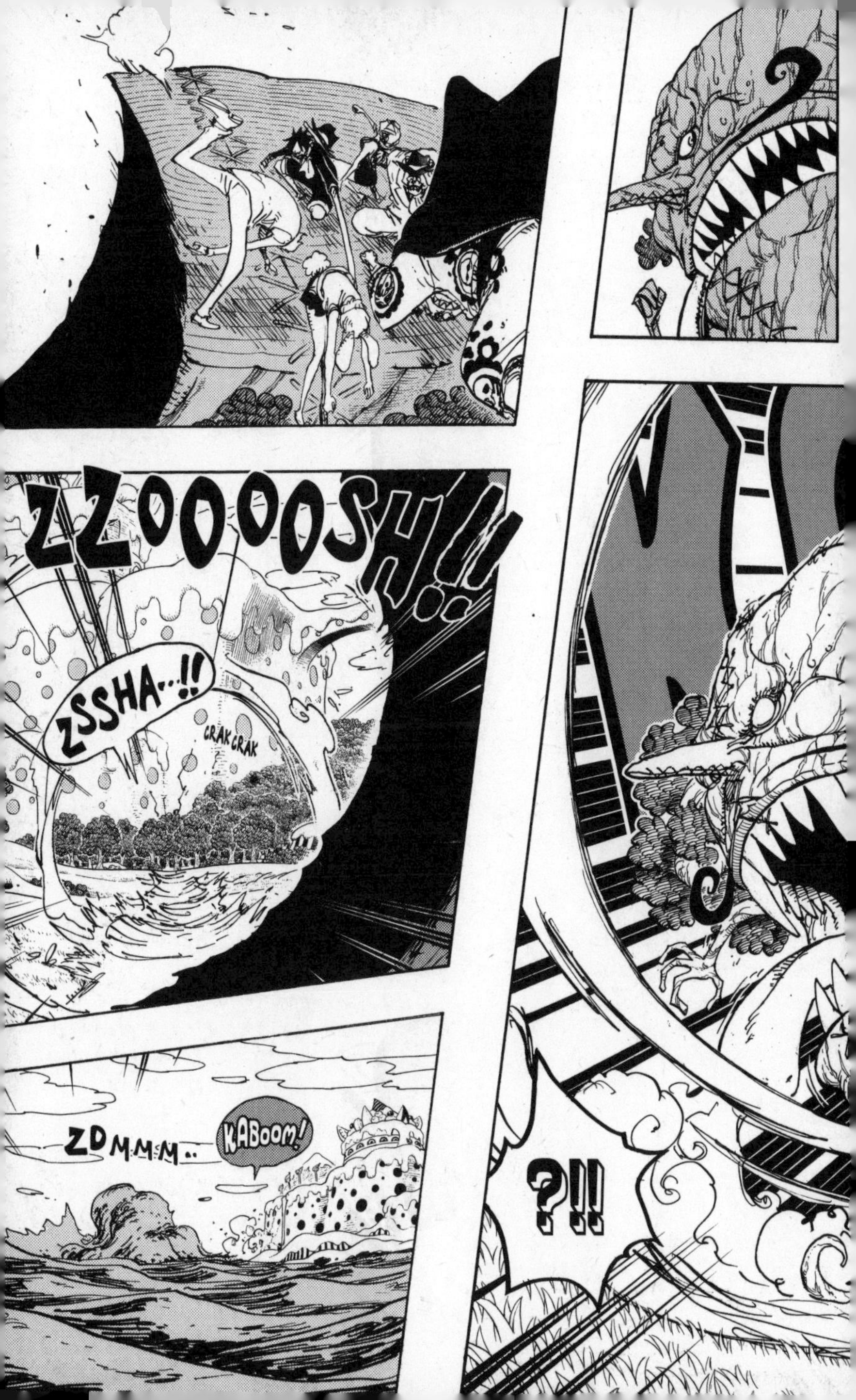
?!!
ZZOOOOSH!!
ZSSHA...!!
CRAK CRAK
KABOOM!
ZDMMM..

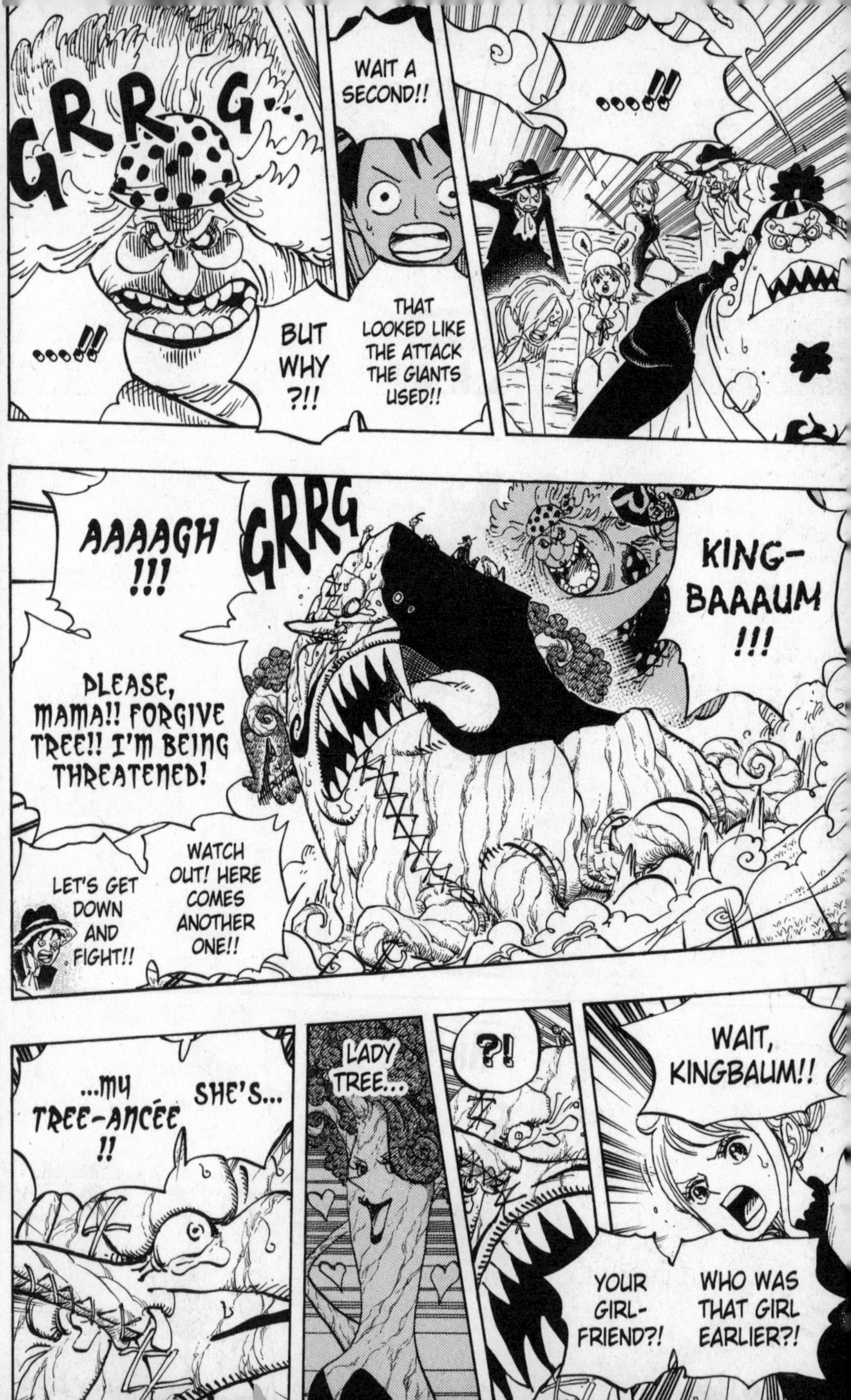
...!!
WAIT A SECOND!!
THAT LOOKED LIKE THE ATTACK THE GIANTS USED!!
BUT WHY ?!!
GRRG...
...!!
KING-BAAAUM!!!
GRRG
AAAAGH!!!
PLEASE, MAMA!! FORGIVE TREE!! I'M BEING THREATENED!
WATCH OUT! HERE COMES ANOTHER ONE!!
LET'S GET DOWN AND FIGHT!!
WAIT, KINGBAUM!!
WHO WAS THAT GIRL EARLIER?!
YOUR GIRL-FRIEND?!
?!
LADY TREE...
SHE'S...
...MY TREE-ANCÉE!!

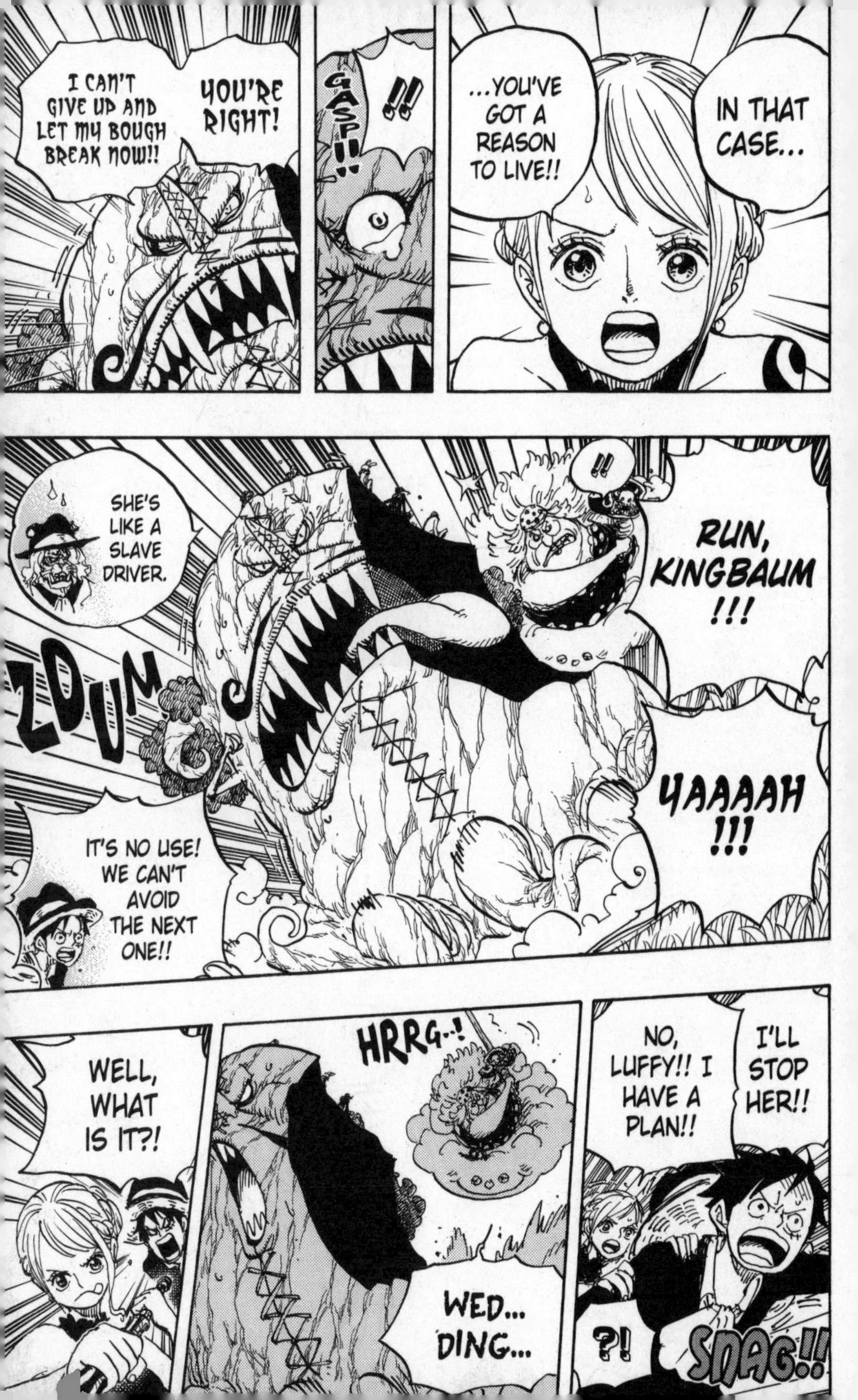
IN THAT CASE...
...YOU'VE GOT A REASON TO LIVE!!
GASP!!
!!
YOU'RE RIGHT!
I CAN'T GIVE UP AND LET MY BOUGH BREAK NOW!!
RUN, KINGBAUM!!!
!!
SHE'S LIKE A SLAVE DRIVER.
YAAAAH!!!
ZDUM
IT'S NO USE! WE CAN'T AVOID THE NEXT ONE!!
I'LL STOP HER!!
NO, LUFFY!! I HAVE A PLAN!!
?!
SNAG!!
HRRG..!
WED... DING...
WELL, WHAT IS IT?!

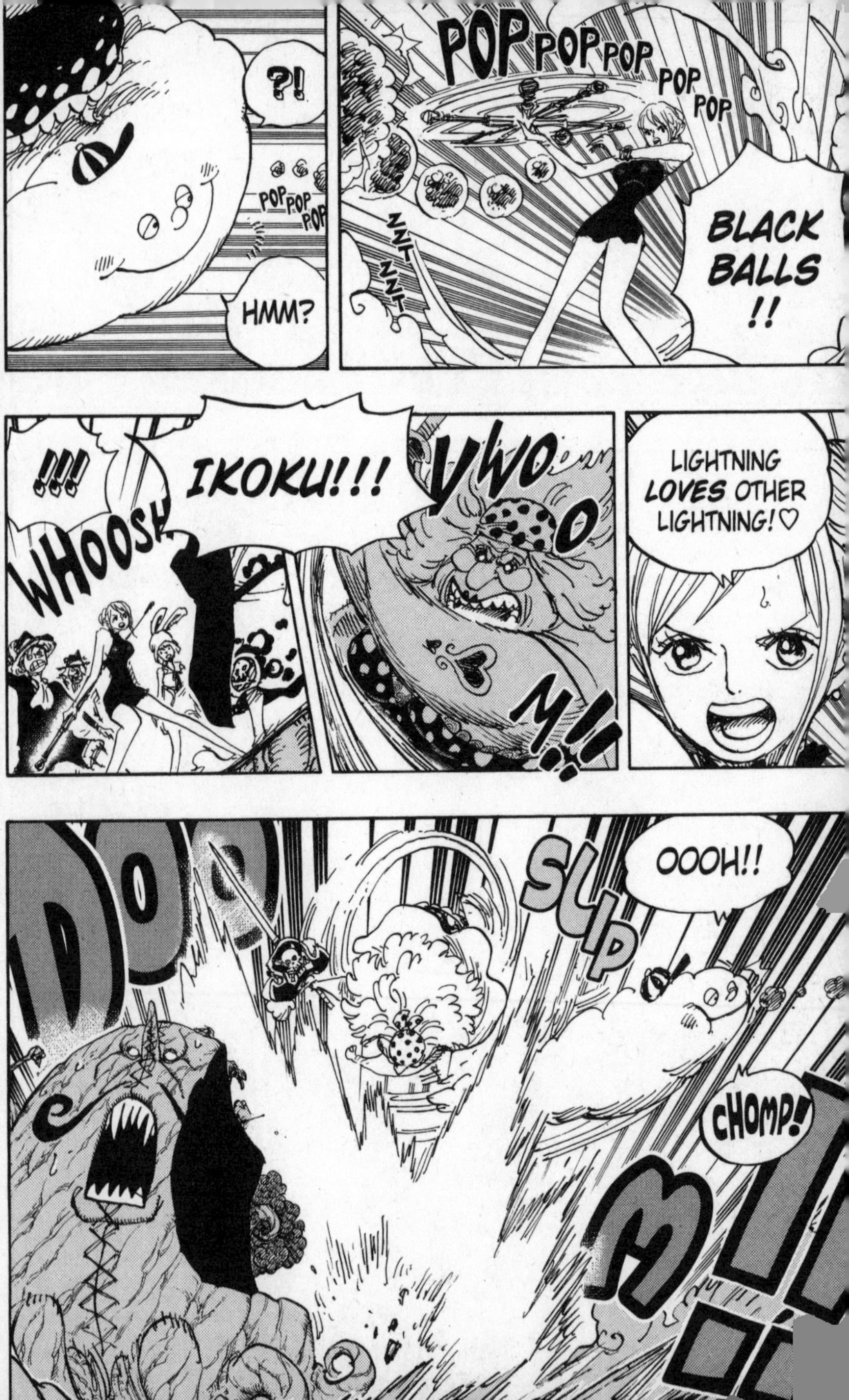
POP POP POP
POP POP
ZZZT
ZZZT
BLACK BALLS!!
?!
POP POP POP
HMM?
LIGHTNING LOVES OTHER LIGHTNING!♡
VWOOOM!!
IKOKU!!!
!!!
WHOOSH
OOOH!!
SLIP
CHOMP!

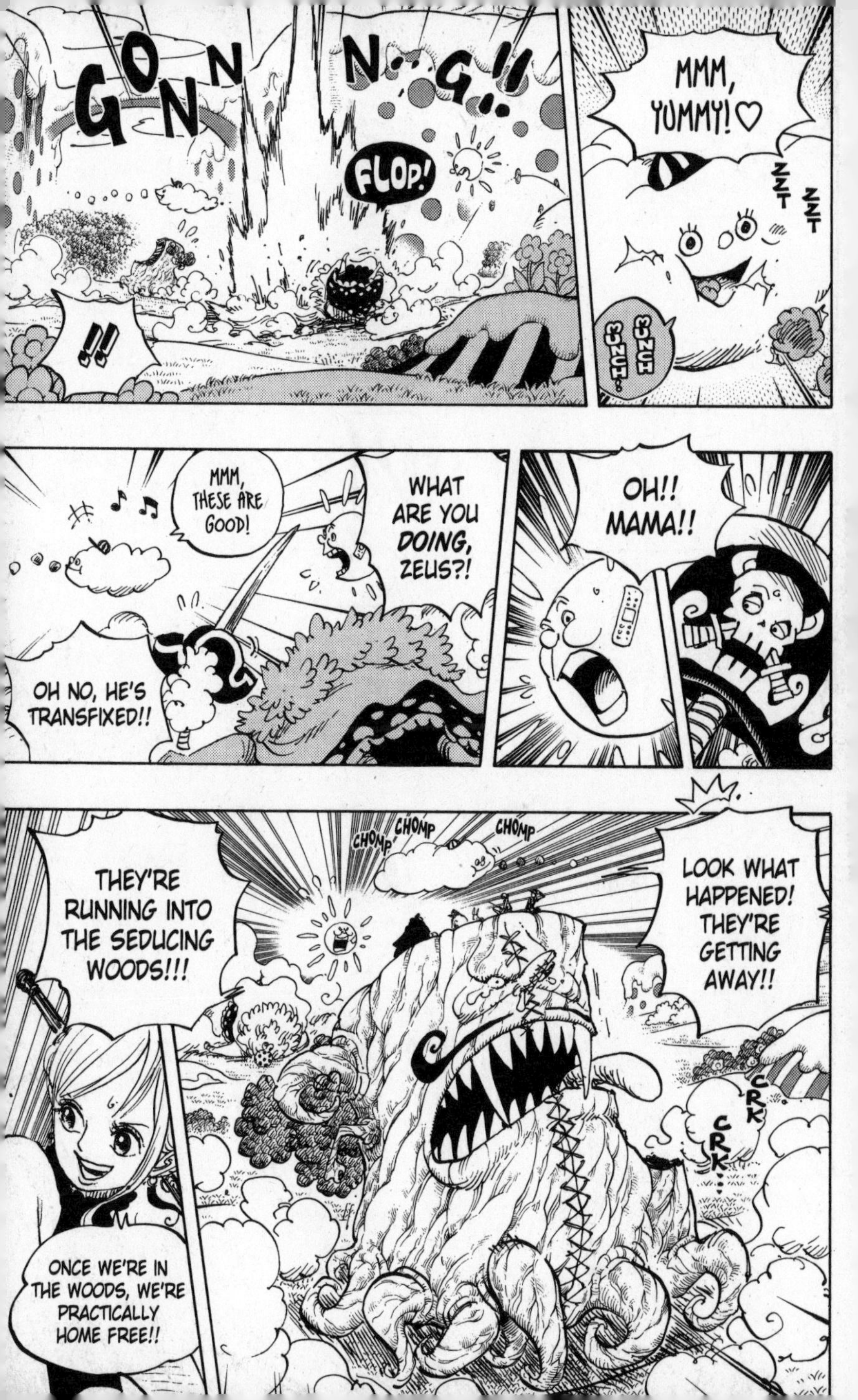
MMM, YUMMY! ♡
ZZT ZZT
MUNCH MUNCH...
GONNNG!!
FLOP!
!!
OH!! MAMA!!
WHAT ARE YOU DOING, ZEUS?!
MMM, THESE ARE GOOD!
OH NO, HE'S TRANSFIXED!!
LOOK WHAT HAPPENED! THEY'RE GETTING AWAY!!
CHOMP CHOMP
CHOMP
CRK CRK...
THEY'RE RUNNING INTO THE SEDUCING WOODS!!!
ONCE WE'RE IN THE WOODS, WE'RE PRACTICALLY HOME FREE!!

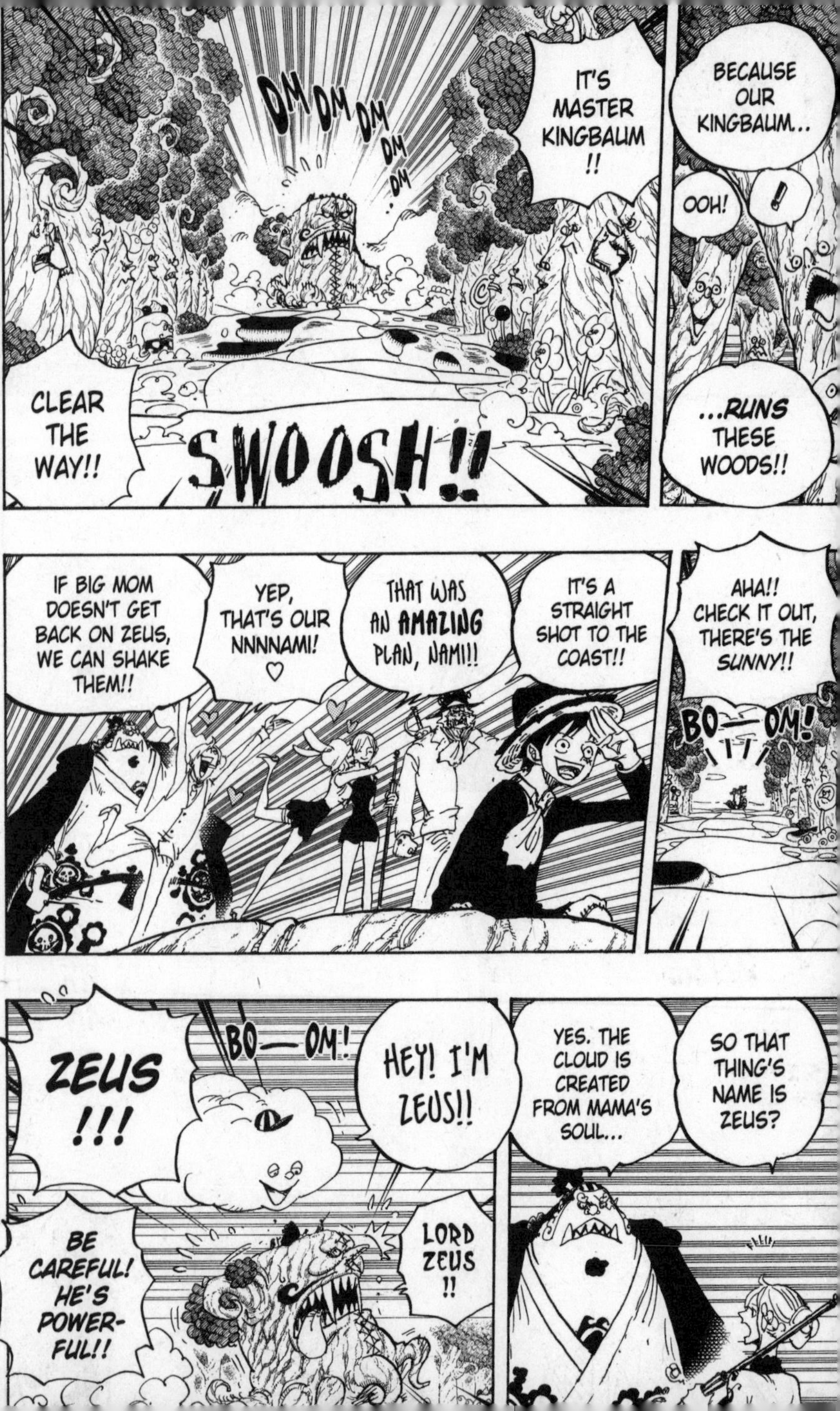
BECAUSE OUR KINGBAUM...
OOH!
!
...RUNS THESE WOODS!!
IT'S MASTER KINGBAUM !!
DM DM DM DM DM
CLEAR THE WAY!!
SWOOSH!!
AHA!! CHECK IT OUT, THERE'S THE SUNNY!!
BO—OM!
IT'S A STRAIGHT SHOT TO THE COAST!!
THAT WAS AN AMAZING PLAN, NAMI!!
YEP, THAT'S OUR NNNNAMI! ♡
IF BIG MOM DOESN'T GET BACK ON ZEUS, WE CAN SHAKE THEM!!
SO THAT THING'S NAME IS ZEUS?
YES. THE CLOUD IS CREATED FROM MAMA'S SOUL...
HEY! I'M ZEUS!!
BO—OM!
ZEUS !!!
LORD ZEUS !!
BE CAREFUL! HE'S POWER-FUL!!

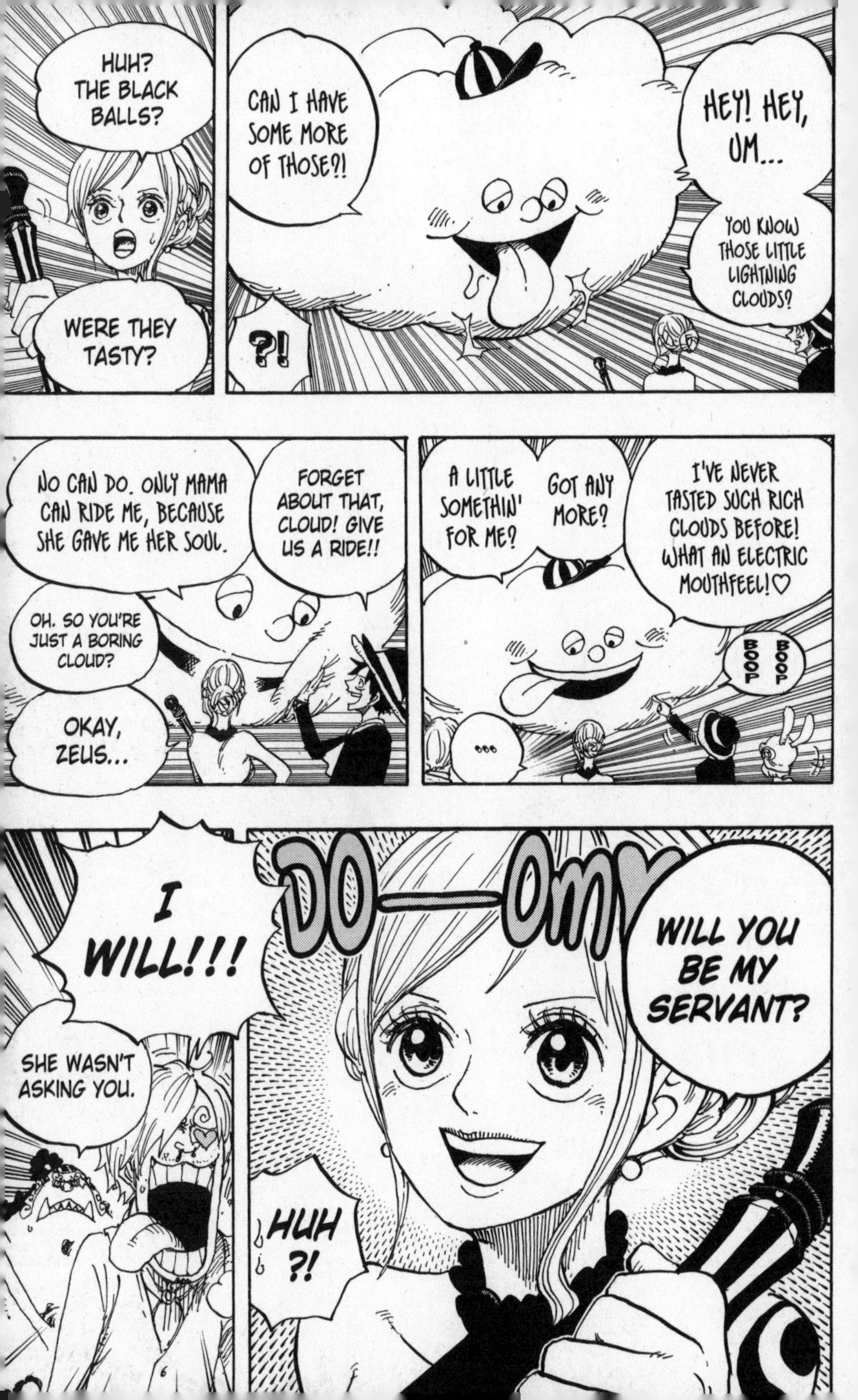
HEY! HEY, UM...
YOU KNOW THOSE LITTLE LIGHTNING CLOUDS?
CAN I HAVE SOME MORE OF THOSE?!
?!
HUH? THE BLACK BALLS?
WERE THEY TASTY?
I'VE NEVER TASTED SUCH RICH CLOUDS BEFORE! WHAT AN ELECTRIC MOUTHFEEL!♡
GOT ANY MORE?
A LITTLE SOMETHIN' FOR ME?
BOOP BOOP
...
FORGET ABOUT THAT, CLOUD! GIVE US A RIDE!!
NO CAN DO. ONLY MAMA CAN RIDE ME, BECAUSE SHE GAVE ME HER SOUL.
OH. SO YOU'RE JUST A BORING CLOUD?
OKAY, ZEUS...
DO—OM
WILL YOU BE MY SERVANT?
HUH?!
I WILL!!!
SHE WASN'T ASKING YOU.

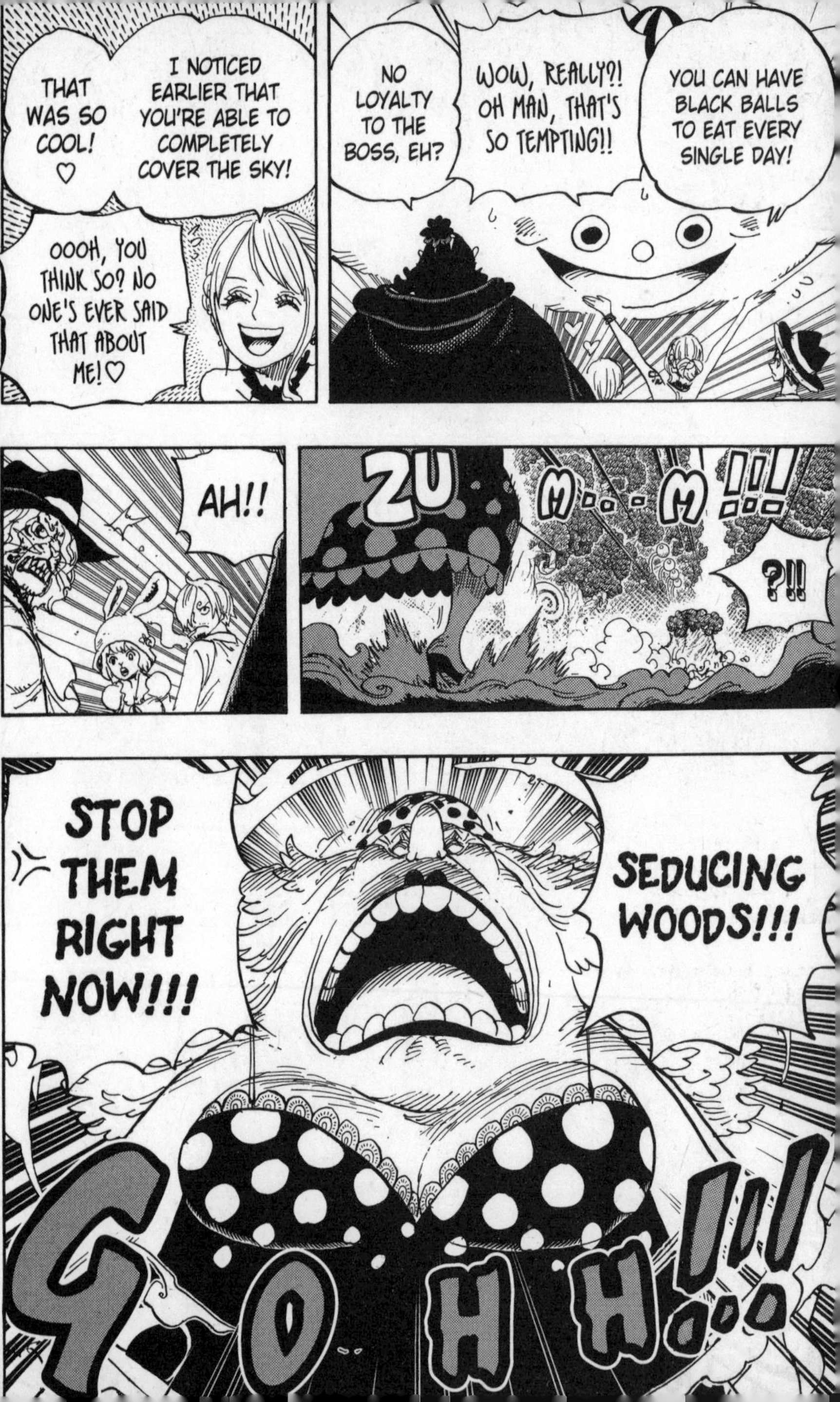
YOU CAN HAVE BLACK BALLS TO EAT EVERY SINGLE DAY!
WOW, REALLY?! OH MAN, THAT'S SO TEMPTING!!
NO LOYALTY TO THE BOSS, EH?
I NOTICED EARLIER THAT YOU'RE ABLE TO COMPLETELY COVER THE SKY!
THAT WAS SO COOL! ♡
OOOH, YOU THINK SO? NO ONE'S EVER SAID THAT ABOUT ME! ♡
ZU
M...M!!!
?!!
AH!!
SEDUCING WOODS!!!
STOP THEM RIGHT NOW!!!
GOHH...!!!

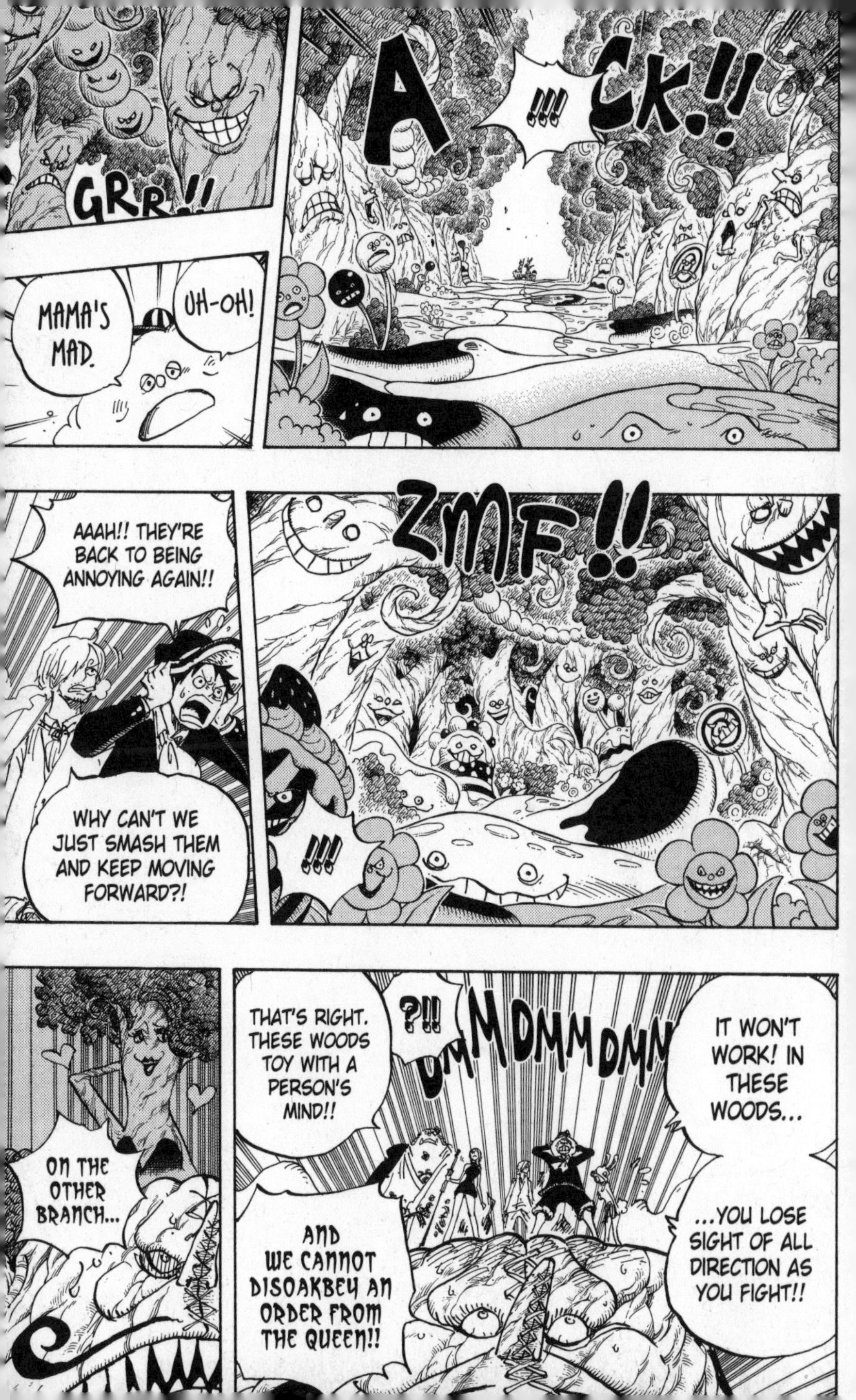
A
!!!
CK!!
GRR!!
UH-OH!
MAMA'S MAD.
ZMF!!
!!!
AAAH!! THEY'RE BACK TO BEING ANNOYING AGAIN!!
WHY CAN'T WE JUST SMASH THEM AND KEEP MOVING FORWARD?!
IT WON'T WORK! IN THESE WOODS...
DMMDMMDMN
?!!
THAT'S RIGHT. THESE WOODS TOY WITH A PERSON'S MIND!!
...YOU LOSE SIGHT OF ALL DIRECTION AS YOU FIGHT!!
AND WE CANNOT DISOAKBEY AN ORDER FROM THE QUEEN!!
ON THE OTHER BRANCH...

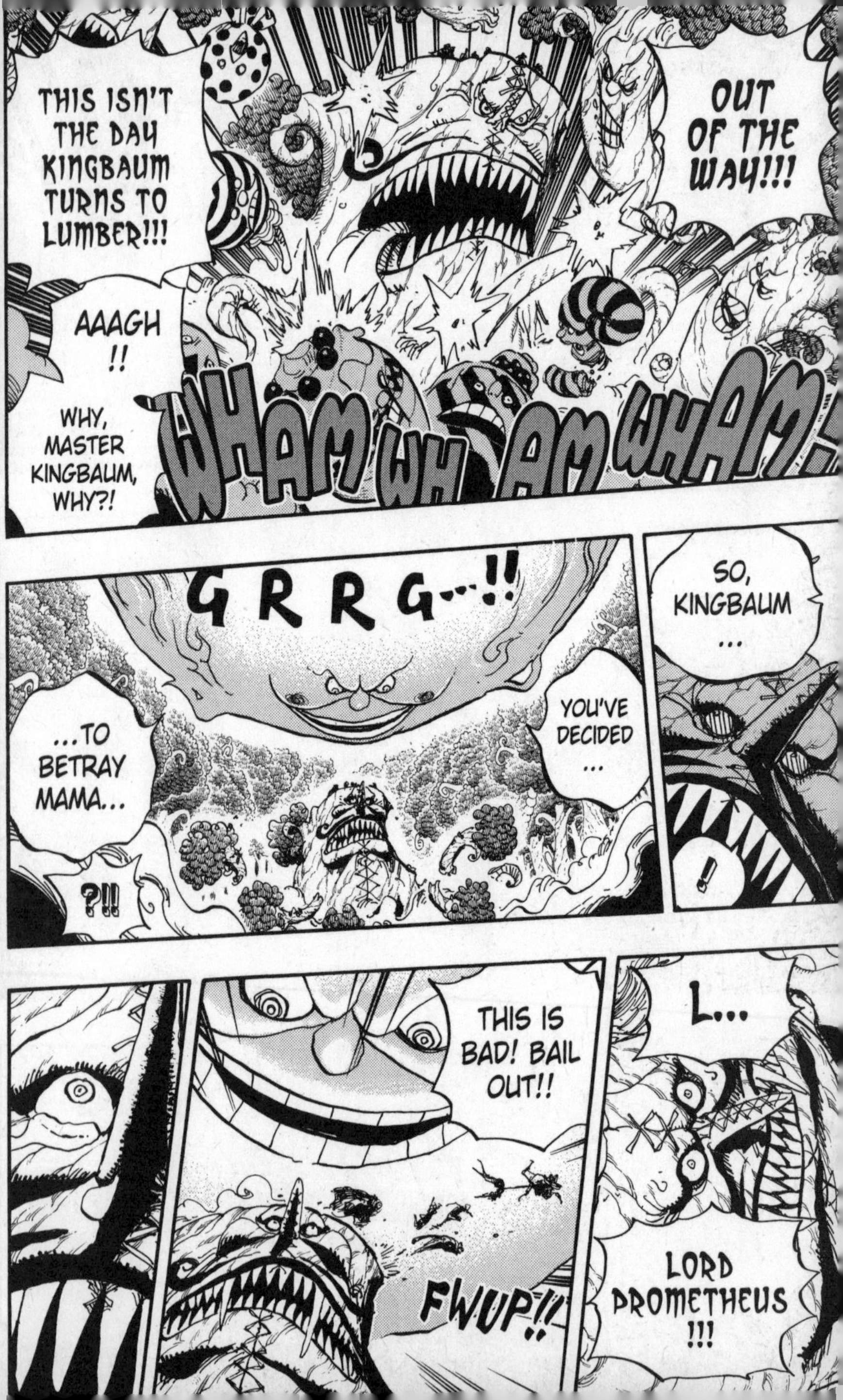
OUT OF THE WAY!!!
THIS ISN'T THE DAY KINGBAUM TURNS TO LUMBER!!!
WHAM WH AM WHAM
AAAGH !!
WHY, MASTER KINGBAUM, WHY?!
SO, KINGBAUM ...
!
GRRRG...!!
YOU'VE DECIDED ...
...TO BETRAY MAMA...
?!!
L...
LORD PROMETHEUS !!!
THIS IS BAD! BAIL OUT!!
FWUP!!

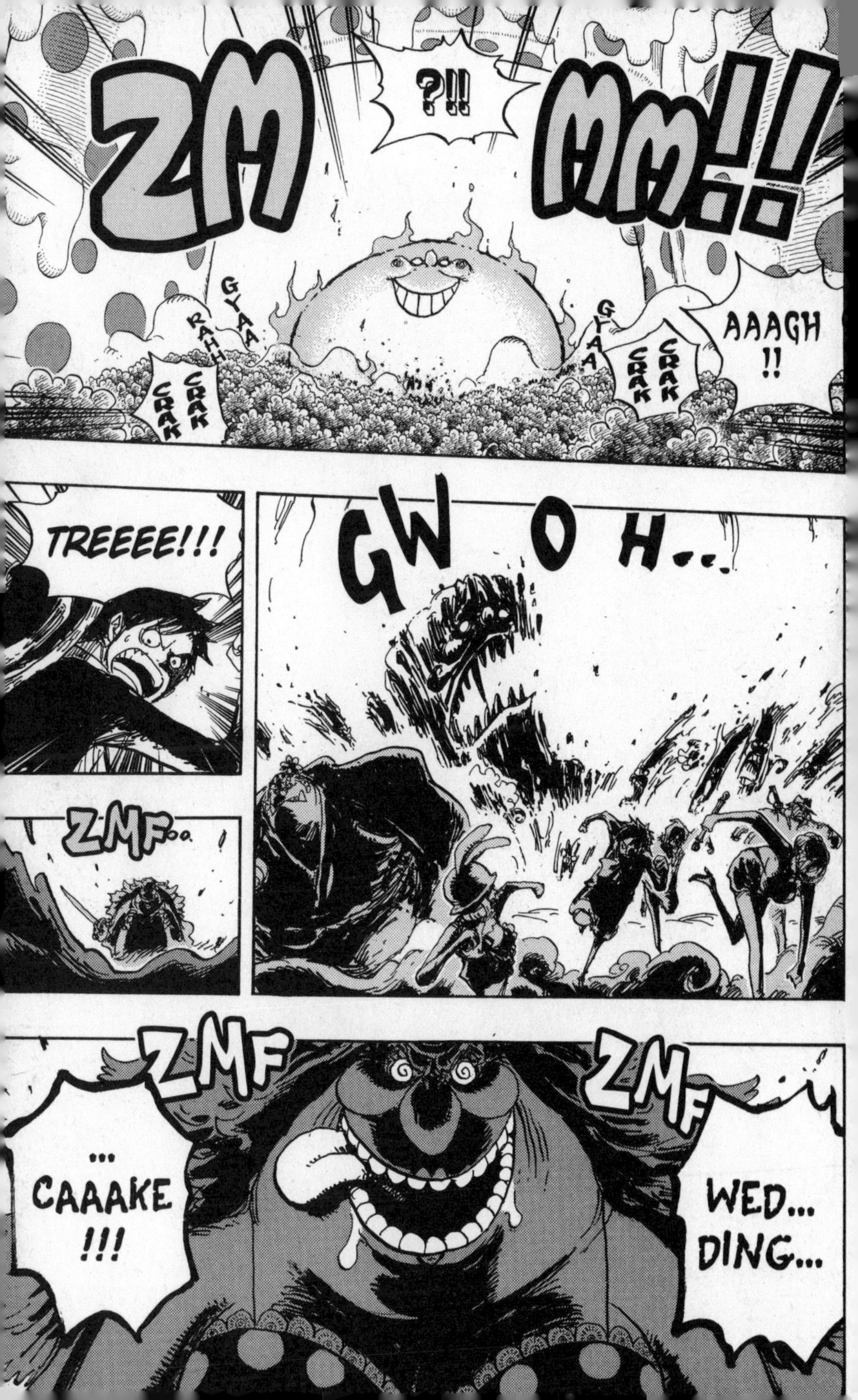

ZM
?!!
MM!!
AAAGH !!
GYAA
CRAK CRAK
GYAA RAHH
CRAK CRAK
GW O H...
TREEEE!!!
ZMF..
ZMF
ZMF
WED... DING...
... CAAAKE !!!

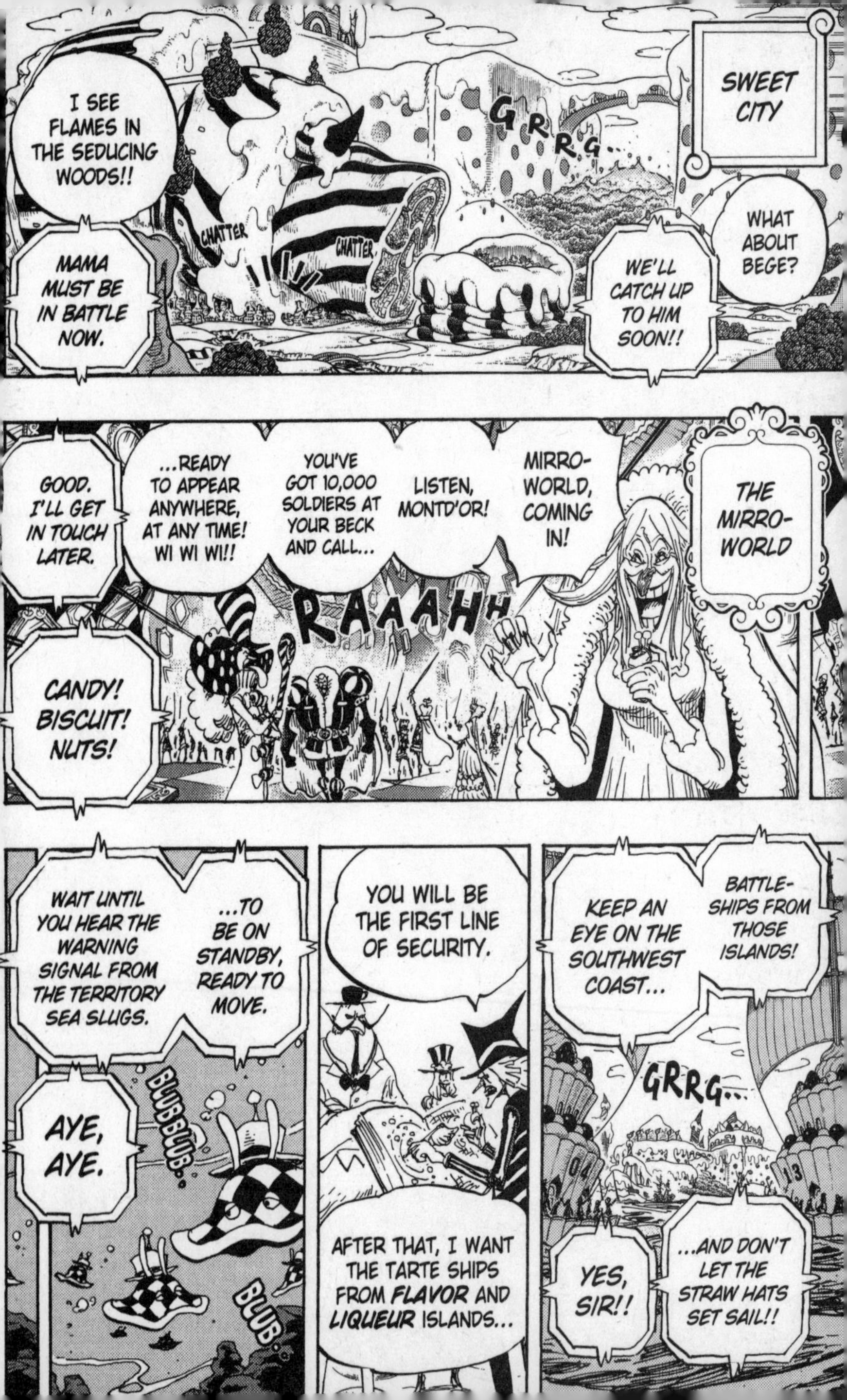
SWEET CITY
WHAT ABOUT BEGE?
WE'LL CATCH UP TO HIM SOON!!
GRRRG...
I SEE FLAMES IN THE SEDUCING WOODS!!
CHATTER
CHATTER
MAMA MUST BE IN BATTLE NOW.
THE MIRRO-WORLD
MIRRO-WORLD, COMING IN!
LISTEN, MONTD'OR!
YOU'VE GOT 10,000 SOLDIERS AT YOUR BECK AND CALL...
...READY TO APPEAR ANYWHERE, AT ANY TIME! WI WI WI!!
GOOD. I'LL GET IN TOUCH LATER.
RAAAHH
CANDY! BISCUIT! NUTS!
BATTLE-SHIPS FROM THOSE ISLANDS!
KEEP AN EYE ON THE SOUTHWEST COAST...
GRRRG...
...AND DON'T LET THE STRAW HATS SET SAIL!!
YES, SIR!!
YOU WILL BE THE FIRST LINE OF SECURITY.
AFTER THAT, I WANT THE TARTE SHIPS FROM FLAVOR AND LIQUEUR ISLANDS...
...TO BE ON STANDBY, READY TO MOVE.
WAIT UNTIL YOU HEAR THE WARNING SIGNAL FROM THE TERRITORY SEA SLUGS.
BLUBBLUB
AYE, AYE.
BLUB

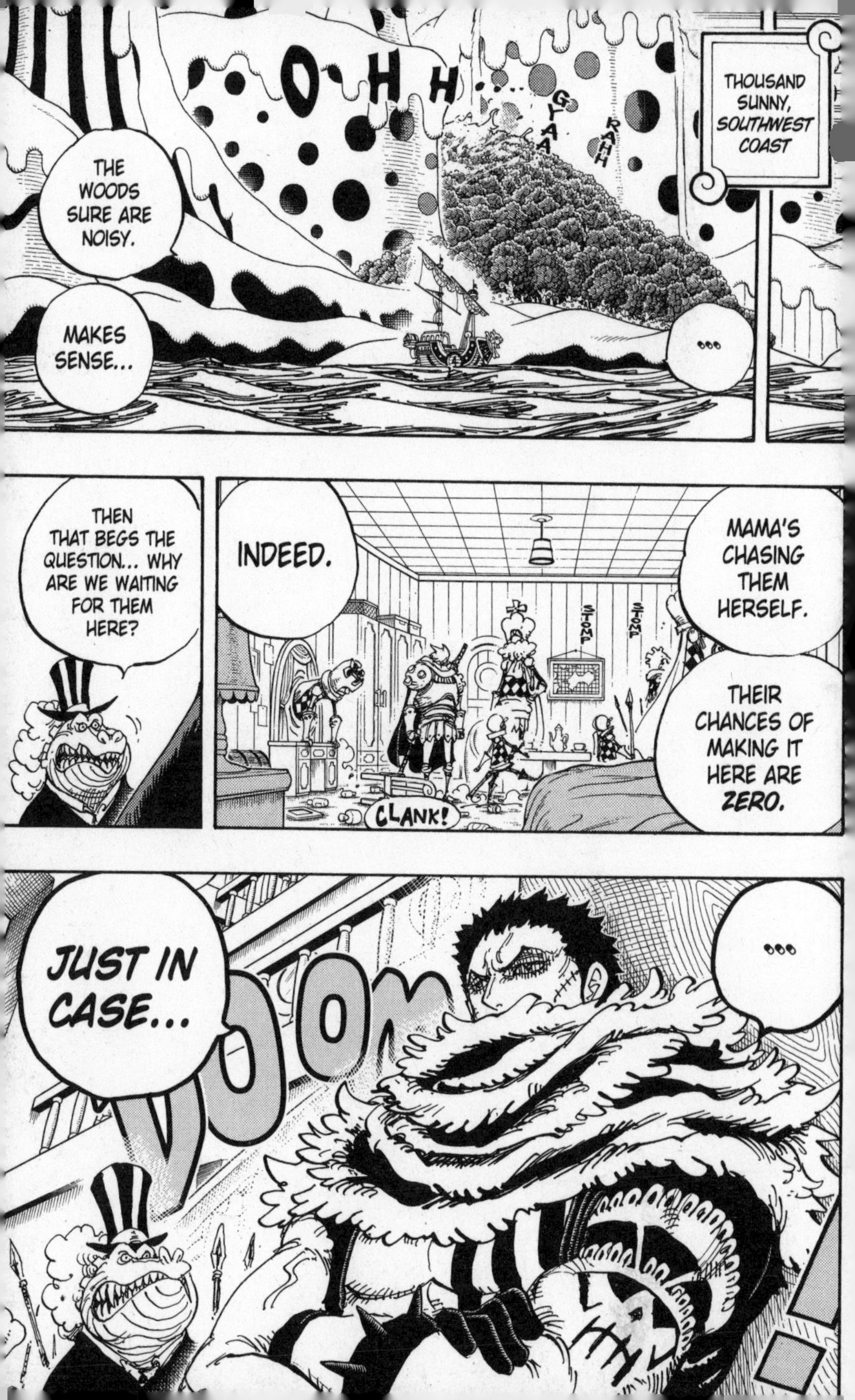
THOUSAND SUNNY, SOUTHWEST COAST
RAHH
GYAAA
OHH...
THE WOODS SURE ARE NOISY.
...
MAKES SENSE...
MAMA'S CHASING THEM HERSELF.
THEIR CHANCES OF MAKING IT HERE ARE ZERO.
STOMP
STOMP
INDEED.
CLANK!
THEN THAT BEGS THE QUESTION... WHY ARE WE WAITING FOR THEM HERE?
...
VOOOM
JUST IN CASE...

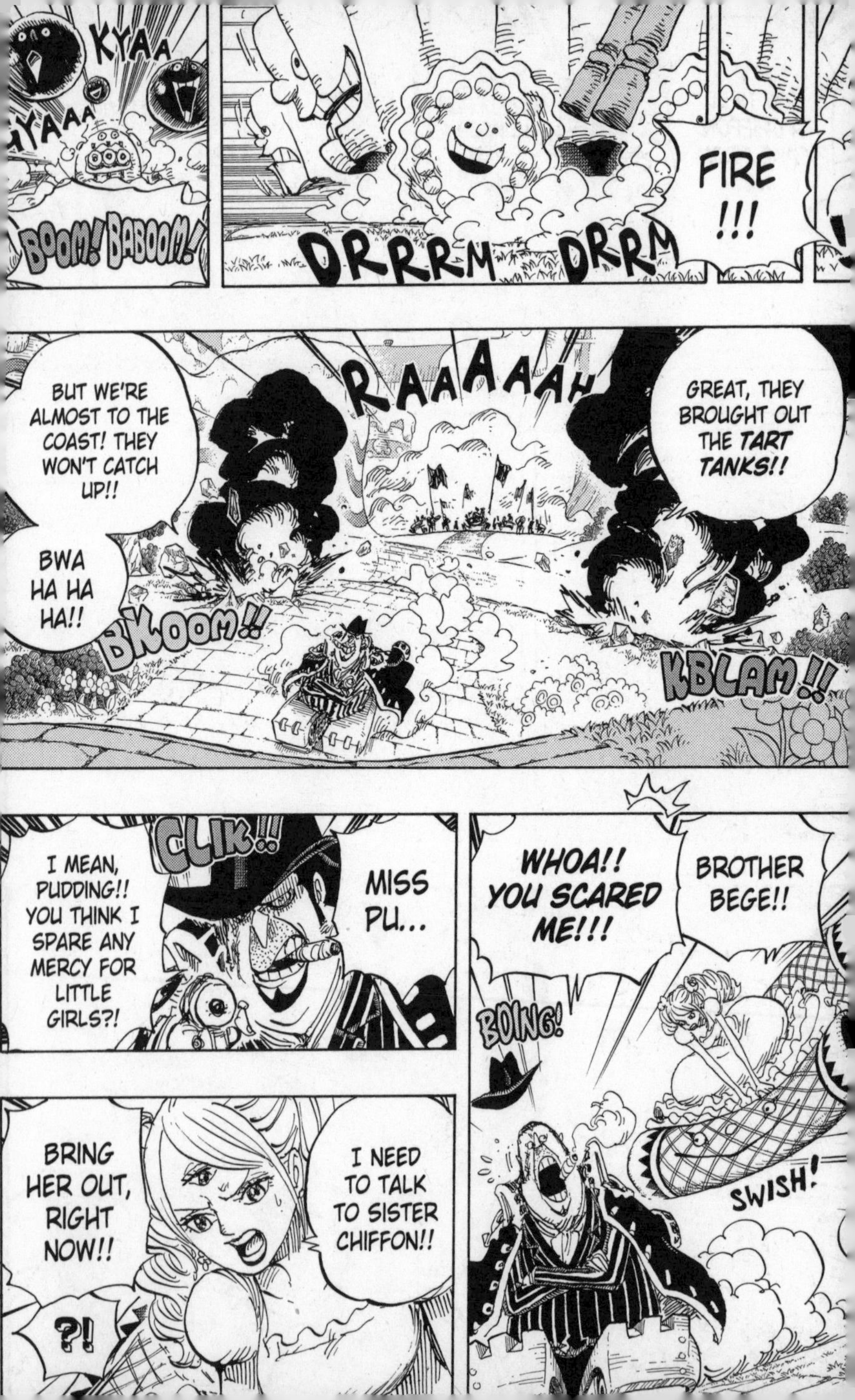
FIRE!!!
DRRRM DRRRM
KYAA
GYAAA
BOOM! BABOOM!
GREAT, THEY BROUGHT OUT THE *TART TANKS!!*
RAAAAAH
KBLAM!!
BUT WE'RE ALMOST TO THE COAST! THEY WON'T CATCH UP!!
BWA HA HA HA!!
BKOOM!!
BROTHER BEGE!!
WHOA!! YOU SCARED ME!!!
BOING!
SWISH!
MISS PU...
I MEAN, PUDDING!! YOU THINK I SPARE ANY MERCY FOR LITTLE GIRLS?!
CLIK!!
I NEED TO TALK TO SISTER CHIFFON!!
BRING HER OUT, RIGHT NOW!!
?!

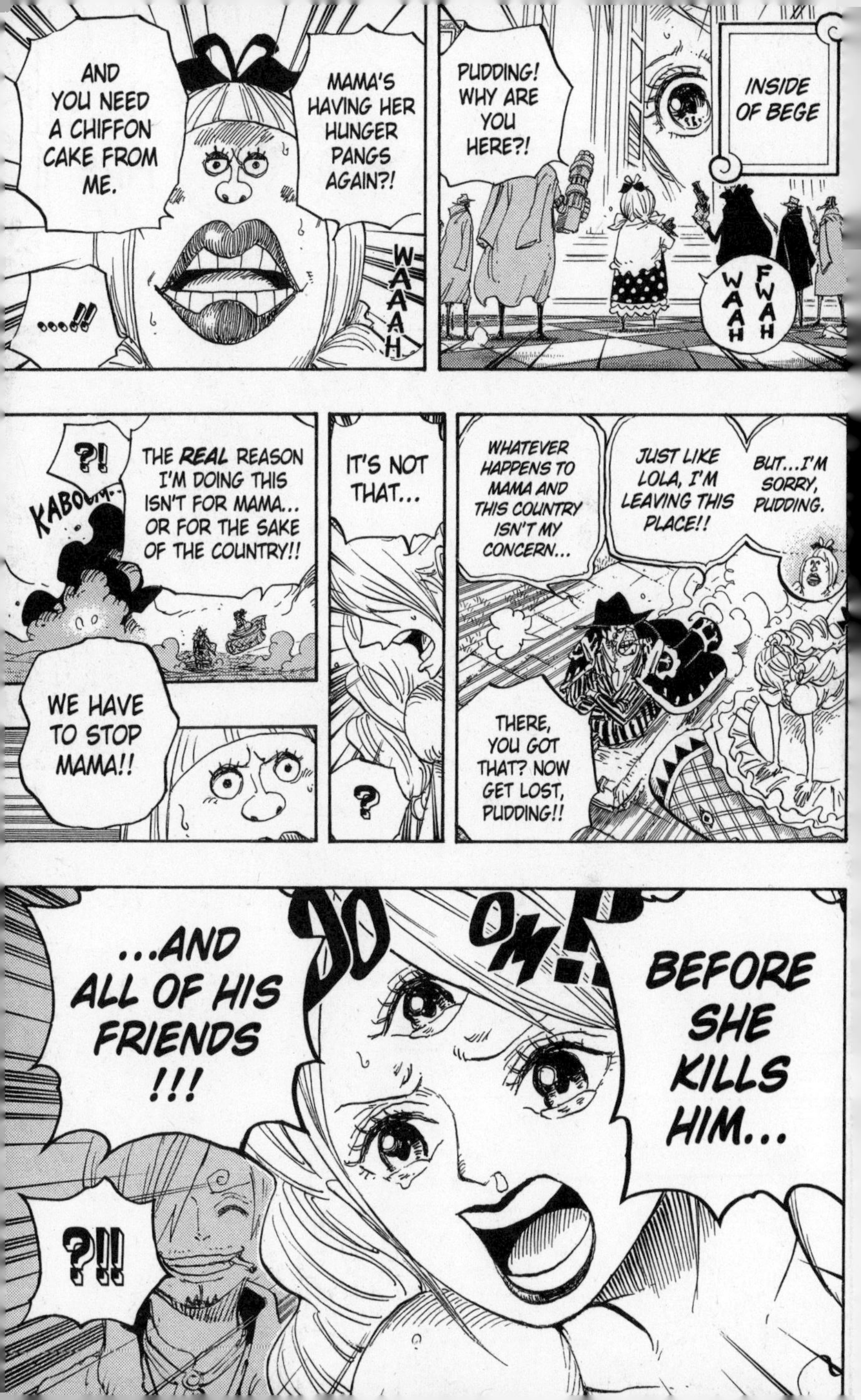
INSIDE OF BEGE
PUDDING! WHY ARE YOU HERE?!
FWAH
WAAH
MAMA'S HAVING HER HUNGER PANGS AGAIN?!
AND YOU NEED A CHIFFON CAKE FROM ME.
WAAAAH
...!!
BUT...I'M SORRY, PUDDING.
JUST LIKE LOLA, I'M LEAVING THIS PLACE!!
WHATEVER HAPPENS TO MAMA AND THIS COUNTRY ISN'T MY CONCERN...
THERE, YOU GOT THAT? NOW GET LOST, PUDDING!!
IT'S NOT THAT...
?
THE **REAL** REASON I'M DOING THIS ISN'T FOR MAMA... OR FOR THE SAKE OF THE COUNTRY!!
?!
KABOOM
WE HAVE TO STOP MAMA!!
BEFORE SHE KILLS HIM...
DOOM!!
...AND ALL OF HIS FRIENDS!!!
?!!

SBS Question Corner

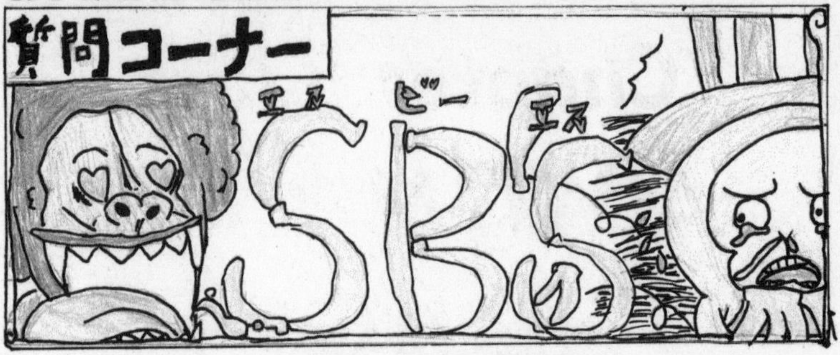

質問コーナー
SBS

(Colo-Colo-Linlin Wasabi, Mie)

Q: Oda Sen…I mean, Odacchi! After reading Volume 86 I became a huge fan of Katakuri. But in Chapter 873, Daifuku (3rd son) refers to Katakuri (2nd son) as just "Katakuri," without the "Brother" honorific. Why did he do that? Are they just twins who don't look like each other? Why is Katakuri the only one who isn't a Minister? Tell me his age and height too!!

--Charlotte Yurie

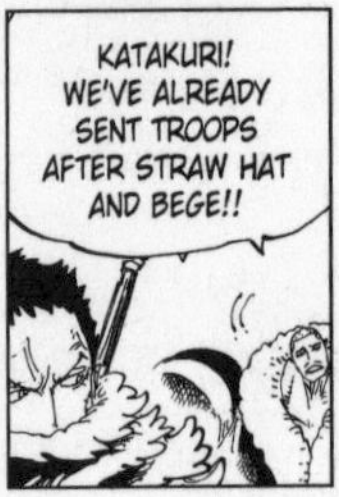

KATAKURI! WE'VE ALREADY SENT TROOPS AFTER STRAW HAT AND BEGE!!

A: Wow, that's a storm of Katakuri questions! Very perceptive of you to suspect that Daifuku is his twin. As a matter of fact, they're 48-year-old triplets!

C. Katakuri
[16' 8"]

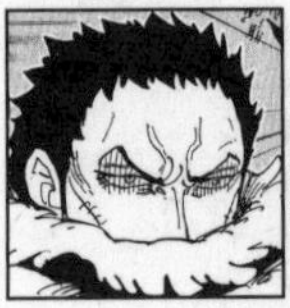

Wheat Island (Flour Town)
Minister of Flour
2nd Son

C. Daifuku
[16']

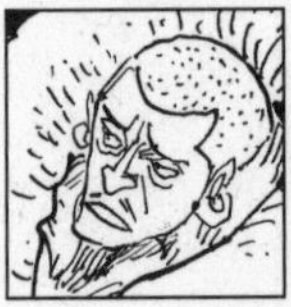

Munchie Island (Beany-Bean Town)
Minister of Beans
3rd Son

C. Oven
[16' 2"]

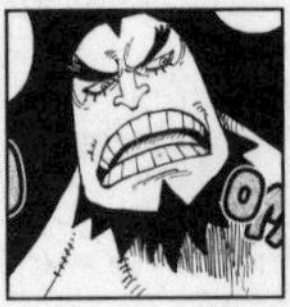

Bakery Island (Puffed Town)
Minister of Baking
4th Son

There are 34 ministers for 34 islands. All of them are Big Mom's children, naturally, and I have them all written down, but I'm currently debating whether I should put all that info out there or not. There's just a ton of background info. And most of it is totally pointless. (laughs)

Q: So once Baron Tamago's Egg-Egg Fruit evolves him into Count Niwatori, how does he go back into egg mode?

--Match and Takeshi

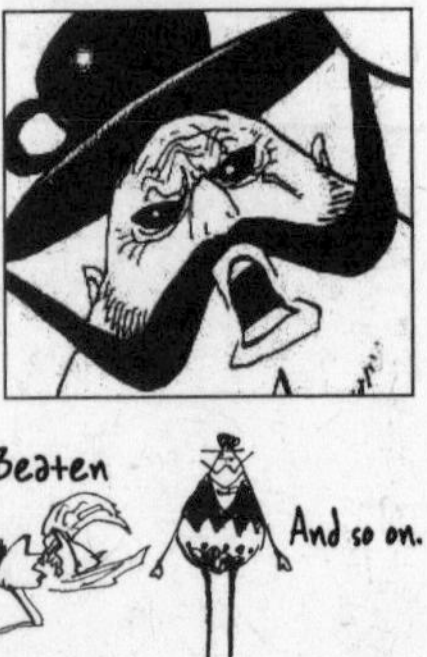

A: Like this. But which came first, the egg form or the chicken form? Nobody knows the answer.

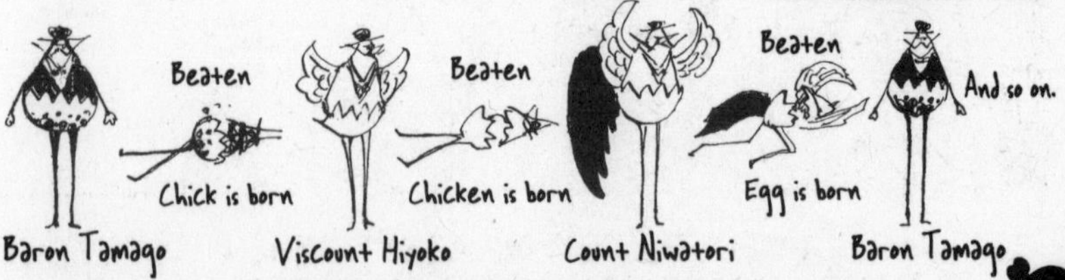

Baron Tamago
Beaten
Chick is born
Viscount Hiyoko
Beaten
Chicken is born
Count Niwatori
Beaten
Egg is born
Baron Tamago
And so on.

Chapter 875:
A WOMAN'S HONOR

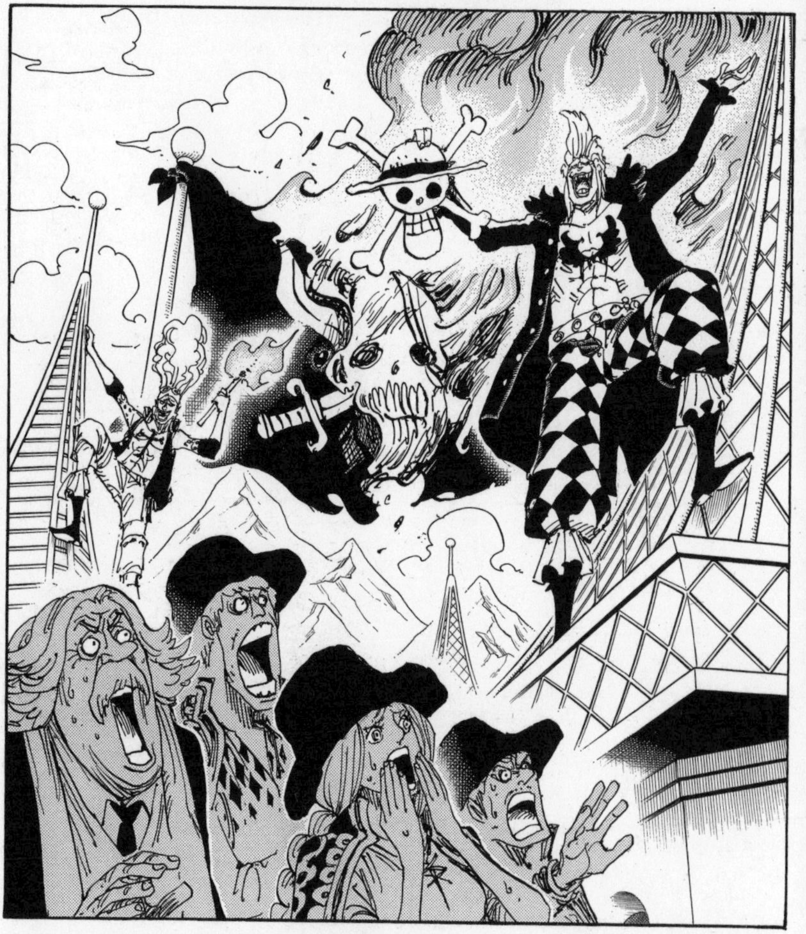

THE SAGA OF THE SELF-PROCLAIMED STRAW HAT FLEET,
VOL. 10, BARTOLOMEO: "EMPEROR OF THE SEA?! SO WHAT?!!"

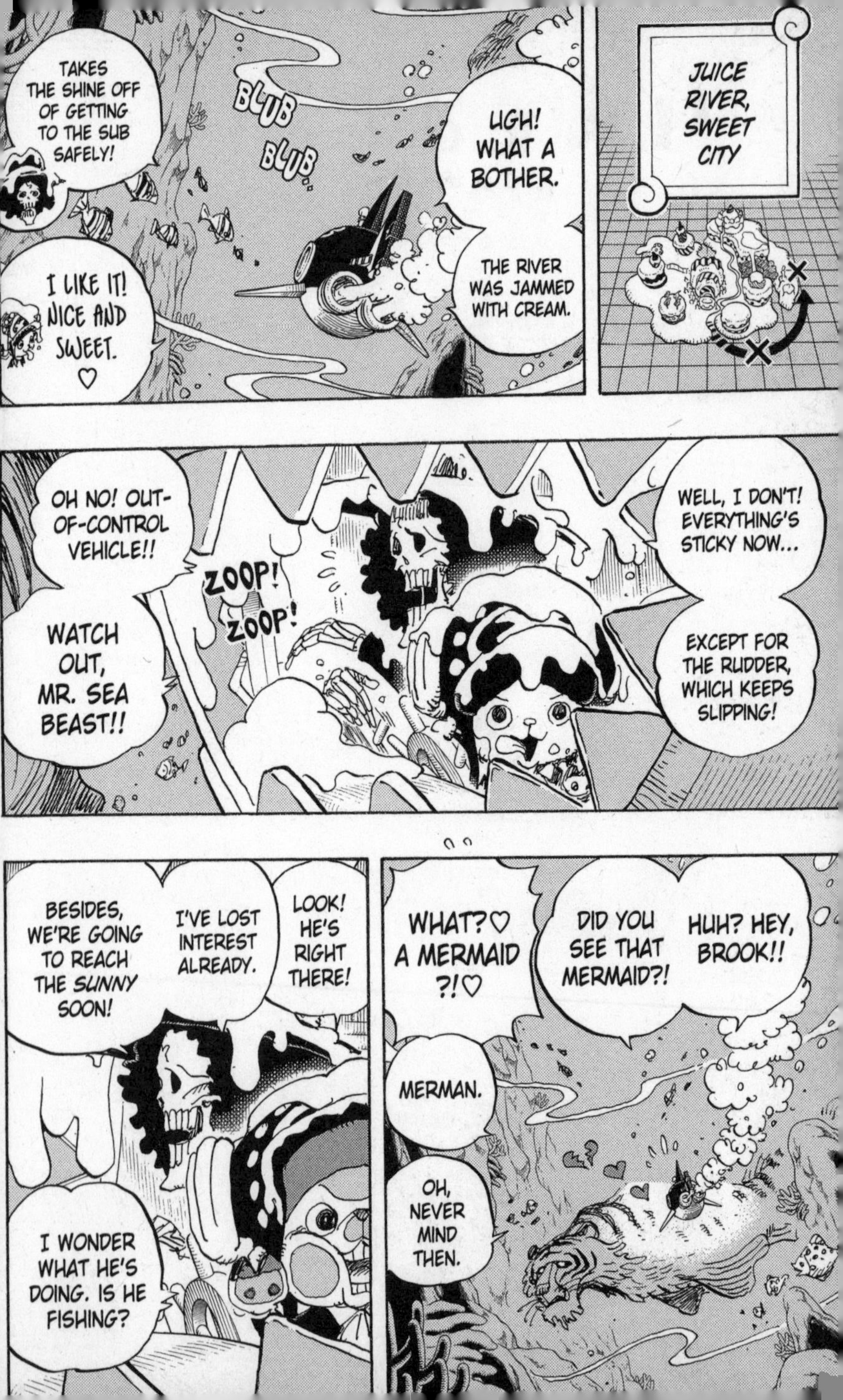
JUICE RIVER, SWEET CITY
UGH! WHAT A BOTHER.
THE RIVER WAS JAMMED WITH CREAM.
BLUB
BLUB
TAKES THE SHINE OFF OF GETTING TO THE SUB SAFELY!
I LIKE IT! NICE AND SWEET. ♡
WELL, I DON'T! EVERYTHING'S STICKY NOW...
EXCEPT FOR THE RUDDER, WHICH KEEPS SLIPPING!
ZOOP!
ZOOP!
OH NO! OUT-OF-CONTROL VEHICLE!!
WATCH OUT, MR. SEA BEAST!!
HUH? HEY, BROOK!!
DID YOU SEE THAT MERMAID?!
WHAT?♡ A MERMAID ?!♡
MERMAN.
OH, NEVER MIND THEN.
LOOK! HE'S RIGHT THERE!
I'VE LOST INTEREST ALREADY.
BESIDES, WE'RE GOING TO REACH THE *SUNNY* SOON!
I WONDER WHAT HE'S DOING. IS HE FISHING?

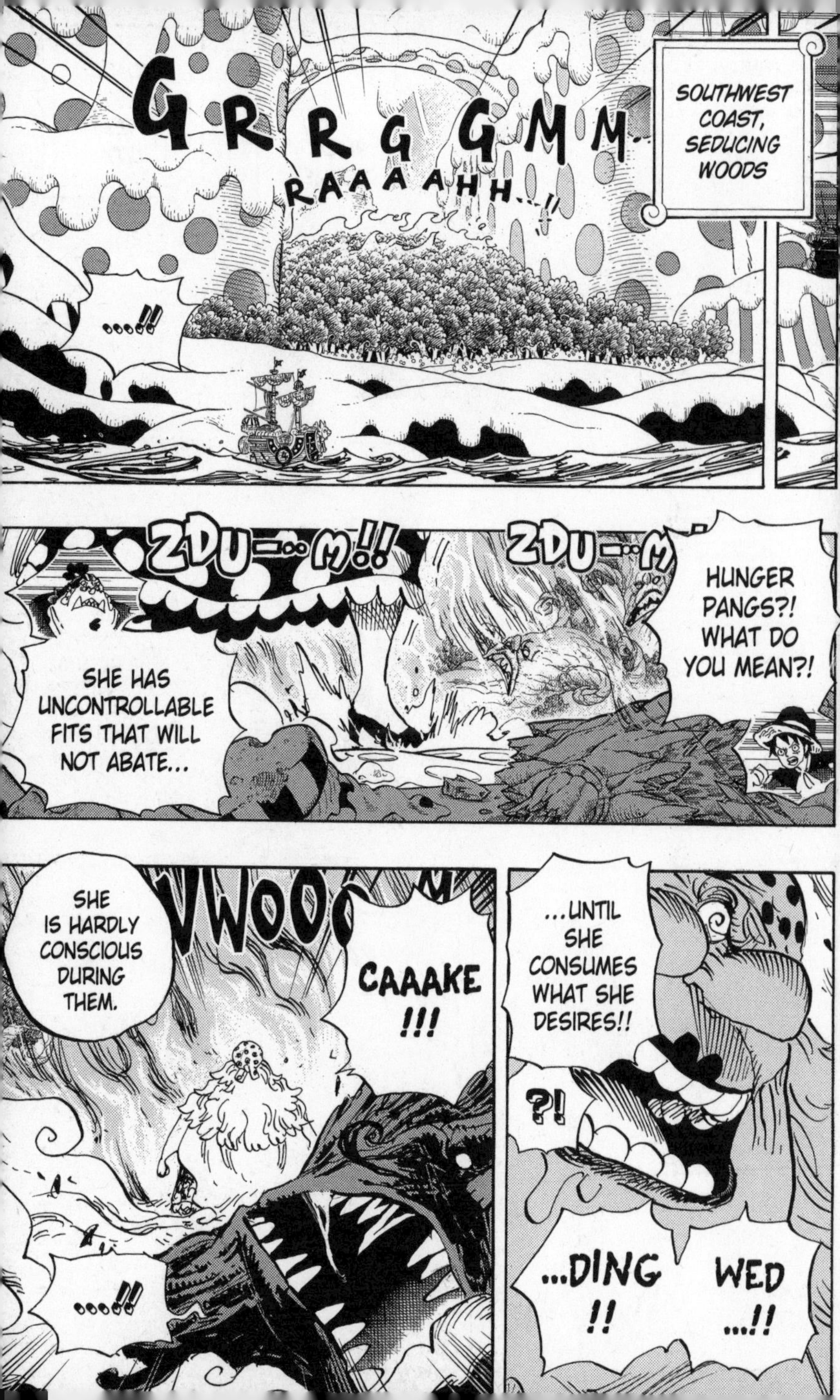
SOUTHWEST COAST, SEDUCING WOODS
GRRRGGMM
RAAAAHH...!!
...!!
HUNGER PANGS?! WHAT DO YOU MEAN?!
ZDU--M
ZDU--M!!
SHE HAS UNCONTROLLABLE FITS THAT WILL NOT ABATE...
...UNTIL SHE CONSUMES WHAT SHE DESIRES!!
?!
WED ...!!
...DING !!
VWOO
SHE IS HARDLY CONSCIOUS DURING THEM.
CAAAKE !!!
...!!

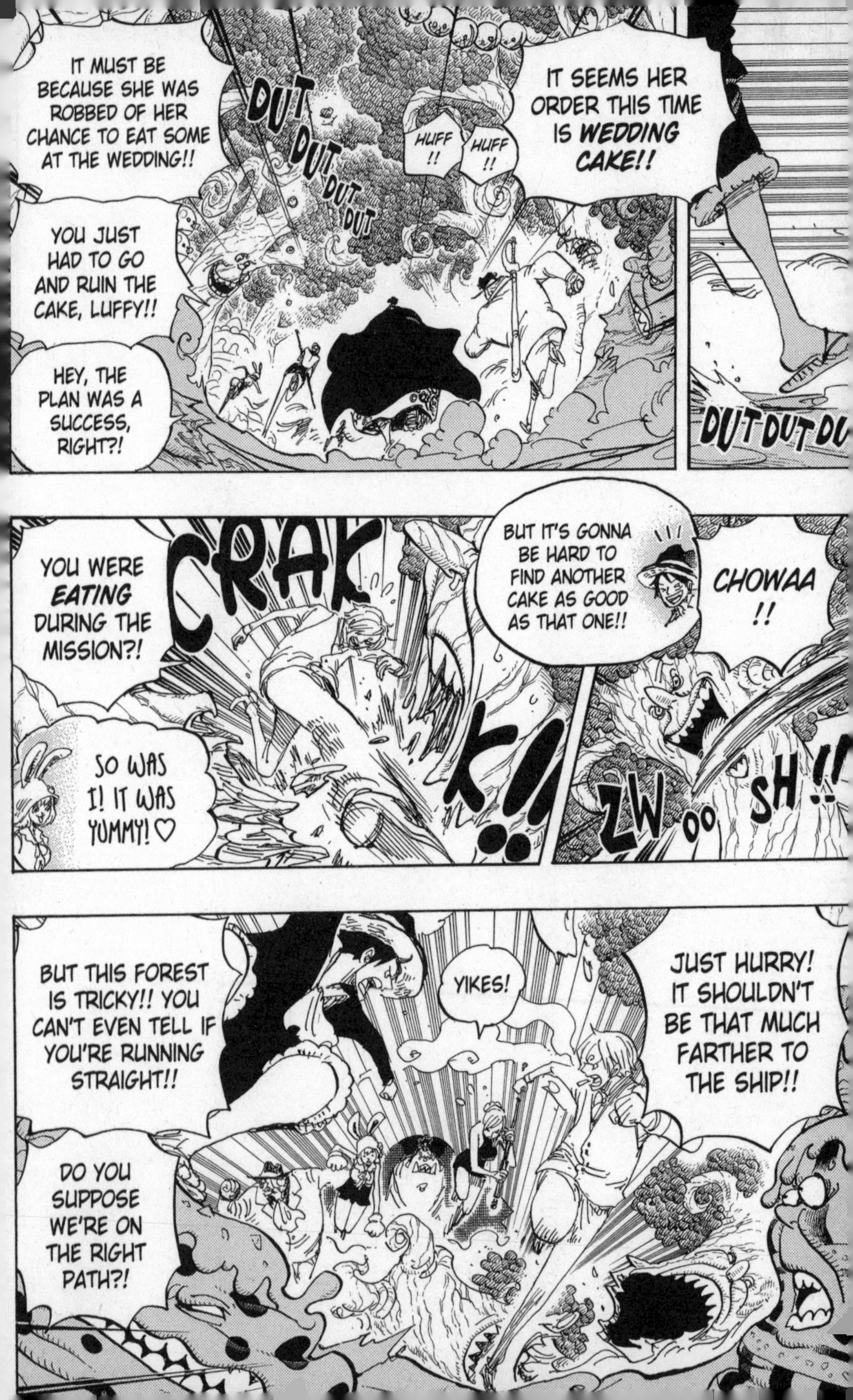
DUT DUT DU
IT SEEMS HER ORDER THIS TIME IS WEDDING CAKE!!
HUFF !!
HUFF !!
DUT DUT DUT DUT
IT MUST BE BECAUSE SHE WAS ROBBED OF HER CHANCE TO EAT SOME AT THE WEDDING!!
YOU JUST HAD TO GO AND RUIN THE CAKE, LUFFY!!
HEY, THE PLAN WAS A SUCCESS, RIGHT?!
BUT IT'S GONNA BE HARD TO FIND ANOTHER CAKE AS GOOD AS THAT ONE!!
CHOWAA !!
ZWOOSH!!
CRAK!!
YOU WERE EATING DURING THE MISSION?!
SO WAS I! IT WAS YUMMY! ♡
JUST HURRY! IT SHOULDN'T BE THAT MUCH FARTHER TO THE SHIP!!
YIKES!
BUT THIS FOREST IS TRICKY!! YOU CAN'T EVEN TELL IF YOU'RE RUNNING STRAIGHT!!
DO YOU SUPPOSE WE'RE ON THE RIGHT PATH?!

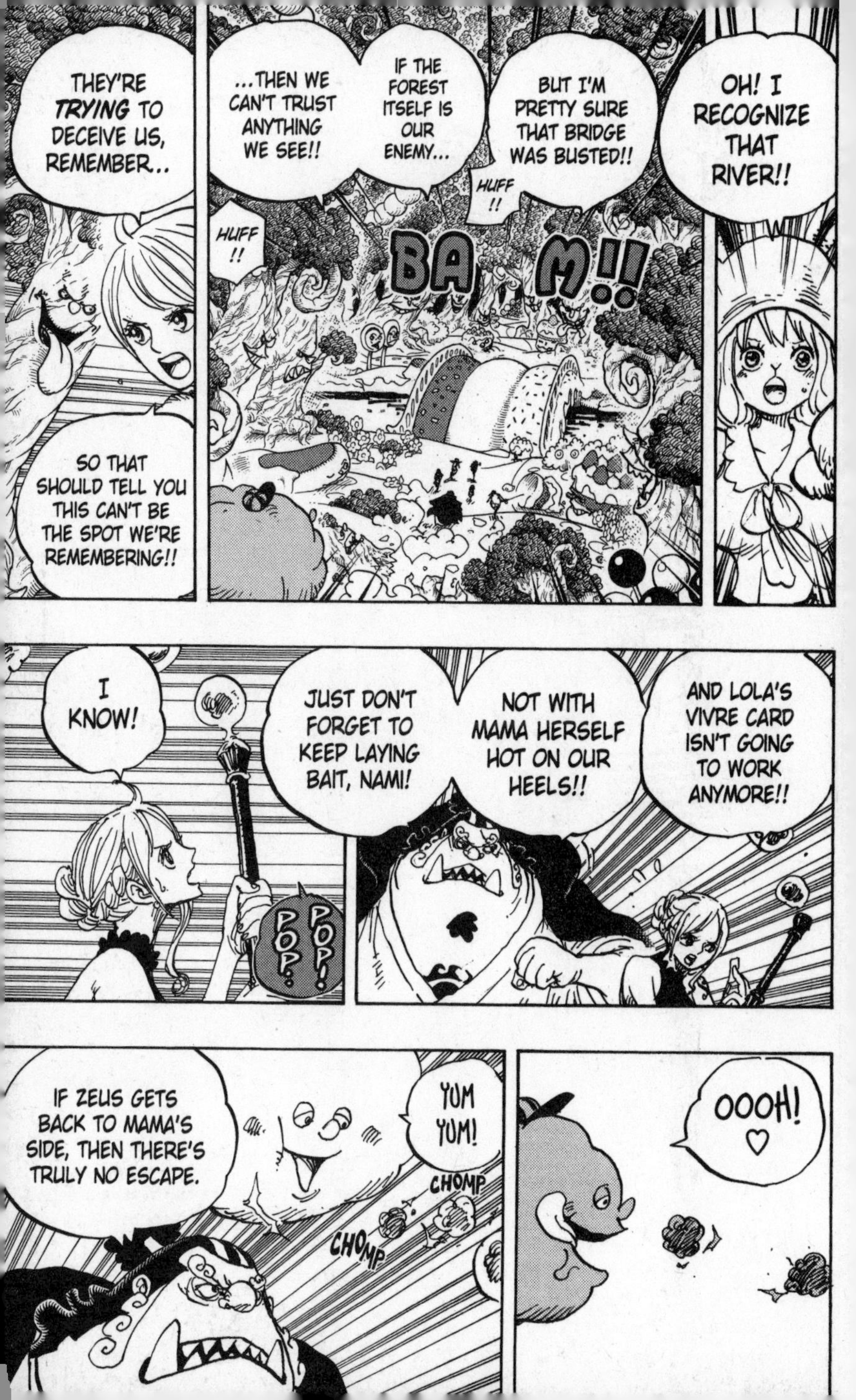
OH! I RECOGNIZE THAT RIVER!!
BUT I'M PRETTY SURE THAT BRIDGE WAS BUSTED!!
HUFF !!
IF THE FOREST ITSELF IS OUR ENEMY...
...THEN WE CAN'T TRUST ANYTHING WE SEE!!
HUFF !!
BA M!!
THEY'RE TRYING TO DECEIVE US, REMEMBER...
SO THAT SHOULD TELL YOU THIS CAN'T BE THE SPOT WE'RE REMEMBERING!!
AND LOLA'S VIVRE CARD ISN'T GOING TO WORK ANYMORE!!
NOT WITH MAMA HERSELF HOT ON OUR HEELS!!
JUST DON'T FORGET TO KEEP LAYING BAIT, NAMI!
I KNOW!
POP! POP!
OOOH! ♡
YUM YUM!
CHOMP
CHOMP
IF ZEUS GETS BACK TO MAMA'S SIDE, THEN THERE'S TRULY NO ESCAPE.

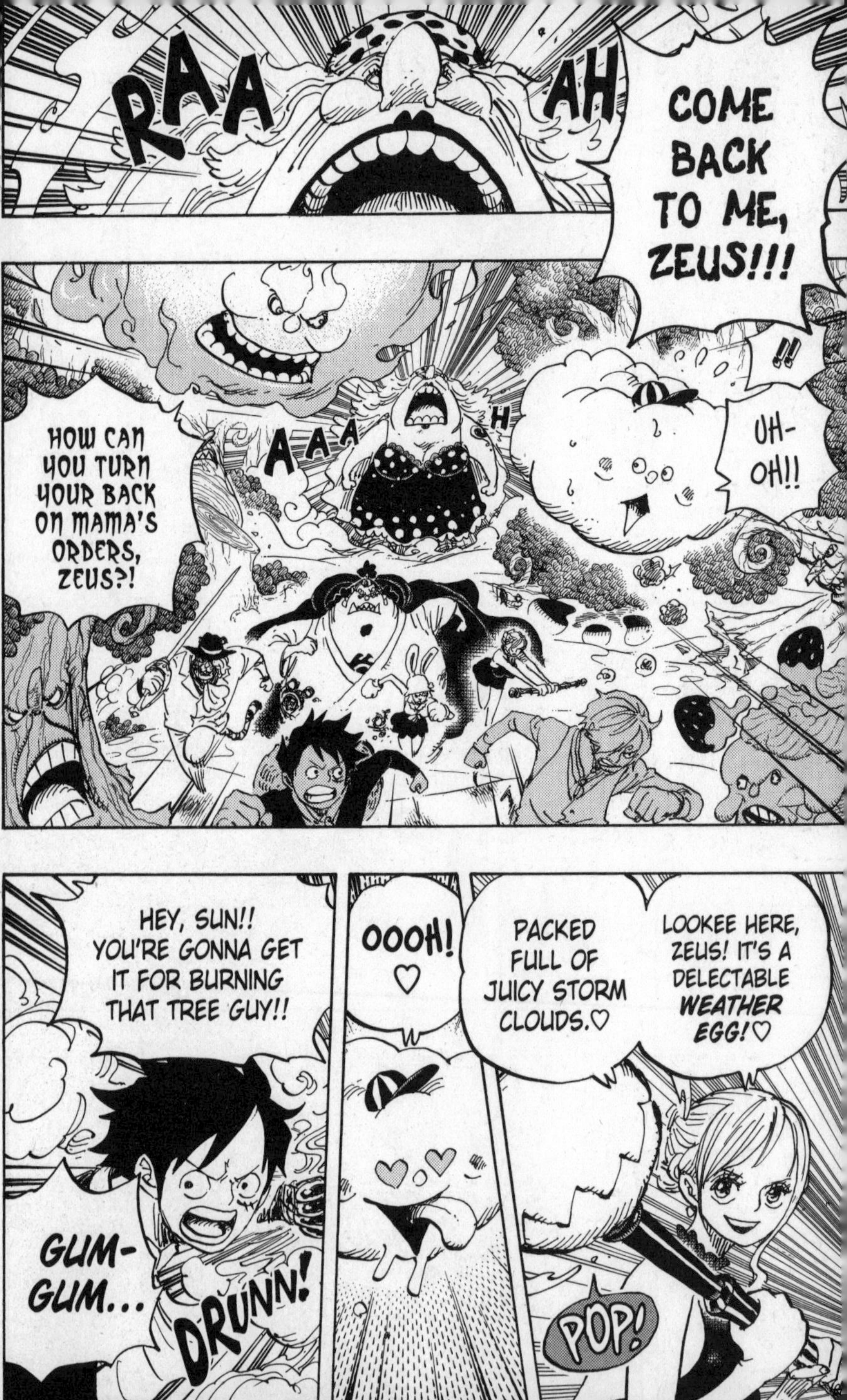
RAAAAH
COME BACK TO ME, ZEUS!!!
AAAAH
!!
UH-OH!!
HOW CAN YOU TURN YOUR BACK ON MAMA'S ORDERS, ZEUS?!
LOOKEE HERE, ZEUS! IT'S A DELECTABLE *WEATHER EGG!*♡
PACKED FULL OF JUICY STORM CLOUDS.♡
POP!
OOOH! ♡
HEY, SUN!! YOU'RE GONNA GET IT FOR BURNING THAT TREE GUY!!
GUM-GUM...
DRUNN!

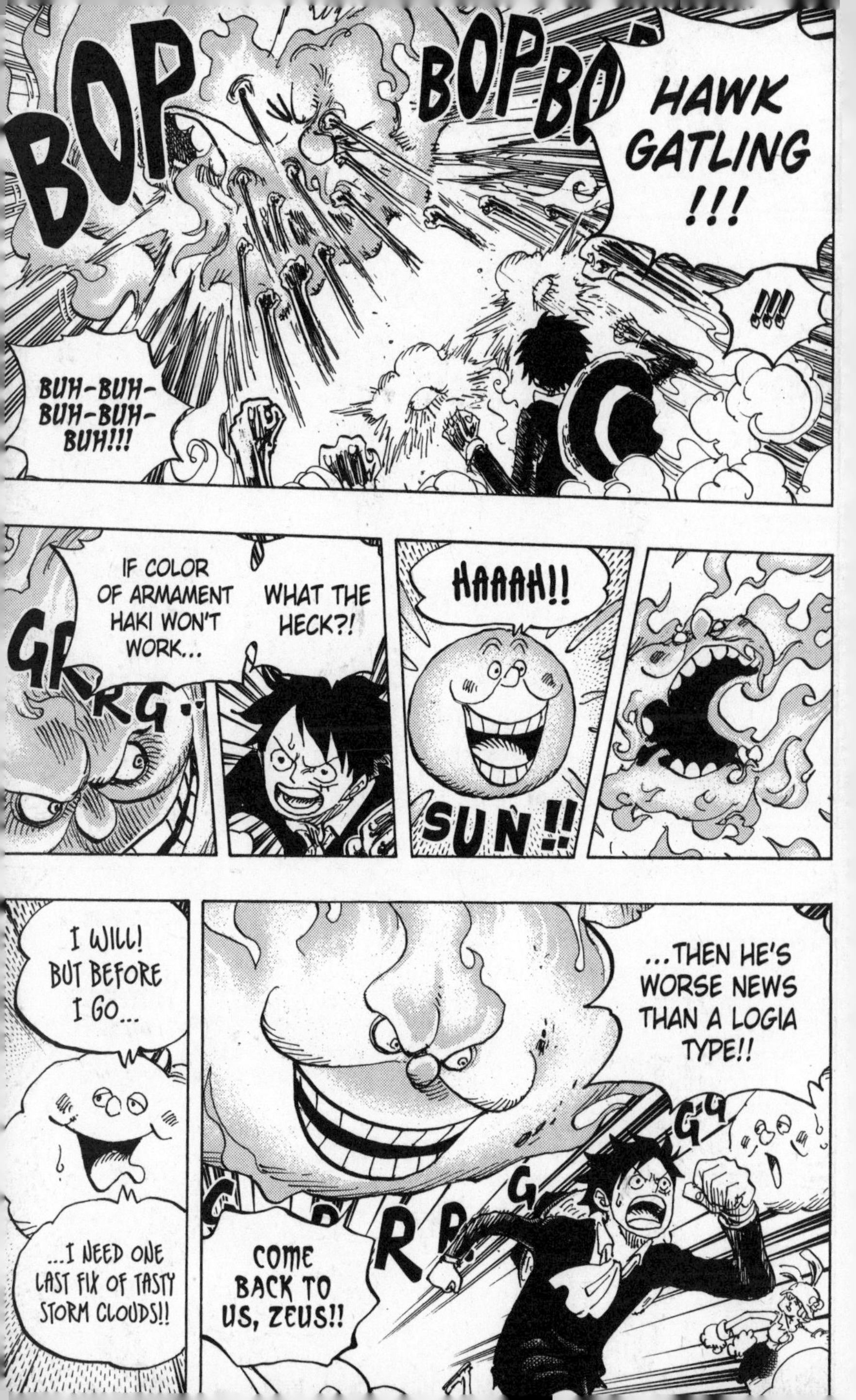
HAWK GATLING!!!
BOP BOP BO
BOP
!!!
BUH-BUH-BUH-BUH-BUH!!!
HAAAH!!
SUN!!
WHAT THE HECK?!
IF COLOR OF ARMAMENT HAKI WON'T WORK...
...THEN HE'S WORSE NEWS THAN A LOGIA TYPE!!
COME BACK TO US, ZEUS!!
I WILL! BUT BEFORE I GO...
...I NEED ONE LAST FIX OF TASTY STORM CLOUDS!!

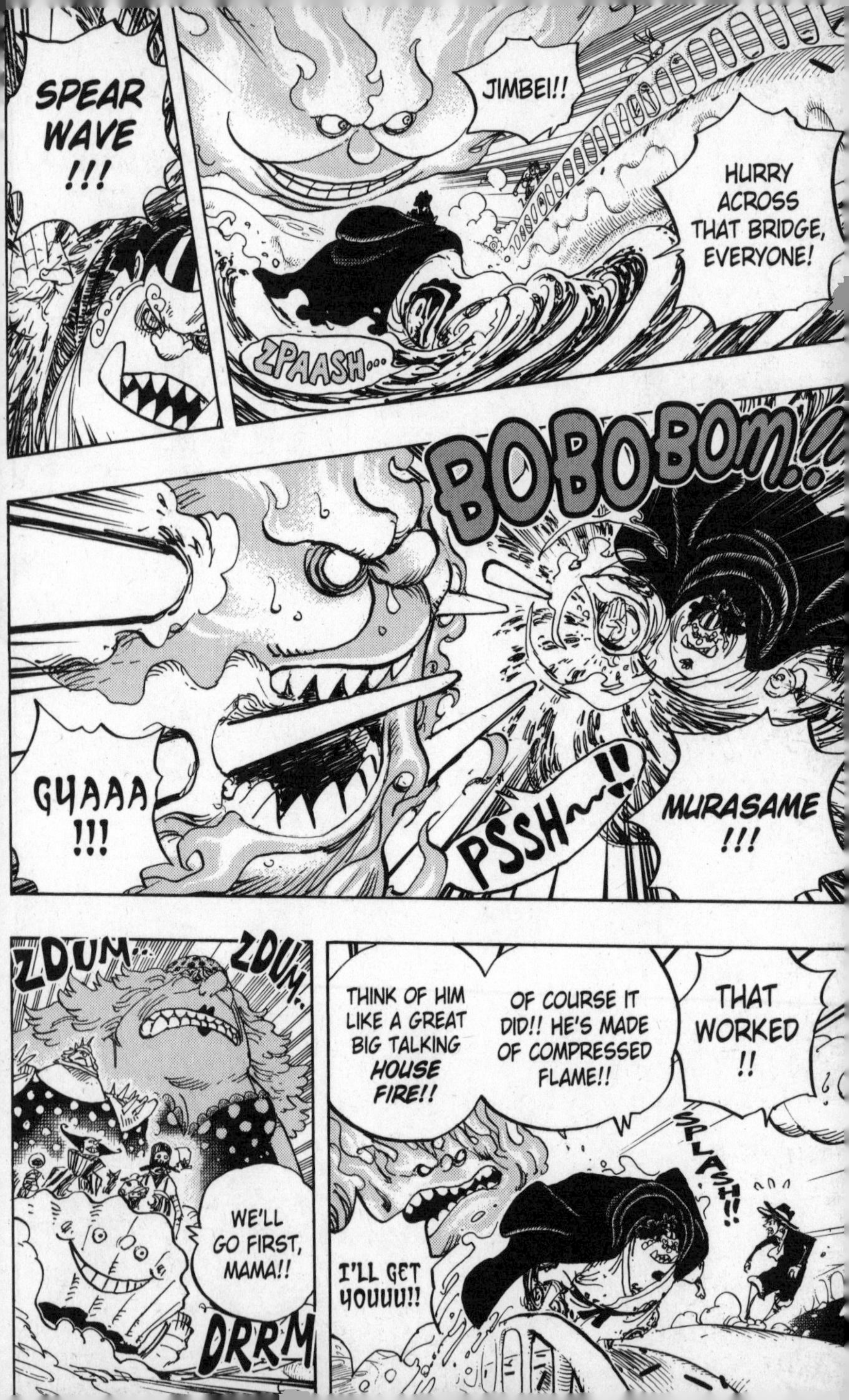
JIMBEI!!
HURRY ACROSS THAT BRIDGE, EVERYONE!
ZPAASH...
SPEAR WAVE!!!
BOBOBOM..!!
MURASAME!!!
PSSH~~!!
GUAAA!!!
THAT WORKED!!
OF COURSE IT DID!! HE'S MADE OF COMPRESSED FLAME!!
THINK OF HIM LIKE A GREAT BIG TALKING HOUSE FIRE!!
SPLASH!!
I'LL GET YOUUU!!
ZDUM..
ZDUM..
WE'LL GO FIRST, MAMA!!
DRRM

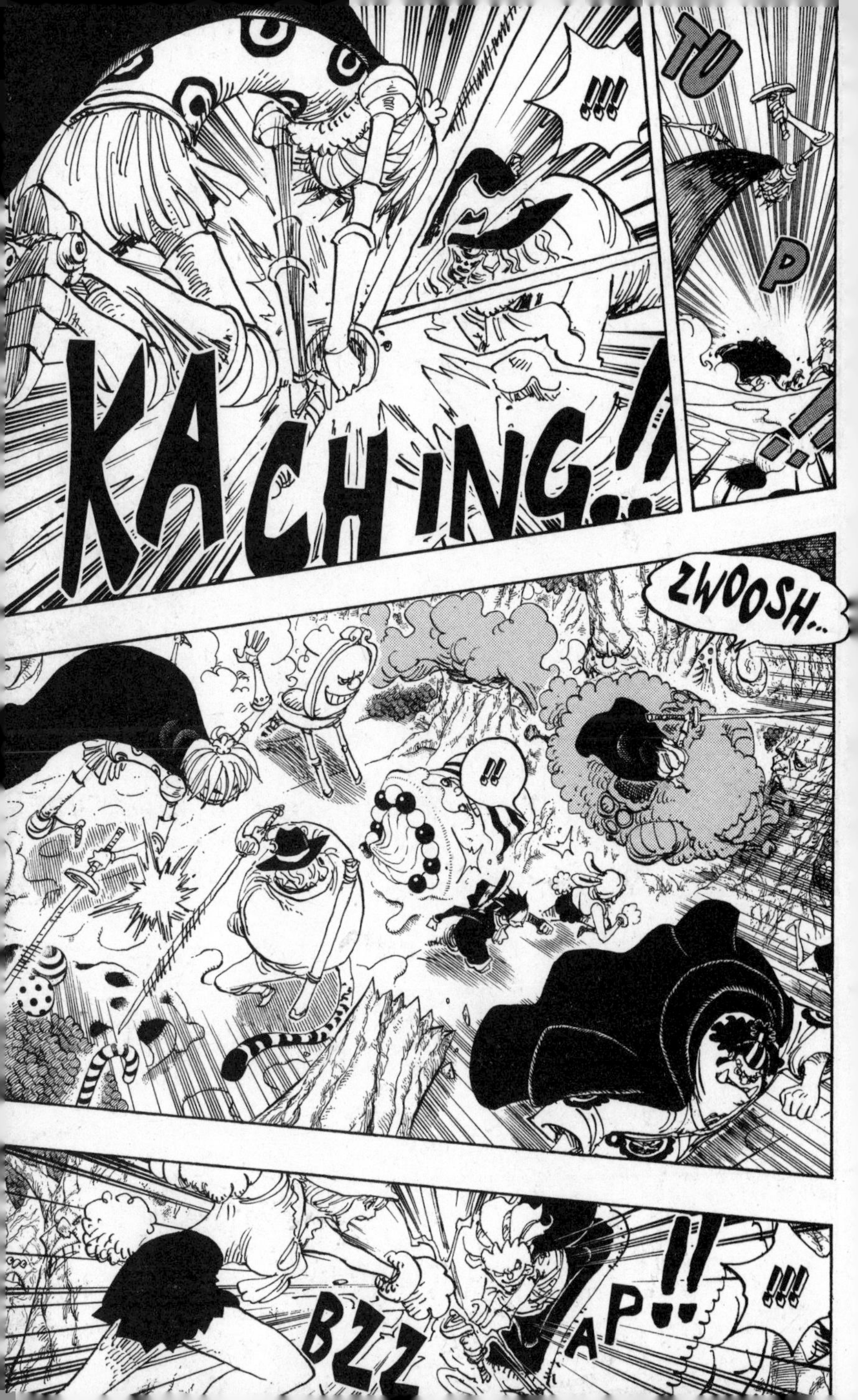

TUP
!!!
KACHING..!!
ZWOOSH...
!!
!!!
BZZAP!!

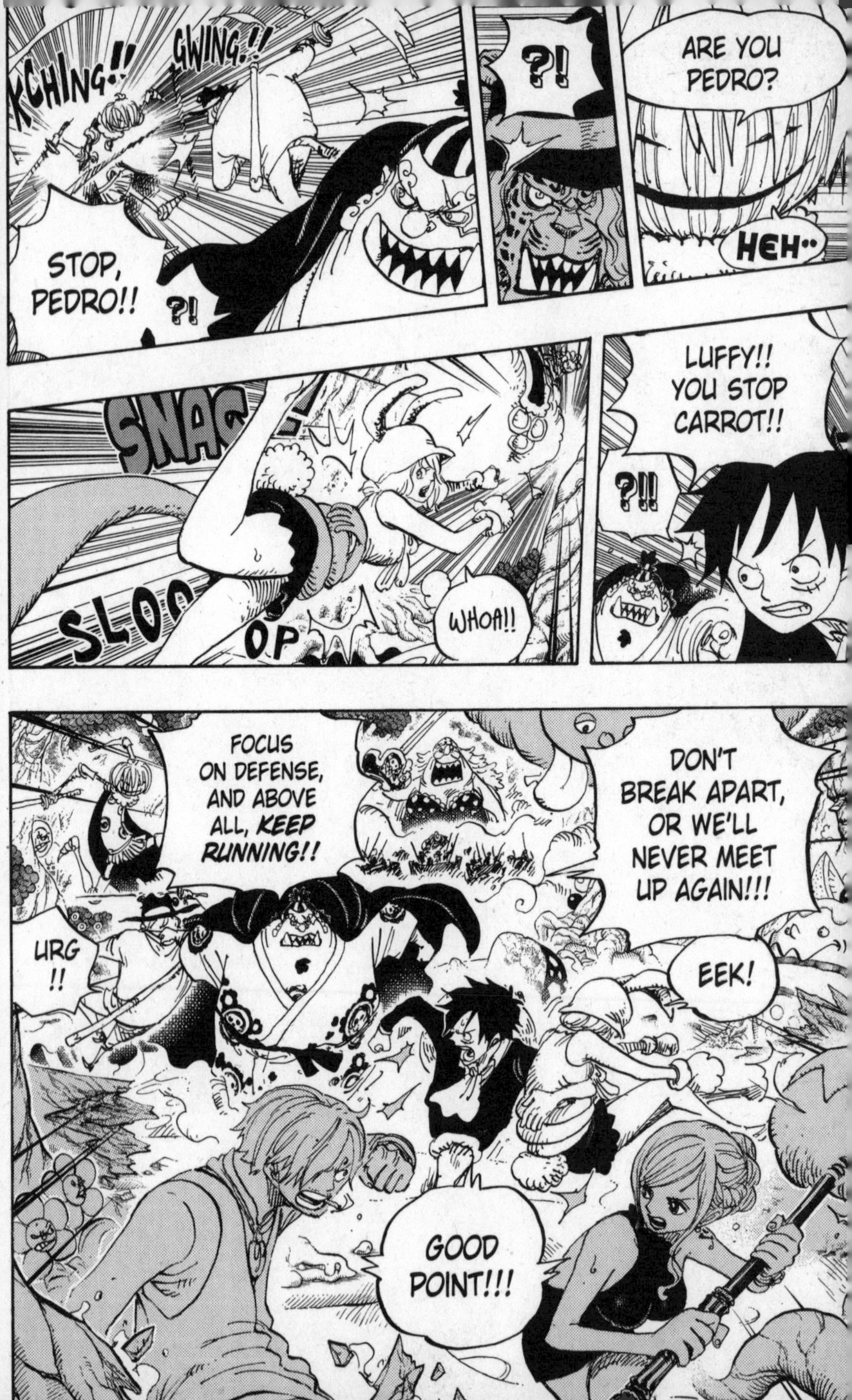
ARE YOU PEDRO?
HEH..
?!
GWING!!
KCHING!!
STOP, PEDRO!!
?!
LUFFY!! YOU STOP CARROT!!
?!!
SNAG
WHOA!!
SLOOOP
DON'T BREAK APART, OR WE'LL NEVER MEET UP AGAIN!!!
FOCUS ON DEFENSE, AND ABOVE ALL, *KEEP RUNNING!!*
EEK!
URG !!
GOOD POINT!!!

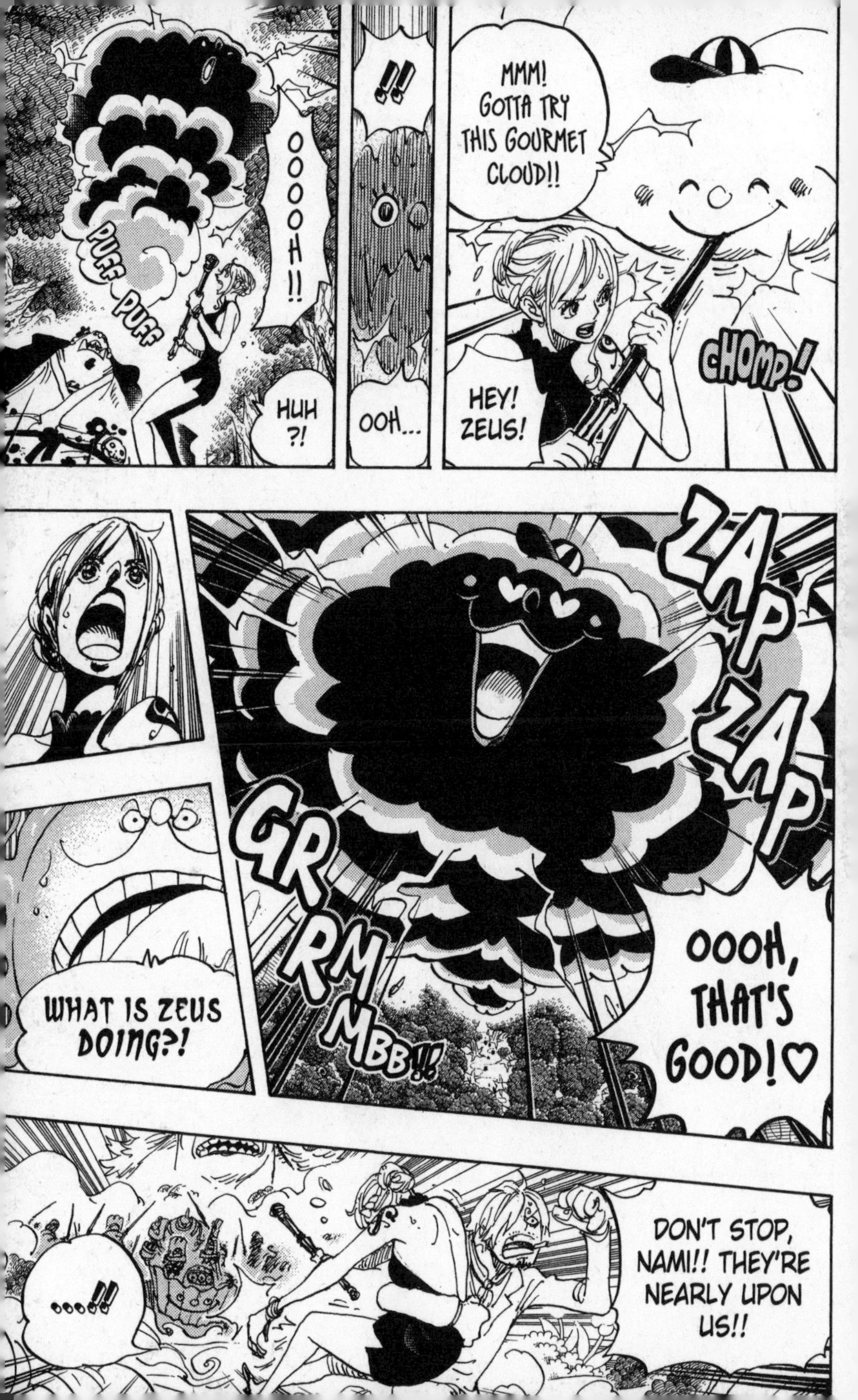
MMM! GOTTA TRY THIS GOURMET CLOUD!!
CHOMP!
HEY! ZEUS!
!!
OOH...
OOOOOH!!
PUFF PUFF
HUH ?!
ZAP ZAP ZAP
GRRMMBB!!
OOOH, THAT'S GOOD!♡
WHAT IS ZEUS DOING?!
DON'T STOP, NAMI!! THEY'RE NEARLY UPON US!!
....!!

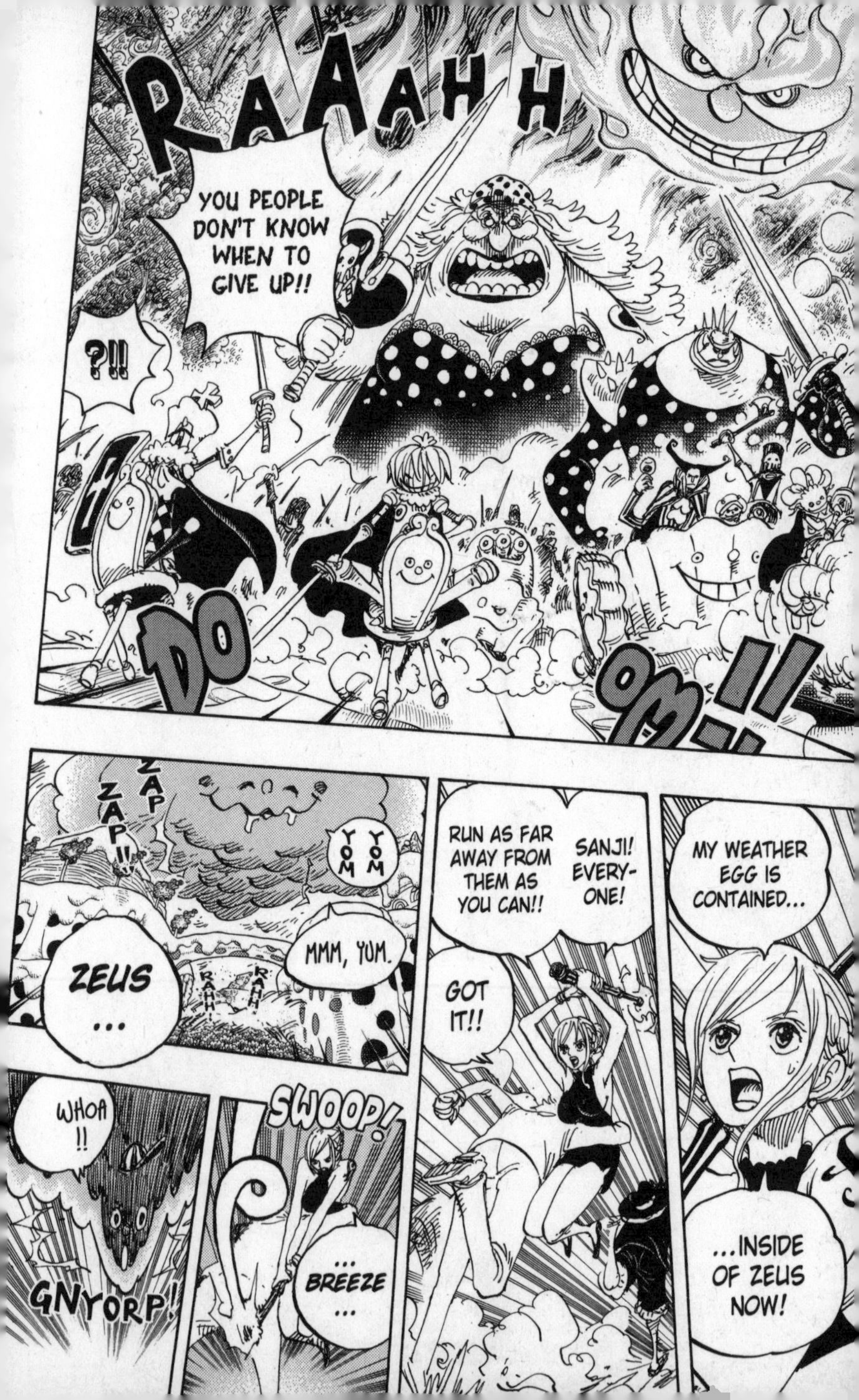
RAAAHH
YOU PEOPLE DON'T KNOW WHEN TO GIVE UP!!
?!!
DOOM!!
MY WEATHER EGG IS CONTAINED...
...INSIDE OF ZEUS NOW!
SANJI! EVERYONE!
RUN AS FAR AWAY FROM THEM AS YOU CAN!!
GOT IT!!
ZAP ZAP ZAP!!
YOM YOM
MMM, YUM.
RAHH RAHH
ZEUS ...
SWOOP!
... BREEZE ...
WHOA !!
GNYORP!

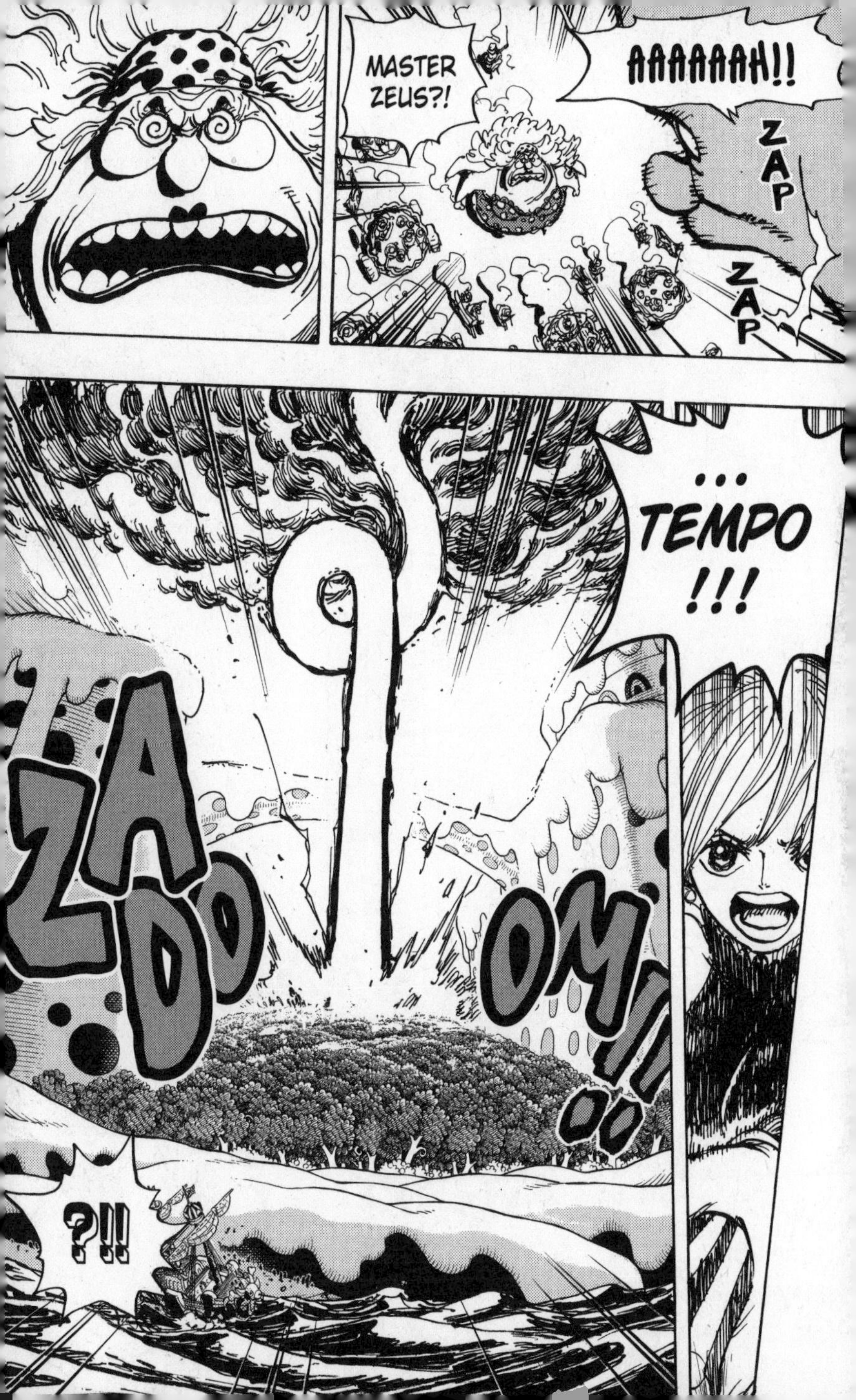
AAAAAAH!!
ZAP
ZAP
MASTER ZEUS?!
... TEMPO !!!
ZADOOM!!
?!!

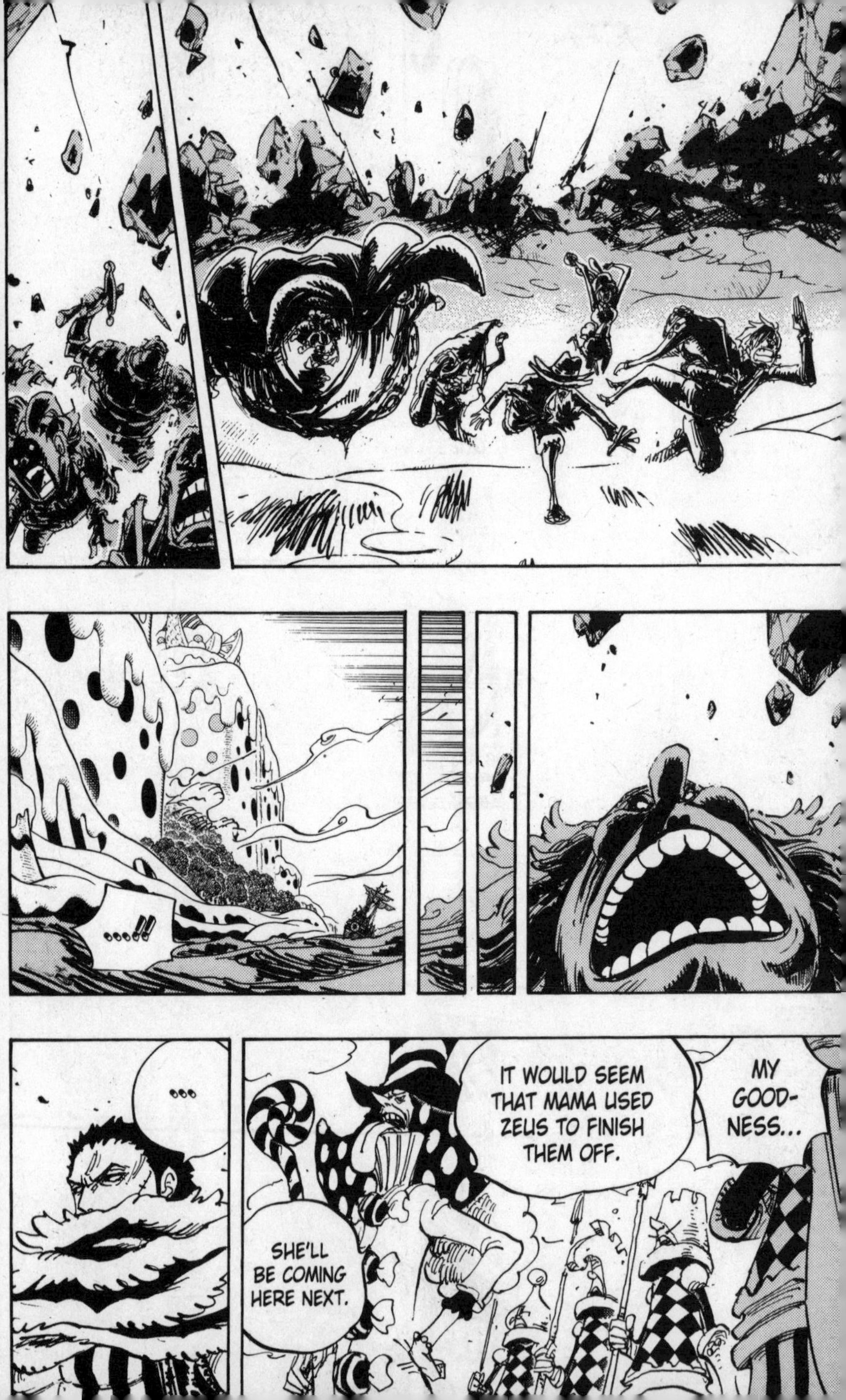
....!!
MY GOOD-NESS...
IT WOULD SEEM THAT MAMA USED ZEUS TO FINISH THEM OFF.
SHE'LL BE COMING HERE NEXT.
...

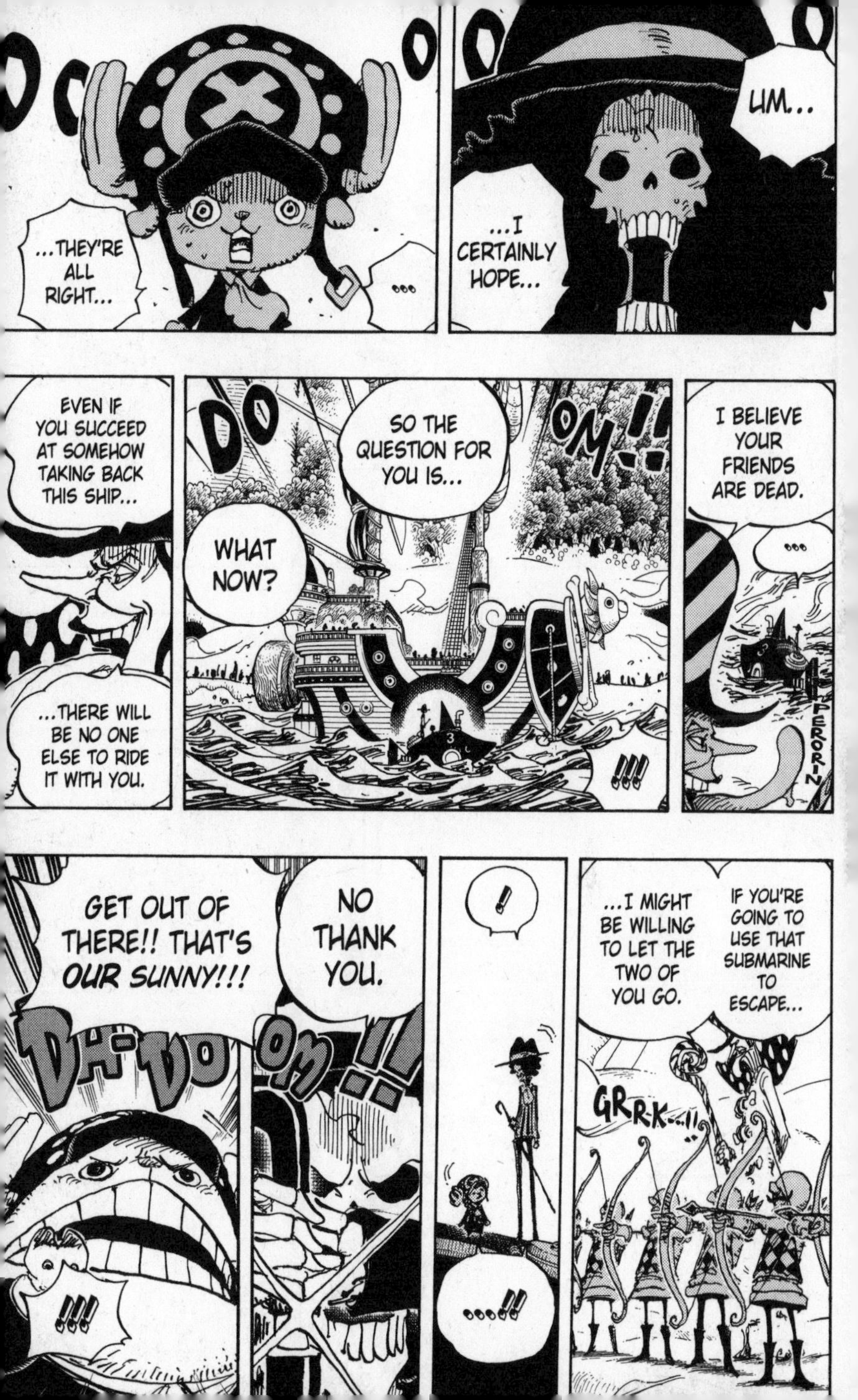
UM...
...I CERTAINLY HOPE...
...
...THEY'RE ALL RIGHT...
I BELIEVE YOUR FRIENDS ARE DEAD.
...
PERORIN
SO THE QUESTION FOR YOU IS...
WHAT NOW?
DO OM!!
!!!
EVEN IF YOU SUCCEED AT SOMEHOW TAKING BACK THIS SHIP...
...THERE WILL BE NO ONE ELSE TO RIDE IT WITH YOU.
IF YOU'RE GOING TO USE THAT SUBMARINE TO ESCAPE...
...I MIGHT BE WILLING TO LET THE TWO OF YOU GO.
GRR-K...!!
!
...!!
NO THANK YOU.
GET OUT OF THERE!! THAT'S OUR SUNNY!!!
DH-DOOM!!
!!!

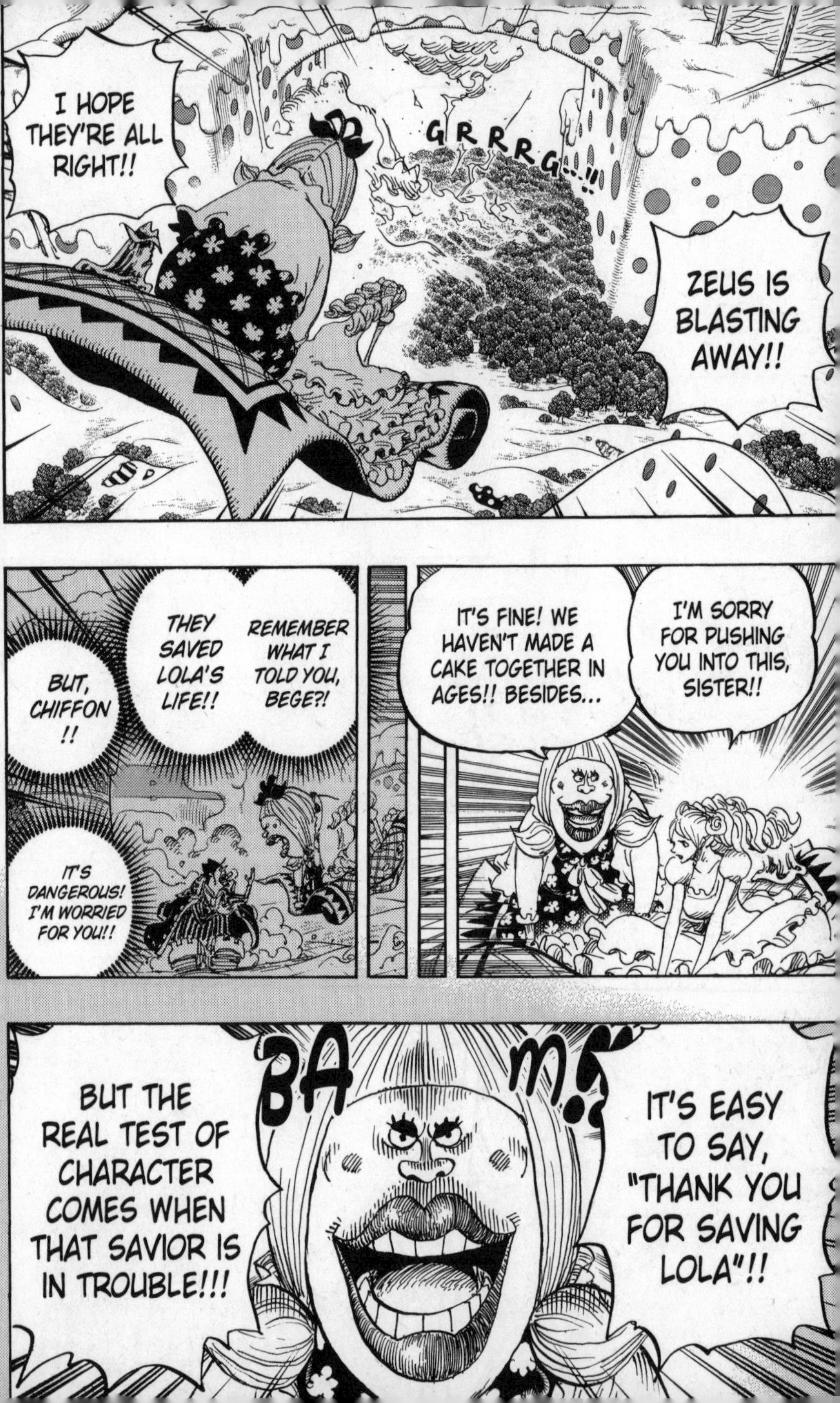
GRRRRG...!!
ZEUS IS BLASTING AWAY!!
I HOPE THEY'RE ALL RIGHT!!
I'M SORRY FOR PUSHING YOU INTO THIS, SISTER!!
IT'S FINE! WE HAVEN'T MADE A CAKE TOGETHER IN AGES!! BESIDES...
REMEMBER WHAT I TOLD YOU, BEGE?!
THEY SAVED LOLA'S LIFE!!
BUT, CHIFFON!!
IT'S DANGEROUS! I'M WORRIED FOR YOU!!
IT'S EASY TO SAY, "THANK YOU FOR SAVING LOLA"!!
BAM!!
BUT THE REAL TEST OF CHARACTER COMES WHEN THAT SAVIOR IS IN TROUBLE!!!

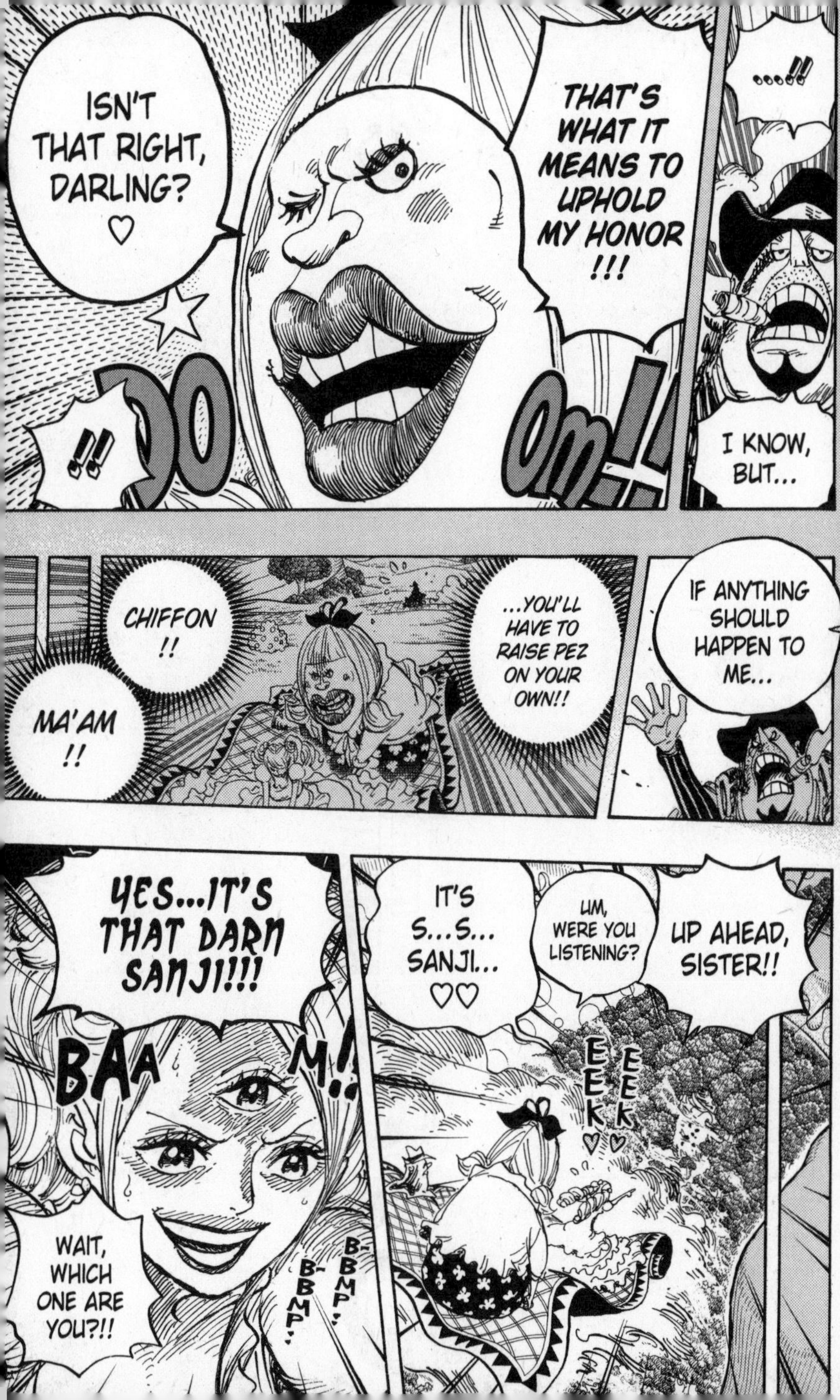

...!!
I KNOW, BUT...
THAT'S WHAT IT MEANS TO UPHOLD MY HONOR!!!
ISN'T THAT RIGHT, DARLING? ♡
!!
DOOM!!
IF ANYTHING SHOULD HAPPEN TO ME...
...YOU'LL HAVE TO RAISE PEZ ON YOUR OWN!!
CHIFFON!!
MA'AM!!
UP AHEAD, SISTER!!
UM, WERE YOU LISTENING?
IT'S S...S... SANJI... ♡♡
EEK ♡
EEK ♡
B-BBMP
B-BBMP
YES...IT'S THAT DARN SANJI!!!
BAAM!!
WAIT, WHICH ONE ARE YOU?!!

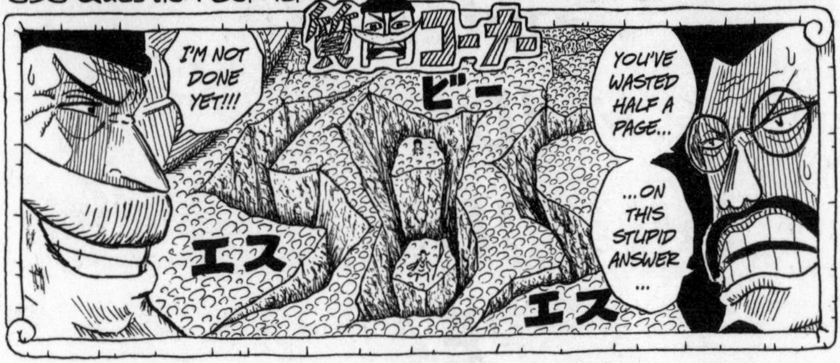
YOU'VE WASTED HALF A PAGE...
...ON THIS STUPID ANSWER ...
I'M NOT DONE YET!!!
ビー
エス
エス

(Igarashi, Oita)

Q: Odacchi!! Hey!! So, I've got a request for you. Swap the genders of Kizaru, Fujitora, Akainu and Aokiji!! Can you do that for me?

--Ouchan

A: Sure. Regret your foolishness!!

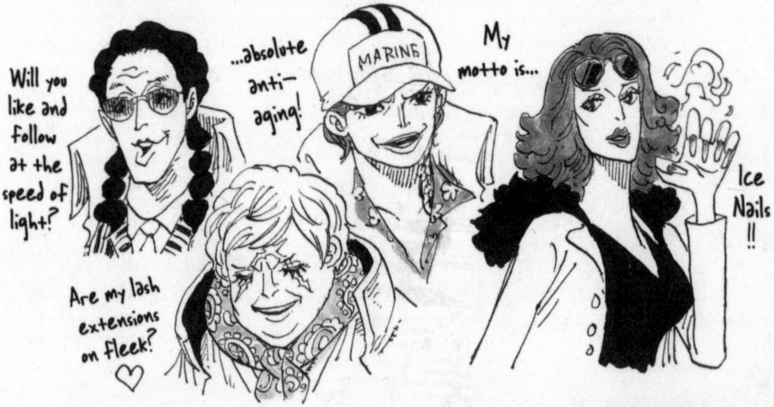
Ice Nails !!
My motto is...
...absolute anti-aging!
MARINE
Will you like and follow at the speed of light?
Are my lash extensions on fleek? ♡

Q: Hello, Mr. Oda! On the cover illustration of Chapter 874, Ace and Sabo look angry. What happened between them? I noticed that Shanks is laughing…

--Chisaki Sakuragi

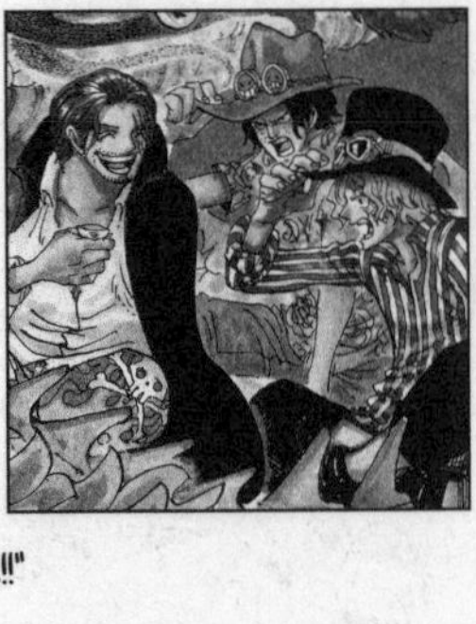

A: Let's listen in for a bit, then.
Ace: "Hey, Mr. Red-Hair! Allow me to apologize for my little brother and thank you for everything you've done for him!!"
Sabo: "My name is Sabo. A pleasure. I'm also Luffy's brother! I must insist on showing my appreciation. Thank you so much. I hope we can count on your continued generosity..."
Shanks: "Ha ha ha! Knock it off, you guys! I get it, I get it. Come here and share a drink with me!!"

A: From what I recall, Ace got a few lessons on good manners from Makino ages ago, so that he could thank Shanks properly when the time came.

Chapter 876: PUDDING COINCIDENTALLY APPEARS!!

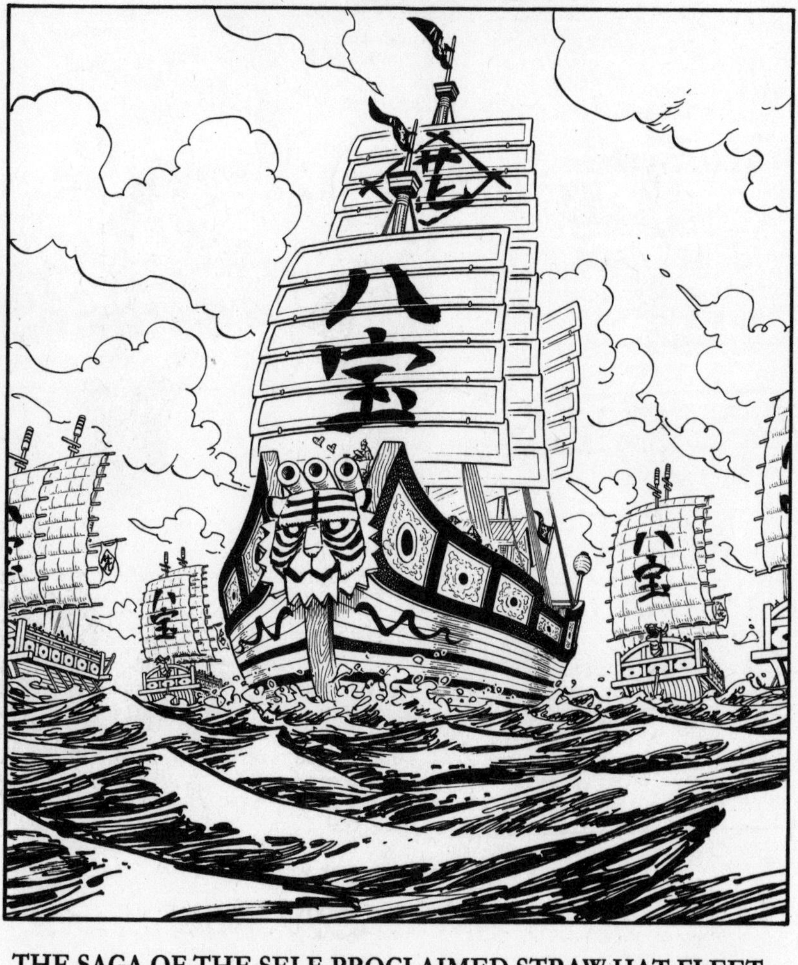

THE SAGA OF THE SELF-PROCLAIMED STRAW HAT FLEET, VOL. 11, SAI: "DON SAI OF THE HAPPOSUI ARMY RETURNS"

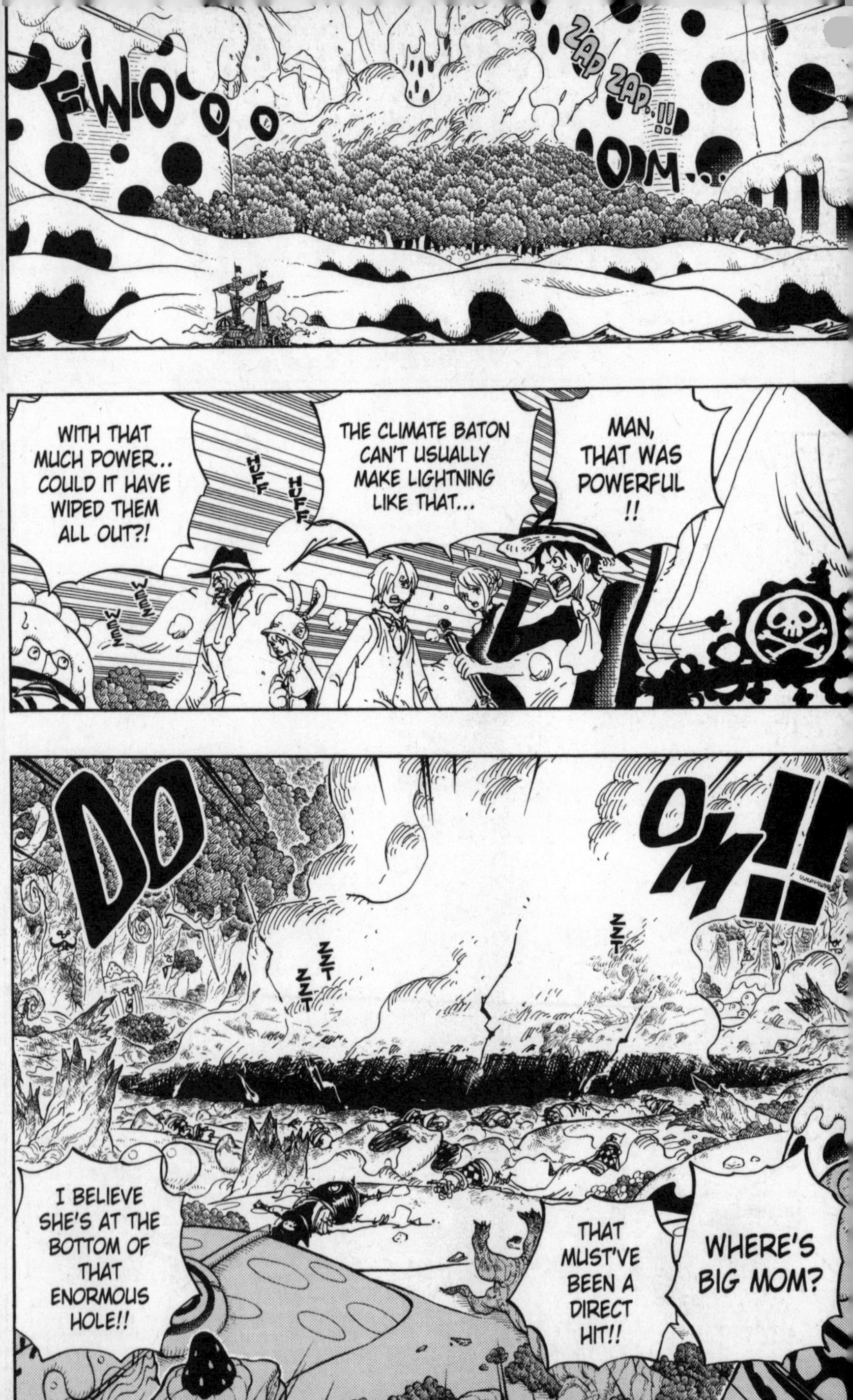
ZAP ZAP..!!
FWOOOOO
OOM..
MAN, THAT WAS POWERFUL!!
THE CLIMATE BATON CAN'T USUALLY MAKE LIGHTNING LIKE THAT...
HUFF HUFF
WEEN WEEN
WITH THAT MUCH POWER... COULD IT HAVE WIPED THEM ALL OUT?!
DO
OM!!
ZZT
ZZT
ZZT
WHERE'S BIG MOM?
THAT MUST'VE BEEN A DIRECT HIT!!
I BELIEVE SHE'S AT THE BOTTOM OF THAT ENORMOUS HOLE!!

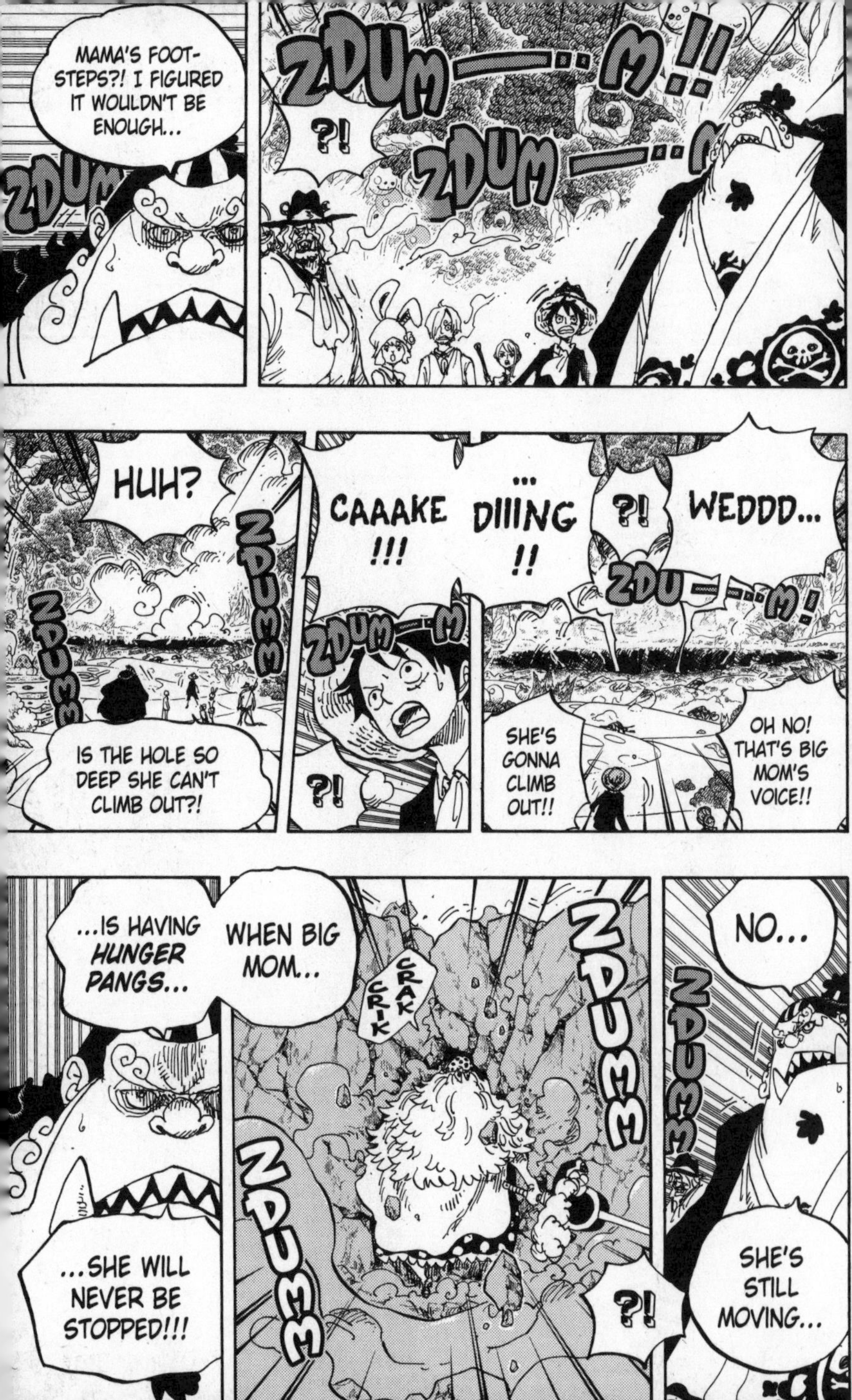
ZDUM—..M!!
?!
ZDUM—..M
MAMA'S FOOT-STEPS?! I FIGURED IT WOULDN'T BE ENOUGH...
ZDUM
WEDDD...
?!
ZDU—..M!
OH NO! THAT'S BIG MOM'S VOICE!!
SHE'S GONNA CLIMB OUT!!
... DIIING !!
CAAAKE !!!
ZDUM—M
?!
HUH?
ZDUMM
ZDUMM
IS THE HOLE SO DEEP SHE CAN'T CLIMB OUT?!
NO...
ZDUMM
SHE'S STILL MOVING...
ZDUMM
CRAK CRAK
CRIK
ZDUMM
?!
WHEN BIG MOM...
...IS HAVING HUNGER PANGS...
...SHE WILL NEVER BE STOPPED!!!

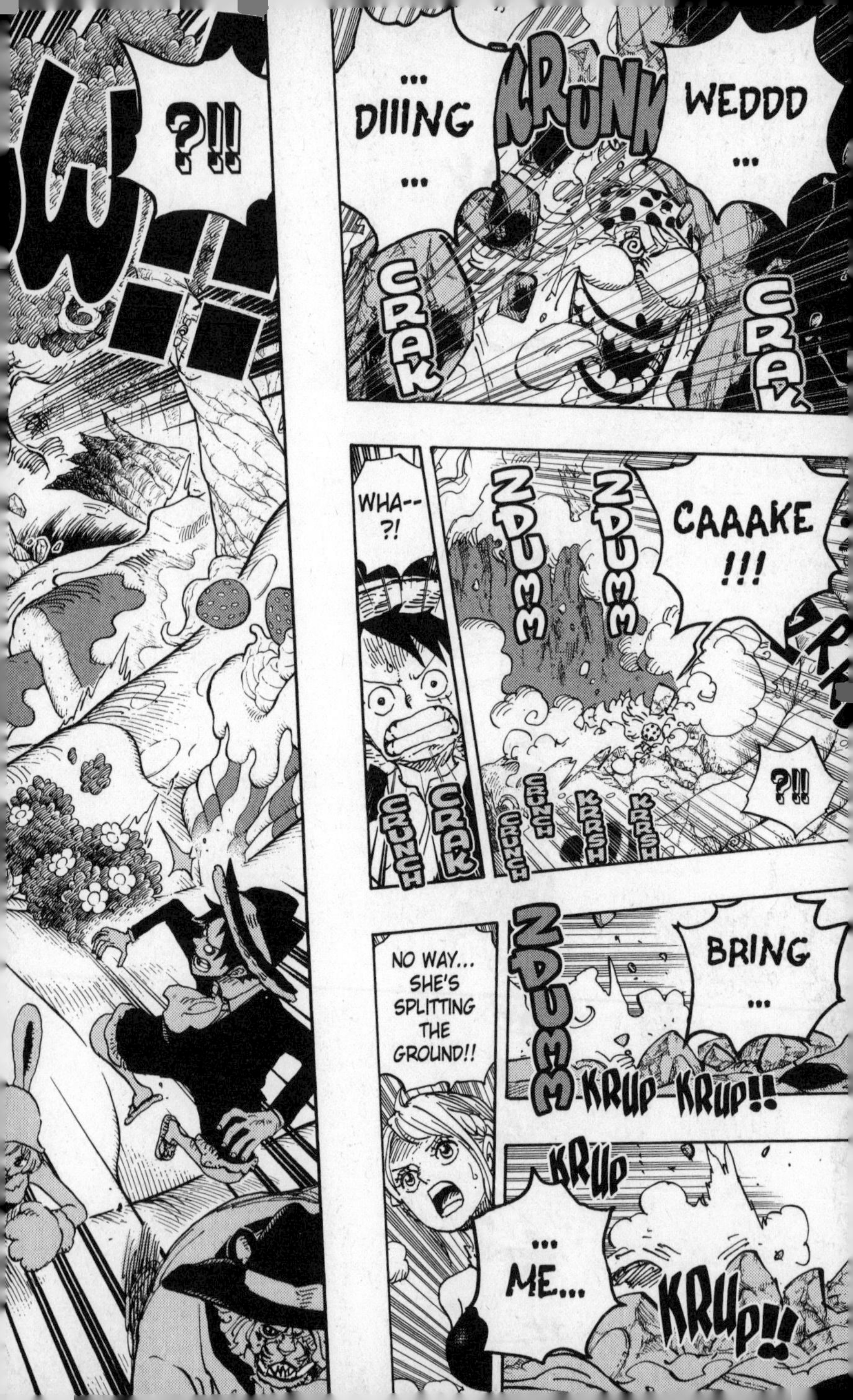
WEDDD ...
KRUNK
... DIIING ...
CRAK
CRAK
CAAAKE !!!
?!!
ZDUMM
ZDUMM
KRRSH
KRRSH
CRUNCH
CRUNCH
WHA-- ?!
CRAK
CRUNCH
BRING ...
ZDUMM
KRUP KRUP!!
NO WAY... SHE'S SPLITTING THE GROUND!!
KRUP
... ME...
KRUP!!
?!!

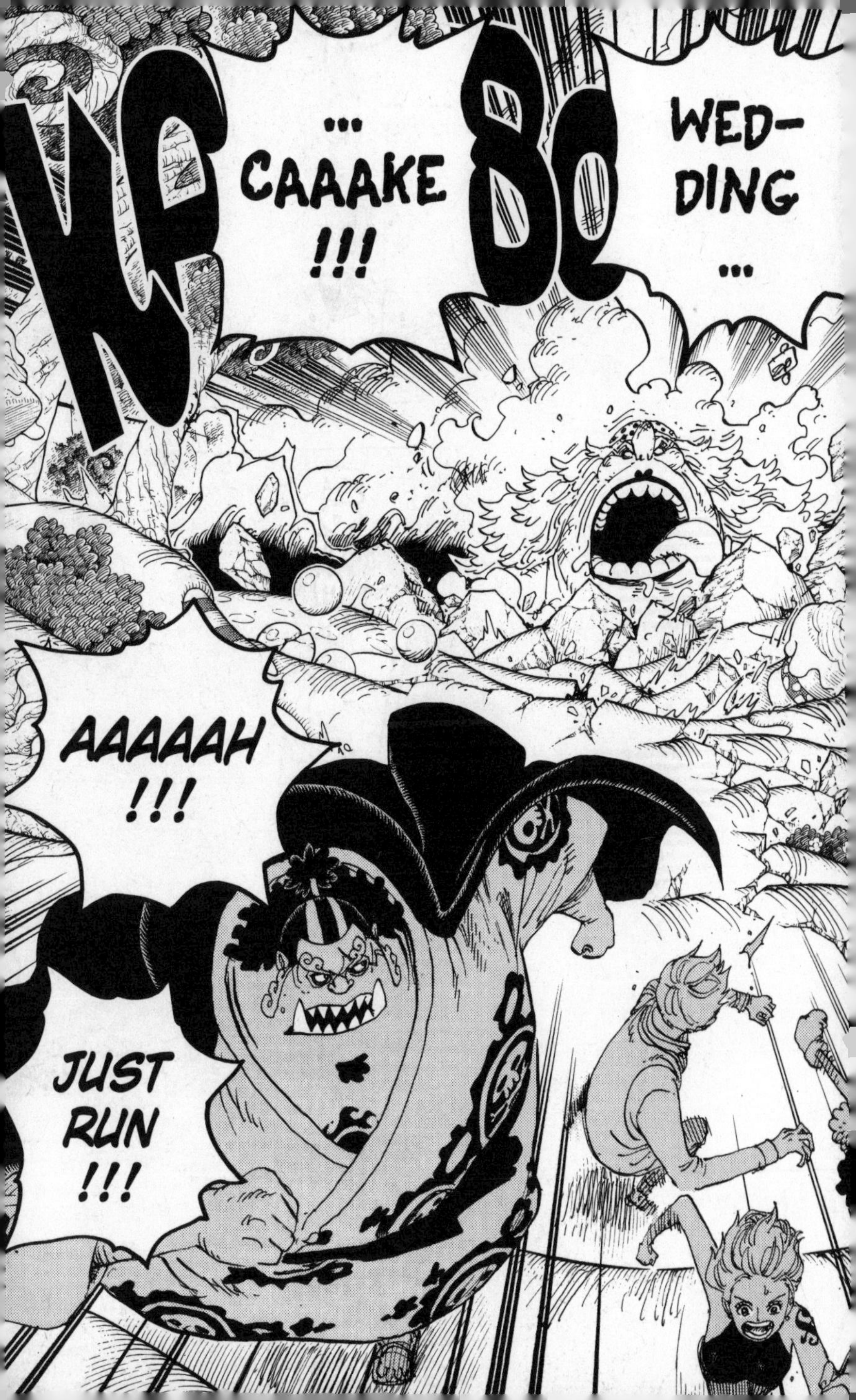
WED-DING ...
KA BO
... CAAAKE !!!
AAAAAH !!!
JUST RUN !!!

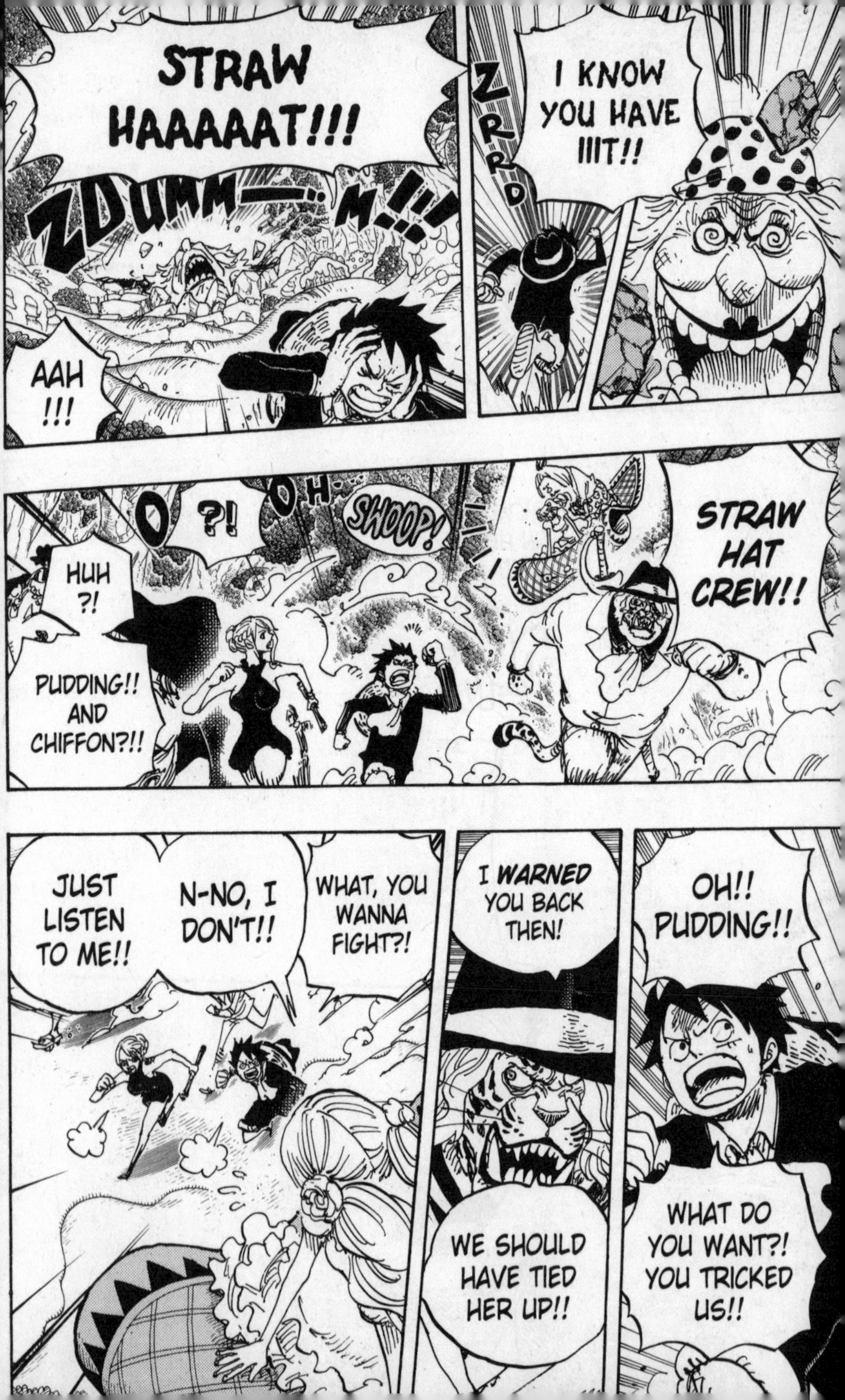

I KNOW YOU HAVE IIIT!!
ZRRRD
STRAW HAAAAAT!!!
ZDUMM—M!!!
AAH !!!
STRAW HAT CREW!!
SHOOP!
OH...
O ?!
HUH ?!
PUDDING!! AND CHIFFON?!!
OH!! PUDDING!!
WHAT DO YOU WANT?! YOU TRICKED US!!
I WARNED YOU BACK THEN!
WE SHOULD HAVE TIED HER UP!!
WHAT, YOU WANNA FIGHT?!
N-NO, I DON'T!!
JUST LISTEN TO ME!!

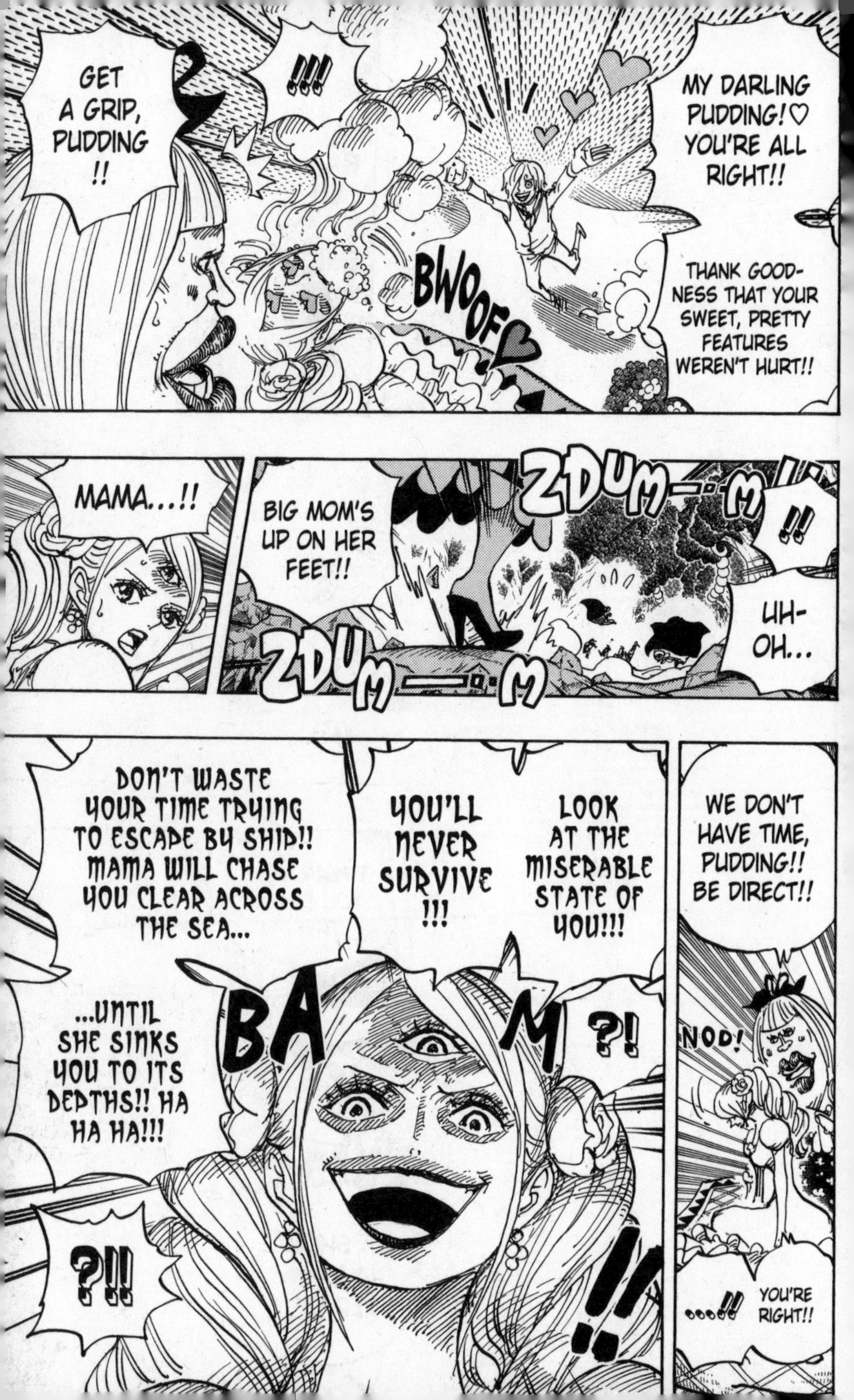
MY DARLING PUDDING!♡ YOU'RE ALL RIGHT!!
THANK GOODNESS THAT YOUR SWEET, PRETTY FEATURES WEREN'T HURT!!
!!!
BWOOF♡
GET A GRIP, PUDDING!!
ZDUM—M
!!
UH-OH...
BIG MOM'S UP ON HER FEET!!
ZDUM—M
MAMA...!!
WE DON'T HAVE TIME, PUDDING!! BE DIRECT!!
NOD!
...!!
YOU'RE RIGHT!!
LOOK AT THE MISERABLE STATE OF YOU!!!
YOU'LL NEVER SURVIVE!!!
DON'T WASTE YOUR TIME TRYING TO ESCAPE BY SHIP!! MAMA WILL CHASE YOU CLEAR ACROSS THE SEA...
BAM
?!
...UNTIL SHE SINKS YOU TO ITS DEPTHS!! HA HA HA!!!
?!!
!!

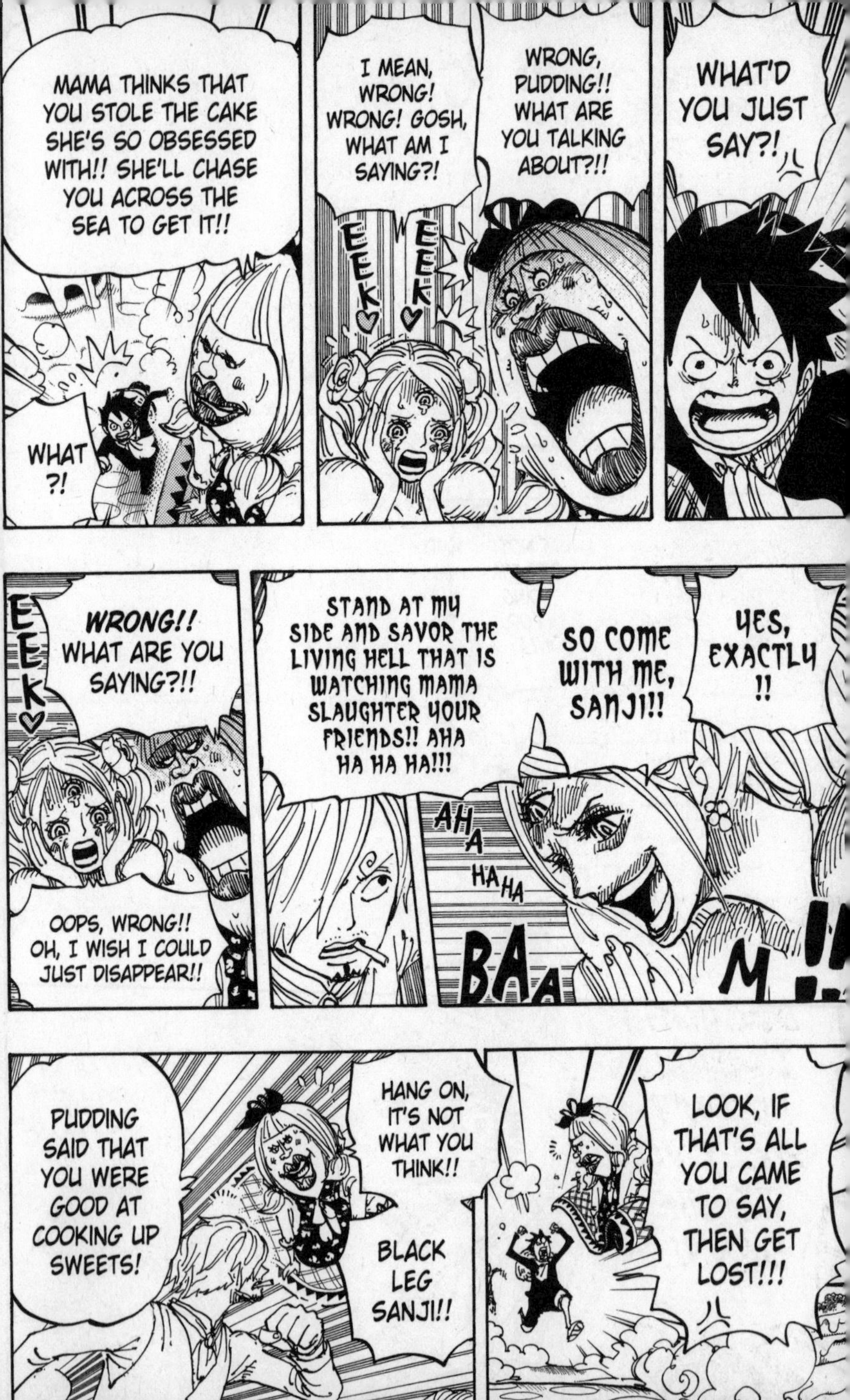
WHAT'D YOU JUST SAY?!
WRONG, PUDDING!! WHAT ARE YOU TALKING ABOUT?!!
I MEAN, WRONG! WRONG! GOSH, WHAT AM I SAYING?!
EEK
EEK
MAMA THINKS THAT YOU STOLE THE CAKE SHE'S SO OBSESSED WITH!! SHE'LL CHASE YOU ACROSS THE SEA TO GET IT!!
WHAT ?!
YES, EXACTLY !!
SO COME WITH ME, SANJI!!
STAND AT MY SIDE AND SAVOR THE LIVING HELL THAT IS WATCHING MAMA SLAUGHTER YOUR FRIENDS!! AHA HA HA HA!!!
AHA HA HA BAA
M!!
EEK
WRONG!! WHAT ARE YOU SAYING?!!
OOPS, WRONG!! OH, I WISH I COULD JUST DISAPPEAR!!
LOOK, IF THAT'S ALL YOU CAME TO SAY, THEN GET LOST!!!
HANG ON, IT'S NOT WHAT YOU THINK!!
PUDDING SAID THAT YOU WERE GOOD AT COOKING UP SWEETS!
BLACK LEG SANJI!!

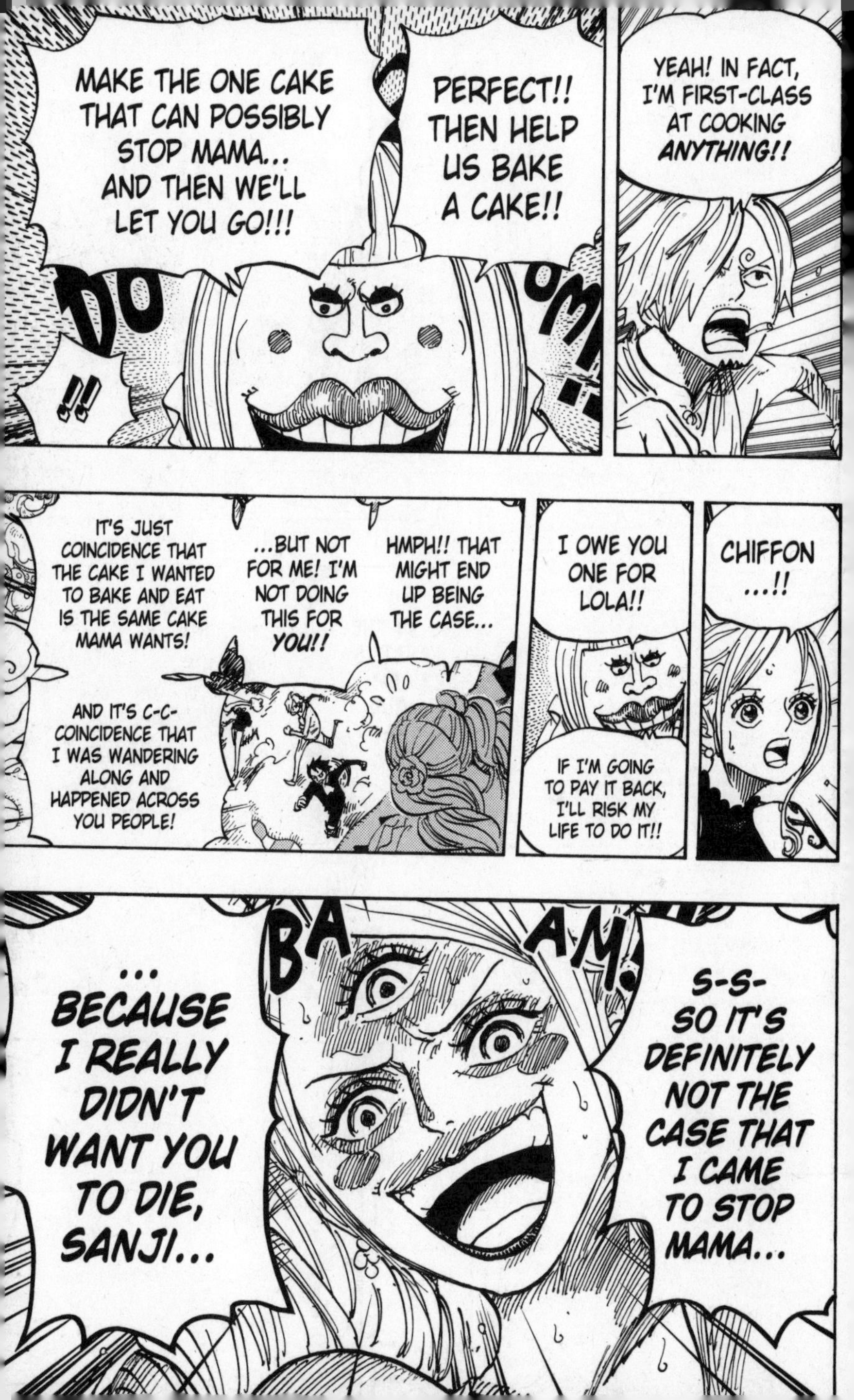

YEAH! IN FACT, I'M FIRST-CLASS AT COOKING ANYTHING!!
PERFECT!! THEN HELP US BAKE A CAKE!!
MAKE THE ONE CAKE THAT CAN POSSIBLY STOP MAMA... AND THEN WE'LL LET YOU GO!!!
DOOM!!
CHIFFON ...!!
I OWE YOU ONE FOR LOLA!!
IF I'M GOING TO PAY IT BACK, I'LL RISK MY LIFE TO DO IT!!
HMPH!! THAT MIGHT END UP BEING THE CASE...
...BUT NOT FOR ME! I'M NOT DOING THIS FOR YOU!!
IT'S JUST COINCIDENCE THAT THE CAKE I WANTED TO BAKE AND EAT IS THE SAME CAKE MAMA WANTS!
AND IT'S C-C-COINCIDENCE THAT I WAS WANDERING ALONG AND HAPPENED ACROSS YOU PEOPLE!
S-S-SO IT'S DEFINITELY NOT THE CASE THAT I CAME TO STOP MAMA...
BAAM
... BECAUSE I REALLY DIDN'T WANT YOU TO DIE, SANJI...

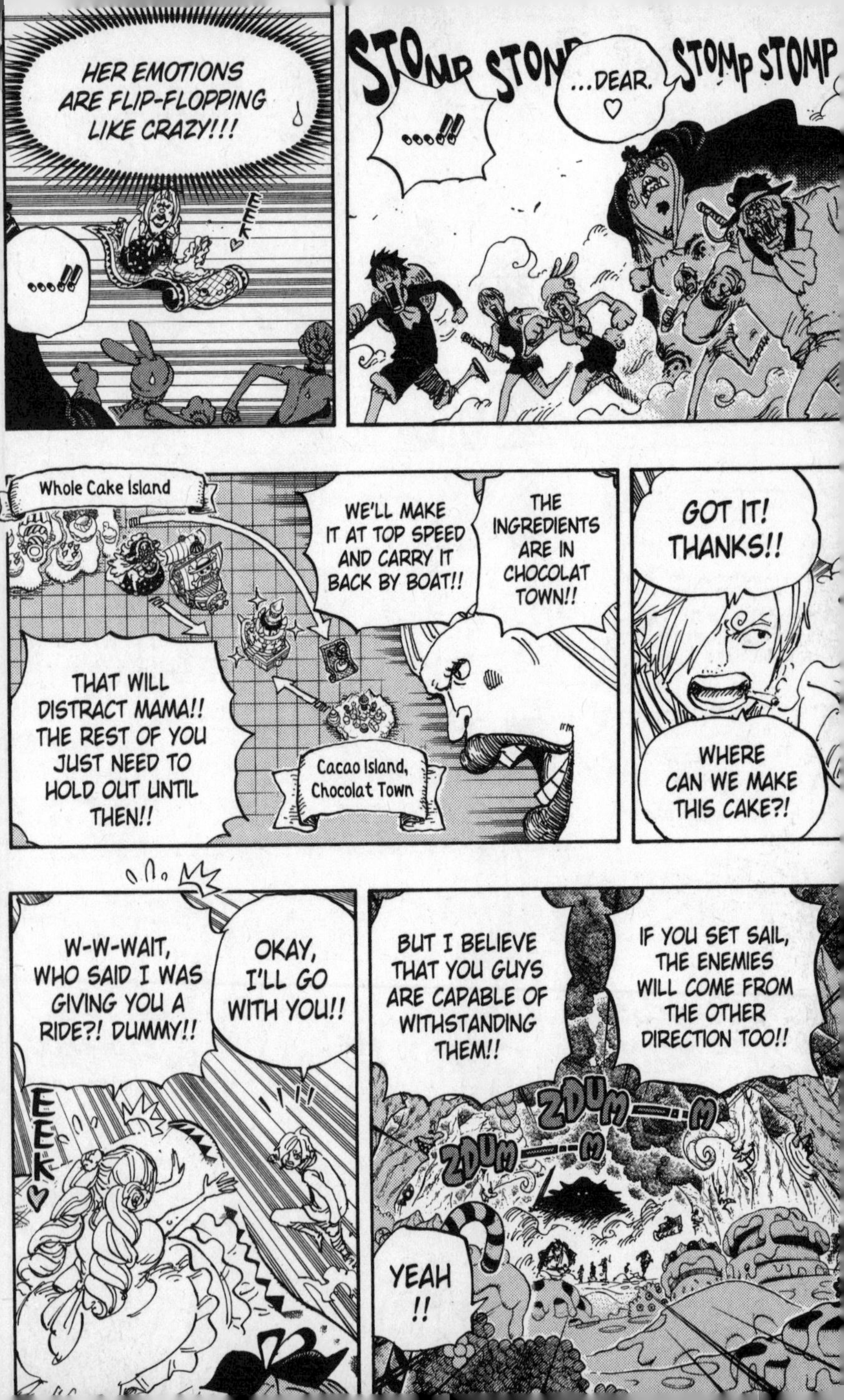
STOMP STOMP
...DEAR. ♡
STOMP STOMP
....!!
HER EMOTIONS ARE FLIP-FLOPPING LIKE CRAZY!!!
EEK ♡
....!!
GOT IT! THANKS!!
WHERE CAN WE MAKE THIS CAKE?!
THE INGREDIENTS ARE IN CHOCOLAT TOWN!!
WE'LL MAKE IT AT TOP SPEED AND CARRY IT BACK BY BOAT!!
Whole Cake Island
THAT WILL DISTRACT MAMA!! THE REST OF YOU JUST NEED TO HOLD OUT UNTIL THEN!!
Cacao Island, Chocolat Town
IF YOU SET SAIL, THE ENEMIES WILL COME FROM THE OTHER DIRECTION TOO!!
BUT I BELIEVE THAT YOU GUYS ARE CAPABLE OF WITHSTANDING THEM!!
ZDUM———M
ZDUM———M
YEAH!!
OKAY, I'LL GO WITH YOU!!
W-W-WAIT, WHO SAID I WAS GIVING YOU A RIDE?! DUMMY!!
EEK ♡

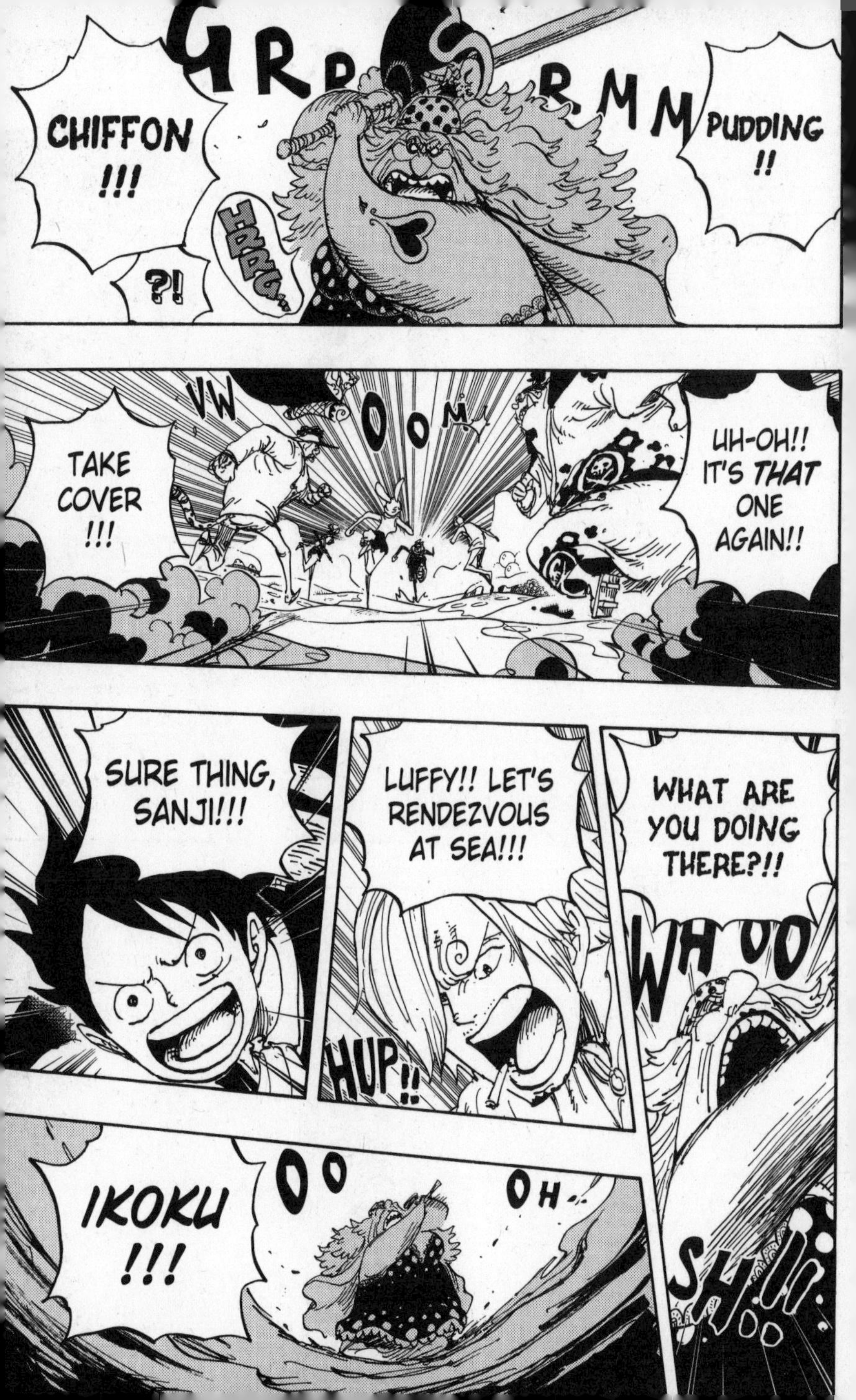
PUDDING!!
GRRRRMM
CHIFFON!!!
HRRG...
?!
UH-OH!! IT'S *THAT* ONE AGAIN!!
VWOOM!
TAKE COVER!!!
WHAT ARE YOU DOING THERE?!!
WHOO
LUFFY!! LET'S RENDEZVOUS AT SEA!!!
HUP!!
SURE THING, SANJI!!!
SHOO
OOOH-
IKOKU!!!

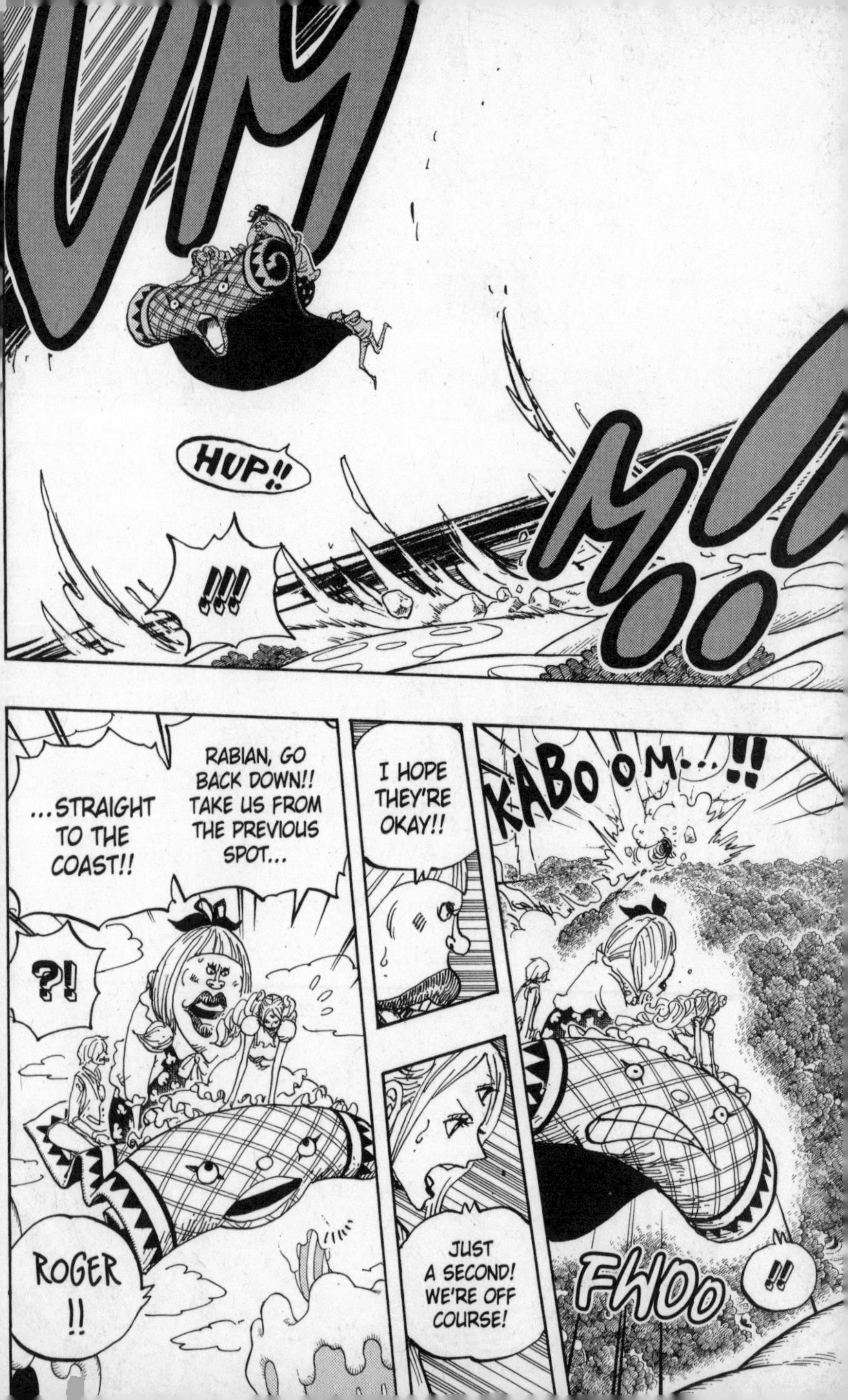
UM
MOO
HUP!!
!!!
KABOOM...!!
FWOO
!!
I HOPE THEY'RE OKAY!!
JUST A SECOND! WE'RE OFF COURSE!
RABIAN, GO BACK DOWN!! TAKE US FROM THE PREVIOUS SPOT...
...STRAIGHT TO THE COAST!!
?!
ROGER!!

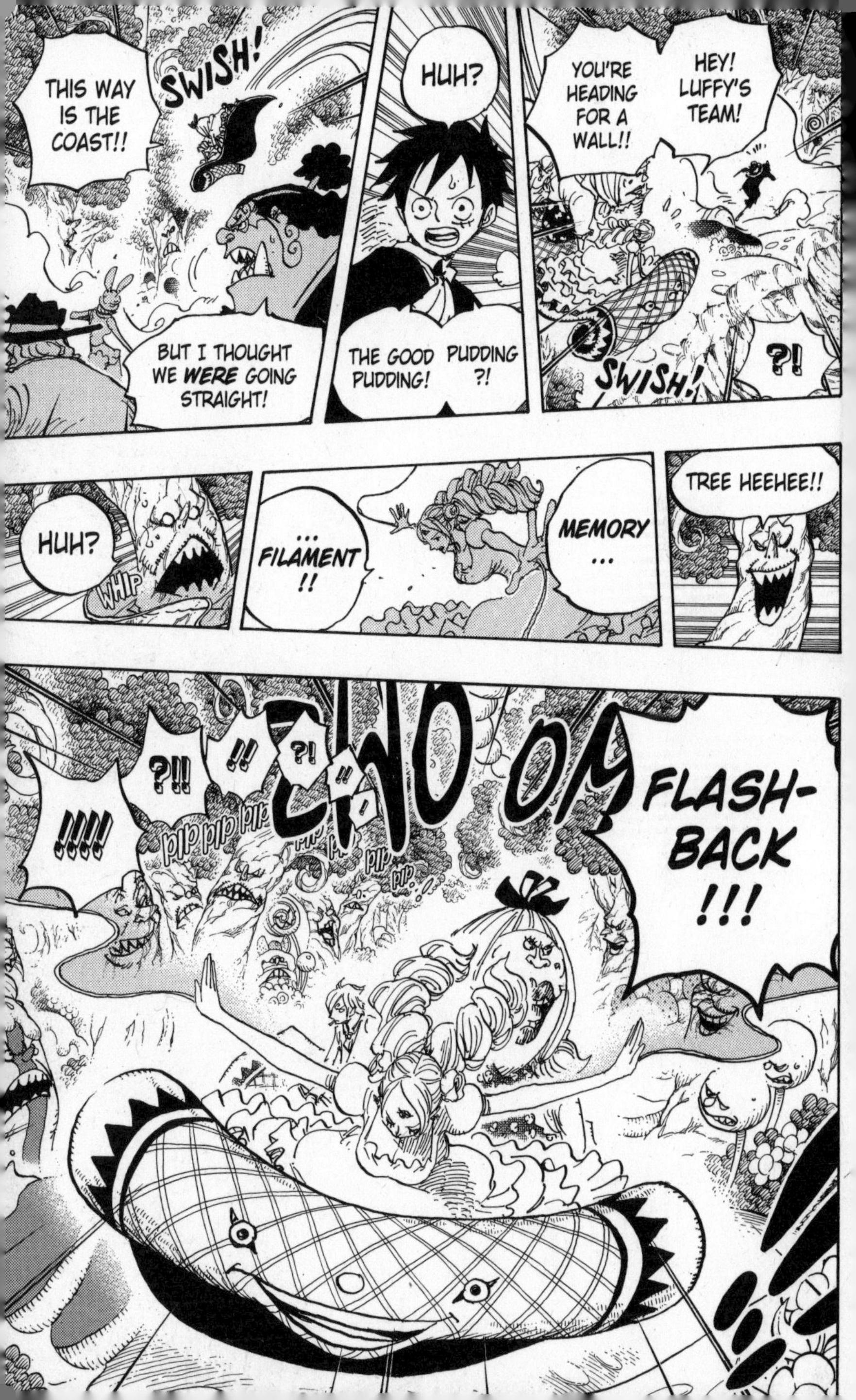
HEY! LUFFY'S TEAM!
YOU'RE HEADING FOR A WALL!!
SWISH!
?!
HUH?
PUDDING ?!
THE GOOD PUDDING!
THIS WAY IS THE COAST!!
SWISH!
BUT I THOUGHT WE *WERE* GOING STRAIGHT!
TREE HEEHEE!!
MEMORY ...
... FILAMENT !!
HUH?
WHIP
FLASH-BACK !!!
!!
?!
!!
?!!
!!!!
pip pip pip
pip pip

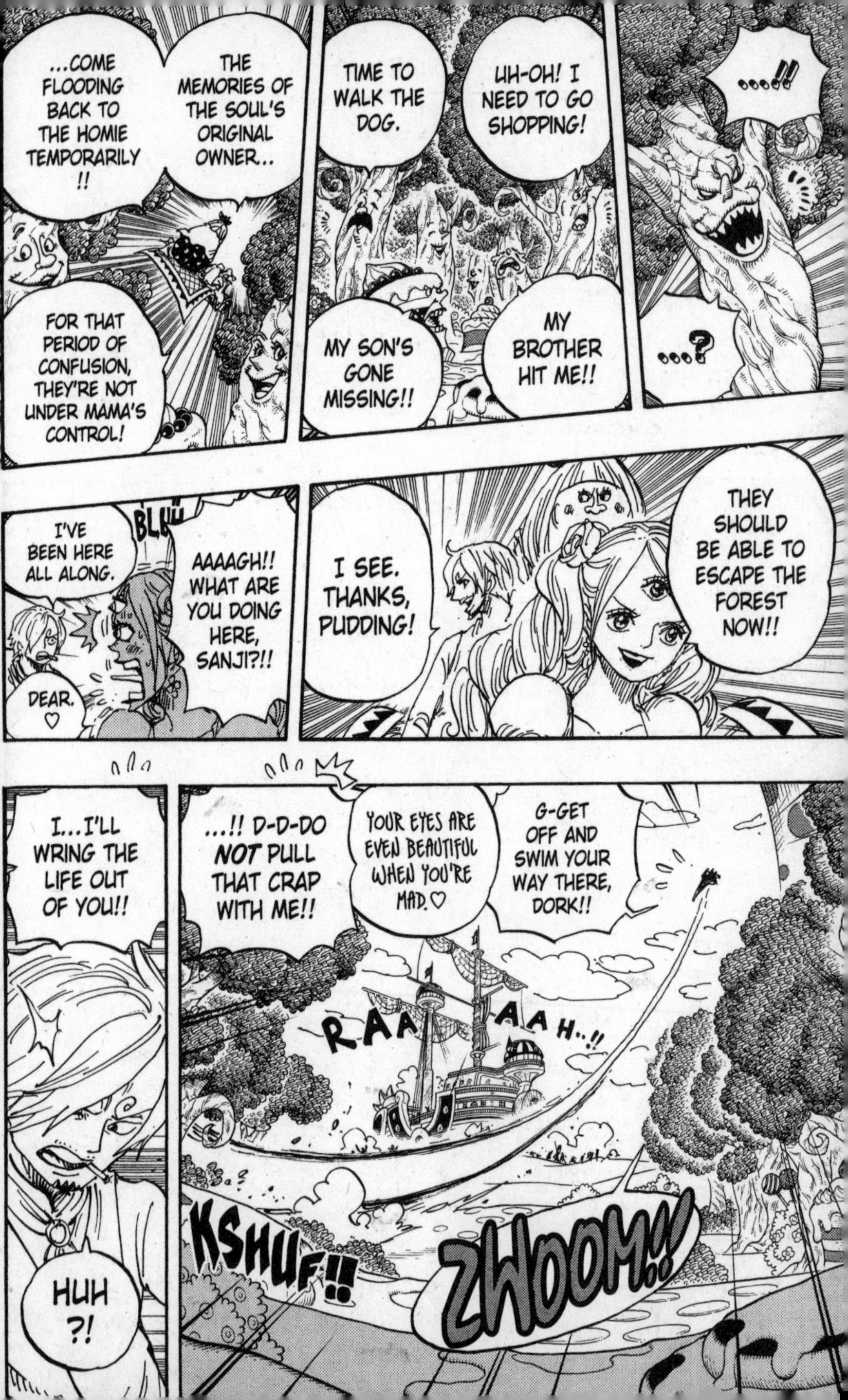
....!!
...?
UH-OH! I NEED TO GO SHOPPING!
TIME TO WALK THE DOG.
MY BROTHER HIT ME!!
MY SON'S GONE MISSING!!
THE MEMORIES OF THE SOUL'S ORIGINAL OWNER...
...COME FLOODING BACK TO THE HOMIE TEMPORARILY!!
FOR THAT PERIOD OF CONFUSION, THEY'RE NOT UNDER MAMA'S CONTROL!
THEY SHOULD BE ABLE TO ESCAPE THE FOREST NOW!!
I SEE. THANKS, PUDDING!
BLU
AAAAGH!! WHAT ARE YOU DOING HERE, SANJI?!!
I'VE BEEN HERE ALL ALONG.
DEAR. ♡
G-GET OFF AND SWIM YOUR WAY THERE, DORK!!
YOUR EYES ARE EVEN BEAUTIFUL WHEN YOU'RE MAD. ♡
...!! D-D-DO NOT PULL THAT CRAP WITH ME!!
RAAAAH..!!
ZHOOM!!
KSHUF!!
I...I'LL WRING THE LIFE OUT OF YOU!!
HUH?!

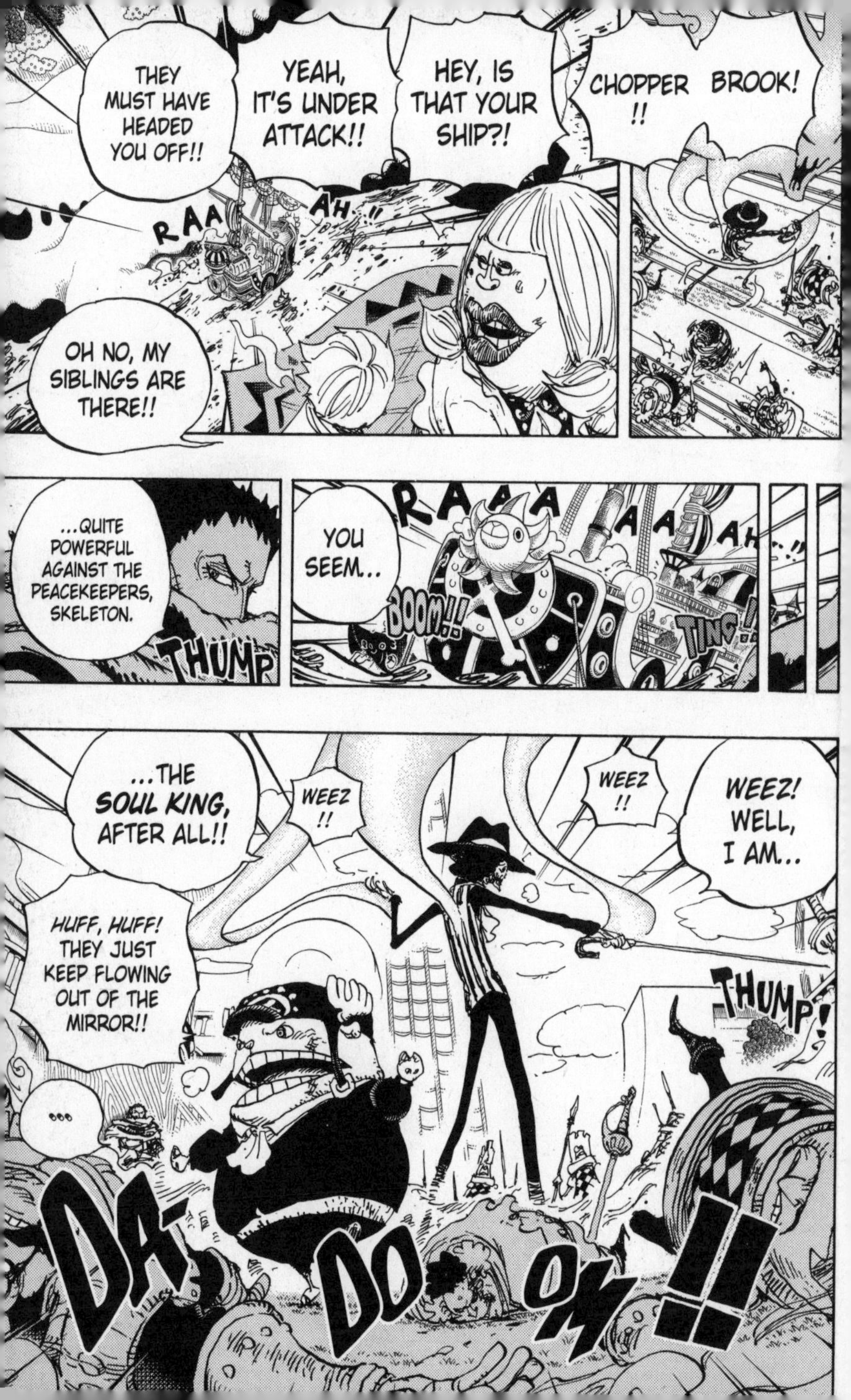
CHOPPER !! BROOK!
HEY, IS THAT YOUR SHIP?!
YEAH, IT'S UNDER ATTACK!!
THEY MUST HAVE HEADED YOU OFF!!
RAAAH!!
OH NO, MY SIBLINGS ARE THERE!!
RAAAAAAH!!
YOU SEEM...
BOOM!!
TING!!
...QUITE POWERFUL AGAINST THE PEACEKEEPERS, SKELETON.
THUMP
WEEZ! WELL, I AM...
WEEZ !!
...THE *SOUL KING*, AFTER ALL!!
WEEZ !!
THUMP!
HUFF, HUFF! THEY JUST KEEP FLOWING OUT OF THE MIRROR!!
...
DA-DO-OM!!

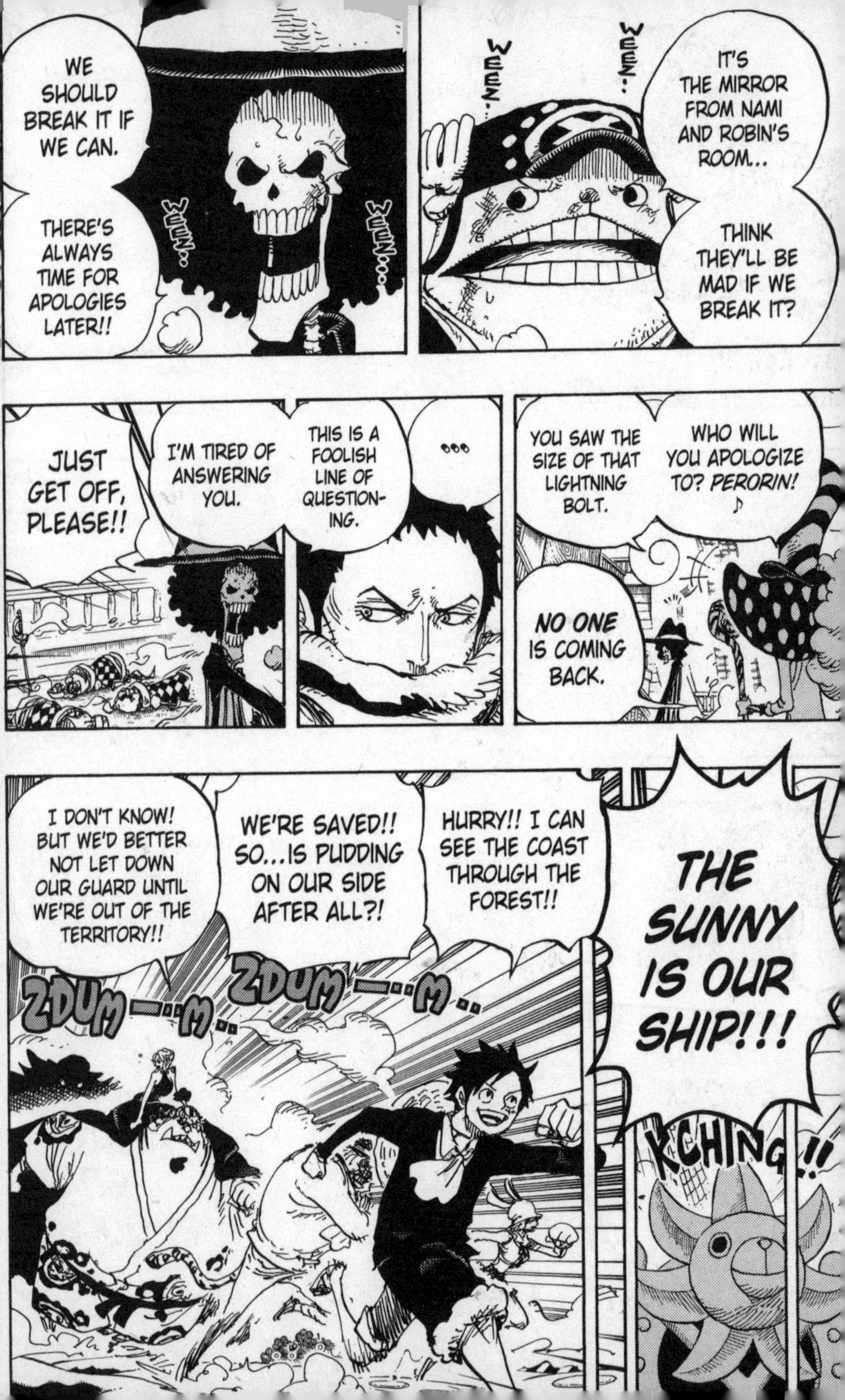
WEEZ...
WEEZ...
IT'S THE MIRROR FROM NAMI AND ROBIN'S ROOM...
THINK THEY'LL BE MAD IF WE BREAK IT?
WE SHOULD BREAK IT IF WE CAN.
THERE'S ALWAYS TIME FOR APOLOGIES LATER!!
WEEZ...
WEEZ...
WHO WILL YOU APOLOGIZE TO? PERORIN! ♪
YOU SAW THE SIZE OF THAT LIGHTNING BOLT.
NO ONE IS COMING BACK.
...
THIS IS A FOOLISH LINE OF QUESTIONING.
I'M TIRED OF ANSWERING YOU.
JUST GET OFF, PLEASE!!
THE SUNNY IS OUR SHIP!!!
KCHING!!
HURRY!! I CAN SEE THE COAST THROUGH THE FOREST!!
WE'RE SAVED!! SO...IS PUDDING ON OUR SIDE AFTER ALL?!
I DON'T KNOW! BUT WE'D BETTER NOT LET DOWN OUR GUARD UNTIL WE'RE OUT OF THE TERRITORY!!
ZDUM---M..
ZDUM---M..

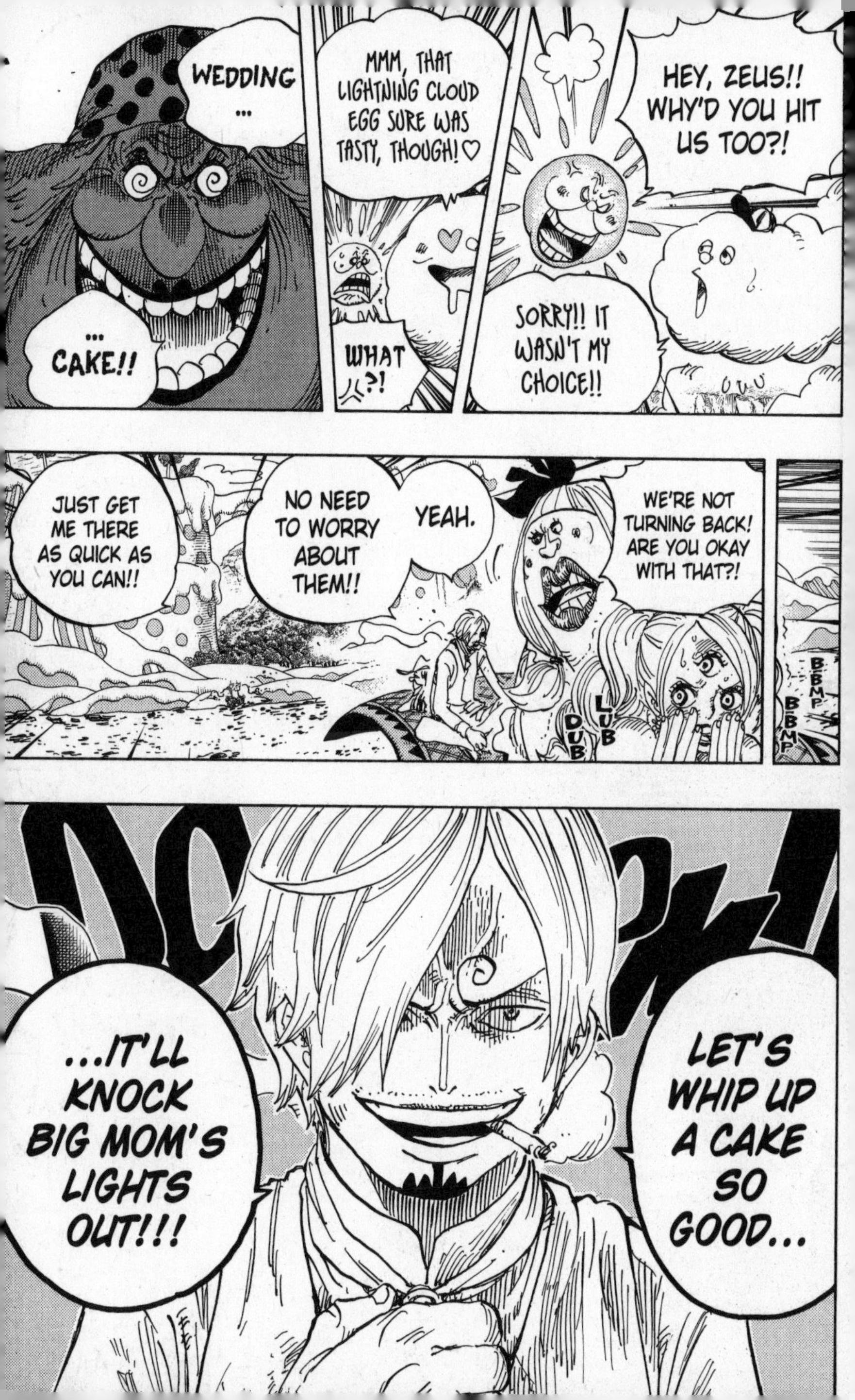
HEY, ZEUS!! WHY'D YOU HIT US TOO?!
SORRY!! IT WASN'T MY CHOICE!!
MMM, THAT LIGHTNING CLOUD EGG SURE WAS TASTY, THOUGH!♡
WHAT?!
WEDDING ...
... CAKE!!
BBMP
BBMP
WE'RE NOT TURNING BACK! ARE YOU OKAY WITH THAT?!
LUB
DUB
YEAH.
NO NEED TO WORRY ABOUT THEM!!
JUST GET ME THERE AS QUICK AS YOU CAN!!
LET'S WHIP UP A CAKE SO GOOD...
...IT'LL KNOCK BIG MOM'S LIGHTS OUT!!!

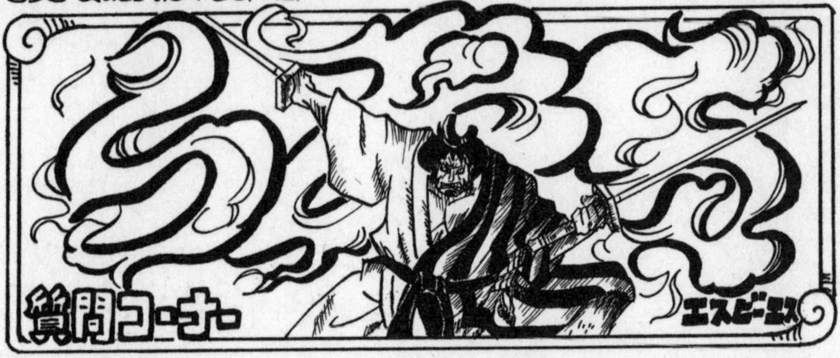
質問コーナー
エスビーエス

(Michi Nakahara, Tottori)

Q: Hello, Oda Sensei. In Chapter 852, there's a scene where Jimbei saves Luffy and Nami. In the process, Nami's clothes get tattered. But on the next page, she's changed outfits! So does that mean that on the previous page, that's Nami rustling up some clothes in the background?! How did she do that?! Tell us, Odacchi! ♡

--Help With My Summer Vacation Homework

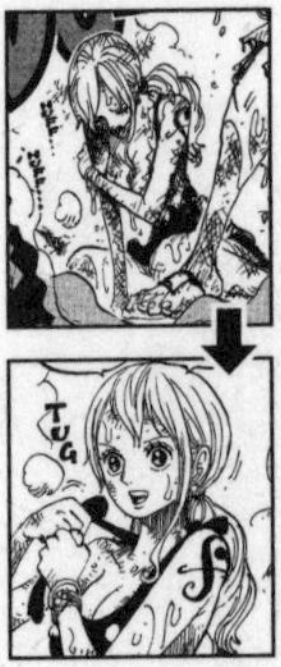
TUG

A: Yes, she's changing. Can't wear those burned-up tatters.

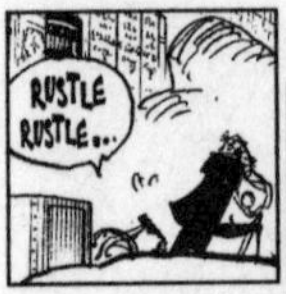
RUSTLE
RUSTLE...

← You can see her rustling here.

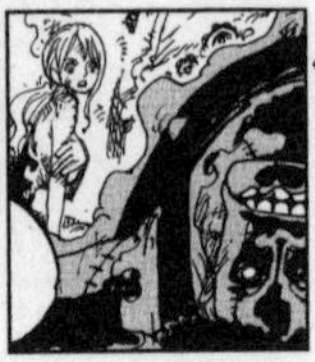

← Now look at the previous panel. Nami's noticed something: the clothes of the defeated soldier.

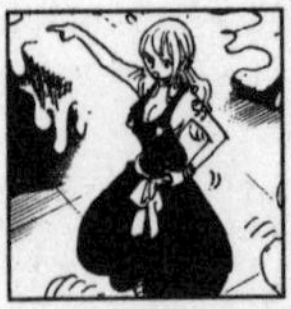

← So she rustles in the corner, then shows up wearing some baggy new clothes. She's trying to wear clothes from a much larger soldier.

She's a looter.

Q: I was looking closely at the *hanafuda* cards Shanks is holding on the cover of Chapter 862…and that hand is called the "Four Lights"!

Like the Four Emperors!!

--Kamiki-kun

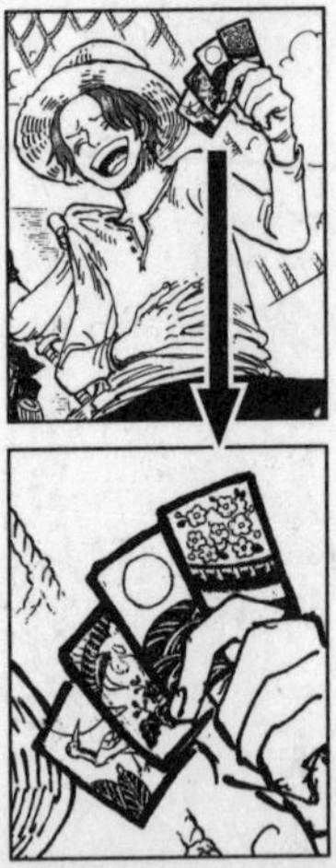

A: Wow, I'm amazed that you noticed that! That's right; there's a hand in *hanafuda* called the "Four Lights." In Japanese it's pronounced very similar to "Four Emperors," which would seem to portend Shanks' future status as one of those Emperors. Very well done.

Chapter 877:
BITTERSWEET

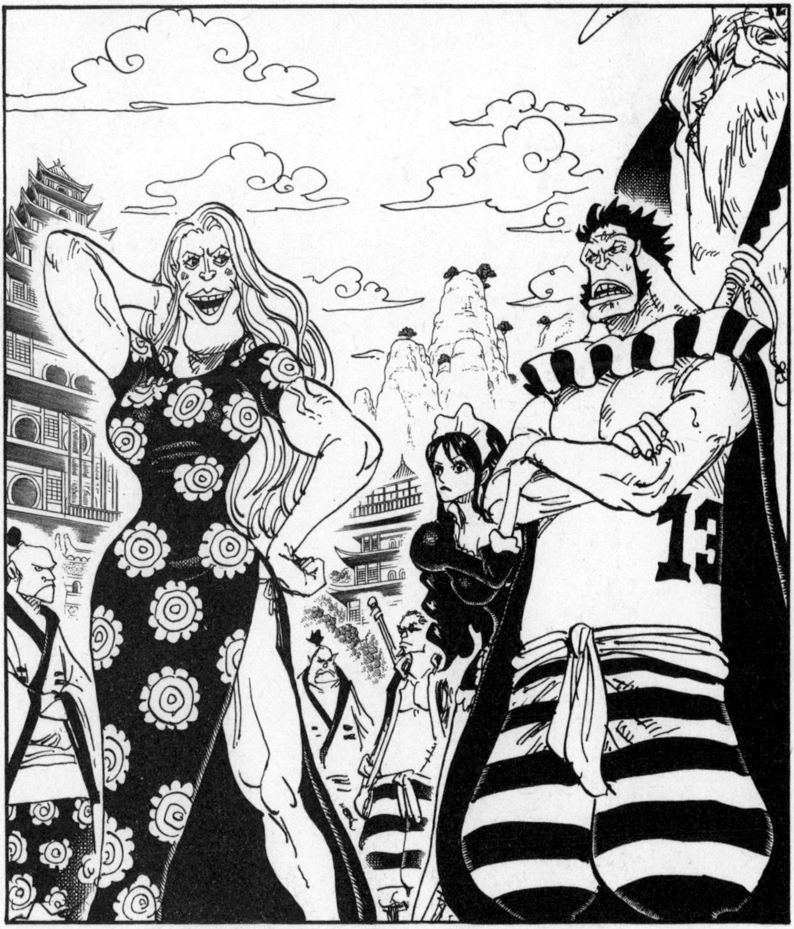
13

THE SAGA OF THE SELF-PROCLAIMED STRAW HAT FLEET, VOL. 12, SAI:
OOKLICIA: "I WAS THINKING ABOUT THE DATE OF OUR WEDDING..."
SAI: "SO, OOKLICIA, ABOUT THAT..."

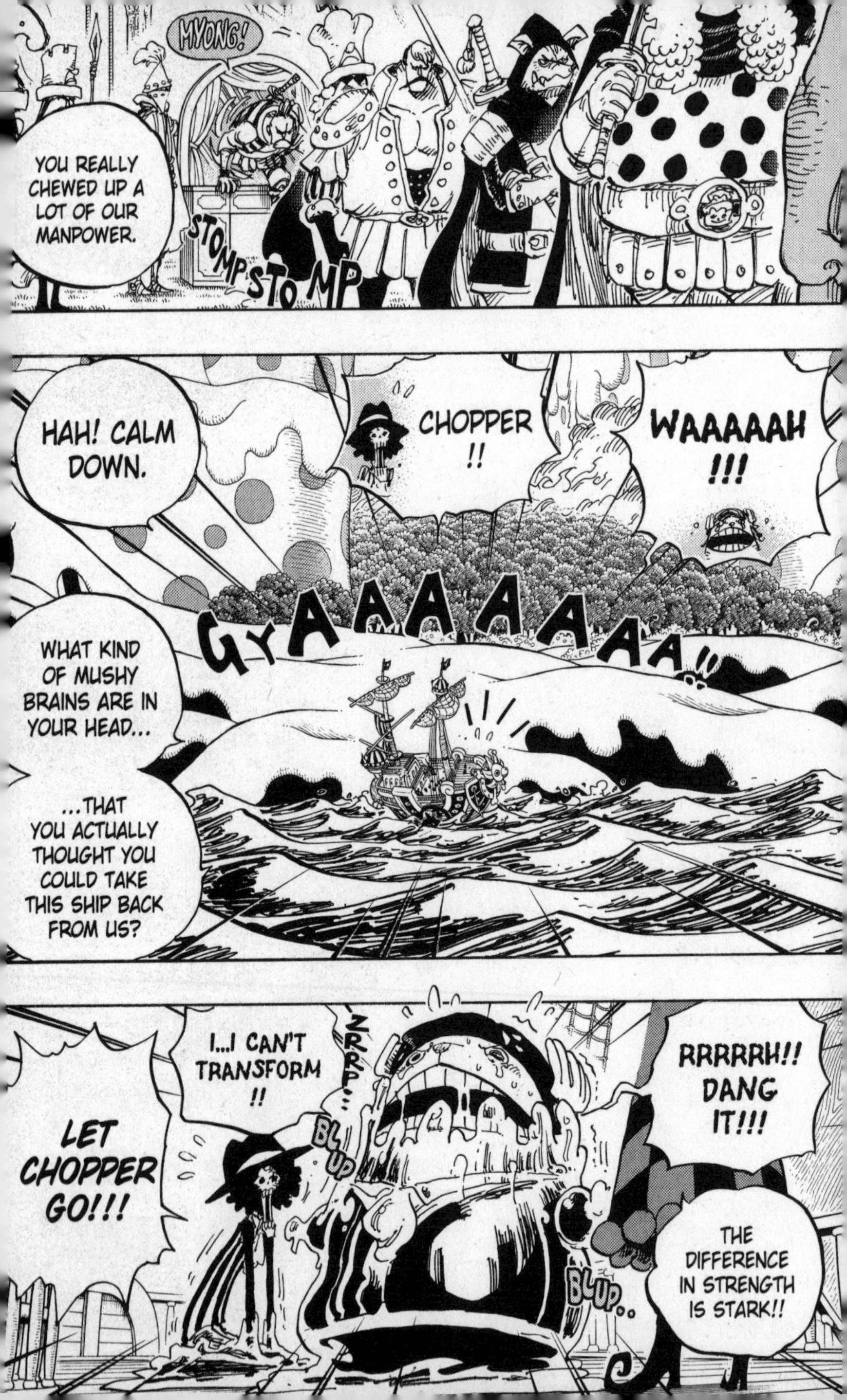
MYONG!
YOU REALLY CHEWED UP A LOT OF OUR MANPOWER.
STOMP STOMP
WAAAAAH!!!
CHOPPER!!
HAH! CALM DOWN.
GYAAAAAAA!!
WHAT KIND OF MUSHY BRAINS ARE IN YOUR HEAD...
...THAT YOU ACTUALLY THOUGHT YOU COULD TAKE THIS SHIP BACK FROM US?
RRRRRH!! DANG IT!!!
ZRRP...
I...I CAN'T TRANSFORM!!
LET CHOPPER GO!!!
BLUP
THE DIFFERENCE IN STRENGTH IS STARK!!
BLUP..

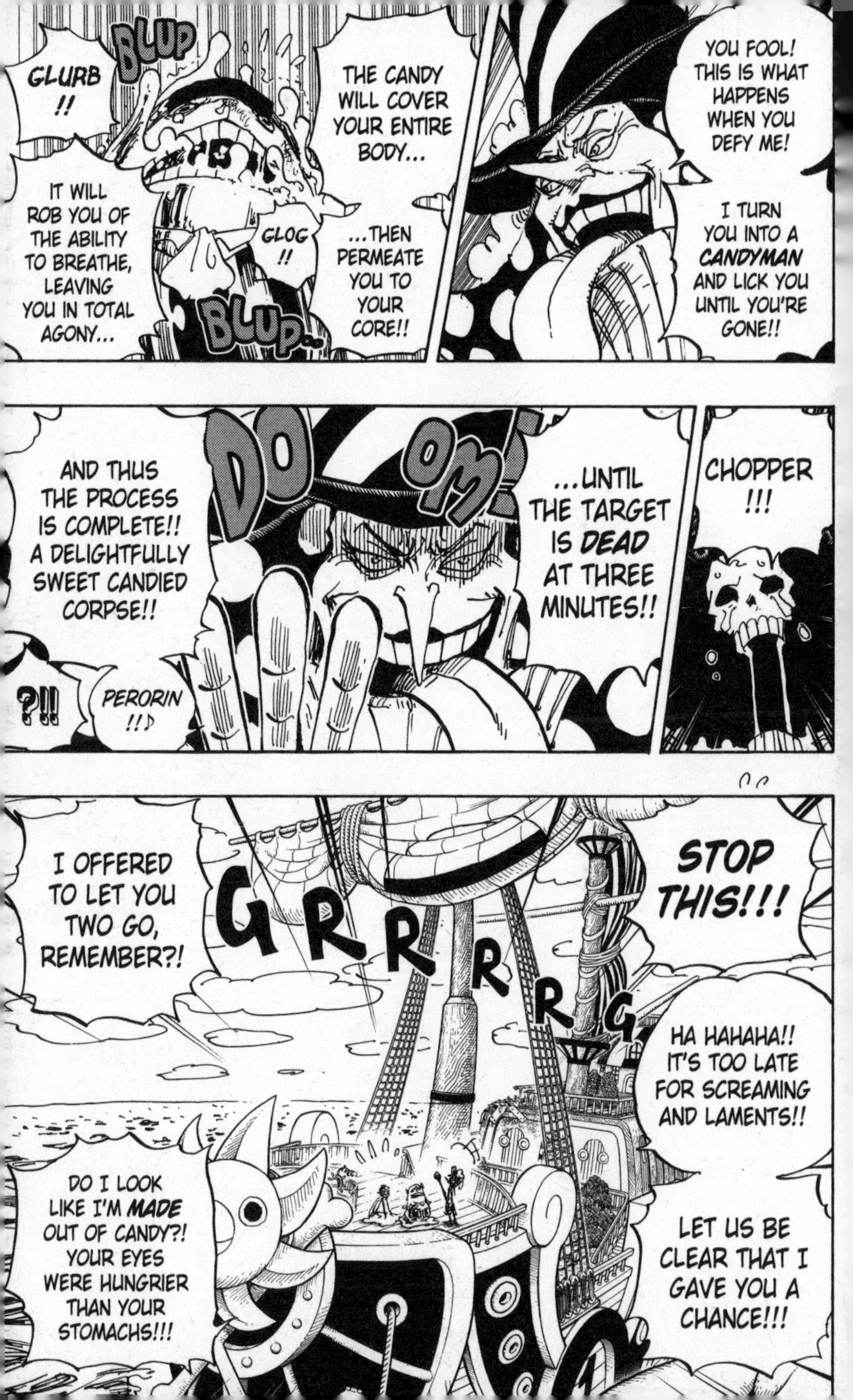
YOU FOOL! THIS IS WHAT HAPPENS WHEN YOU DEFY ME!
I TURN YOU INTO A *CANDYMAN* AND LICK YOU UNTIL YOU'RE GONE!!
THE CANDY WILL COVER YOUR ENTIRE BODY...
BLUP
GLURB !!
...THEN PERMEATE YOU TO YOUR CORE!!
GLOG !!
IT WILL ROB YOU OF THE ABILITY TO BREATHE, LEAVING YOU IN TOTAL AGONY...
BLUP..
CHOPPER !!!
DOOM!
...UNTIL THE TARGET IS *DEAD* AT THREE MINUTES!!
AND THUS THE PROCESS IS COMPLETE!! A DELIGHTFULLY SWEET CANDIED CORPSE!!
PERORIN !!♪
?!!
STOP THIS!!!
I OFFERED TO LET YOU TWO GO, REMEMBER?!
GRRRRRG
HA HAHAHA!! IT'S TOO LATE FOR SCREAMING AND LAMENTS!!
LET US BE CLEAR THAT I GAVE YOU A CHANCE!!!
DO I LOOK LIKE I'M *MADE* OUT OF CANDY?! YOUR EYES WERE HUNGRIER THAN YOUR STOMACHS!!!

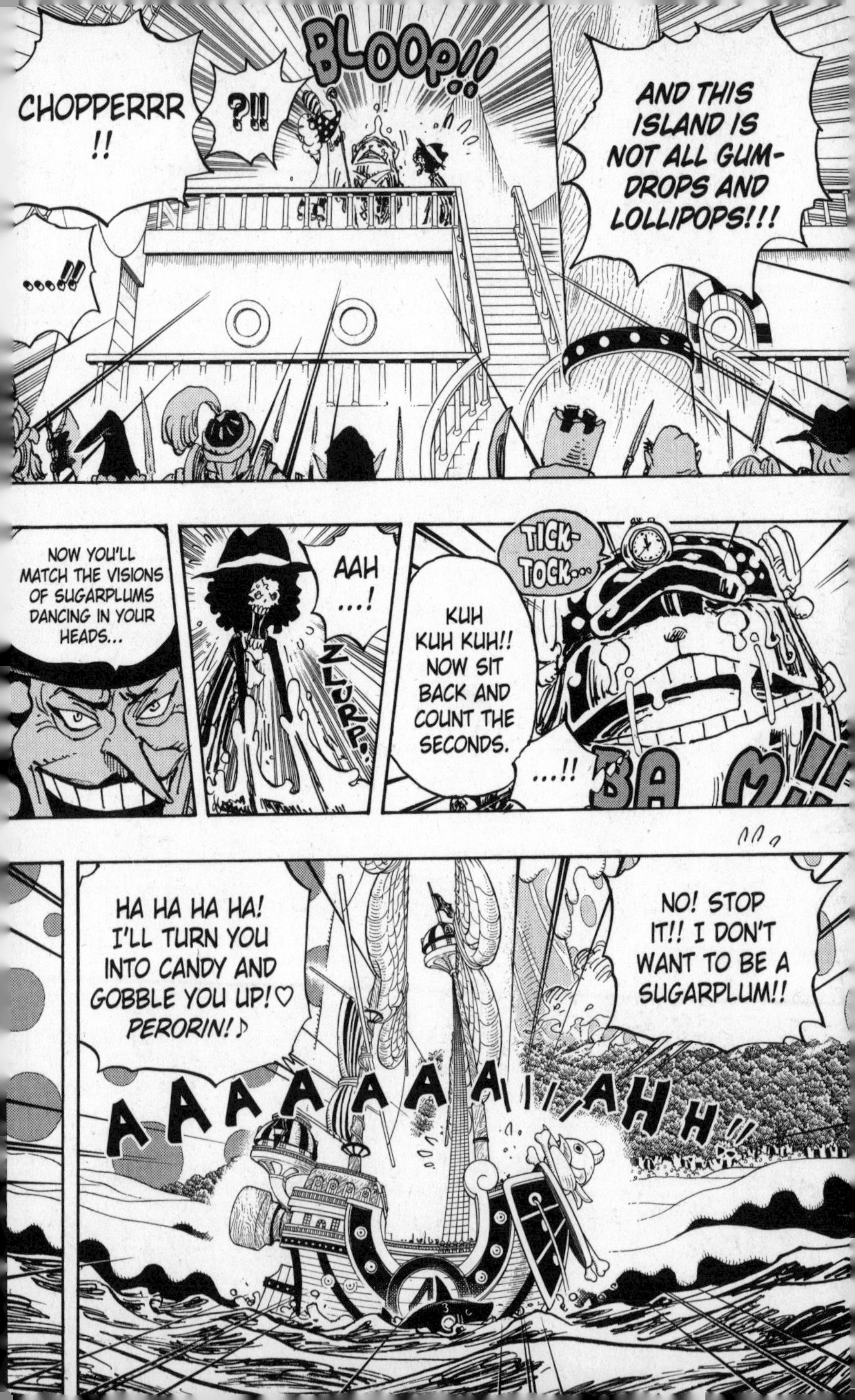
AND THIS ISLAND IS NOT ALL GUM-DROPS AND LOLLIPOPS!!!
BLOOP!!
?!!
CHOPPERRR !!
....!!
TICK-TOCK...
KUH KUH KUH!! NOW SIT BACK AND COUNT THE SECONDS.
...!!
BAM!!
AAH ...!
ZLURP.
NOW YOU'LL MATCH THE VISIONS OF SUGARPLUMS DANCING IN YOUR HEADS...
NO! STOP IT!! I DON'T WANT TO BE A SUGARPLUM!!
HA HA HA HA! I'LL TURN YOU INTO CANDY AND GOBBLE YOU UP!♡ PERORIN!♪
AAAAAAAAHH!!

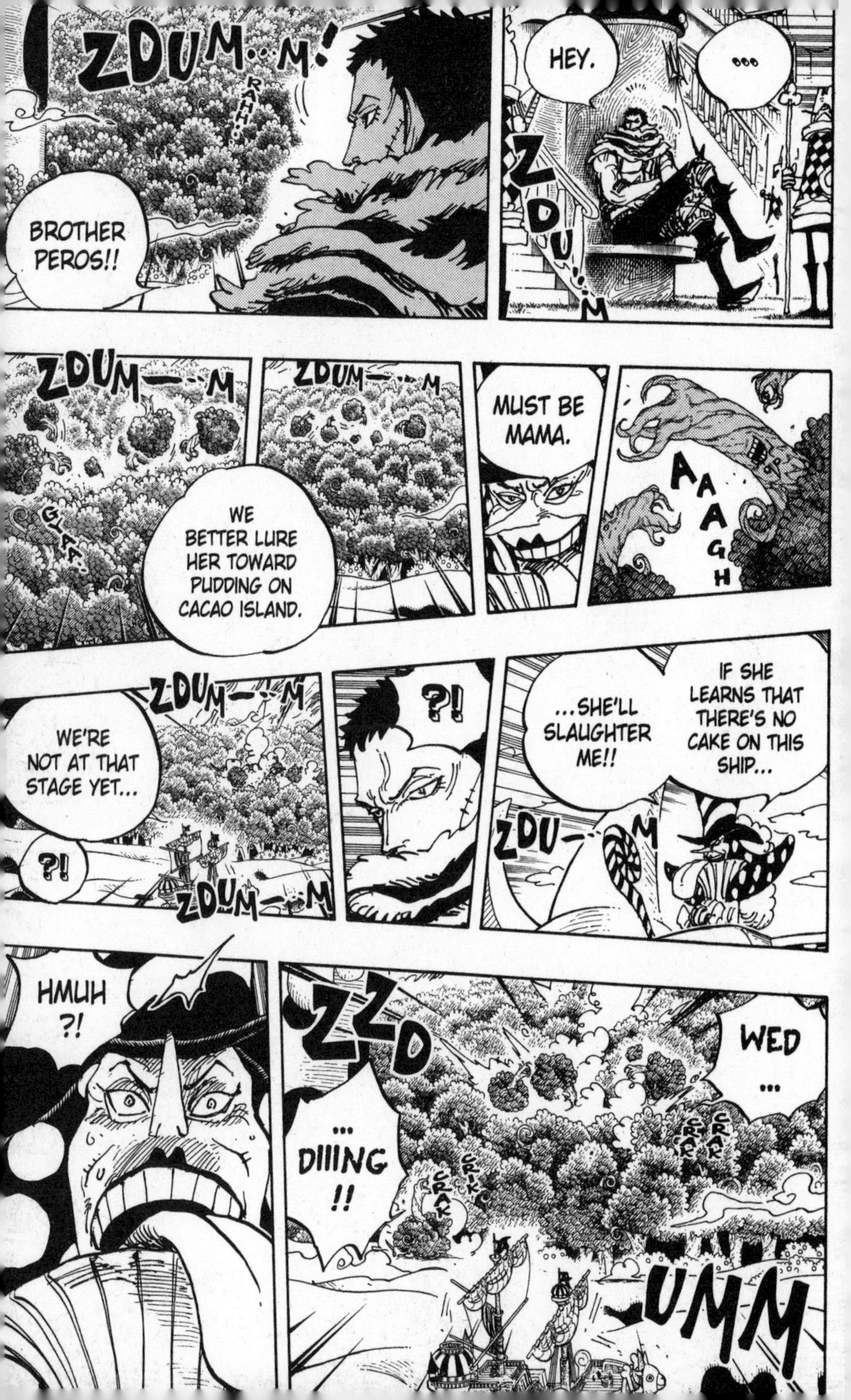
...
HEY.
ZDU...M
ZDUM...M!
RAHH...
BROTHER PEROS!!
AAAGH
MUST BE MAMA.
ZDUM—...M
WE BETTER LURE HER TOWARD PUDDING ON CACAO ISLAND.
ZDUM—...M
GYAA
IF SHE LEARNS THAT THERE'S NO CAKE ON THIS SHIP...
...SHE'LL SLAUGHTER ME!!
ZDU—...M
?!
ZDUM—...M
WE'RE NOT AT THAT STAGE YET...
?!
ZDUM—...M
WED...
CRAK CRAK
ZZD
...DIIING!!
CRIK CRAK
UMM
HMUH?!

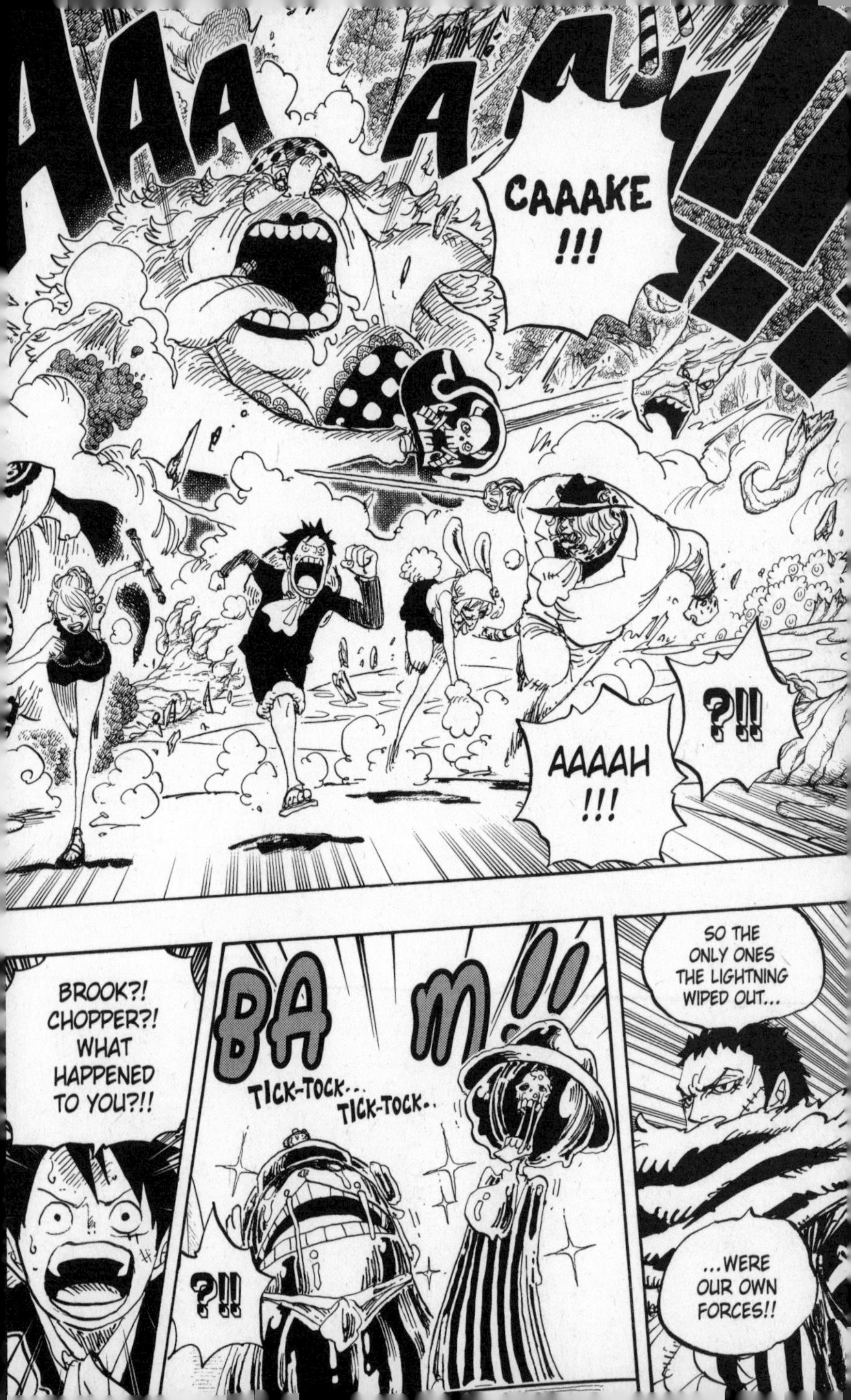
AAAAA!!!
CAAAKE !!!
?!!
AAAAH !!!
SO THE ONLY ONES THE LIGHTNING WIPED OUT...
...WERE OUR OWN FORCES!!
BAM!!
TICK-TOCK... TICK-TOCK..
?!!
BROOK?! CHOPPER?! WHAT HAPPENED TO YOU?!!

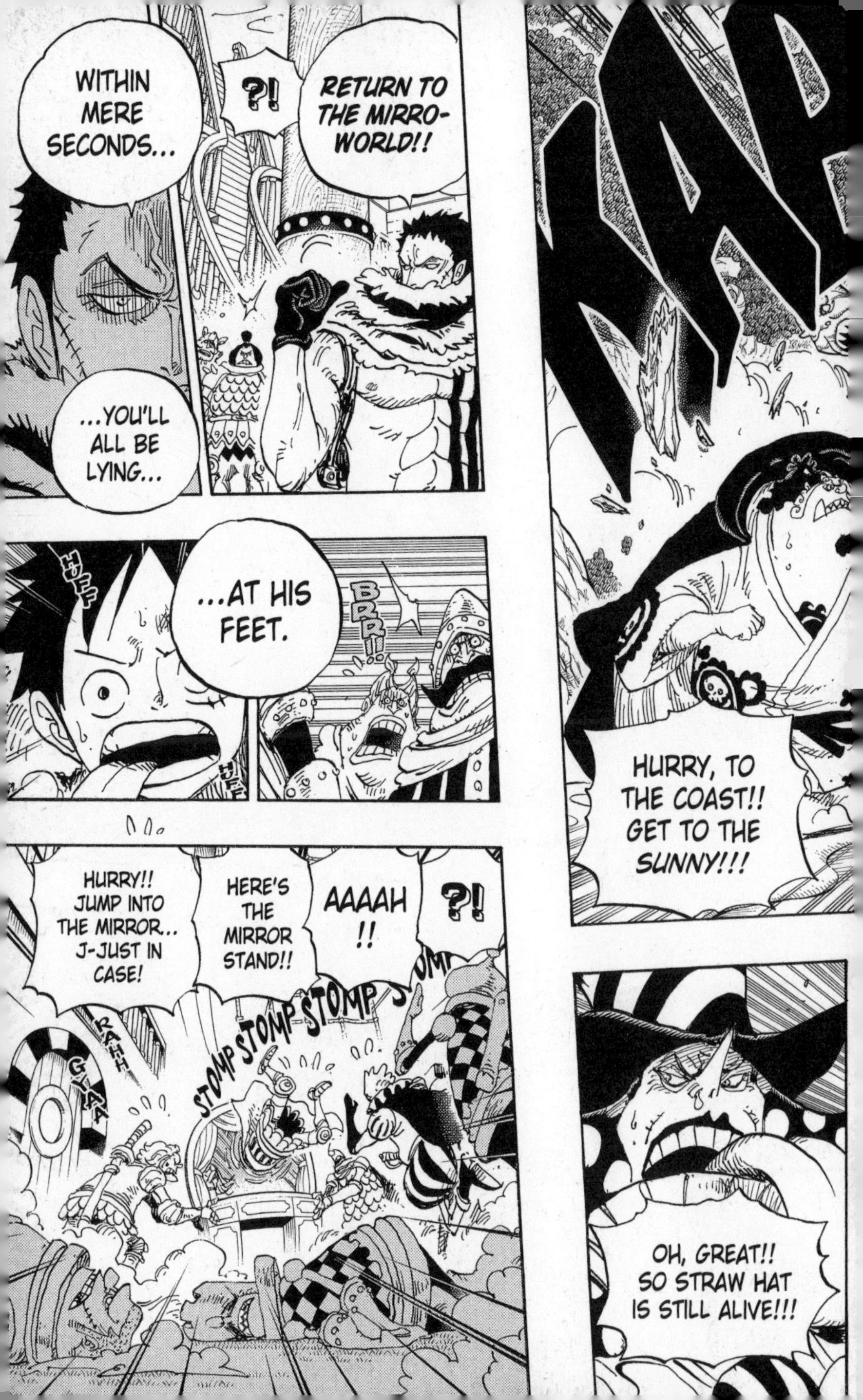
HURRY, TO THE COAST!! GET TO THE SUNNY!!!
OH, GREAT!! SO STRAW HAT IS STILL ALIVE!!!
RETURN TO THE MIRRO-WORLD!!
?!
WITHIN MERE SECONDS...
...YOU'LL ALL BE LYING...
BRR!!
...AT HIS FEET.
HUFF
HUFF
?!
AAAAH !!
HERE'S THE MIRROR STAND!!
HURRY!! JUMP INTO THE MIRROR... J-JUST IN CASE!
STOMP STOMP STOMP
RAHH
GYAA

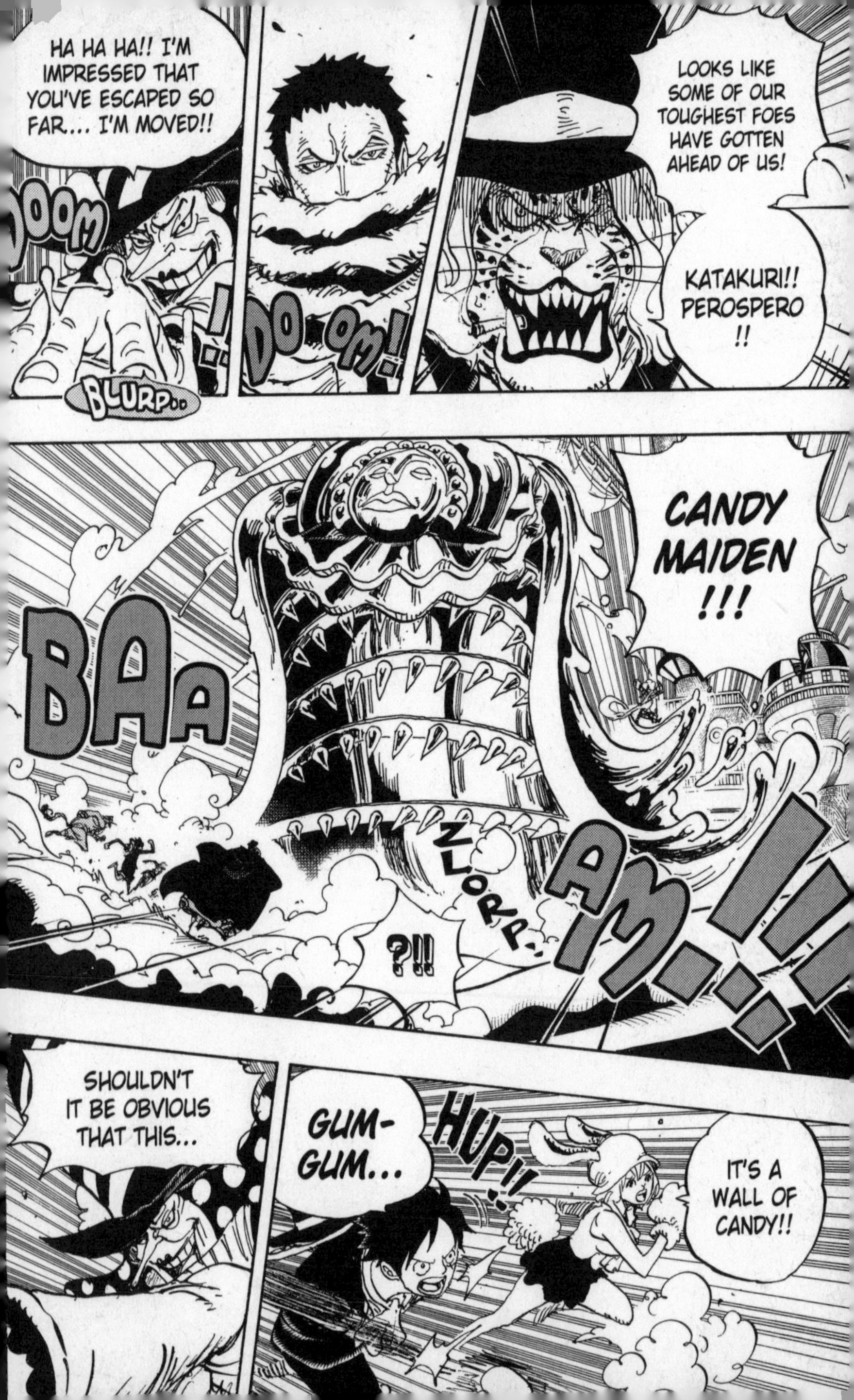
LOOKS LIKE SOME OF OUR TOUGHEST FOES HAVE GOTTEN AHEAD OF US!
KATAKURI!! PEROSPERO !!
DO..OM!!
HA HA HA!! I'M IMPRESSED THAT YOU'VE ESCAPED SO FAR.... I'M MOVED!!
OOOM
BLURP..
CANDY MAIDEN !!!
BAAAM..!!
ZLORP..
?!!
IT'S A WALL OF CANDY!!
HUP!!
GUM-GUM...
SHOULDN'T IT BE OBVIOUS THAT THIS...

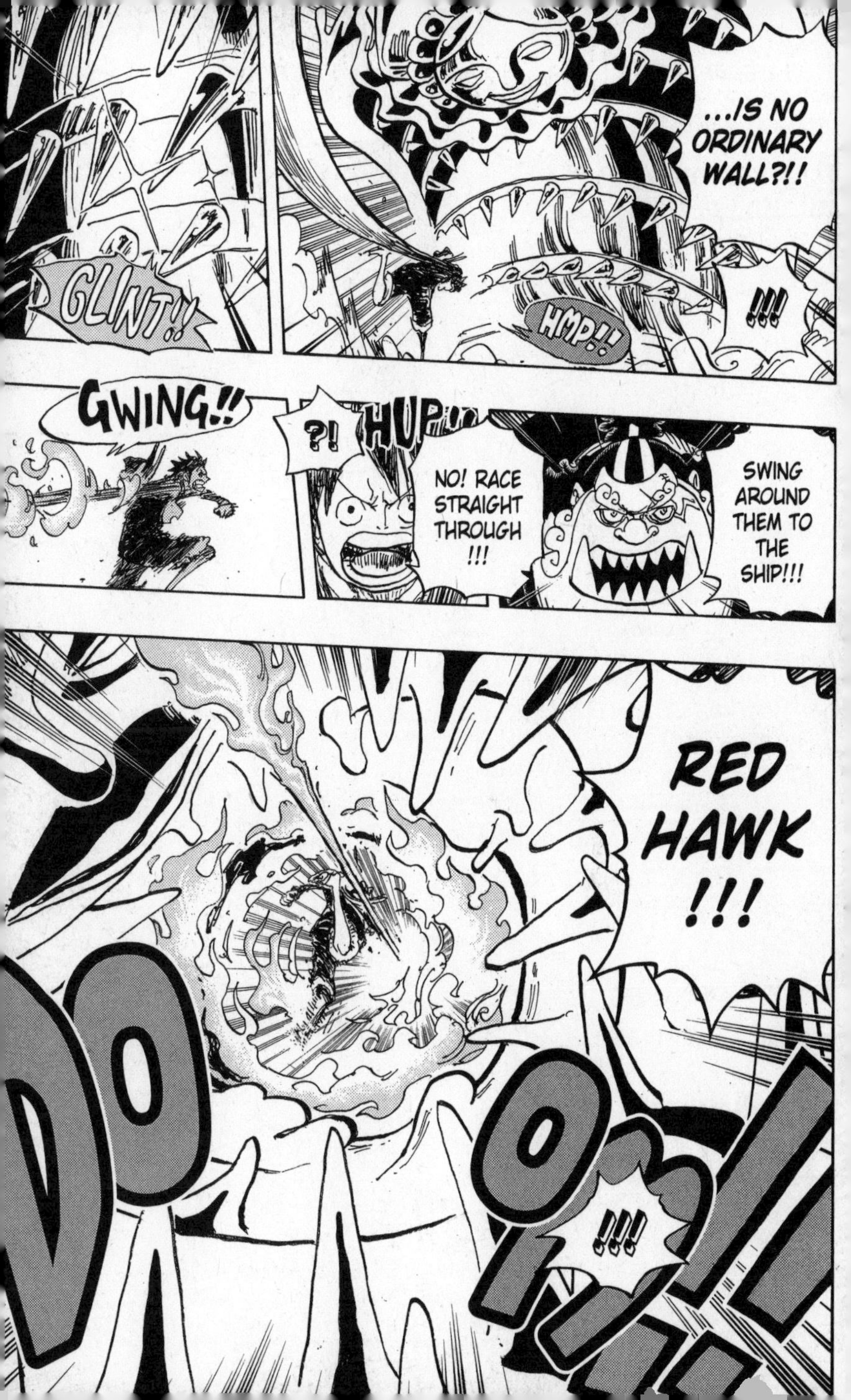
...IS NO ORDINARY WALL?!!
HMP!!
!!!
GLINT!!
SWING AROUND THEM TO THE SHIP!!!
HUP!!
?!
NO! RACE STRAIGHT THROUGH!!!
GWING!!
RED HAWK!!!
!!!

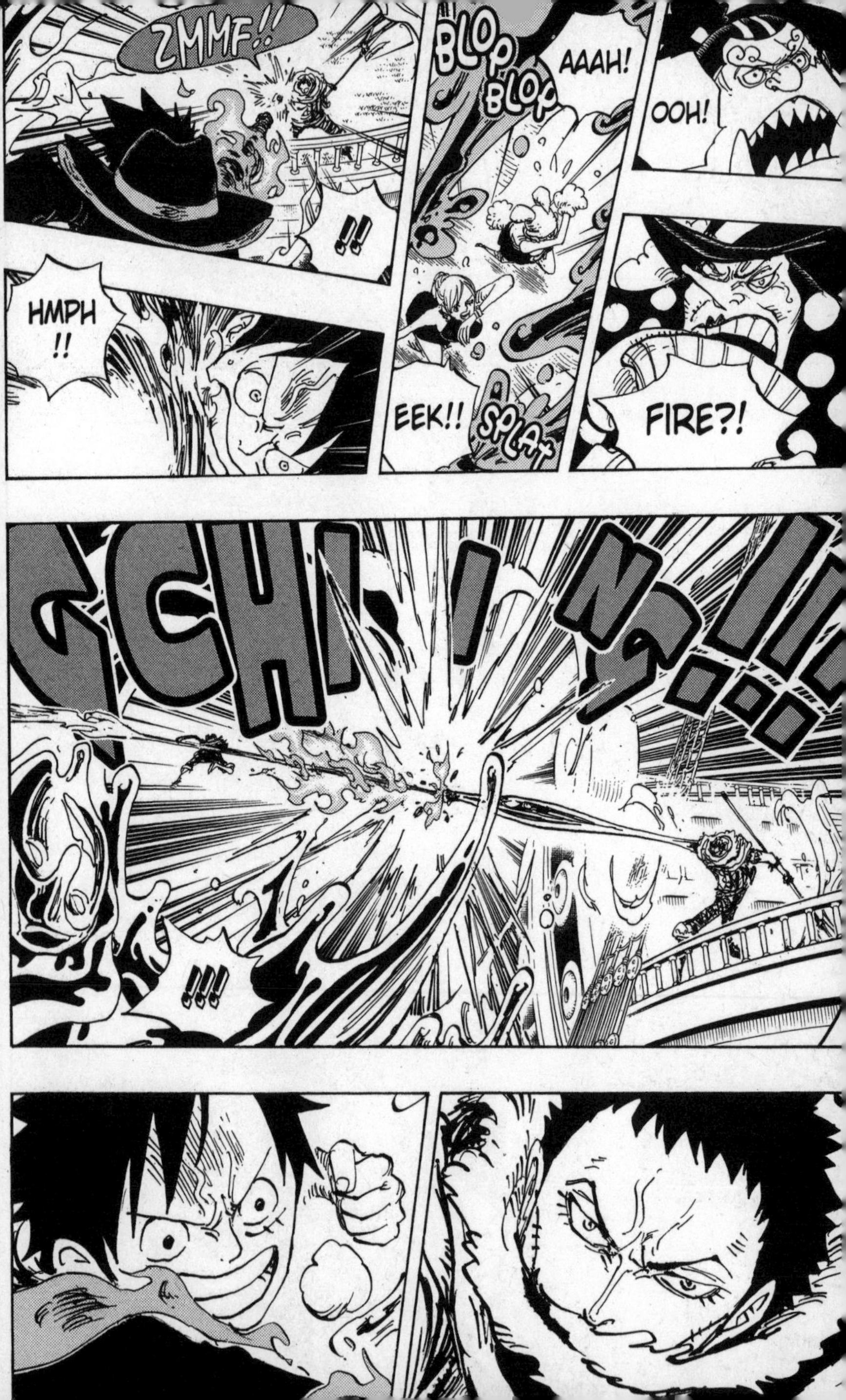

OOH!
FIRE?!
BLOP BLOP
AAAH!
EEK!!
SPLAT
ZMMF!!
!!
HMPH !!
CHIIN!!!
!!!

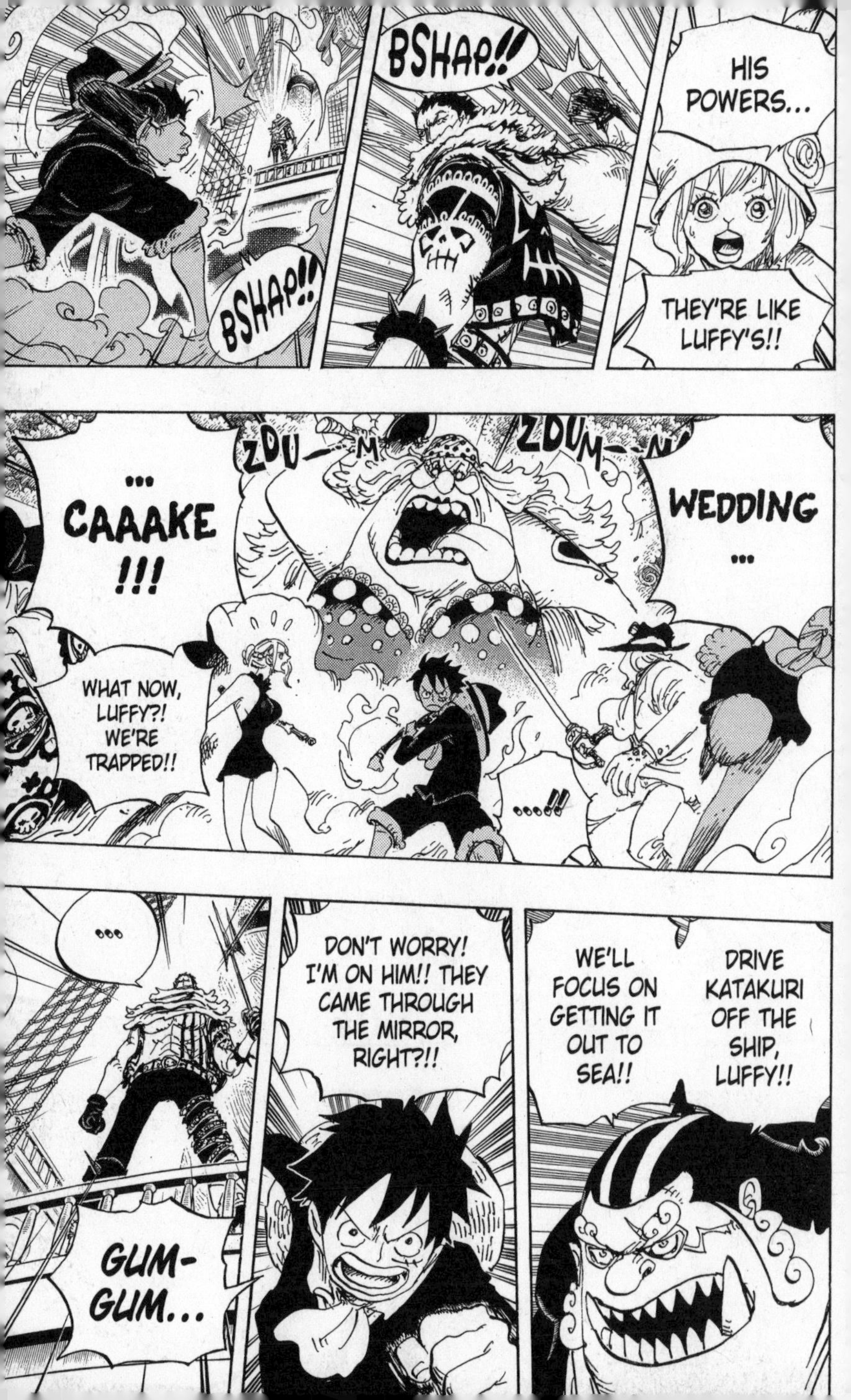
HIS POWERS...
THEY'RE LIKE LUFFY'S!!
BSHAP!!
BSHAP!!
WEDDING ...
ZDUM--N
ZDU--M
... CAAAKE !!!
....!!
WHAT NOW, LUFFY?! WE'RE TRAPPED!!
DRIVE KATAKURI OFF THE SHIP, LUFFY!!
WE'LL FOCUS ON GETTING IT OUT TO SEA!!
DON'T WORRY! I'M ON HIM!! THEY CAME THROUGH THE MIRROR, RIGHT?!!
...
GUM-GUM...

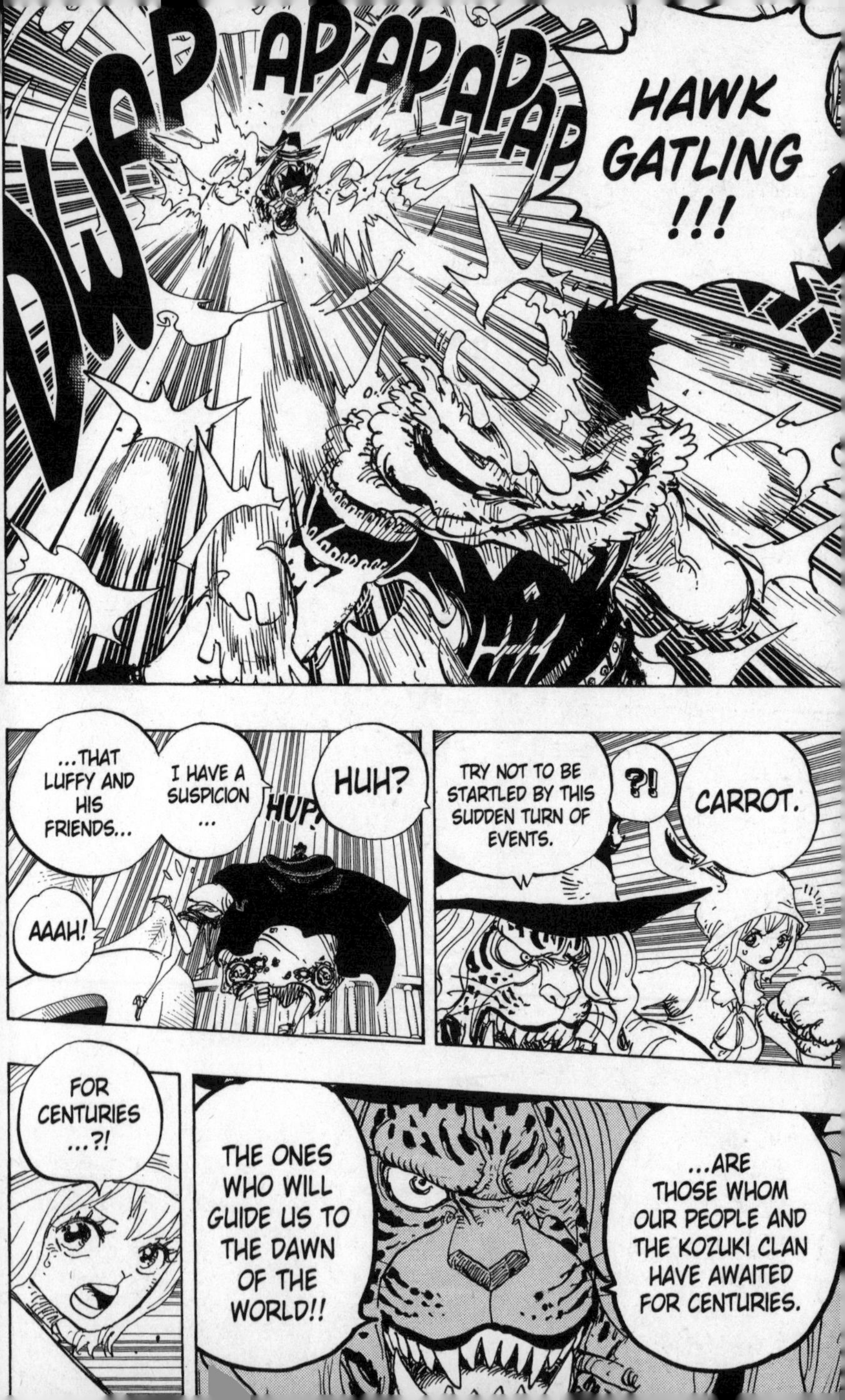
HAWK GATLING !!!
DWAP APAPAPAPAP
CARROT.
?!
TRY NOT TO BE STARTLED BY THIS SUDDEN TURN OF EVENTS.
HUH?
HUP!
I HAVE A SUSPICION ...
...THAT LUFFY AND HIS FRIENDS...
AAAH!
...ARE THOSE WHOM OUR PEOPLE AND THE KOZUKI CLAN HAVE AWAITED FOR CENTURIES.
THE ONES WHO WILL GUIDE US TO THE DAWN OF THE WORLD!!
FOR CENTURIES ...?!

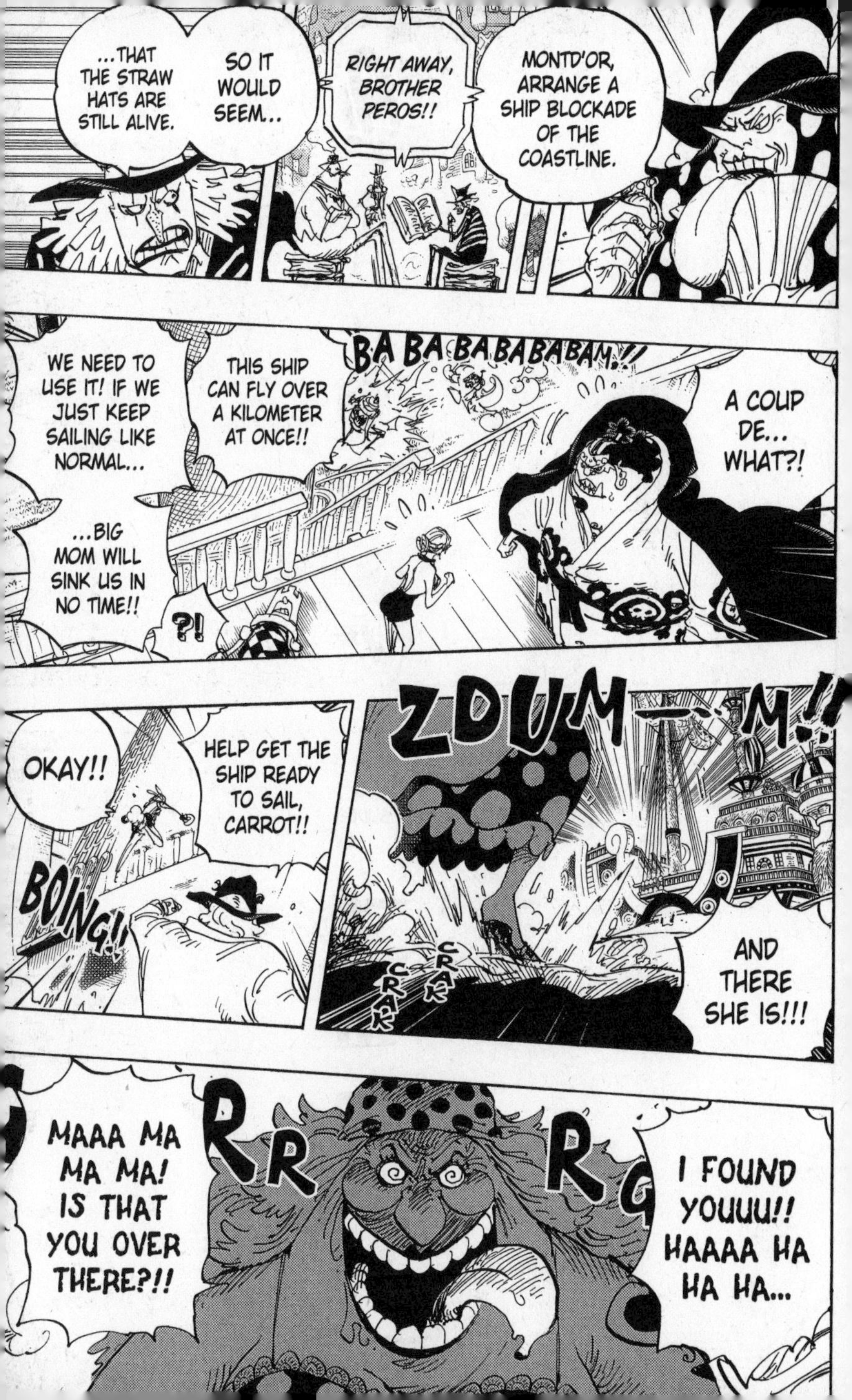
MONTD'OR, ARRANGE A SHIP BLOCKADE OF THE COASTLINE.
RIGHT AWAY, BROTHER PEROS!!
SO IT WOULD SEEM...
...THAT THE STRAW HATS ARE STILL ALIVE.
BA BA BA BABABABAM!!
A COUP DE... WHAT?!
THIS SHIP CAN FLY OVER A KILOMETER AT ONCE!!
WE NEED TO USE IT! IF WE JUST KEEP SAILING LIKE NORMAL...
...BIG MOM WILL SINK US IN NO TIME!!
?!
ZDUM—M!!
AND THERE SHE IS!!!
CRAK
CRAK
HELP GET THE SHIP READY TO SAIL, CARROT!!
OKAY!!
BOING!!
I FOUND YOUUU!! HAAAA HA HA HA...
RRRG
MAAA MA MA MA! IS THAT YOU OVER THERE?!!

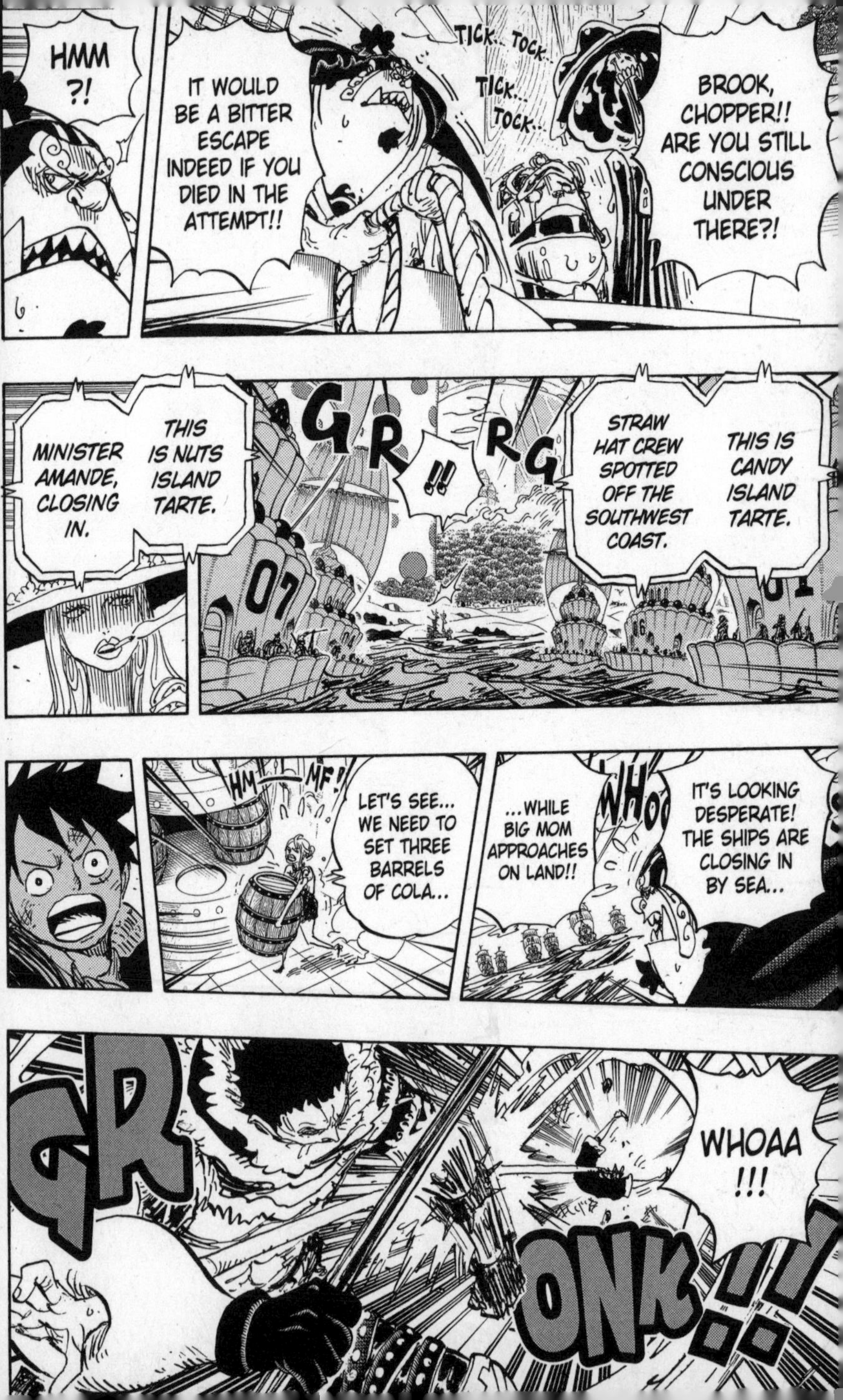
TICK... TOCK...
TICK... TOCK...
BROOK, CHOPPER!! ARE YOU STILL CONSCIOUS UNDER THERE?!
IT WOULD BE A BITTER ESCAPE INDEED IF YOU DIED IN THE ATTEMPT!!
HMM ?!
THIS IS CANDY ISLAND TARTE.
STRAW HAT CREW SPOTTED OFF THE SOUTHWEST COAST.
GRRG!!
THIS IS NUTS ISLAND TARTE.
MINISTER AMANDE, CLOSING IN.
IT'S LOOKING DESPERATE! THE SHIPS ARE CLOSING IN BY SEA...
...WHILE BIG MOM APPROACHES ON LAND!!
WHO
HM—MF!
LET'S SEE... WE NEED TO SET THREE BARRELS OF COLA...
WHOAA !!!
GR
ONK..!!

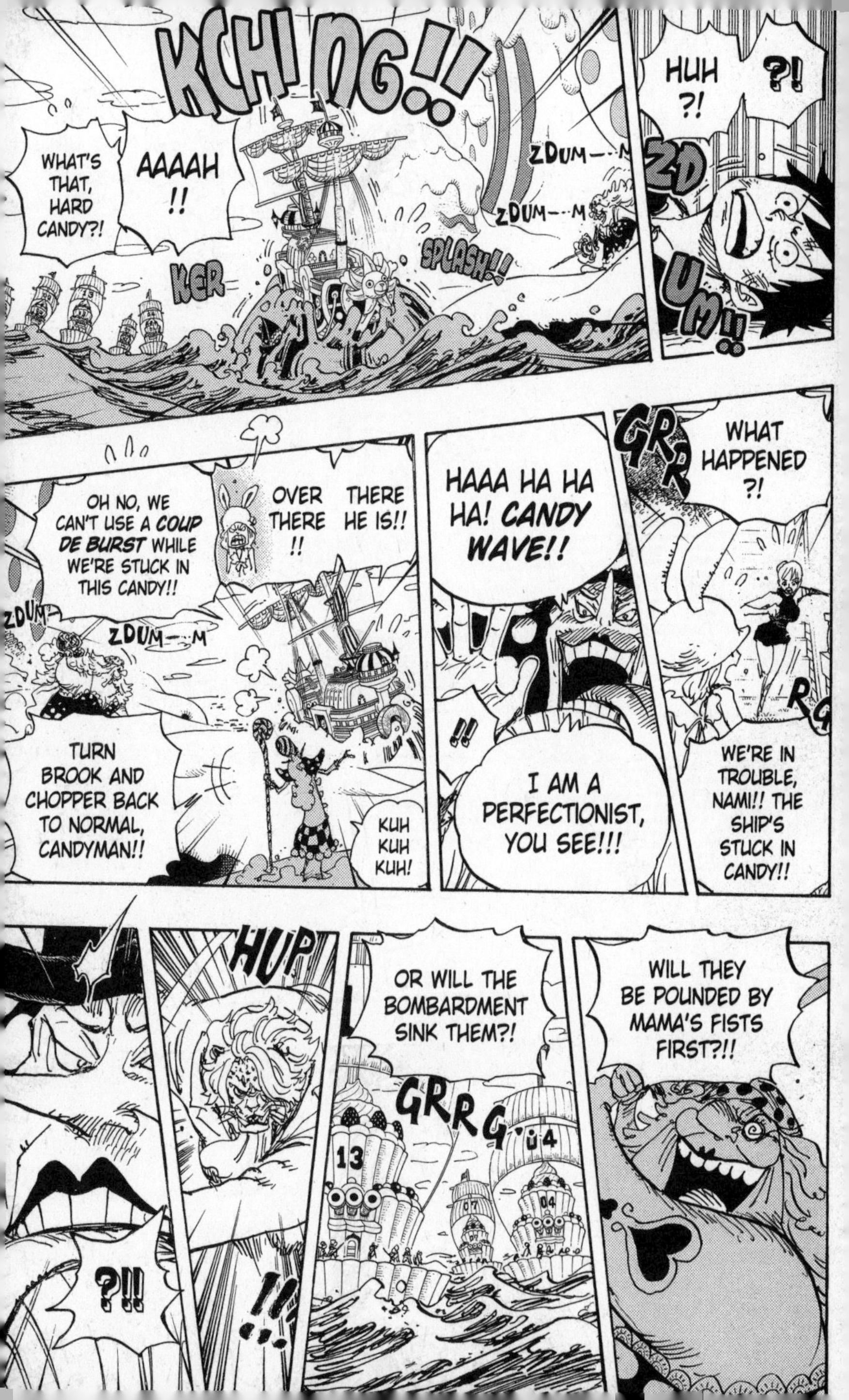
HUH ?!
?!
ZD
UM!!
KCHING!!
ZDUM--M
ZDUM--M
SPLASH!!
AAAAH !!
WHAT'S THAT, HARD CANDY?!
KER
GRR
WHAT HAPPENED ?!
RG
WE'RE IN TROUBLE, NAMI!! THE SHIP'S STUCK IN CANDY!!
HAAA HA HA HA! *CANDY WAVE!!*
!!
I AM A PERFECTIONIST, YOU SEE!!!
THERE HE IS!!
OVER THERE !!
OH NO, WE CAN'T USE A *COUP DE BURST* WHILE WE'RE STUCK IN THIS CANDY!!
ZDUM
ZDUM--M
TURN BROOK AND CHOPPER BACK TO NORMAL, CANDYMAN!!
KUH KUH KUH!
WILL THEY BE POUNDED BY MAMA'S FISTS FIRST?!!
OR WILL THE BOMBARDMENT SINK THEM?!
GRRG
HUP
!!
?!!

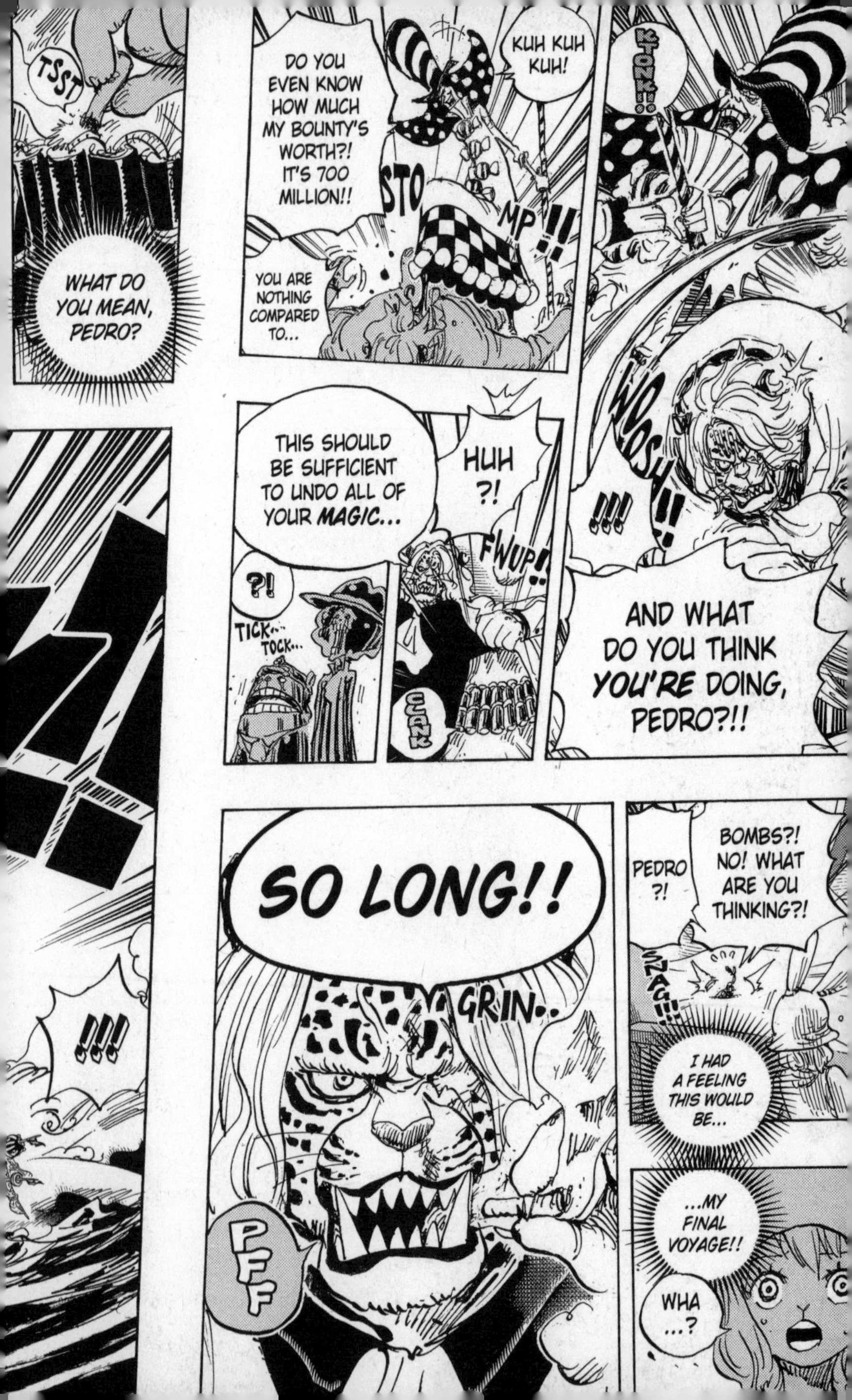
KTONK!!
KUH KUH KUH!
DO YOU EVEN KNOW HOW MUCH MY BOUNTY'S WORTH?! IT'S 700 MILLION!!
STOMP!!
YOU ARE NOTHING COMPARED TO...
TSST
WHAT DO YOU MEAN, PEDRO?
WOOSH!!
!!!
AND WHAT DO YOU THINK YOU'RE DOING, PEDRO?!!
HUH ?!
FWUP!!
THIS SHOULD BE SUFFICIENT TO UNDO ALL OF YOUR MAGIC...
CLANK
?!
TICK... TOCK...
PEDRO ?!
BOMBS?! NO! WHAT ARE YOU THINKING?!
SNAG!!
I HAD A FEELING THIS WOULD BE...
...MY FINAL VOYAGE!!
WHA ...?
SO LONG!!
GRIN..
PFF
!!!
TSST

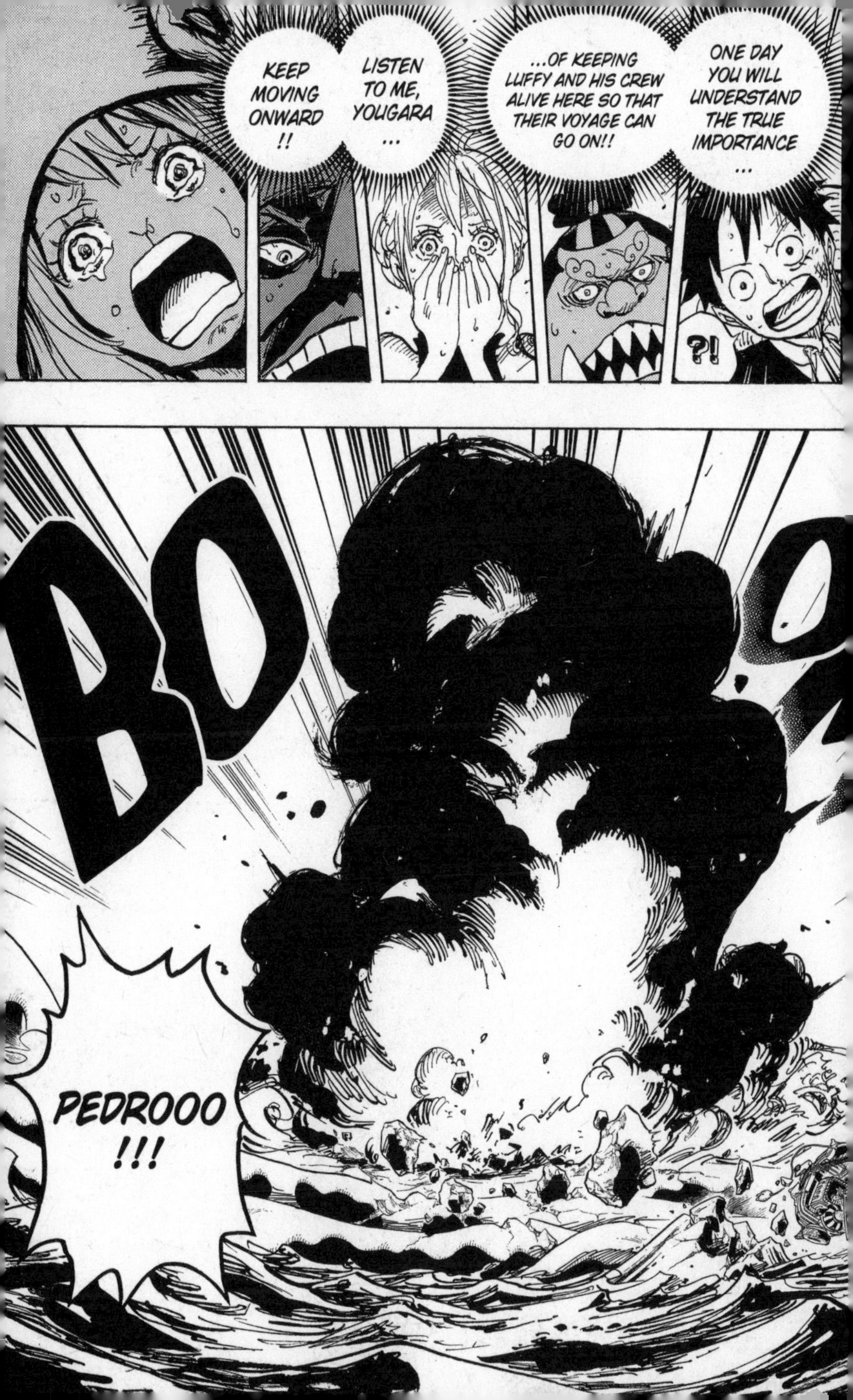
?!
ONE DAY YOU WILL UNDERSTAND THE TRUE IMPORTANCE ...
...OF KEEPING LUFFY AND HIS CREW ALIVE HERE SO THAT THEIR VOYAGE CAN GO ON!!
LISTEN TO ME, YOUGARA ...
KEEP MOVING ONWARD !!
BO
PEDROOO !!!

PEDRO OF THE MINK GUARDIANS

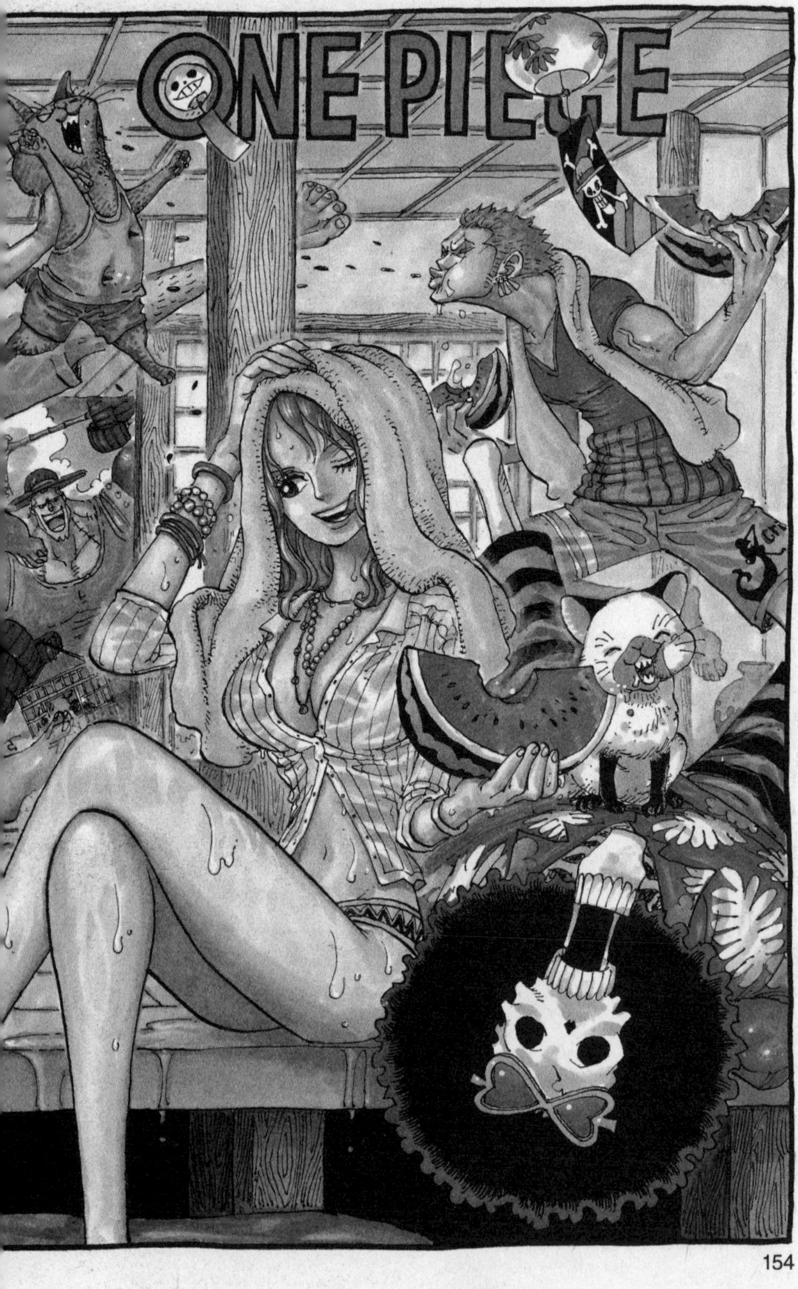
ONE PIECE

Chapter 878: COMMANDER

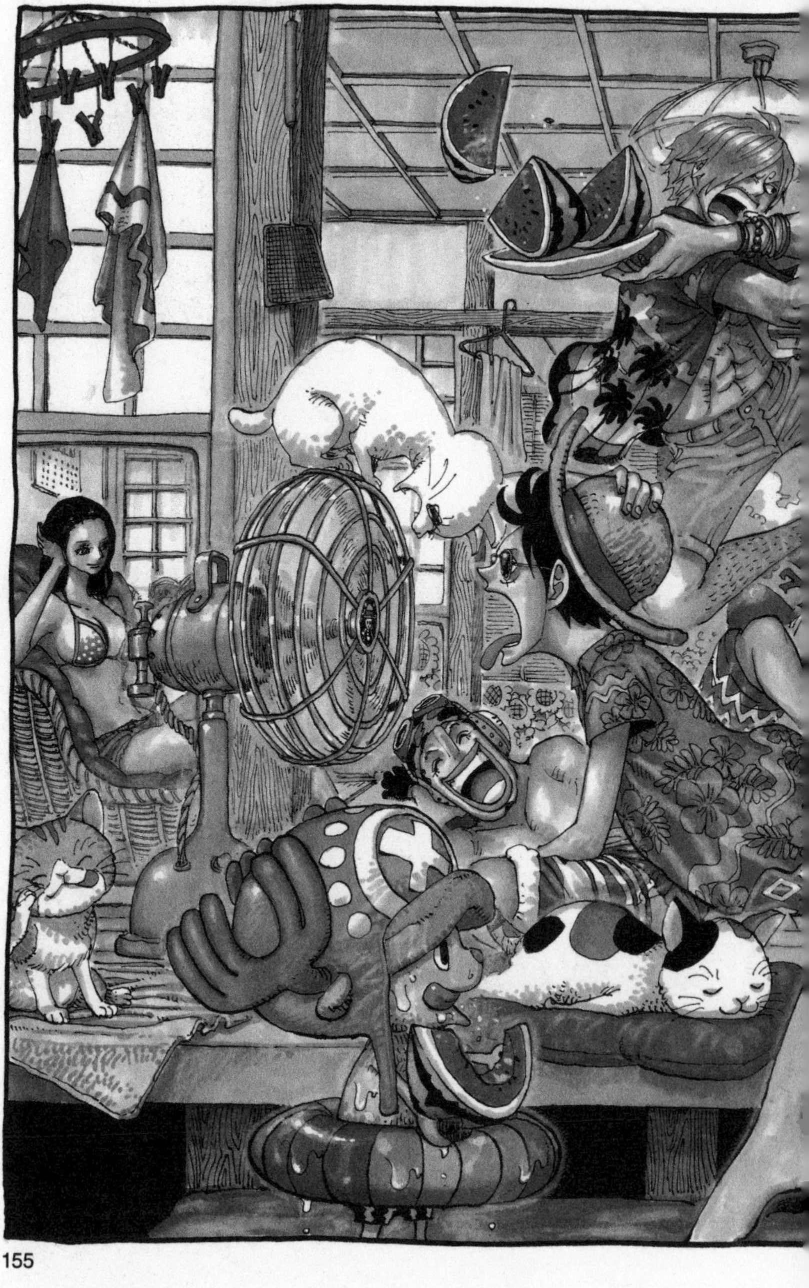

vol.87
ONE PIECE

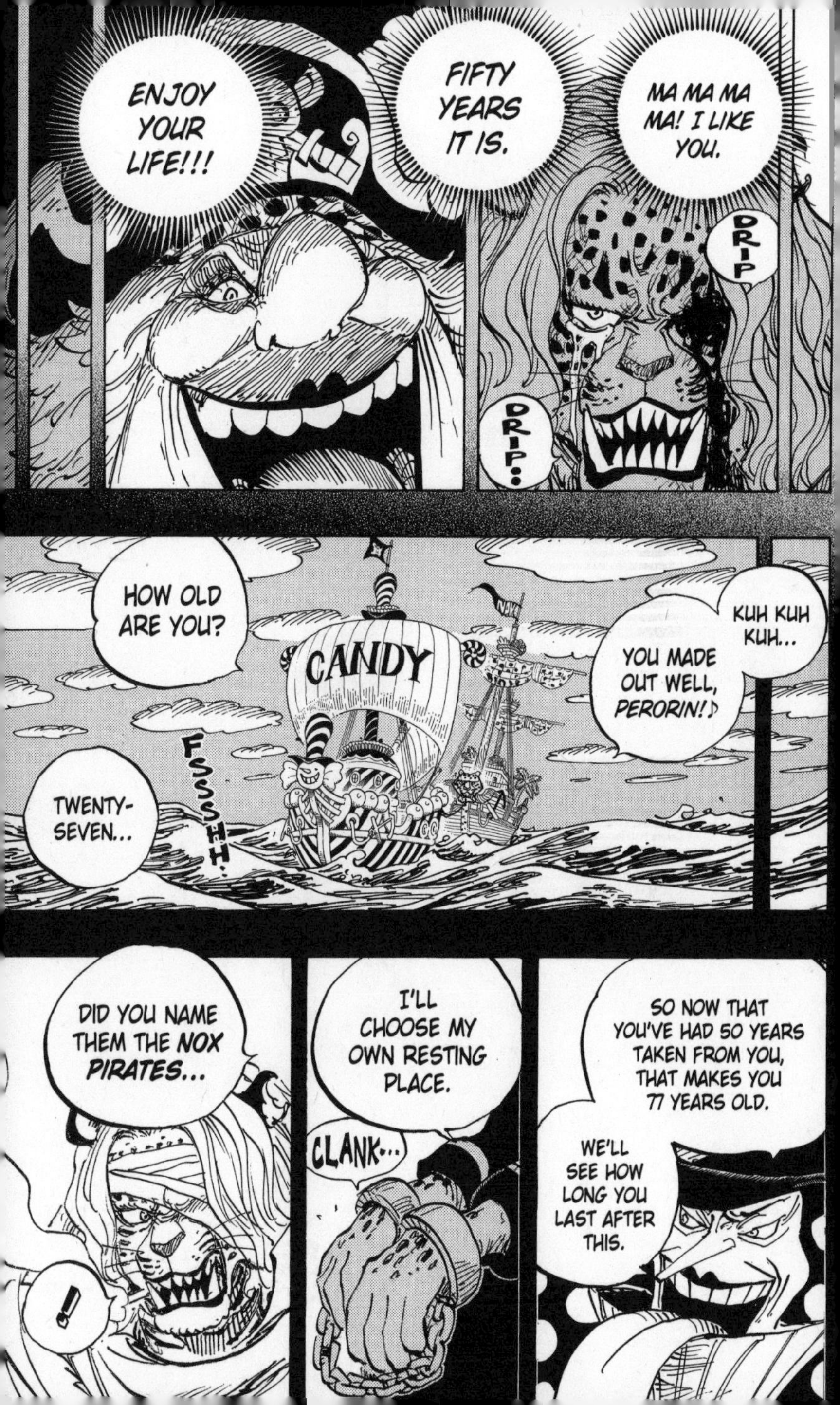
MA MA MA MA! I LIKE YOU.
FIFTY YEARS IT IS.
ENJOY YOUR LIFE!!!
DRIP
DRIP..
KUH KUH KUH...
YOU MADE OUT WELL, PERORIN!♪
CANDY
HOW OLD ARE YOU?
FSSSHH
TWENTY-SEVEN...
SO NOW THAT YOU'VE HAD 50 YEARS TAKEN FROM YOU, THAT MAKES YOU 77 YEARS OLD.
WE'LL SEE HOW LONG YOU LAST AFTER THIS.
I'LL CHOOSE MY OWN RESTING PLACE.
CLANK...
DID YOU NAME THEM THE NOX PIRATES...
!

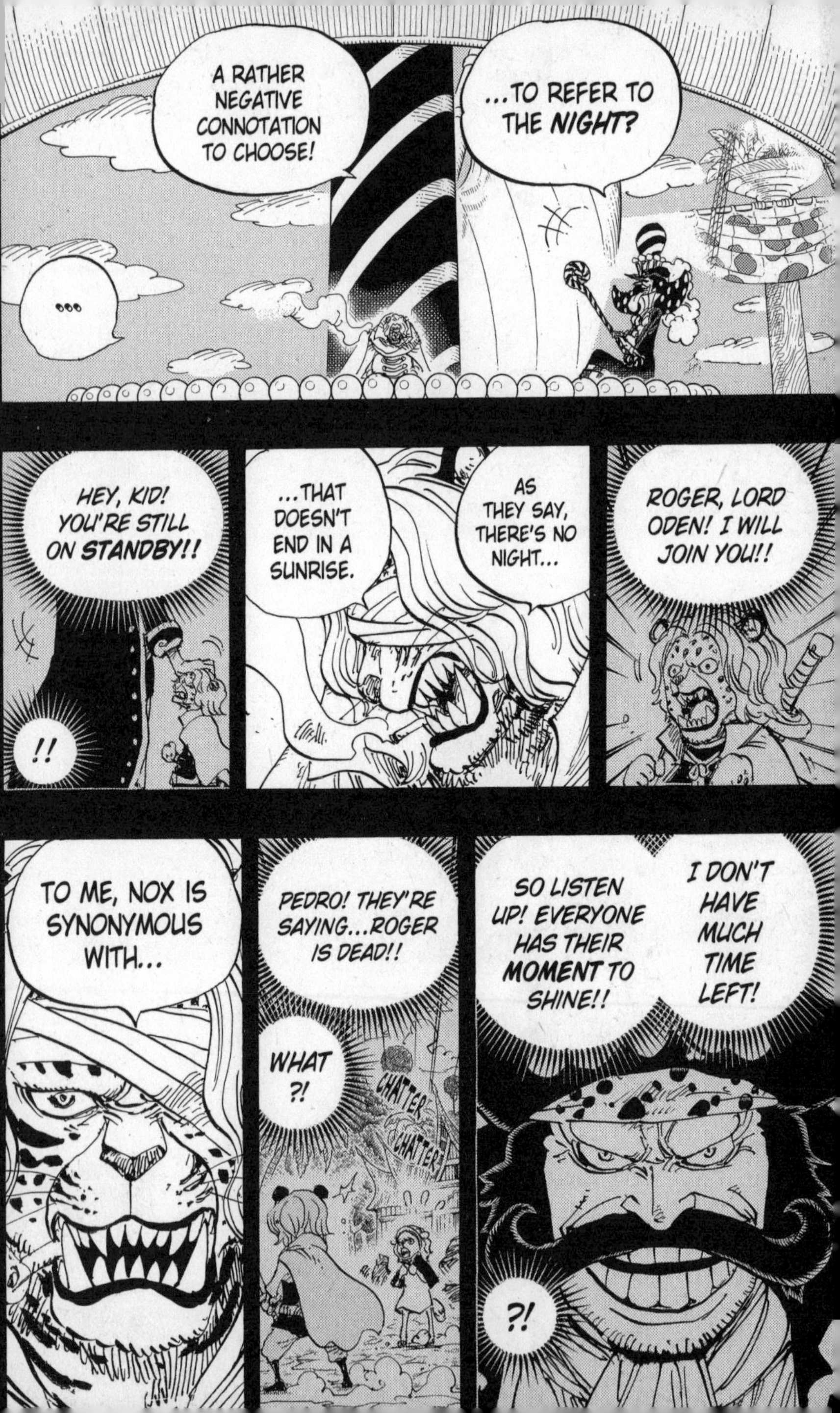
...TO REFER TO THE NIGHT?
A RATHER NEGATIVE CONNOTATION TO CHOOSE!
...
ROGER, LORD ODEN! I WILL JOIN YOU!!
AS THEY SAY, THERE'S NO NIGHT...
...THAT DOESN'T END IN A SUNRISE.
HEY, KID! YOU'RE STILL ON STANDBY!!
!!
I DON'T HAVE MUCH TIME LEFT!
SO LISTEN UP! EVERYONE HAS THEIR MOMENT TO SHINE!!
?!
PEDRO! THEY'RE SAYING...ROGER IS DEAD!!
WHAT ?!
CHATTER
CHATTER
TO ME, NOX IS SYNONYMOUS WITH...

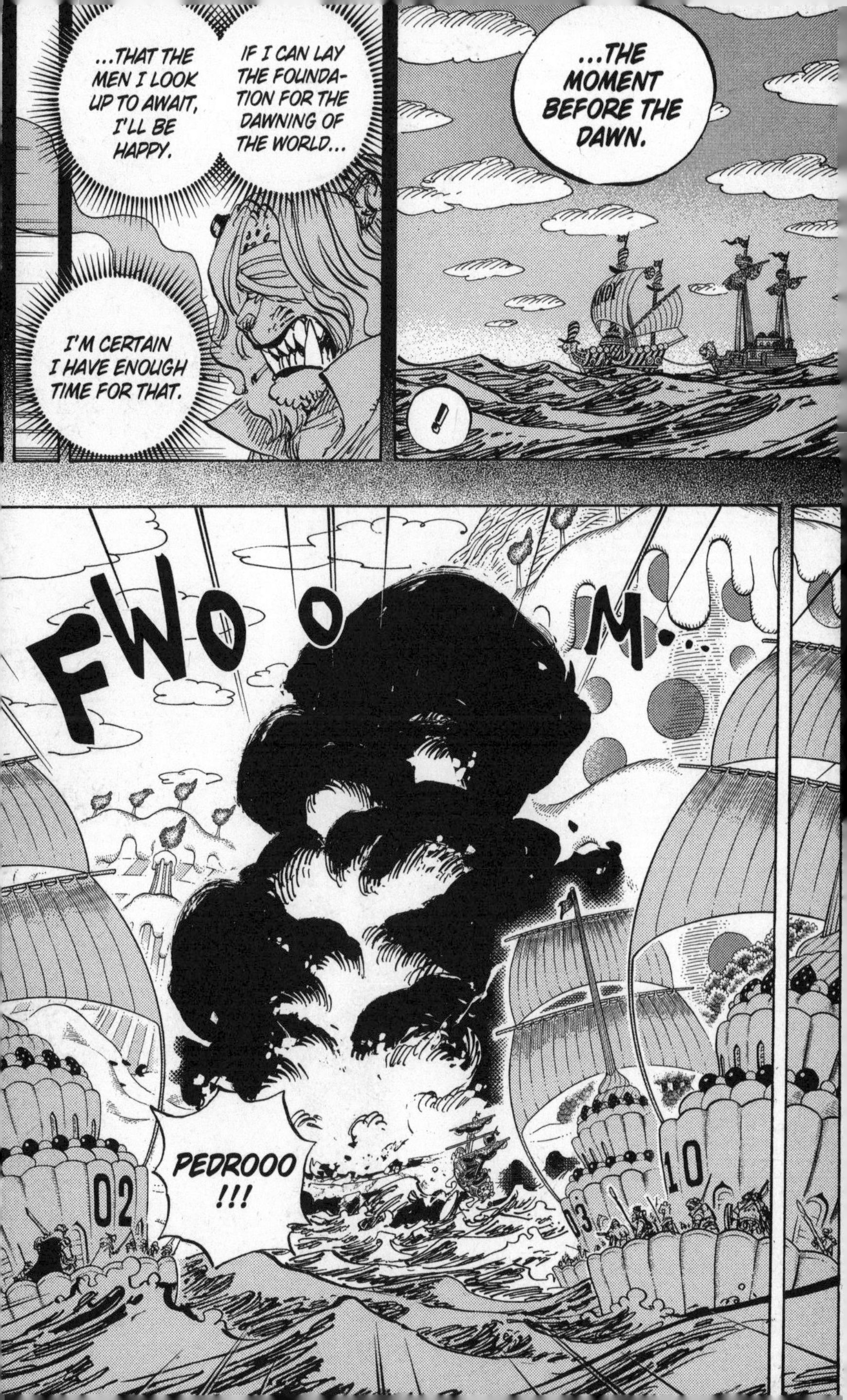
...THE MOMENT BEFORE THE DAWN.
!
IF I CAN LAY THE FOUNDATION FOR THE DAWNING OF THE WORLD...
...THAT THE MEN I LOOK UP TO AWAIT, I'LL BE HAPPY.
I'M CERTAIN I HAVE ENOUGH TIME FOR THAT.
FWOOOM...
PEDROOO!!!
02
03
10

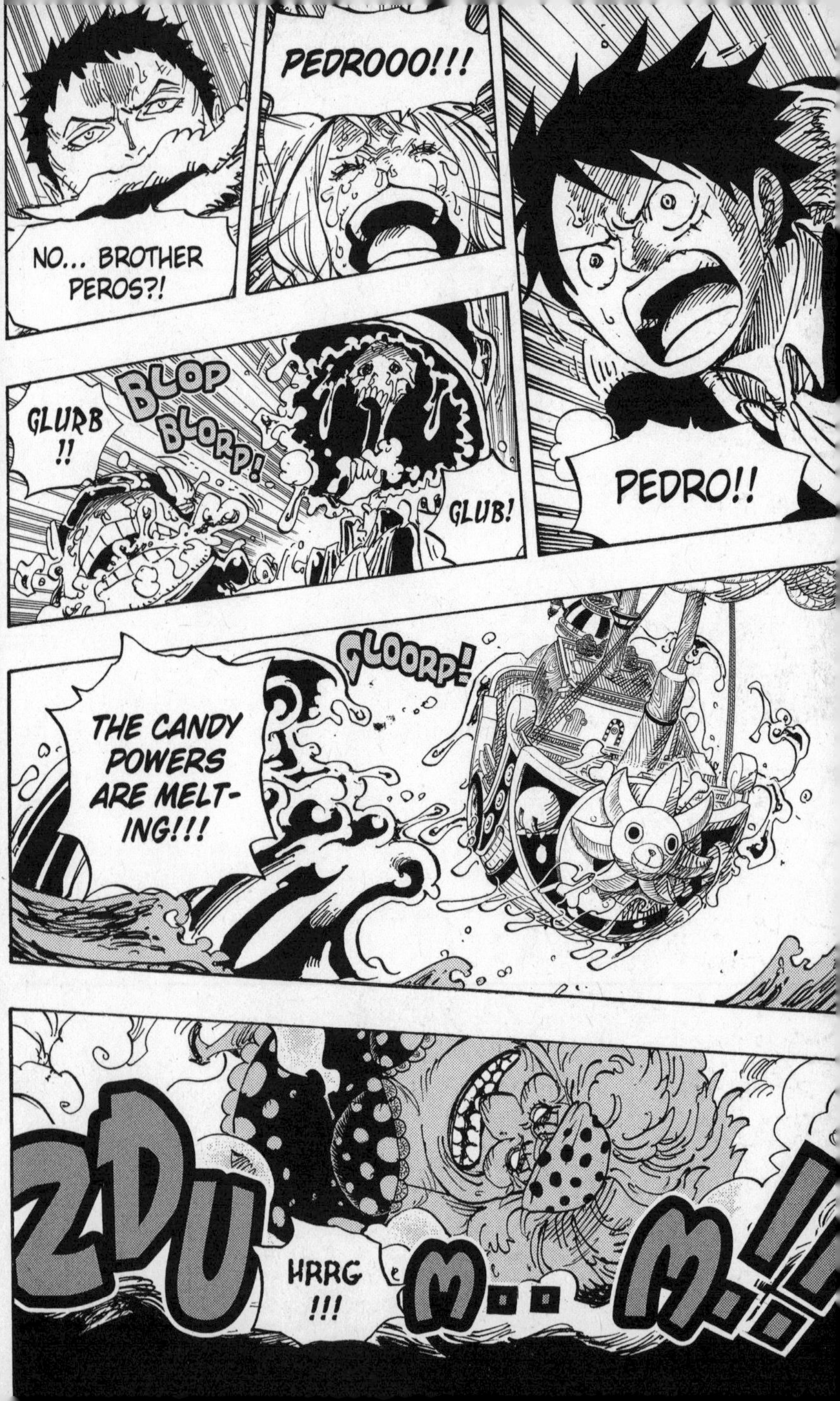
PEDRO!!
PEDROOO!!!
NO... BROTHER PEROS?!
GLUB!
BLOP BLORP!
GLURB !!
GLOORP!
THE CANDY POWERS ARE MELT-ING!!!
ZDUM...M.!!
HRRG !!!

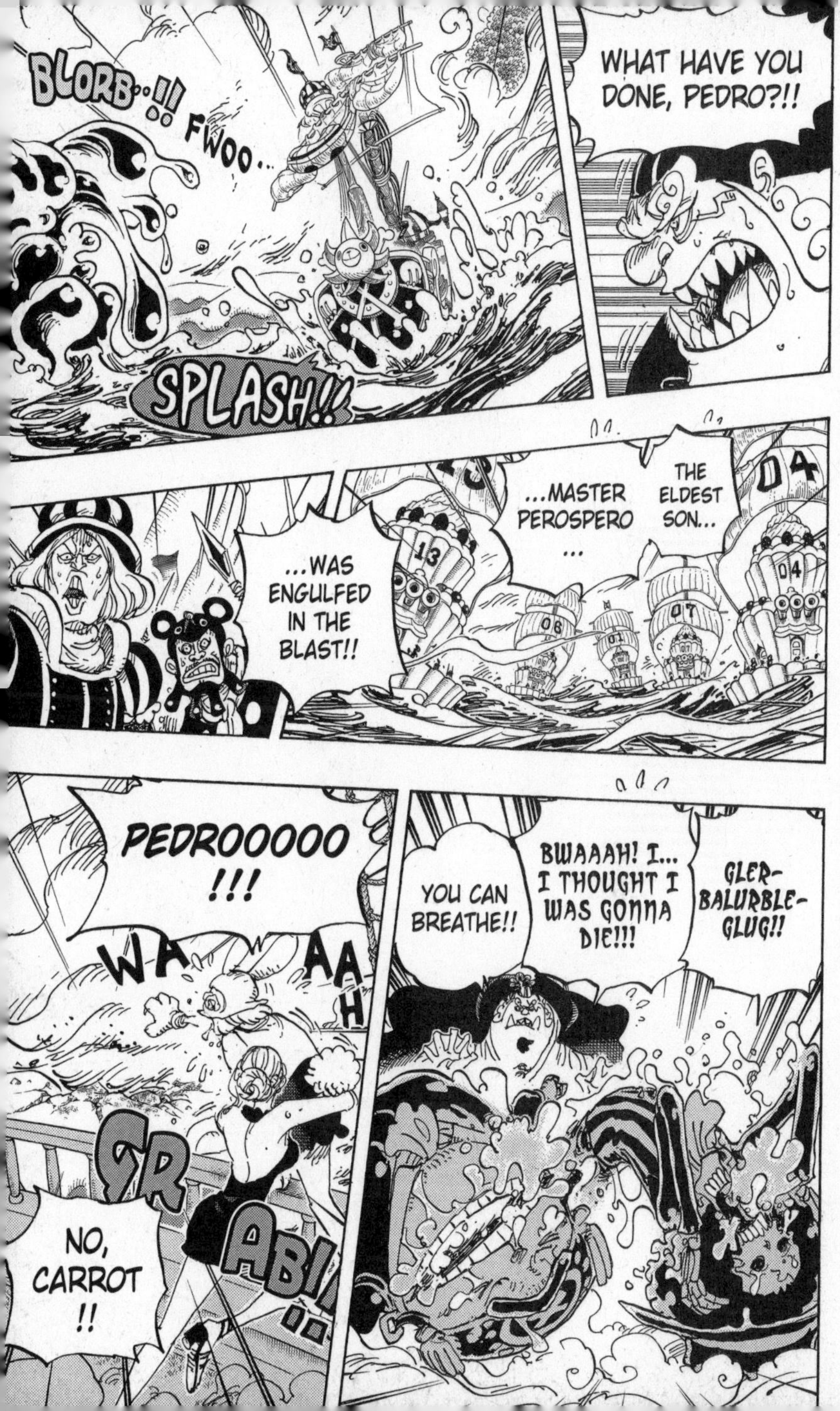
WHAT HAVE YOU DONE, PEDRO?!!
BLORB..!!
FWOO...
SPLASH!!
THE ELDEST SON...
...MASTER PEROSPERO ...
...WAS ENGULFED IN THE BLAST!!
GLER-BALURBLE-GLUG!!
BWAAAH! I... I THOUGHT I WAS GONNA DIE!!!
YOU CAN BREATHE!!
PEDROOOOO !!!
WAAAH
GRAB!!
NO, CARROT !!

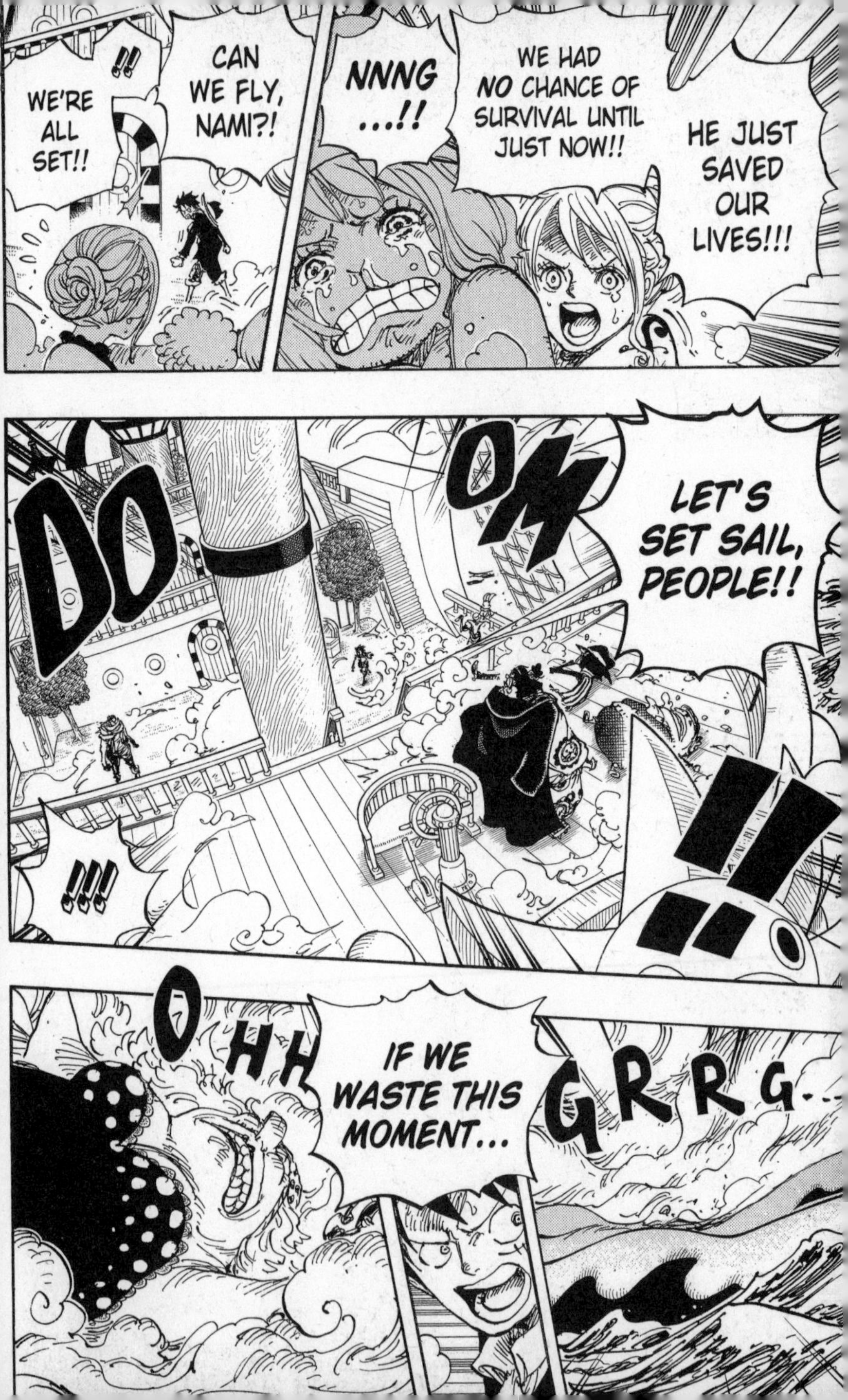
HE JUST SAVED OUR LIVES!!!
WE HAD NO CHANCE OF SURVIVAL UNTIL JUST NOW!!
NNNG ...!!
CAN WE FLY, NAMI?!
!!
WE'RE ALL SET!!
LET'S SET SAIL, PEOPLE!!
!!
DO OM
!!!
GRRRG...
IF WE WASTE THIS MOMENT...
OHH

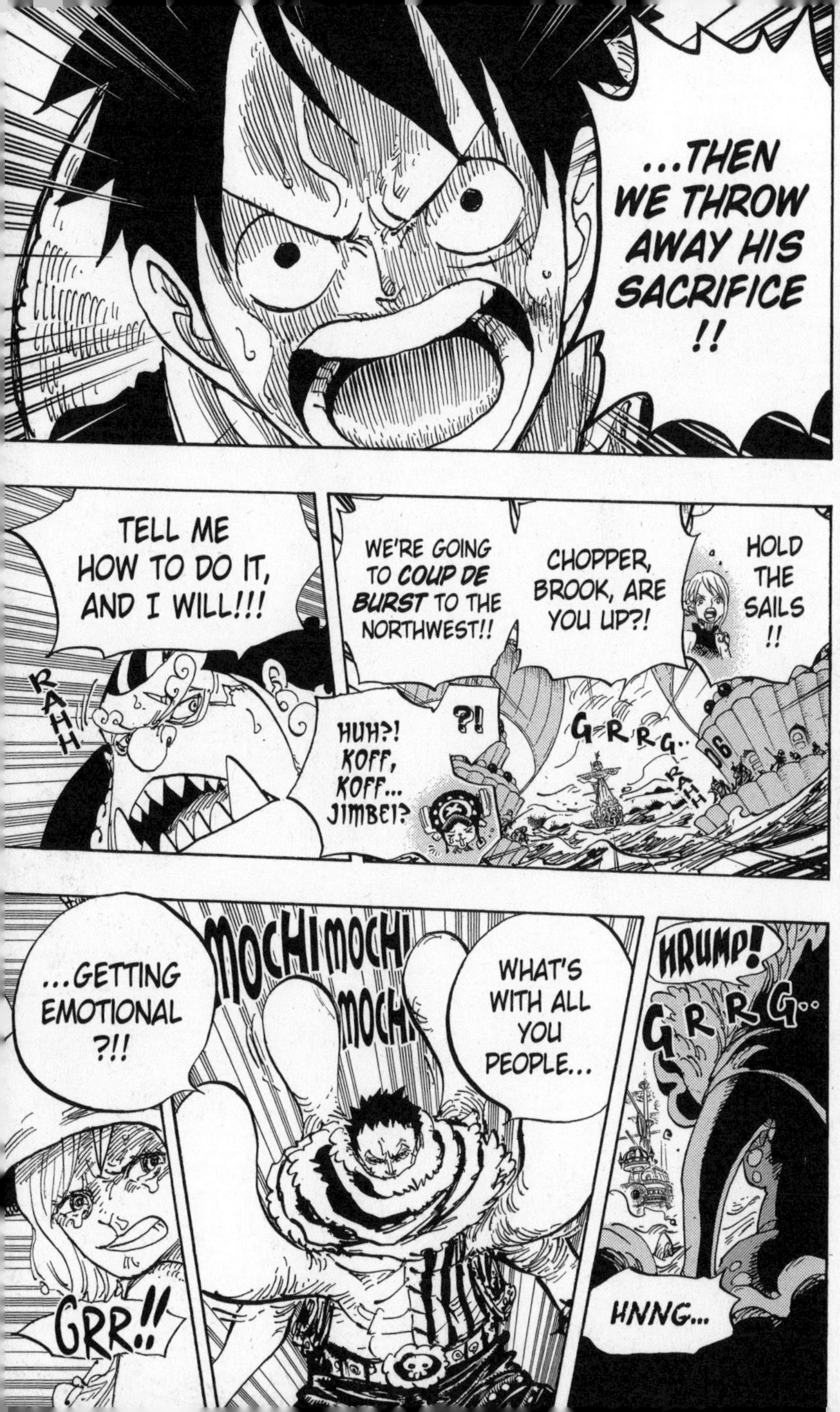
...THEN WE THROW AWAY HIS SACRIFICE!!
HOLD THE SAILS!!
CHOPPER, BROOK, ARE YOU UP?!
WE'RE GOING TO ***COUP DE BURST*** TO THE NORTHWEST!!
?!
HUH?! KOFF, KOFF... JIMBEI?
GRRG..
RAHH
TELL ME HOW TO DO IT, AND I WILL!!!
RAHH
HRUMP!
GRRG..
HNNG...
WHAT'S WITH ALL YOU PEOPLE...
MOCHI MOCHI MOCHI
...GETTING EMOTIONAL?!!
GRR!!

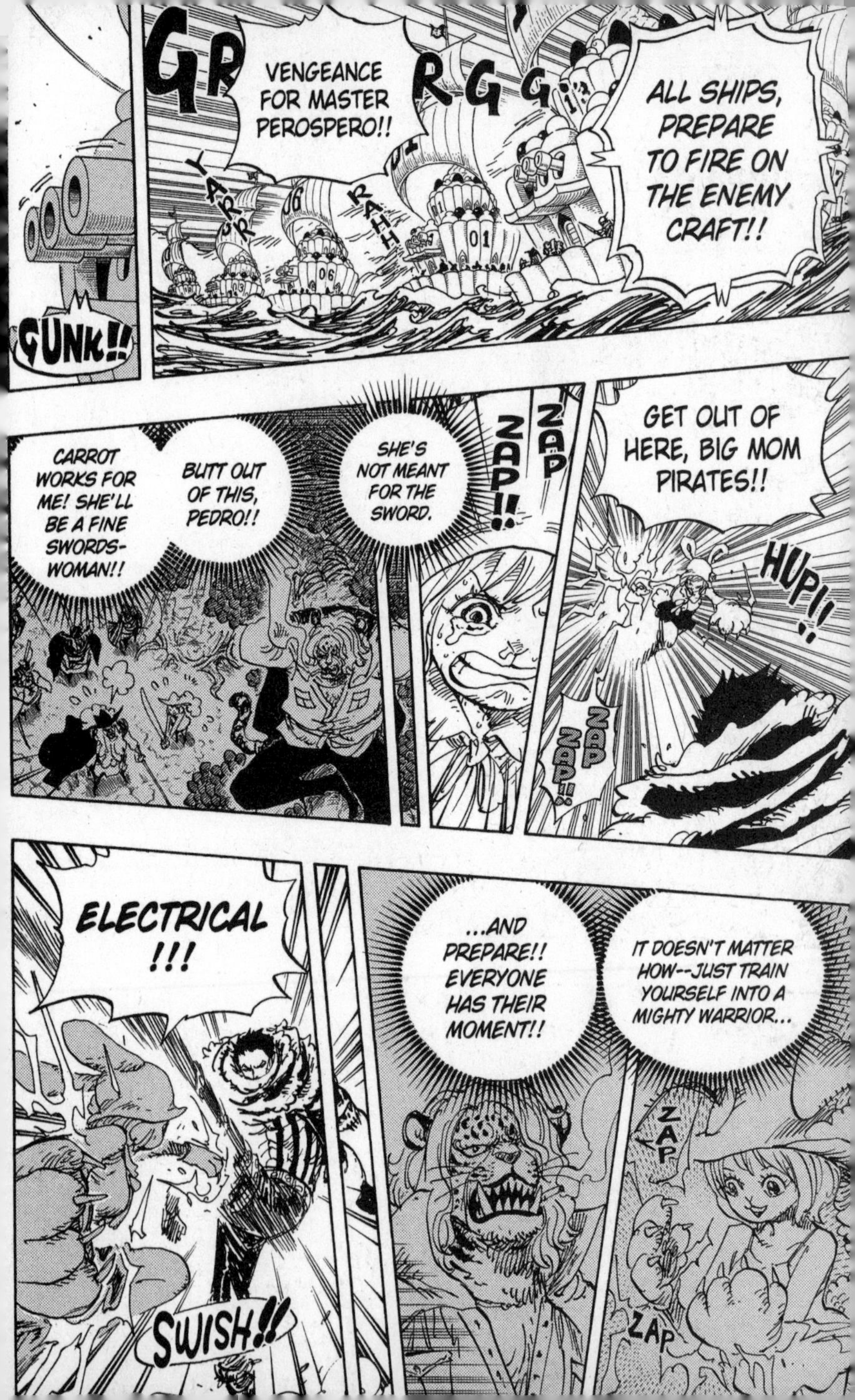
ALL SHIPS, PREPARE TO FIRE ON THE ENEMY CRAFT!!
GR
RGG G
VENGEANCE FOR MASTER PEROSPERO!!
RAHH
YARRR
GUNK!!
GET OUT OF HERE, BIG MOM PIRATES!!
HUP!!
ZAP ZAP!!
ZAP ZAP!!
SHE'S NOT MEANT FOR THE SWORD.
BUTT OUT OF THIS, PEDRO!!
CARROT WORKS FOR ME! SHE'LL BE A FINE SWORDS-WOMAN!!
IT DOESN'T MATTER HOW--JUST TRAIN YOURSELF INTO A MIGHTY WARRIOR...
ZAP
ZAP
...AND PREPARE!! EVERYONE HAS THEIR MOMENT!!
ELECTRICAL!!!
SWISH!!

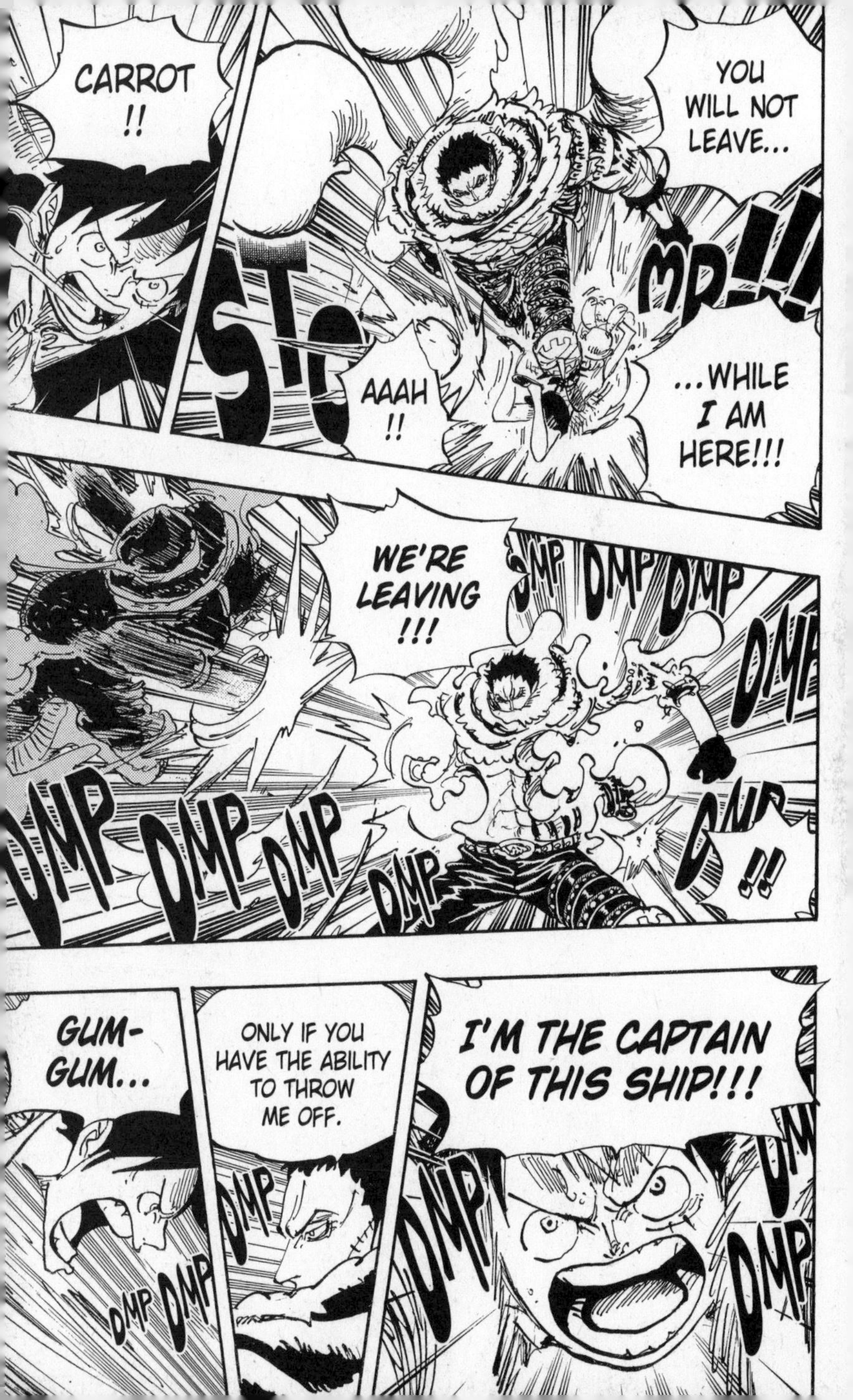

YOU WILL NOT LEAVE...
...WHILE I AM HERE!!!
AAAH !!
CARROT !!
WE'RE LEAVING !!!
DMP DMP DMP
DMP
DMP DMP DMP DMP
I'M THE CAPTAIN OF THIS SHIP!!!
DMP
ONLY IF YOU HAVE THE ABILITY TO THROW ME OFF.
DMP
GUM-GUM...
DMP DMP

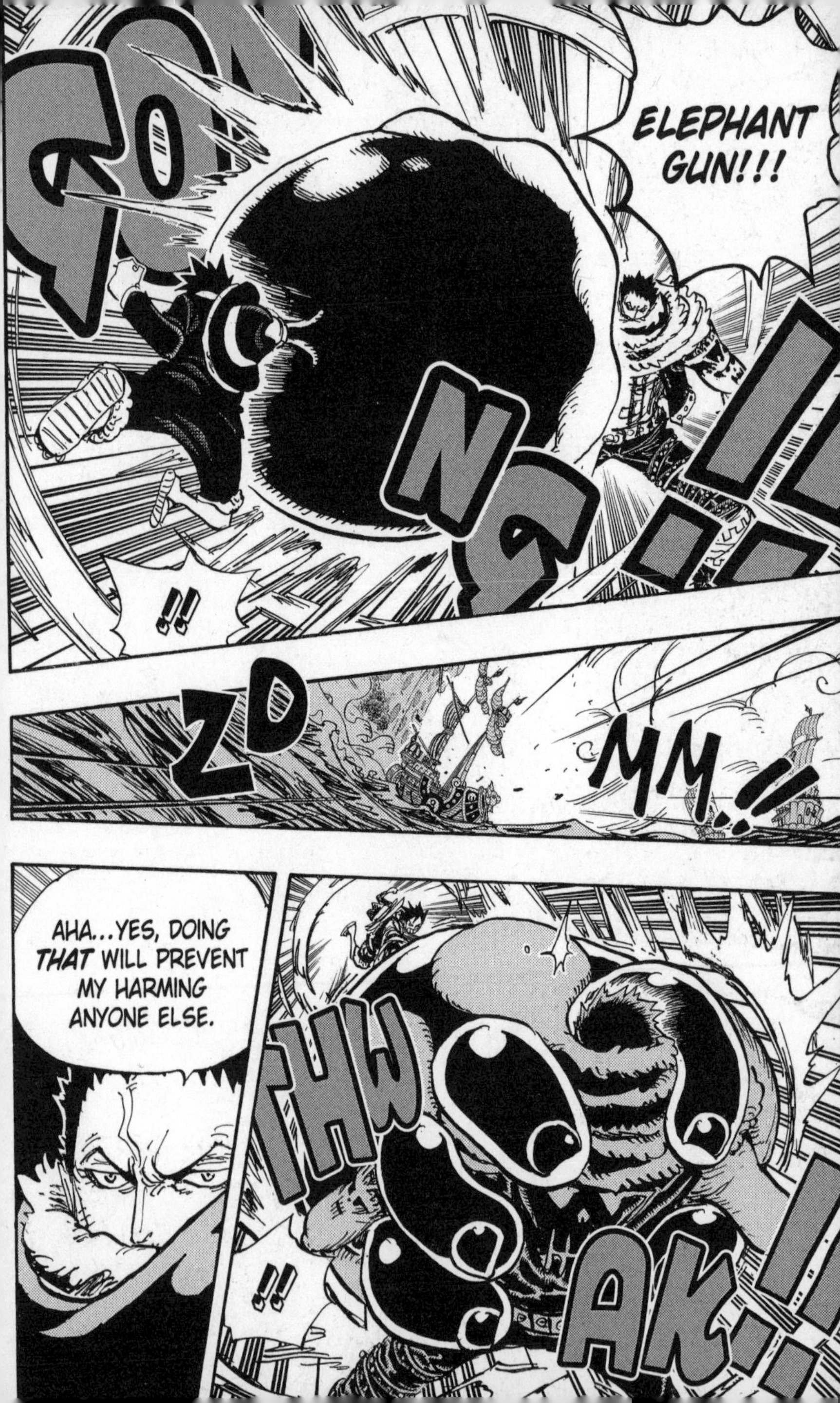
ELEPHANT GUN!!!
GONG!!
!!
ZDMM!!
THWSAK!!
!!
AHA...YES, DOING *THAT* WILL PREVENT MY HARMING ANYONE ELSE.

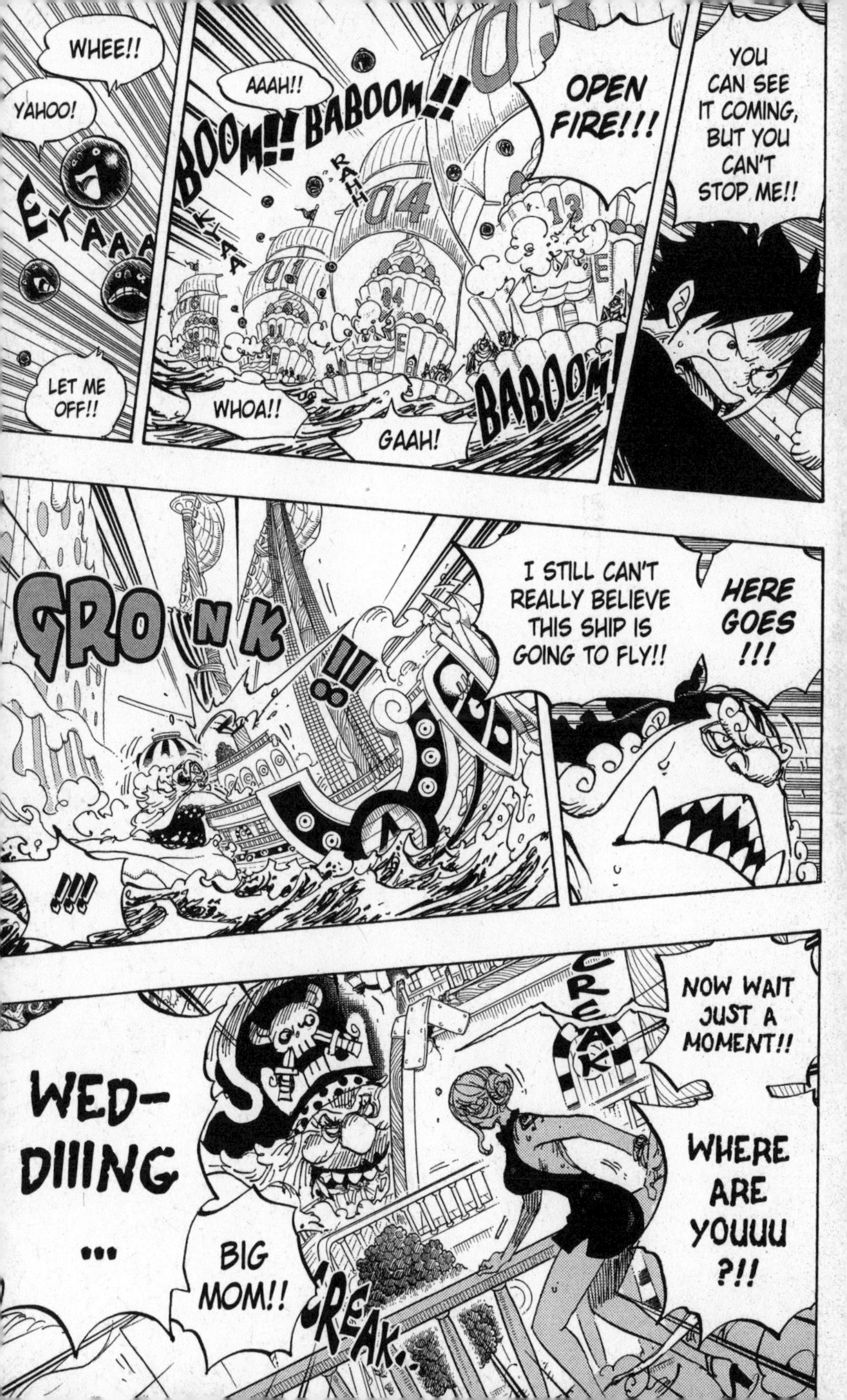

YOU CAN SEE IT COMING, BUT YOU CAN'T STOP ME!!
OPEN FIRE!!!
AAAH!!
BOOM!! BABOOM!!
RAHH
KYAA
BABOOM!
WHOA!!
GAAH!
WHEE!!
YAHOO!
EYAAA
LET ME OFF!!
HERE GOES!!!
I STILL CAN'T REALLY BELIEVE THIS SHIP IS GOING TO FLY!!
GRONK
!!
!!!
NOW WAIT JUST A MOMENT!!
WHERE ARE YOUUU?!!
CREAK
CREAK..
BIG MOM!!
WED-DIIING...

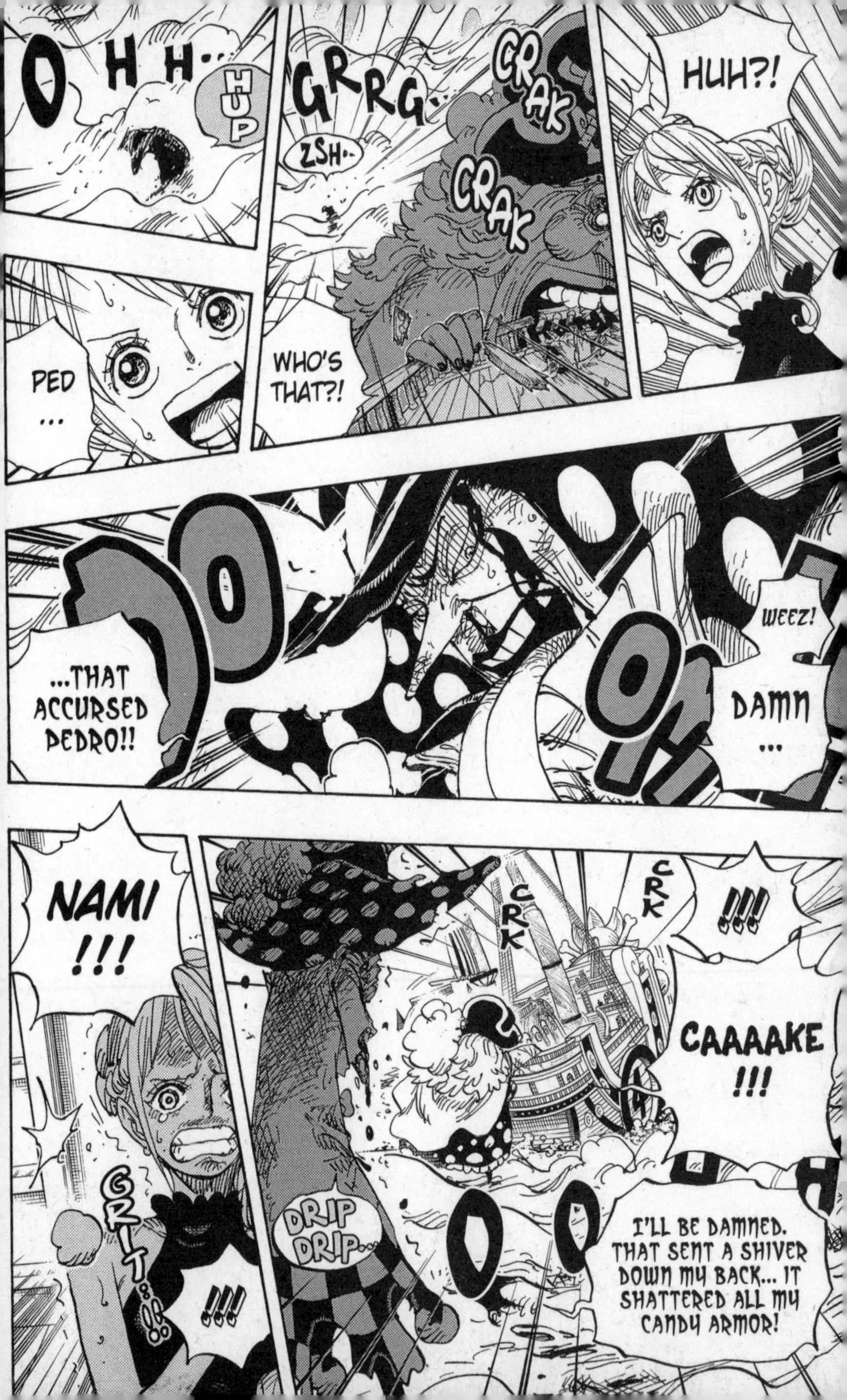
HUH?!
GRRRG..
CRAK
CRAK
ZSH..
WHO'S THAT?!
OHH...
HUP
PED ...
WEEZ!
DAMN ...
...THAT ACCURSED PEDRO!!
!!!
CRK
CRK
CAAAAKE !!!
I'LL BE DAMNED. THAT SENT A SHIVER DOWN MY BACK... IT SHATTERED ALL MY CANDY ARMOR!
DRIP DRIP..
NAMI !!!
GRIT
!!!

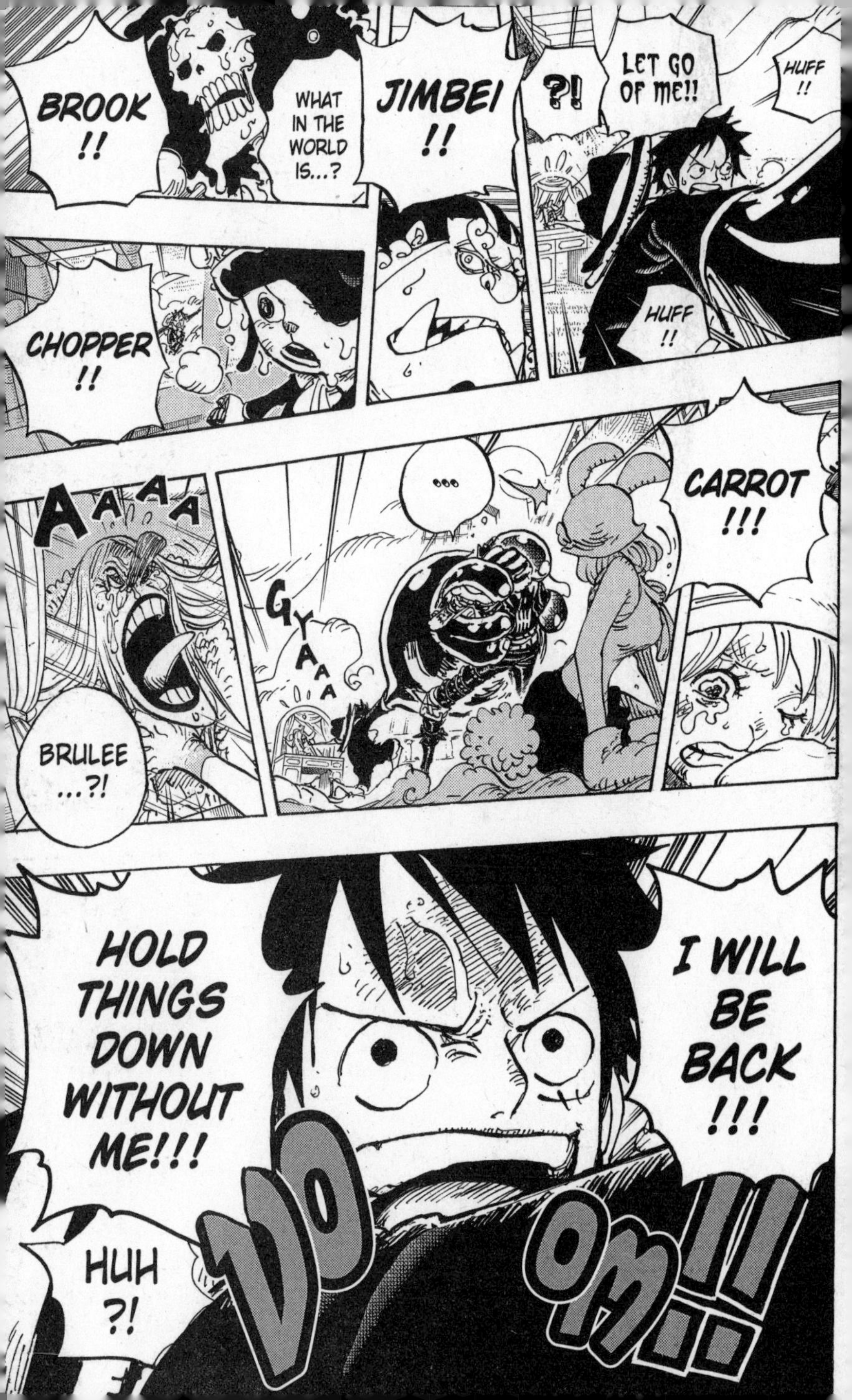
HUFF !!
LET GO OF ME!!
?!
HUFF !!
JIMBEI !!
WHAT IN THE WORLD IS...?
BROOK !!
CHOPPER !!
CARROT !!!
...
GYAAAA
AAAA
BRULEE ...?!
I WILL BE BACK !!!
VOOM!!
HOLD THINGS DOWN WITHOUT ME!!!
HUH ?!

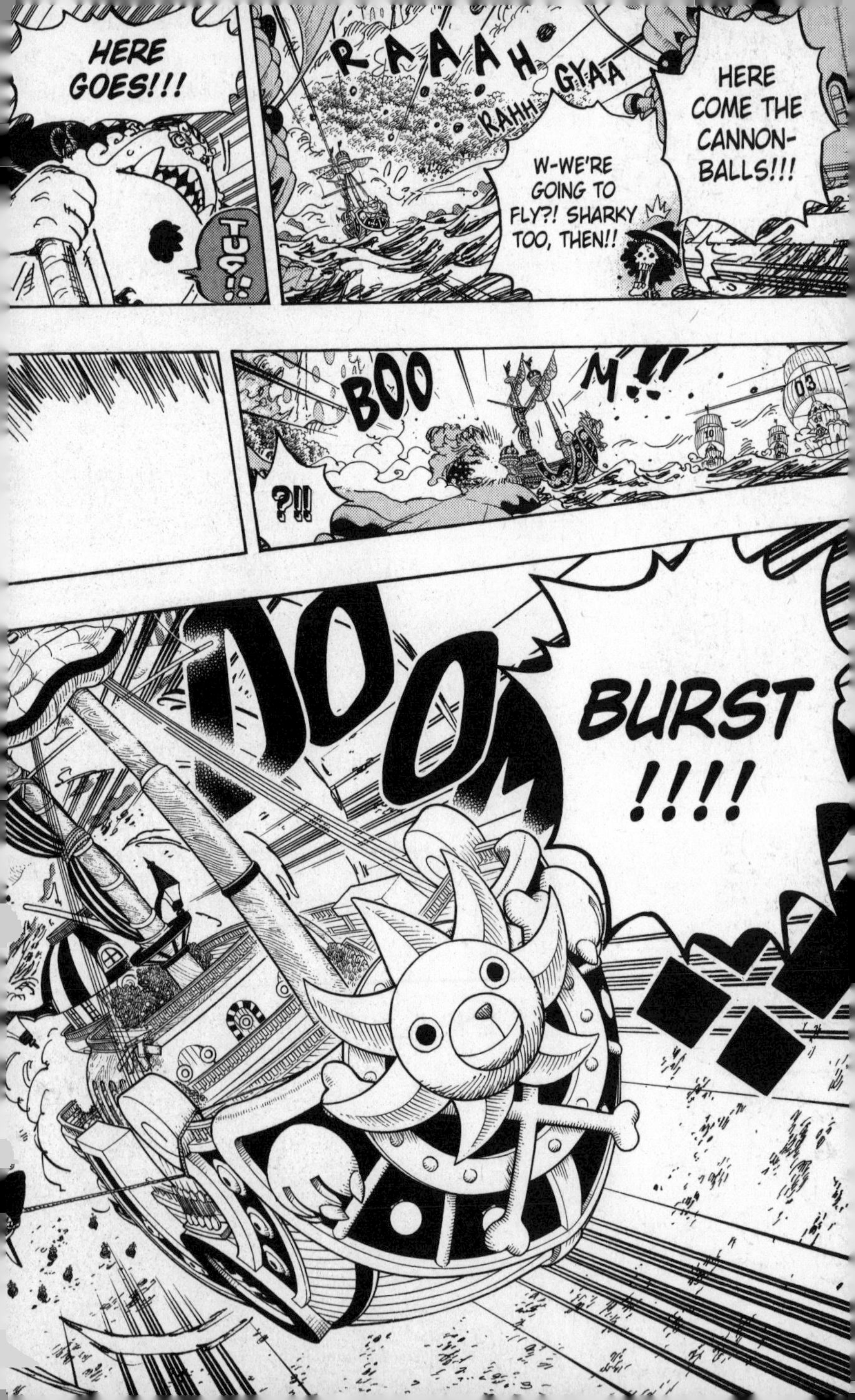
HERE COME THE CANNON-BALLS!!!
W-WE'RE GOING TO FLY?! SHARKY TOO, THEN!!
RAAAAH
GYAA
RAHH
HERE GOES!!!
TUG!!
BOOM!!
?!!
DOOM
BURST!!!!

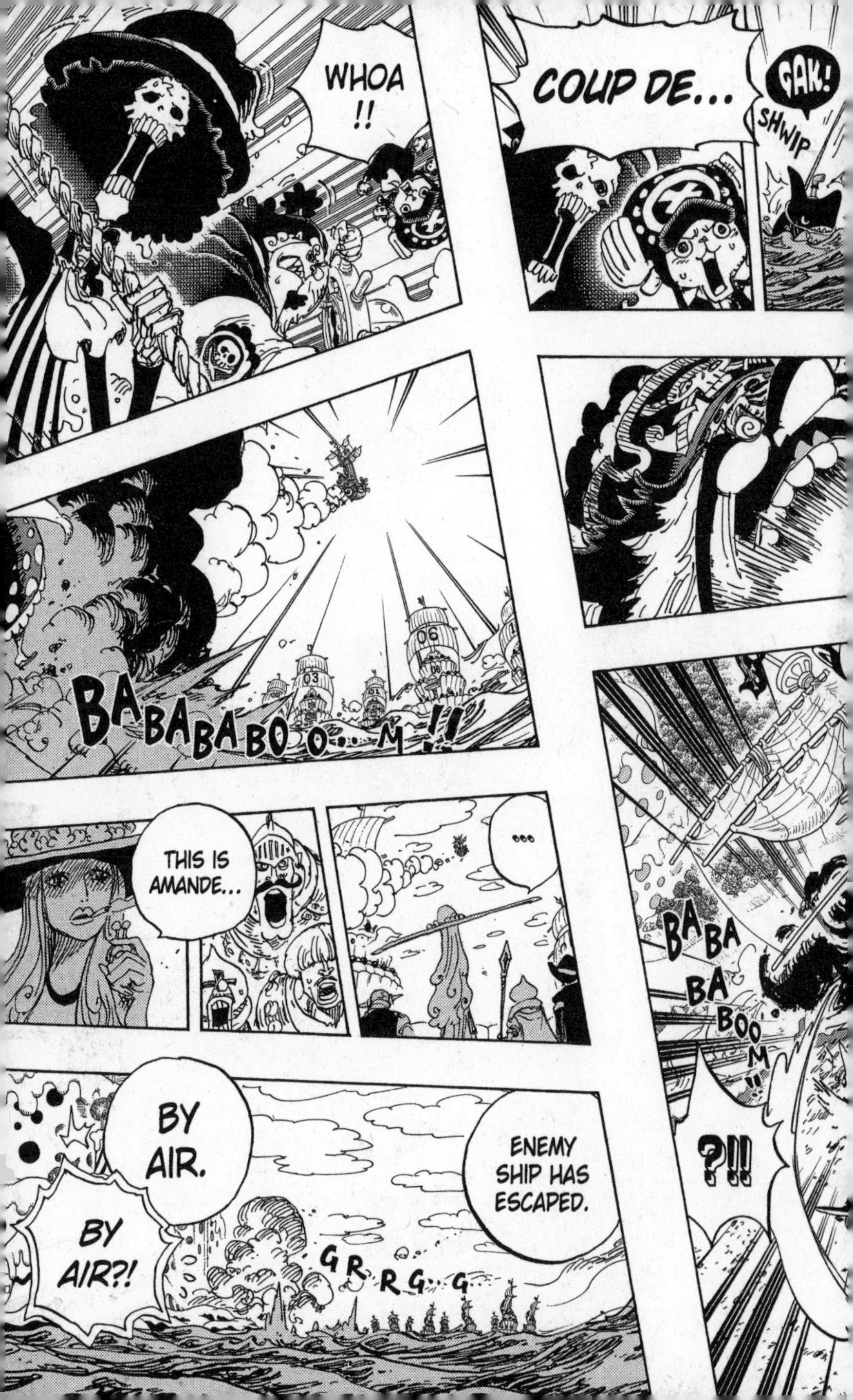

GAK!
SHWIP
COUP DE...
WHOA !!
BABABABOO...M!!
BA BA BA BOOM!!
?!!
...
THIS IS AMANDE...
ENEMY SHIP HAS ESCAPED.
BY AIR.
BY AIR?!
GRRGG

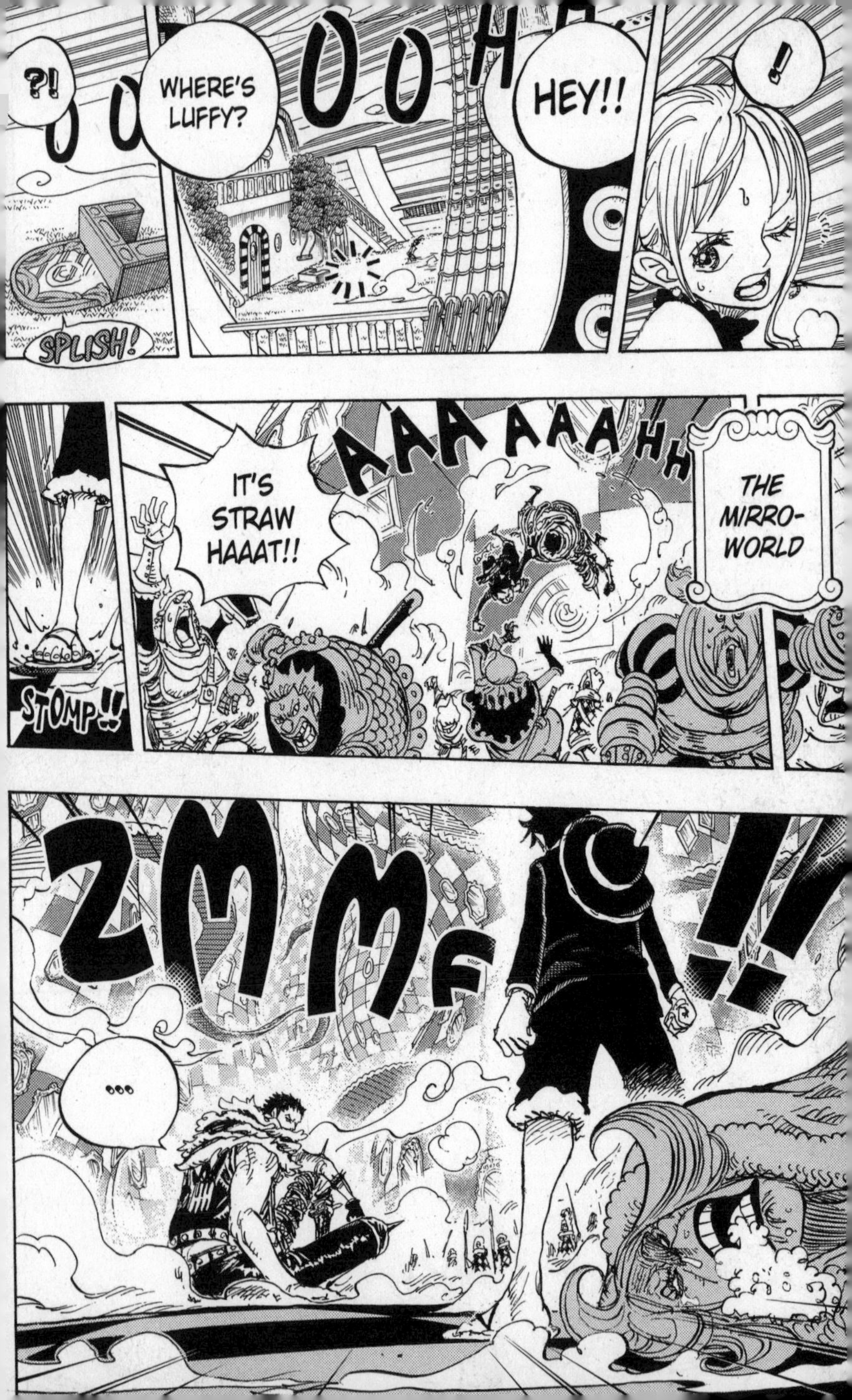
!
HEY!!
OOOOOH
WHERE'S LUFFY?
?!
SPLISH!
THE MIRRO-WORLD
AAAAAAHH
IT'S STRAW HAAAT!!
STOMP!!
ZMMF!!
...

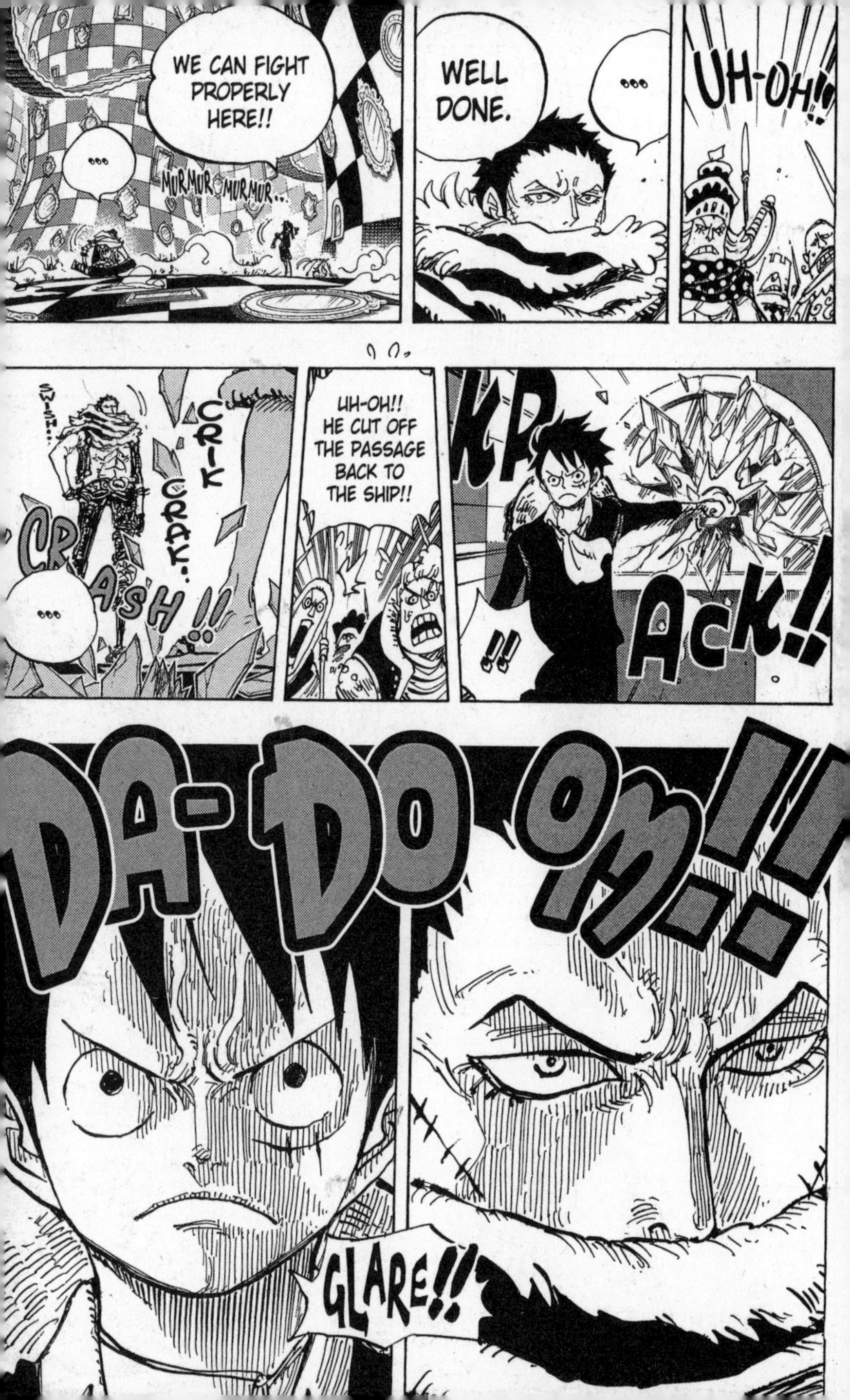
UH-OH!!
...
WELL DONE.
WE CAN FIGHT PROPERLY HERE!!
...
MURMUR MURMUR...
KR
ACK!!
!!
UH-OH!! HE CUT OFF THE PASSAGE BACK TO THE SHIP!!
SWISH..
CRIK
CRAK..
CRASH!!
...
DA-DOOM!!
GLARE!!

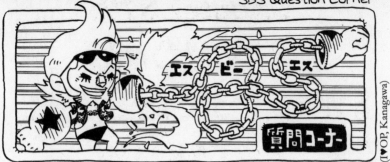

(I♥OP, Kanagawa)

Q: Hiya, Odacchi! ☆ My birthday is May 24, but there are no characters who share it! (cries) So if you don't mind, I'd like to suggest (5) *Go-han wa* (2) *Ninjin* (4) *Shi-rousagi* ("The white bunny whose food is carrots") for Carrot's birthday! How about that?

--Ryo

A: Whaaaat?! ↯ Okay. I find your reasoning very cute.

Q: Hello. Let's keep on filling up that birthday calendar!

Rebecca: [B looks like 8] is the hidden [*maboro-shi*(4)] princess → August 4

Scarlet: Scarle-to [10] is Rebecca [2 C's] mother [*haha*(8)] → October 28

How about those?

--Shin

A: Wait, wait, wait... Okay, cool.
I have an announcement! There's no way we can display all the birthday suggestion letters here, so I think we're going to reveal them on the internet now. That way, we'll be able to properly attribute all your pen names as we fill in the birthday calendar on One-piece.com. Has your birthday been filled in yet? You can check it out on the home page for the series (*Only in Japanese). As always, you can still submit ideas through the SBS.

Q: You wrote that both Kid and Killer hate curry udon noodles. What happened to them in the past...??

--Karin

A: When they were young, they both experienced their first crush on a girl named Broth Splatterina. The trio were having thick udon noodles in curry-flavored soup for lunch one day, until they looked up and saw that their dear Splatterina was simply covered in brown sauce. When they laughed at the sight of her, she beat them both up and never spoke to them again. Ahhh, the bittersweet memories of youth. That's all! See you next volume!!

Chapter 879:
BIG MOM'S SWEET 3 GENERAL, KATAKURI

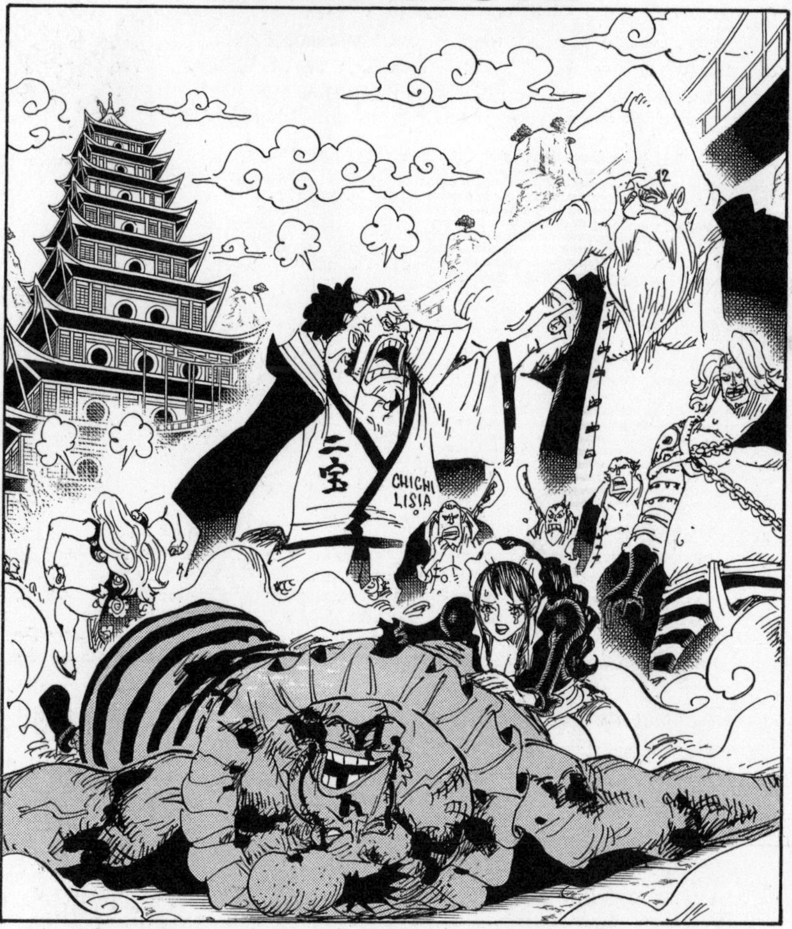
CHICHI
LISIA

THE SAGA OF THE SELF-PROCLAIMED STRAW HAT FLEET, VOL. 13, SAI: "A PRICE TO PAY FOR BETROTHAL ANNULMENT"

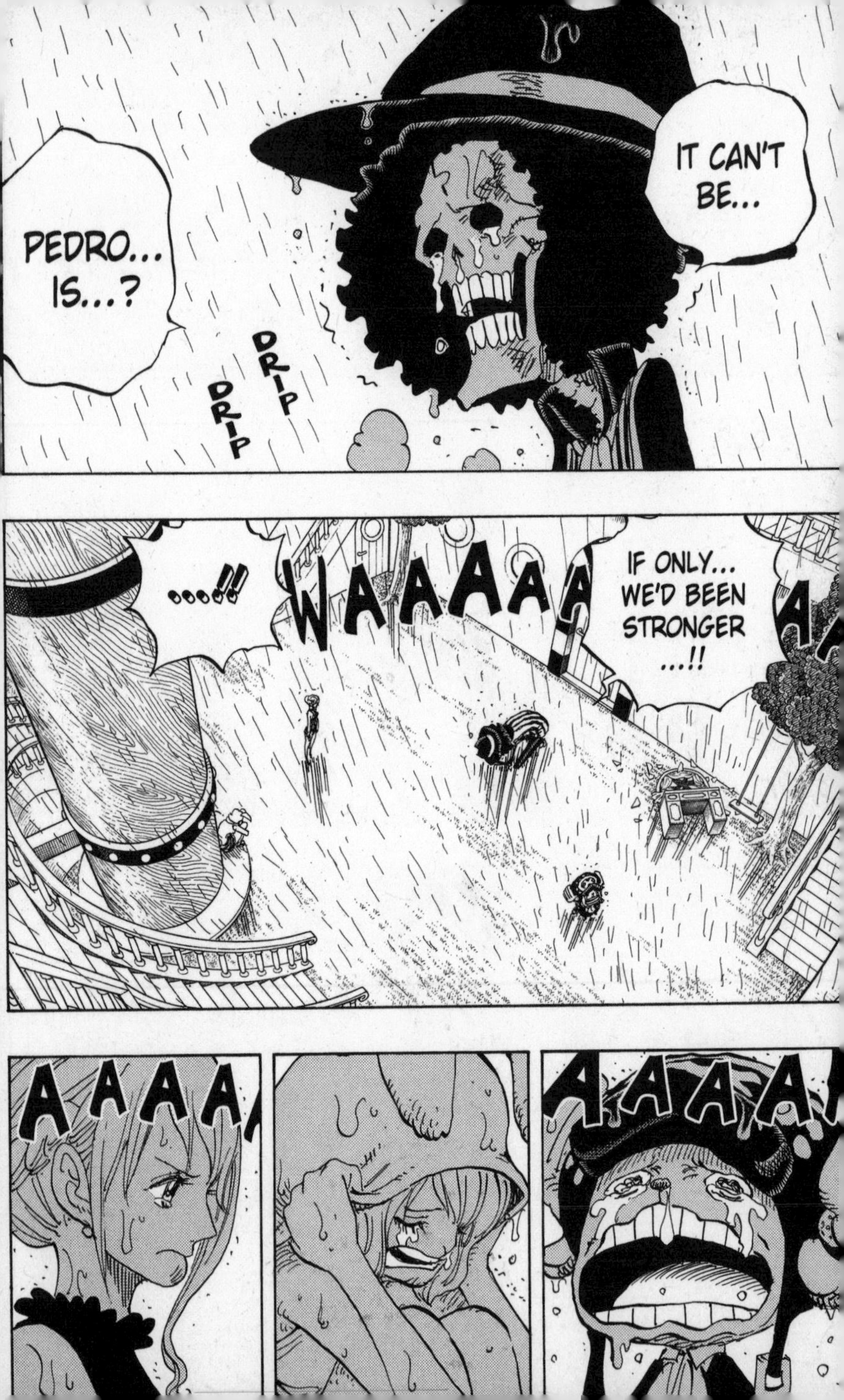
IT CAN'T BE...
DRIP
DRIP
PEDRO... IS...?
IF ONLY... WE'D BEEN STRONGER ...!!
WAAAAAA
....!!
AAAA
AAAA

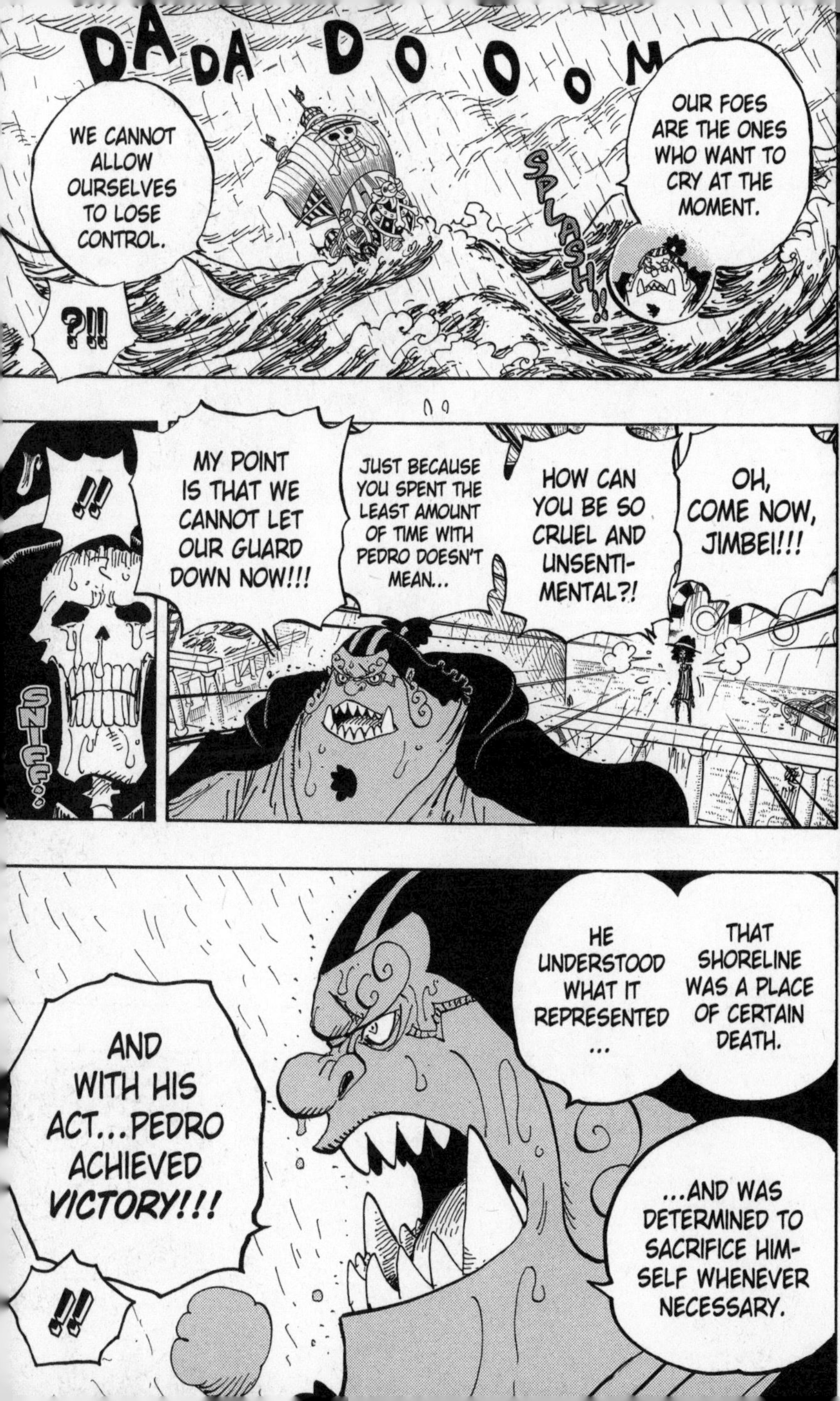
DADA DOOOOM
OUR FOES ARE THE ONES WHO WANT TO CRY AT THE MOMENT.
SPLASH!!
WE CANNOT ALLOW OURSELVES TO LOSE CONTROL.
?!!
OH, COME NOW, JIMBEI!!!
HOW CAN YOU BE SO CRUEL AND UNSENTI-MENTAL?!
JUST BECAUSE YOU SPENT THE LEAST AMOUNT OF TIME WITH PEDRO DOESN'T MEAN...
MY POINT IS THAT WE CANNOT LET OUR GUARD DOWN NOW!!!
!!
SNIFF...
THAT SHORELINE WAS A PLACE OF CERTAIN DEATH.
HE UNDERSTOOD WHAT IT REPRESENTED...
...AND WAS DETERMINED TO SACRIFICE HIM-SELF WHENEVER NECESSARY.
AND WITH HIS ACT...PEDRO ACHIEVED VICTORY!!!
!!

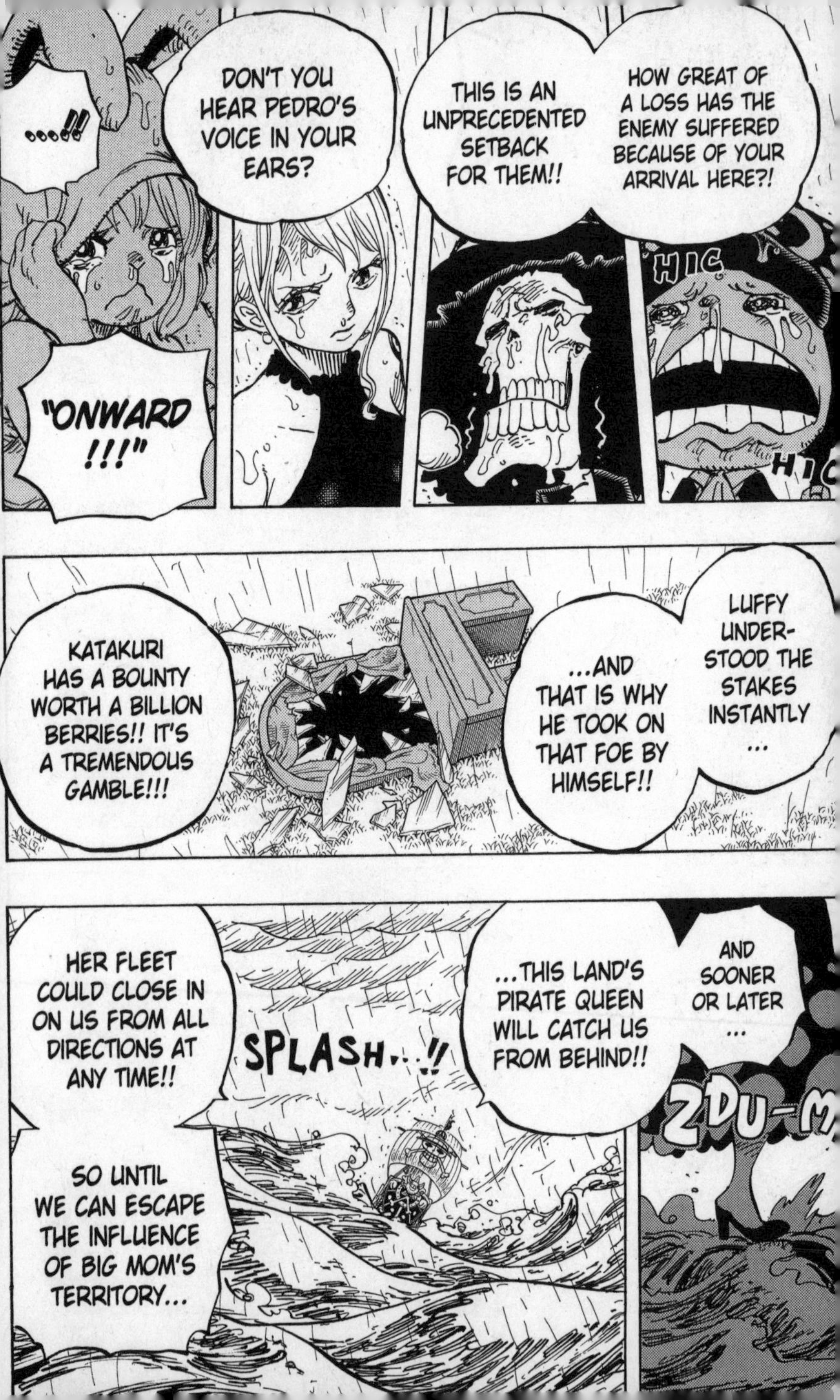
HOW GREAT OF A LOSS HAS THE ENEMY SUFFERED BECAUSE OF YOUR ARRIVAL HERE?!
HIC
HIC
THIS IS AN UNPRECEDENTED SETBACK FOR THEM!!
DON'T YOU HEAR PEDRO'S VOICE IN YOUR EARS?
...!!
"ONWARD!!!"
LUFFY UNDER-STOOD THE STAKES INSTANTLY...
...AND THAT IS WHY HE TOOK ON THAT FOE BY HIMSELF!!
KATAKURI HAS A BOUNTY WORTH A BILLION BERRIES!! IT'S A TREMENDOUS GAMBLE!!!
AND SOONER OR LATER...
ZDU-M
...THIS LAND'S PIRATE QUEEN WILL CATCH US FROM BEHIND!!
HER FLEET COULD CLOSE IN ON US FROM ALL DIRECTIONS AT ANY TIME!!
SPLASH...!!
SO UNTIL WE CAN ESCAPE THE INFLUENCE OF BIG MOM'S TERRITORY...

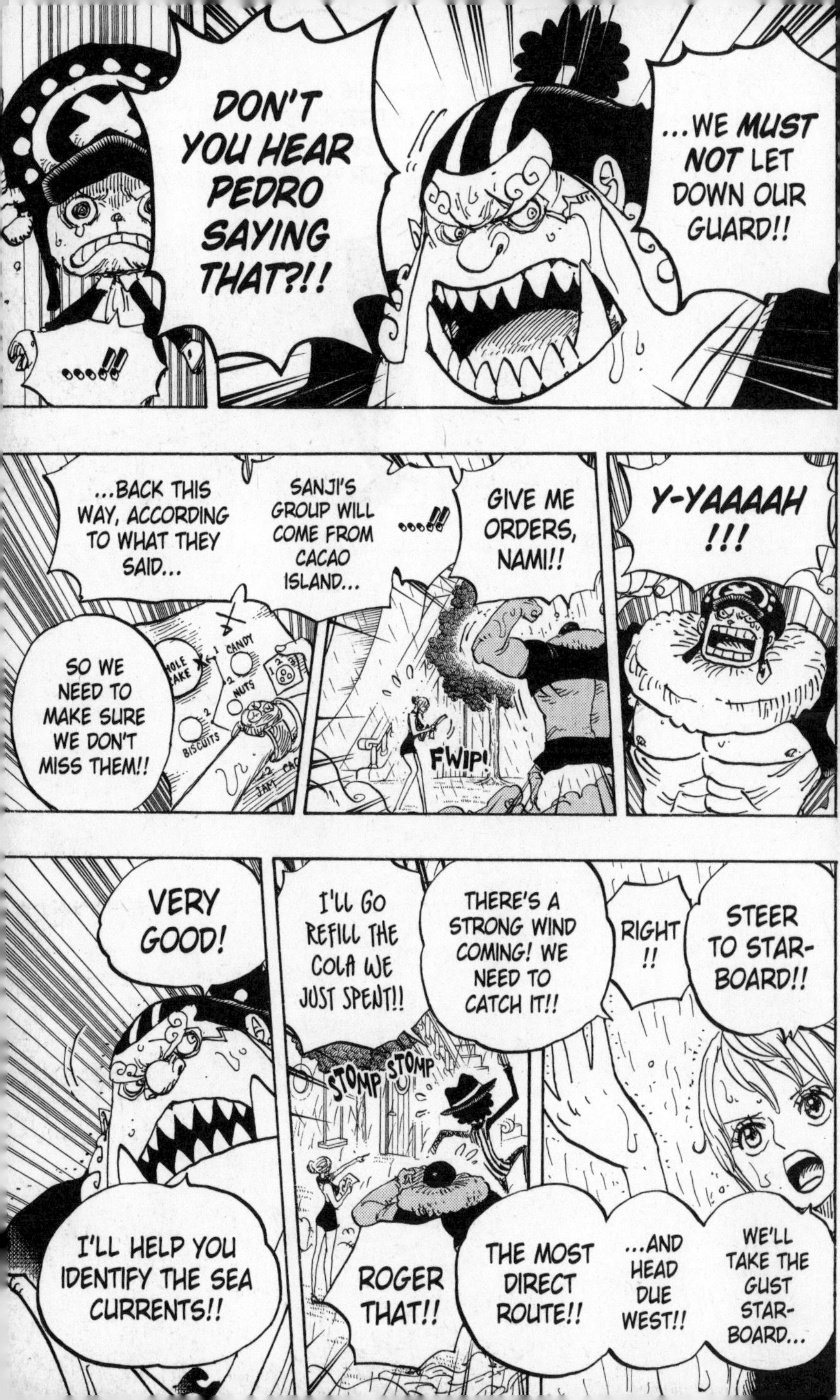
...WE MUST NOT LET DOWN OUR GUARD!!
DON'T YOU HEAR PEDRO SAYING THAT?!!
....!!
Y-YAAAAH !!!
GIVE ME ORDERS, NAMI!!
....!!
FWIP!
SANJI'S GROUP WILL COME FROM CACAO ISLAND...
...BACK THIS WAY, ACCORDING TO WHAT THEY SAID...
CANDY
NUTS
BISCUITS
JAM
SO WE NEED TO MAKE SURE WE DON'T MISS THEM!!
STEER TO STAR-BOARD!!
RIGHT !!
WE'LL TAKE THE GUST STAR-BOARD...
...AND HEAD DUE WEST!!
THE MOST DIRECT ROUTE!!
THERE'S A STRONG WIND COMING! WE NEED TO CATCH IT!!
I'LL GO REFILL THE COLA WE JUST SPENT!!
STOMP STOMP
ROGER THAT!!
VERY GOOD!
I'LL HELP YOU IDENTIFY THE SEA CURRENTS!!

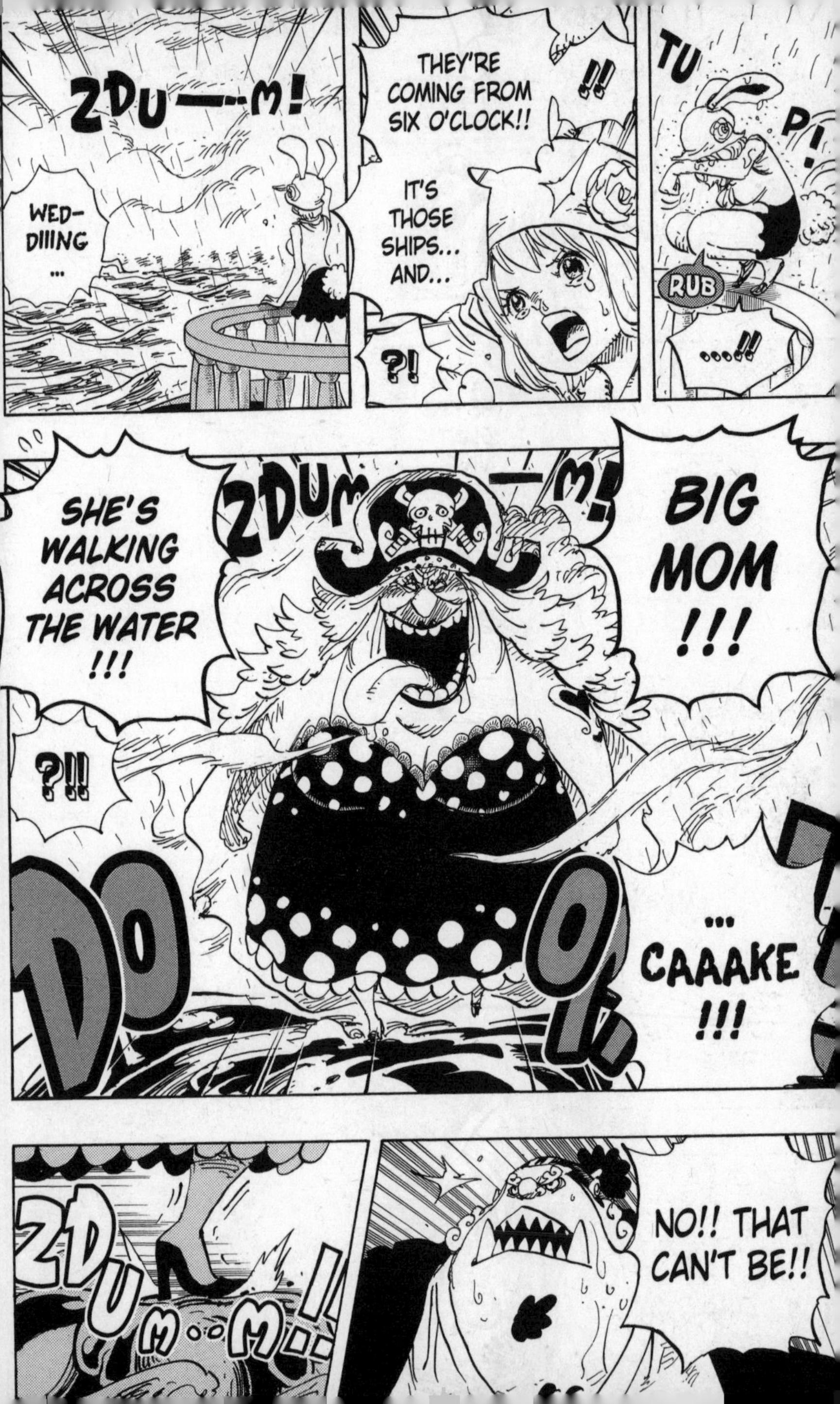

TU
P!
RUB
...!!
THEY'RE COMING FROM SIX O'CLOCK!!
!!
IT'S THOSE SHIPS... AND...
?!
ZDU——M!
WED-DIIING ...
BIG MOM !!!
ZDUM——M!
SHE'S WALKING ACROSS THE WATER !!!
?!!
... CAAAKE !!!
NO!! THAT CAN'T BE!!
ZDUM..M!!

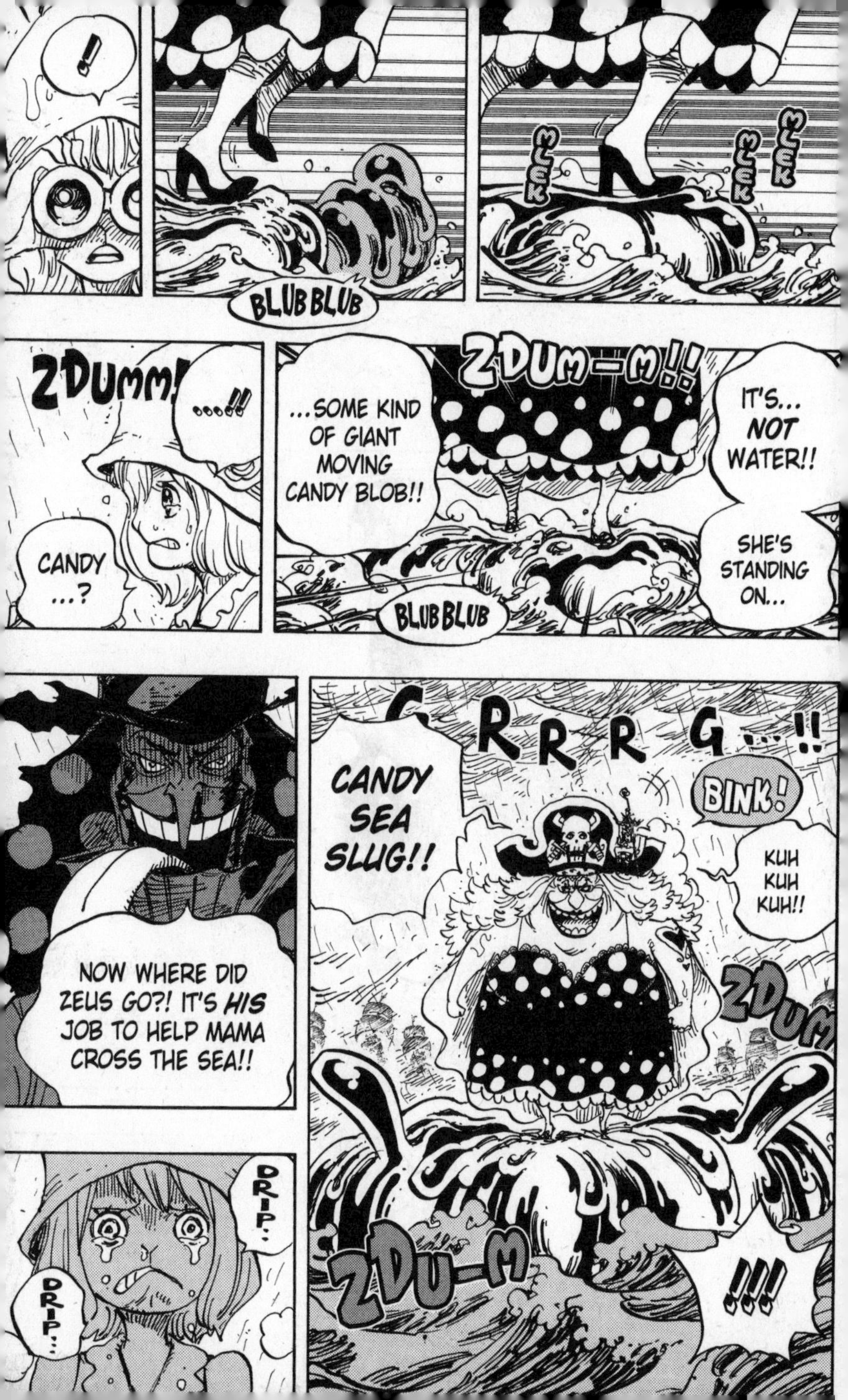
MLEK
MLEK
MLEK
BLUB BLUB
!
ZDUM-M!!
IT'S... NOT WATER!!
SHE'S STANDING ON...
...SOME KIND OF GIANT MOVING CANDY BLOB!!
BLUB BLUB
ZDUMM!
....!!
CANDY ...?
GRRRRG...!!
BINK!
KUH KUH KUH!!
CANDY SEA SLUG!!
ZDUM
ZDU-M
!!!
NOW WHERE DID ZEUS GO?! IT'S HIS JOB TO HELP MAMA CROSS THE SEA!!
DRIP..
DRIP...

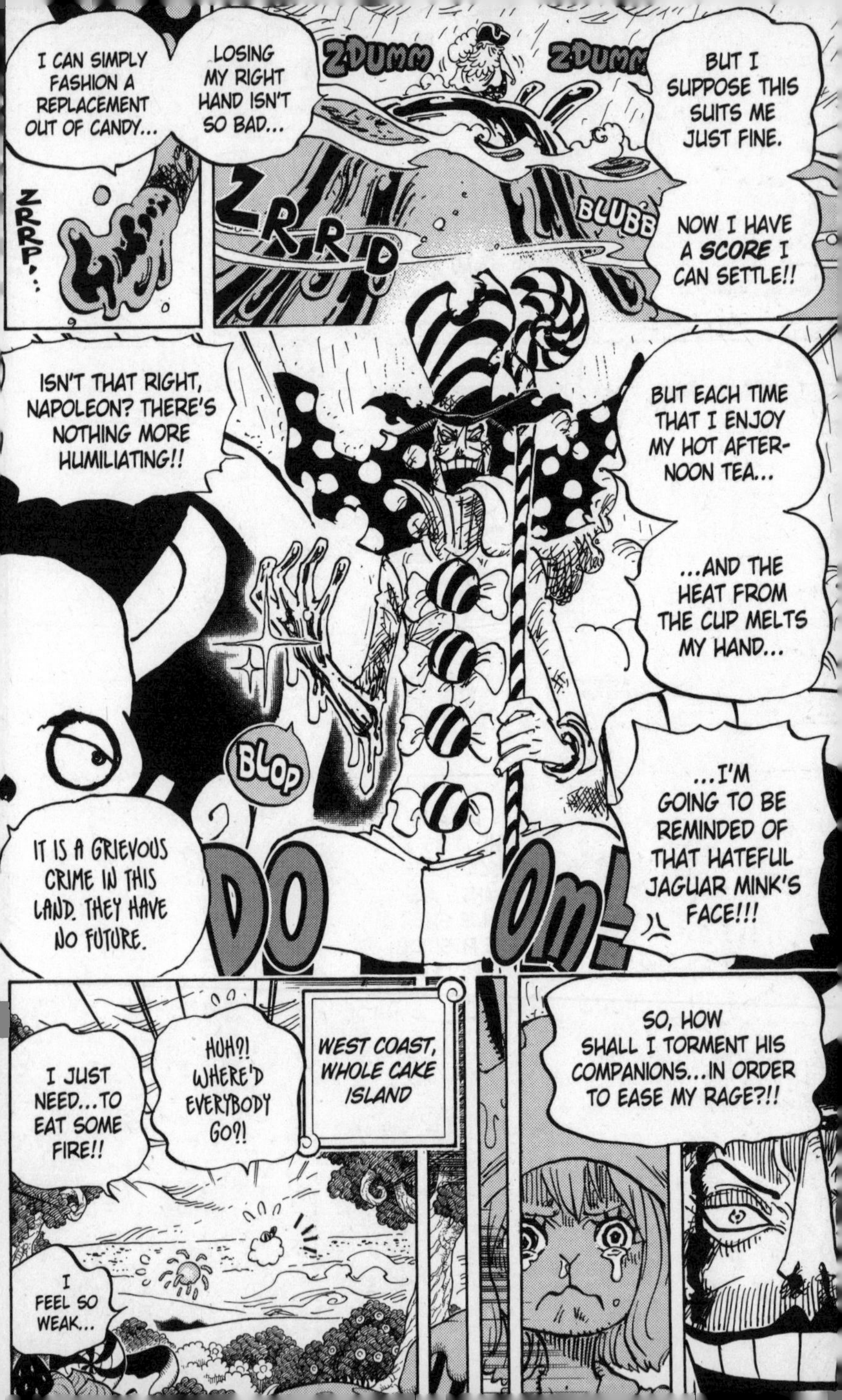
ZDUMM
ZDUMM
BUT I SUPPOSE THIS SUITS ME JUST FINE.
NOW I HAVE A SCORE I CAN SETTLE!!
BLUBB
ZRRRD
LOSING MY RIGHT HAND ISN'T SO BAD...
I CAN SIMPLY FASHION A REPLACEMENT OUT OF CANDY...
ZRRP..
BUT EACH TIME THAT I ENJOY MY HOT AFTER-NOON TEA...
ISN'T THAT RIGHT, NAPOLEON? THERE'S NOTHING MORE HUMILIATING!!
...AND THE HEAT FROM THE CUP MELTS MY HAND...
...I'M GOING TO BE REMINDED OF THAT HATEFUL JAGUAR MINK'S FACE!!!
DOOOM!
BLOP
IT IS A GRIEVOUS CRIME IN THIS LAND. THEY HAVE NO FUTURE.
SO, HOW SHALL I TORMENT HIS COMPANIONS...IN ORDER TO EASE MY RAGE?!!
WEST COAST, WHOLE CAKE ISLAND
HUH?! WHERE'D EVERYBODY GO?!
I JUST NEED...TO EAT SOME FIRE!!
I FEEL SO WEAK...

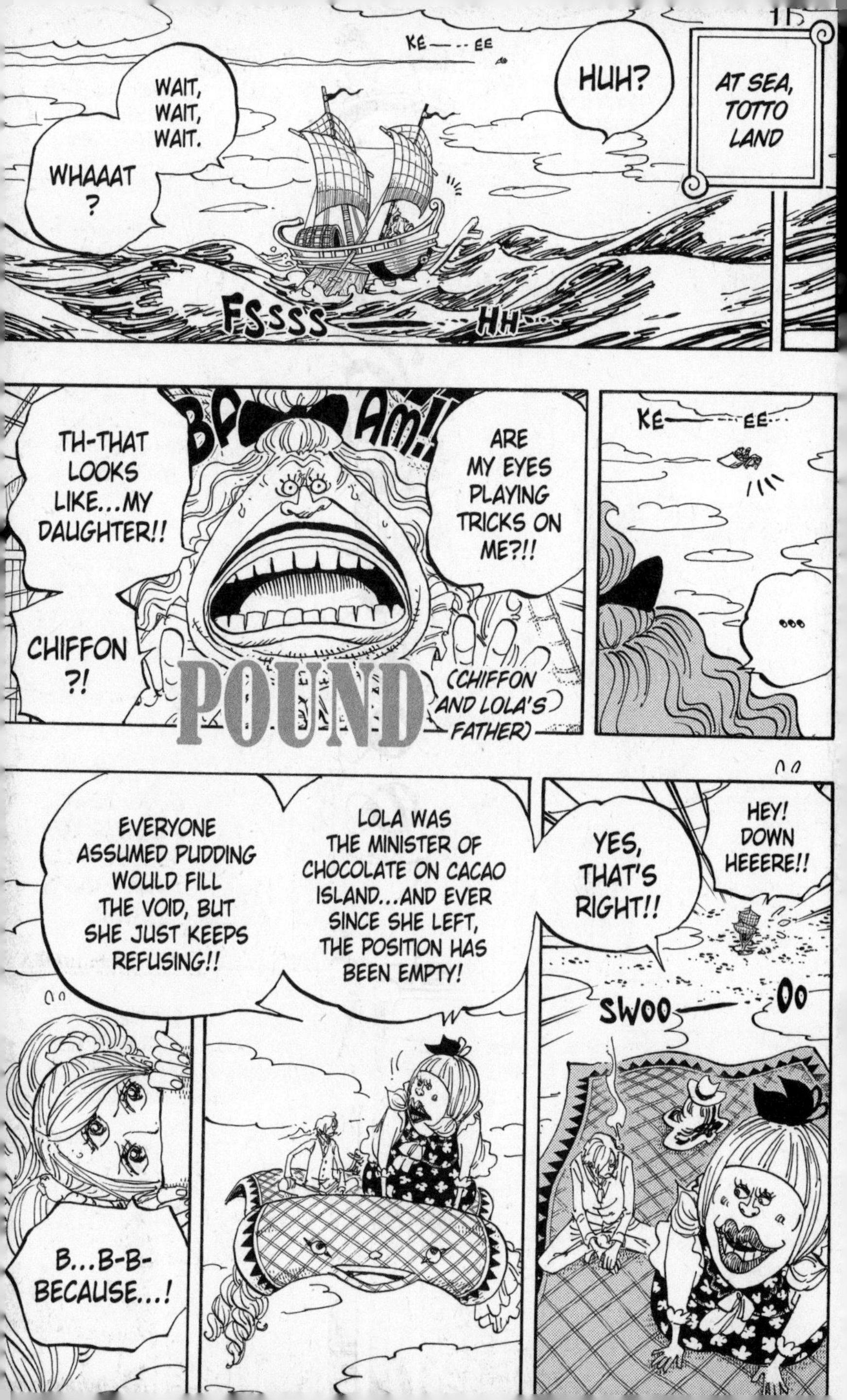

AT SEA, TOTTO LAND
HUH?
KE—--EE
WAIT, WAIT, WAIT.
WHAAAT?
FSSSS——HH...
KE———EE
...
ARE MY EYES PLAYING TRICKS ON ME?!!
BA AM!!
TH-THAT LOOKS LIKE...MY DAUGHTER!!
CHIFFON?!
POUND
(CHIFFON AND LOLA'S FATHER)
HEY! DOWN HEEERE!!
SWOO——OO
YES, THAT'S RIGHT!!
LOLA WAS THE MINISTER OF CHOCOLATE ON CACAO ISLAND...AND EVER SINCE SHE LEFT, THE POSITION HAS BEEN EMPTY!
EVERYONE ASSUMED PUDDING WOULD FILL THE VOID, BUT SHE JUST KEEPS REFUSING!!
B...B-B-BECAUSE...!

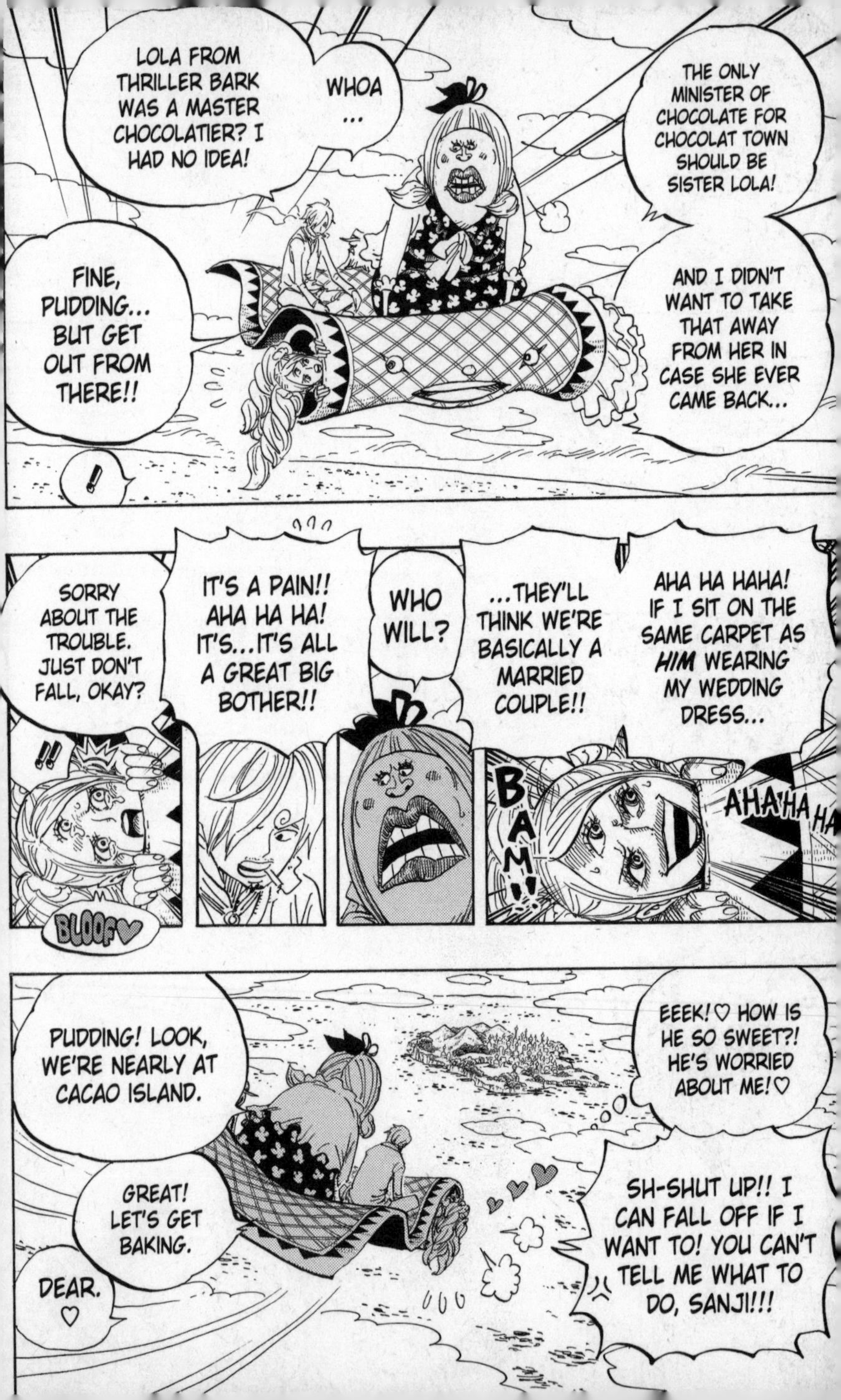
THE ONLY MINISTER OF CHOCOLATE FOR CHOCOLAT TOWN SHOULD BE SISTER LOLA!
WHOA ...
LOLA FROM THRILLER BARK WAS A MASTER CHOCOLATIER? I HAD NO IDEA!
AND I DIDN'T WANT TO TAKE THAT AWAY FROM HER IN CASE SHE EVER CAME BACK...
FINE, PUDDING... BUT GET OUT FROM THERE!!
!
AHA HA HAHA! IF I SIT ON THE SAME CARPET AS *HIM* WEARING MY WEDDING DRESS...
...THEY'LL THINK WE'RE BASICALLY A MARRIED COUPLE!!
BAM!!
AHA HA HA HA
WHO WILL?
IT'S A PAIN!! AHA HA HA! IT'S...IT'S ALL A GREAT BIG BOTHER!!
SORRY ABOUT THE TROUBLE. JUST DON'T FALL, OKAY?
!!
BLOOF♥
EEEK!♡ HOW IS HE SO SWEET?! HE'S WORRIED ABOUT ME!♡
PUDDING! LOOK, WE'RE NEARLY AT CACAO ISLAND.
SH-SHUT UP!! I CAN FALL OFF IF I WANT TO! YOU CAN'T TELL ME WHAT TO DO, SANJI!!!
GREAT! LET'S GET BAKING.
DEAR. ♡

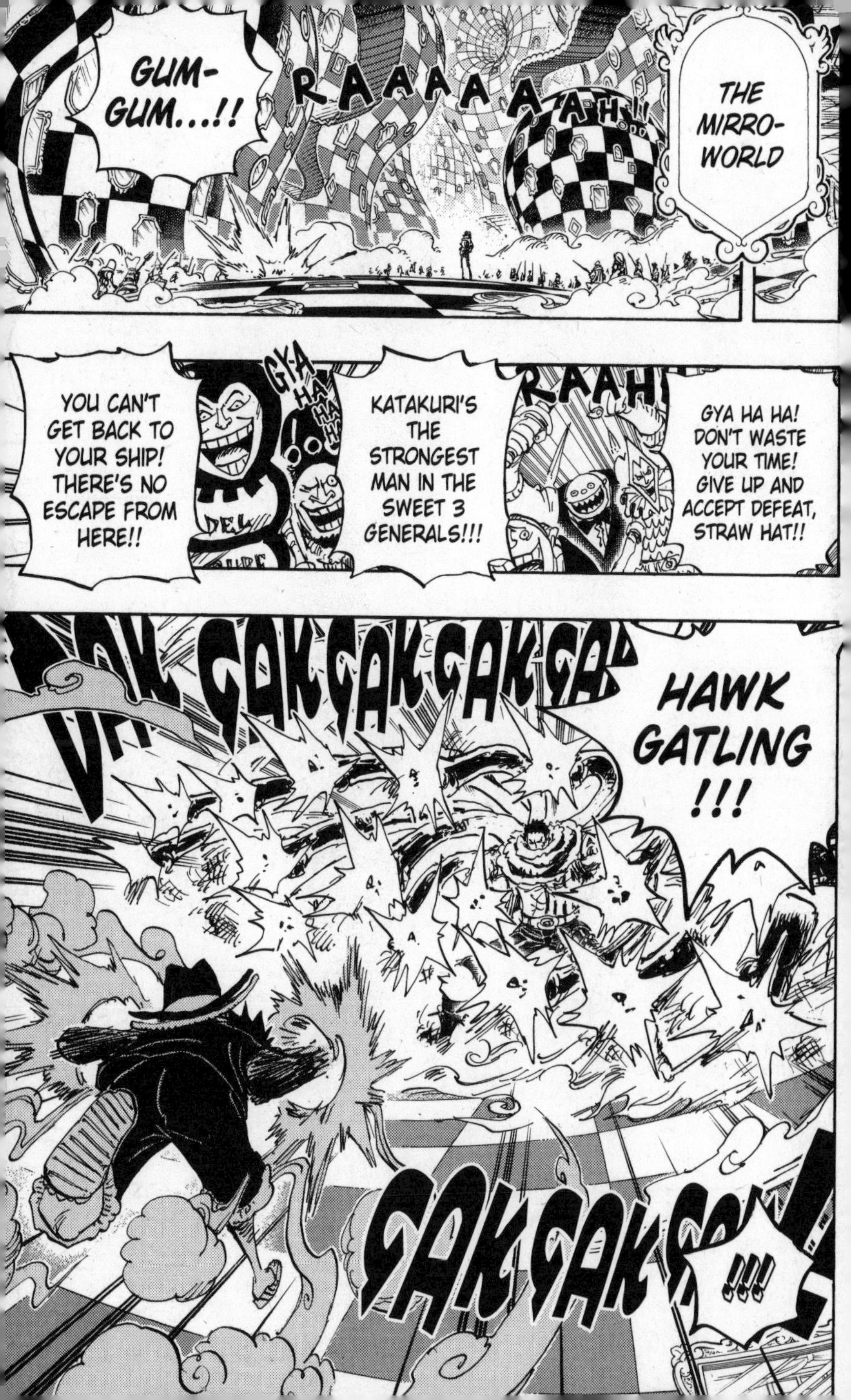
THE MIRRO-WORLD
RAAAAAAAH!!
GUM-GUM...!!
RAAH!
GYA HA HA! DON'T WASTE YOUR TIME! GIVE UP AND ACCEPT DEFEAT, STRAW HAT!!
KATAKURI'S THE STRONGEST MAN IN THE SWEET 3 GENERALS!!!
GYA HA HA HA
YOU CAN'T GET BACK TO YOUR SHIP! THERE'S NO ESCAPE FROM HERE!!
HAWK GATLING!!!
GAK GAK GAK GAK
!!!

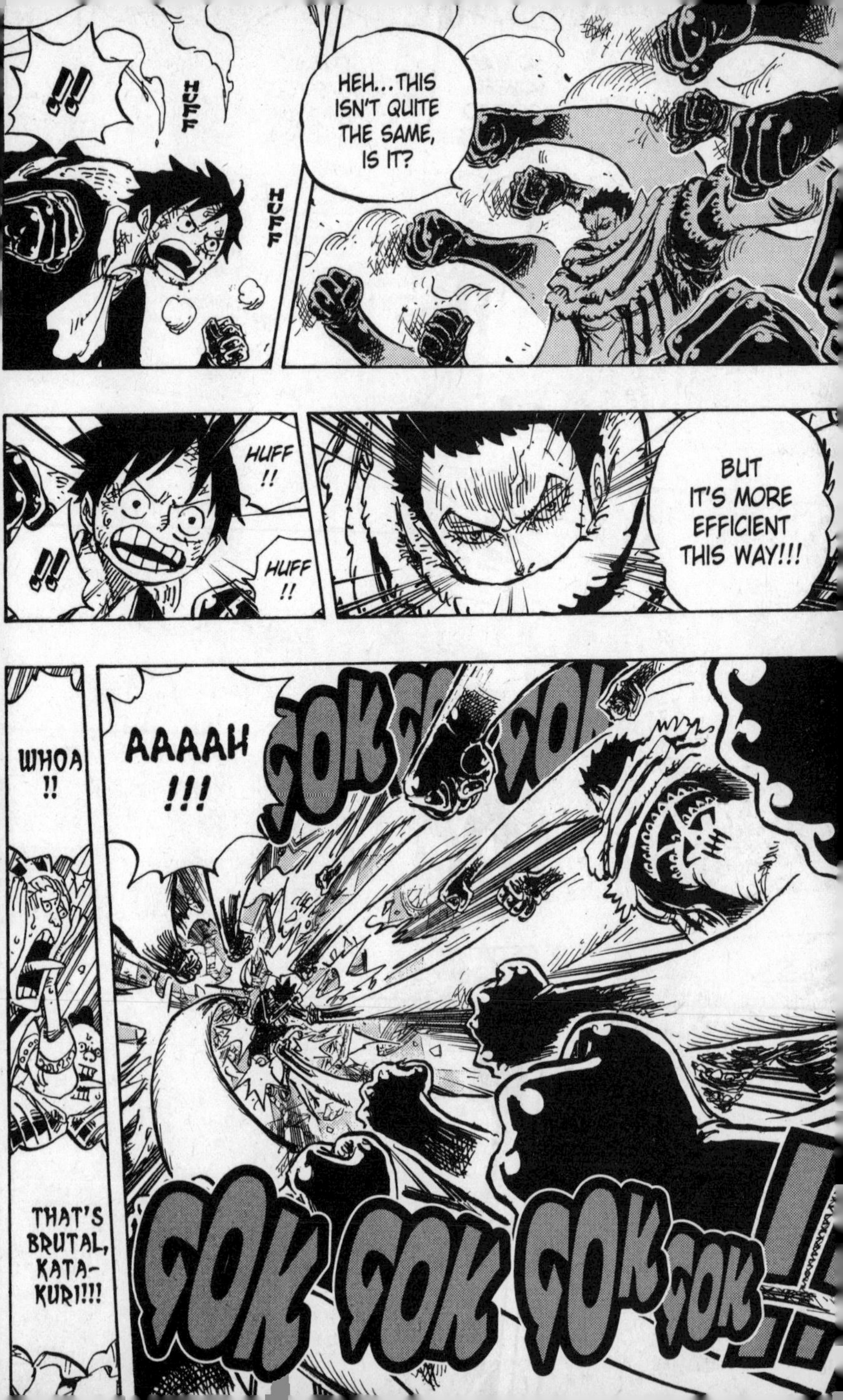
HEH...THIS ISN'T QUITE THE SAME, IS IT?
!!
HUFF
HUFF
BUT IT'S MORE EFFICIENT THIS WAY!!!
HUFF !!
!!
HUFF !!
GOK GOK GOK
AAAAH !!!
GOK GOK GOK GOK GOK !!
WHOA !!
THAT'S BRUTAL, KATA-KURI!!!!

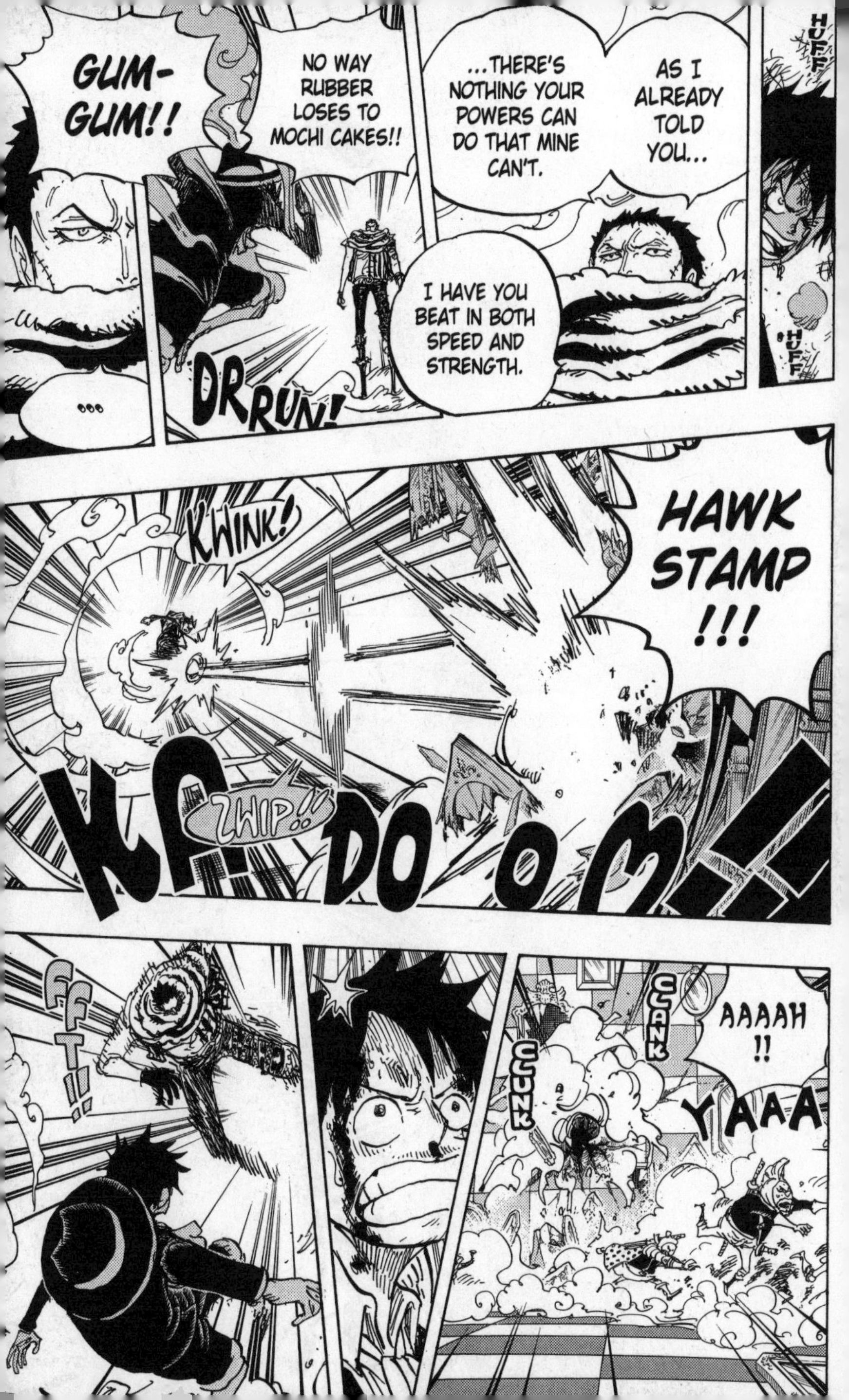
HUFF
HUFF
AS I ALREADY TOLD YOU...
...THERE'S NOTHING YOUR POWERS CAN DO THAT MINE CAN'T.
I HAVE YOU BEAT IN BOTH SPEED AND STRENGTH.
NO WAY RUBBER LOSES TO MOCHI CAKES!!
DRRUN!
GUM-GUM!!
...
HAWK STAMP!!!
KWINK!
ZWIP!!
KA-DOOOM!!
AAAAH!!
CLANK
CLUNK
YAAA
FFT!!

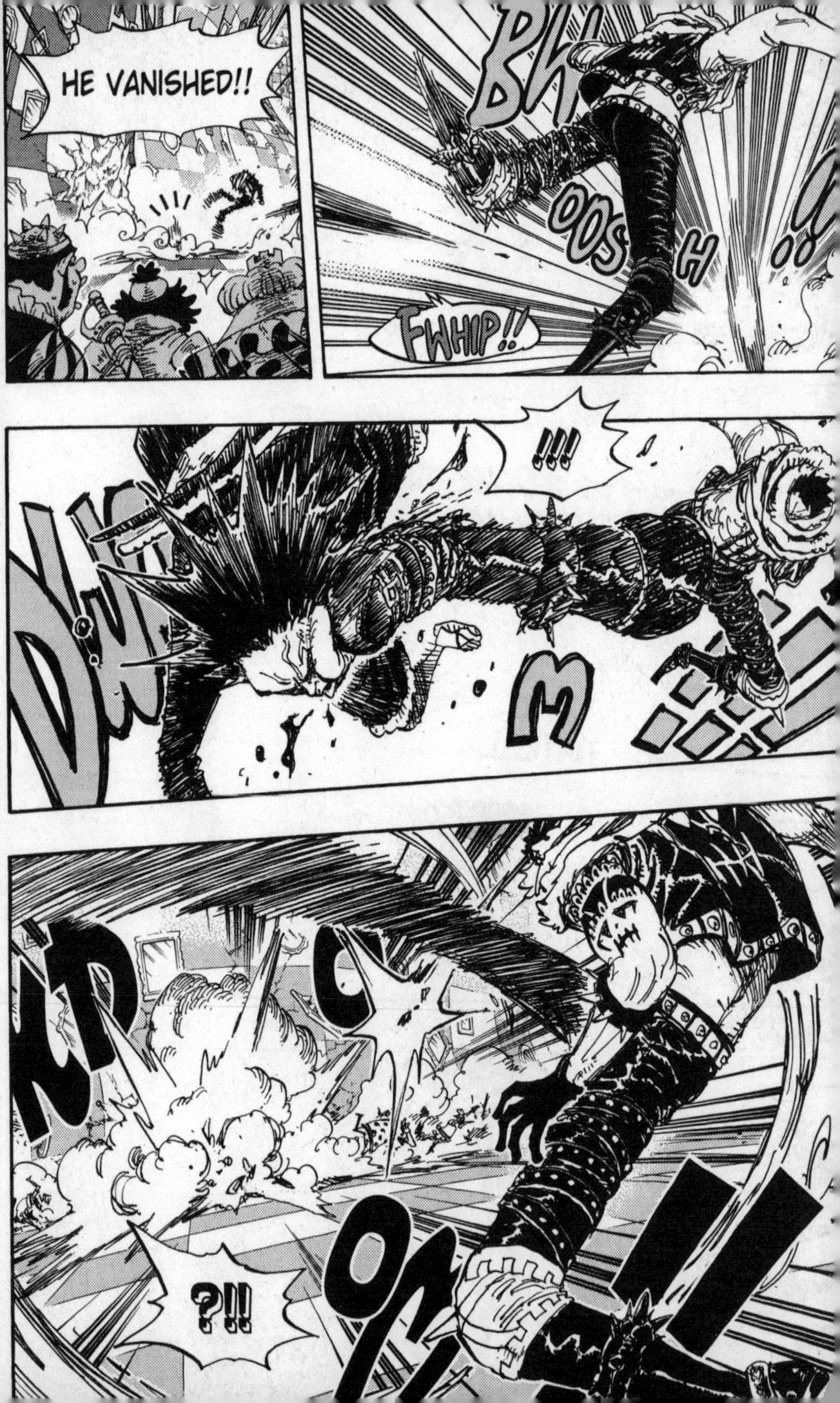
FWHIP!!
HE VANISHED!!
!!!
?!!

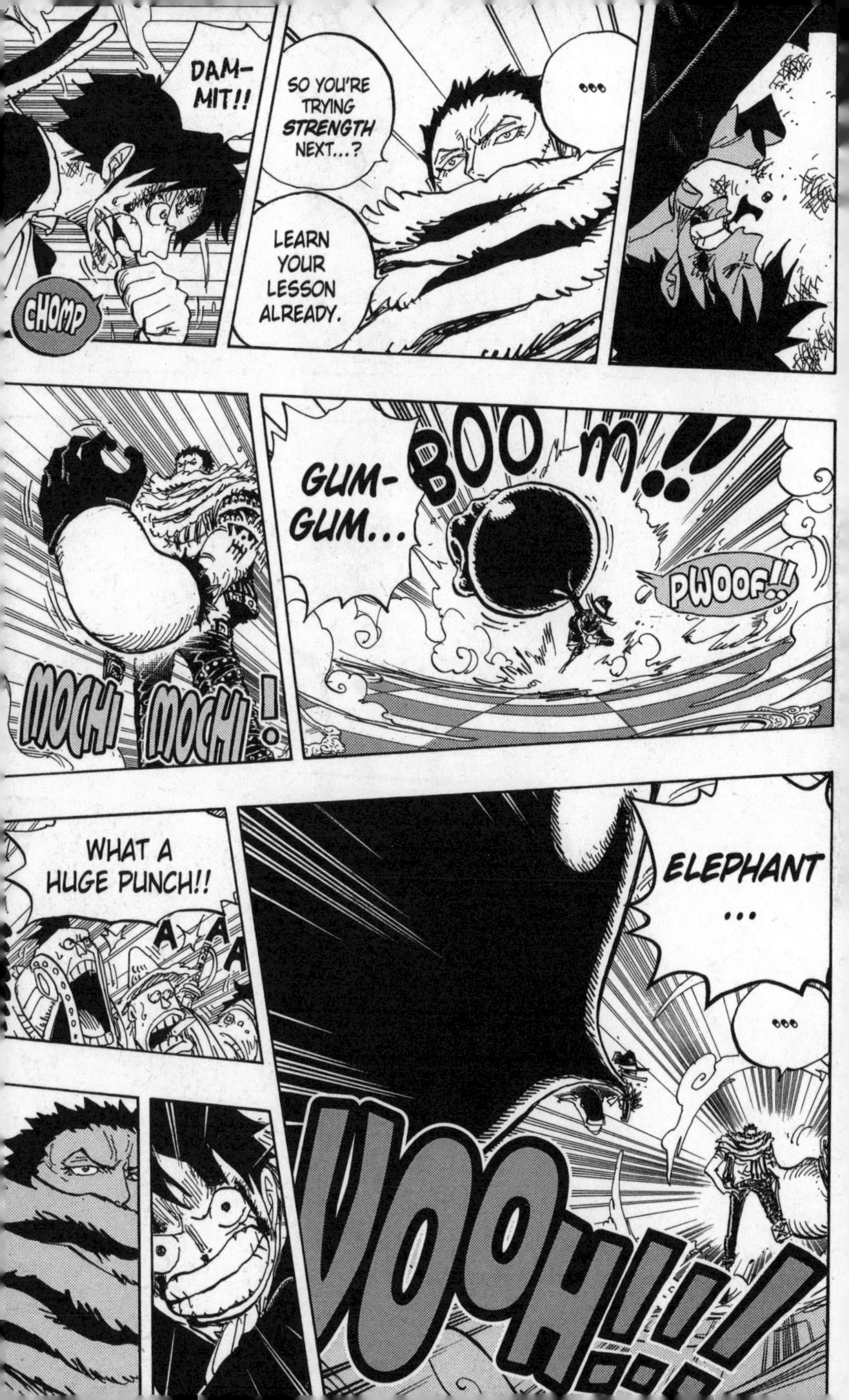
...
SO YOU'RE TRYING STRENGTH NEXT...?
LEARN YOUR LESSON ALREADY.
DAM-MIT!!
CHOMP
BOOM!!
PWOOF!!
GUM-GUM...
MOCHI MOCHI!
ELEPHANT ...
...
VOOH!!!
WHAT A HUGE PUNCH!!
AAA

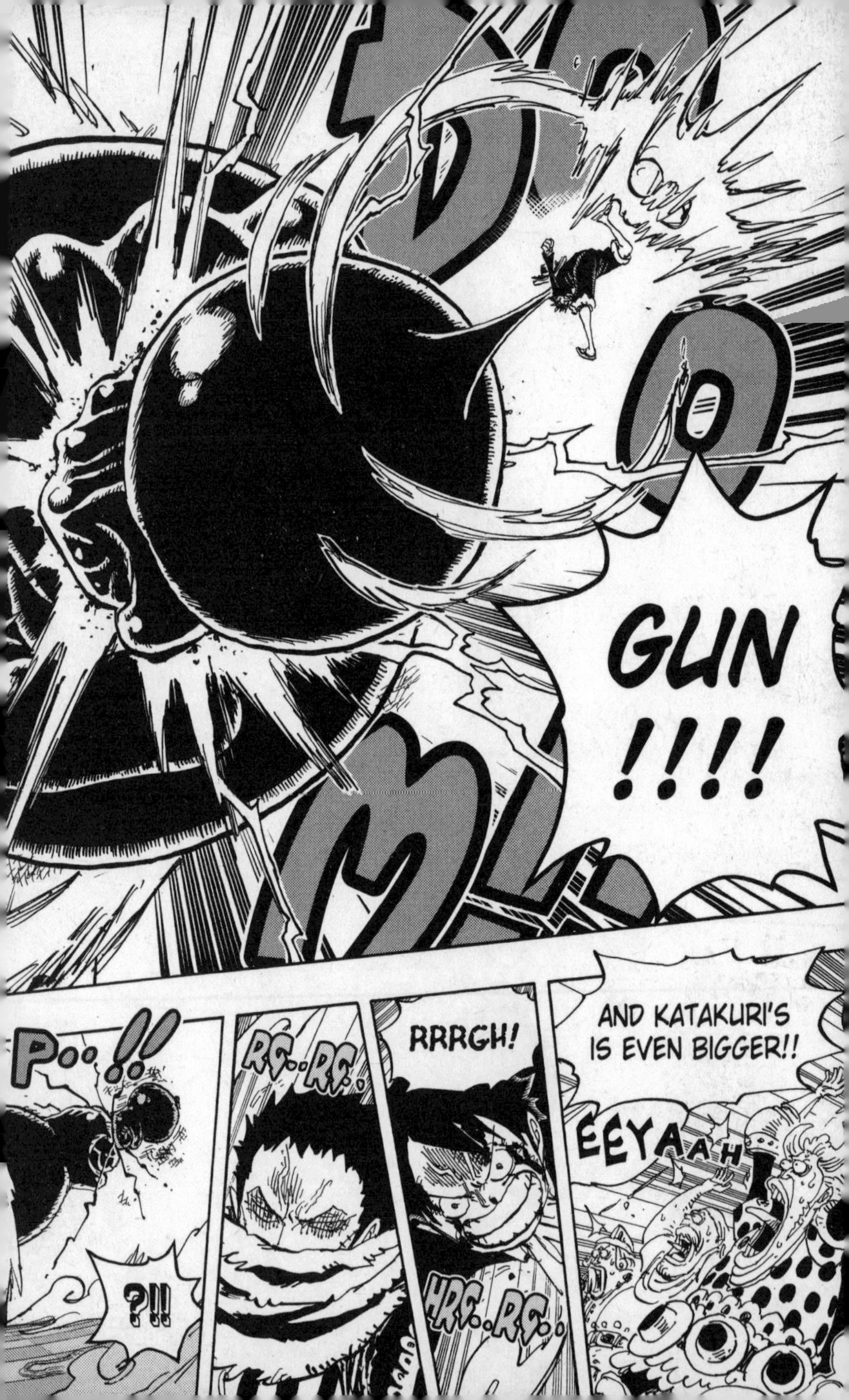
GUN
!!!!
AND KATAKURI'S
IS EVEN BIGGER!!
EEYAAH
RRRGH!
HRG..RG..
RG..RG.
PO..!!
?!!

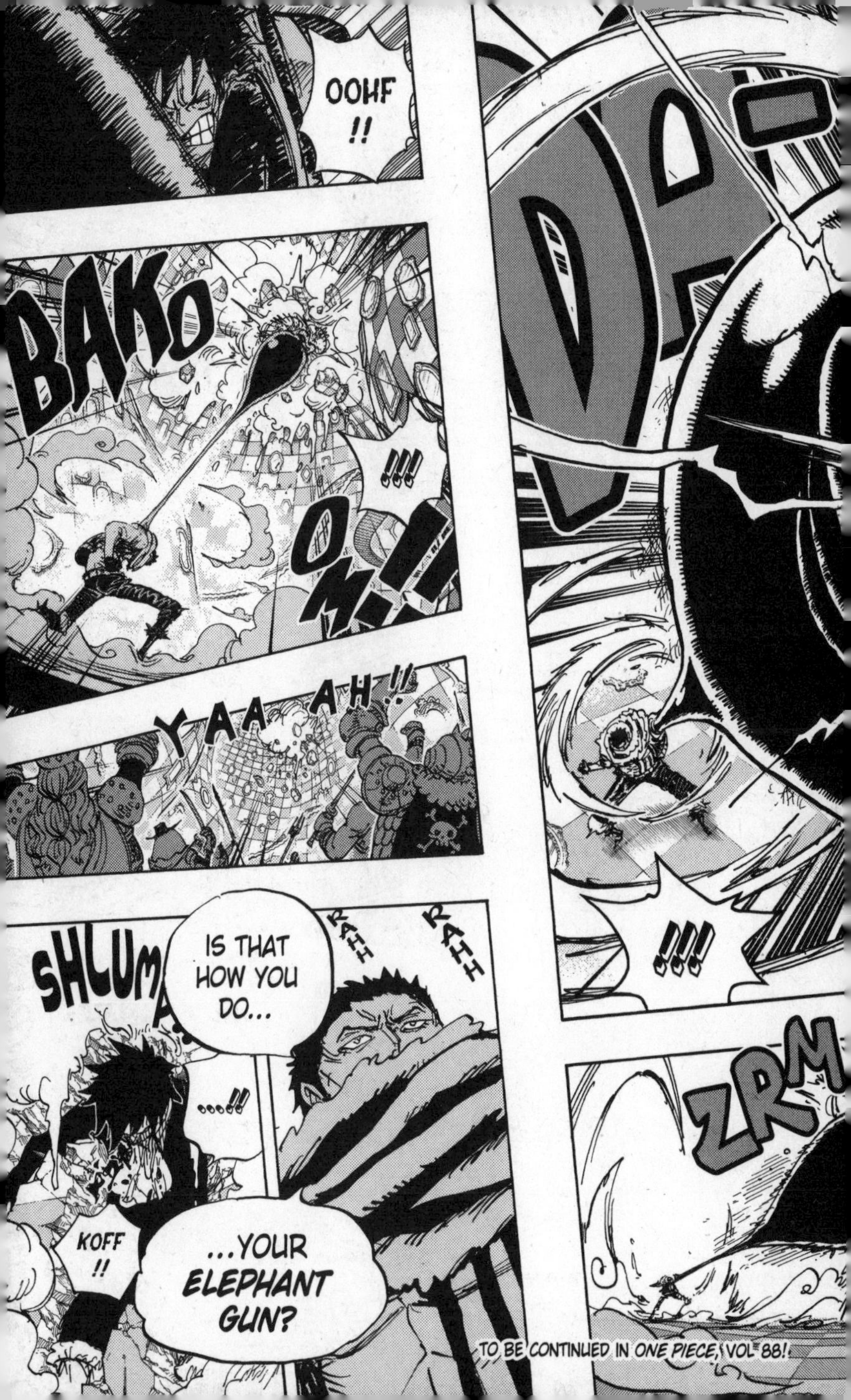
DOA
!!!
ZRM
OOHF !!
BAKOOM
!!!
YAAAAH!!
SHLUMP
RAHH RAHH
IS THAT HOW YOU DO...
...!!
KOFF !!
...YOUR ELEPHANT GUN?

TO BE CONTINUED IN ONE PIECE, VOL. 88!

CHARACTER FULL RESULTS

ANNOUNCED AT LAST!!

OVER 80,000 VOTES CAST!!

That's the highest number of votes cast in any poll, now including Whole Cake Island characters.

#1 MONKEY D. LUFFY

(1) ➡

11,737 votes

The six-time consecutive champion!!

How long will his momentum last?! The way he's always standing at the front is fitting for the hero of the story!!

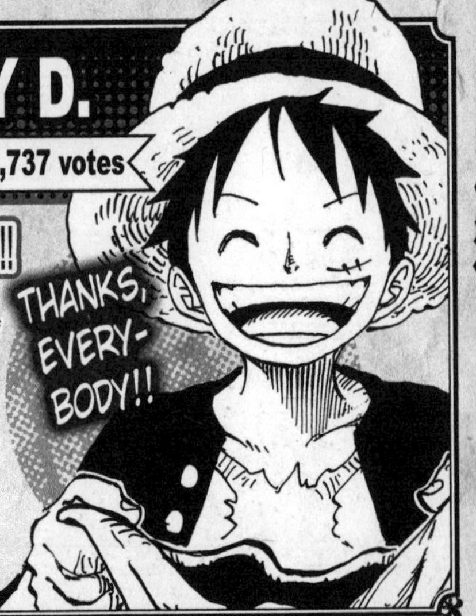
THANKS, EVERY-BODY!!

#30

(9) ⬇

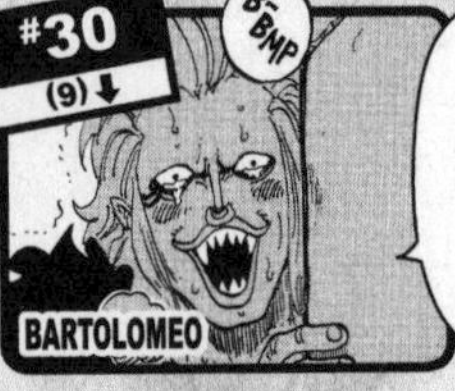
B-BMP
OF COURSE MISTAH LUFFY'S UP HERE!!

BARTOLOMEO

#2 RORONOA ZOLO

(3) ⬆

10,442 votes

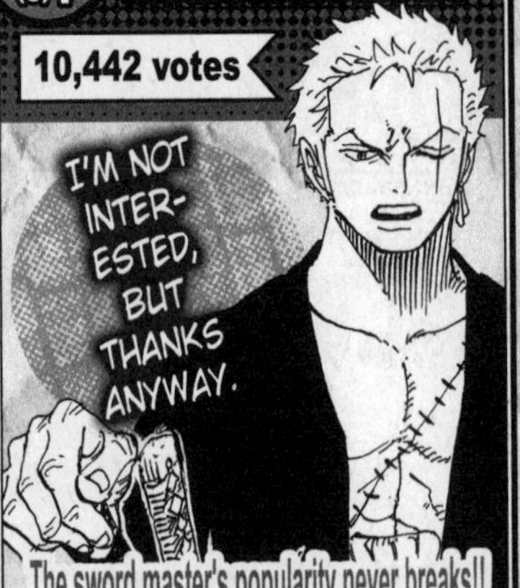
I'M NOT INTER-ESTED, BUT THANKS ANYWAY.

The sword master's popularity never breaks!!

#3 SANJI

(4) ⬆

10,215 votes

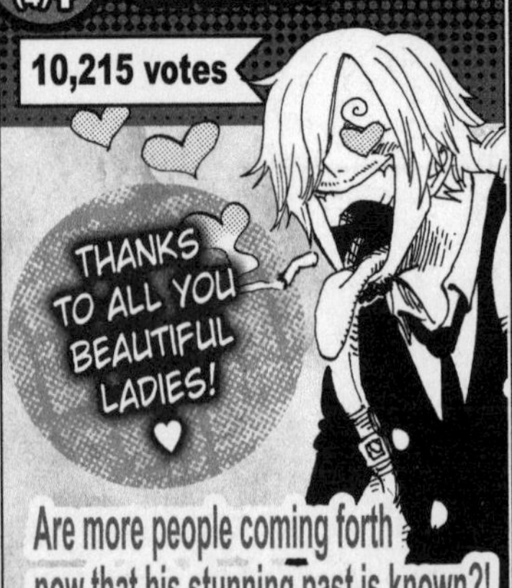
THANKS TO ALL YOU BEAUTIFUL LADIES! ♥

Are more people coming forth now that his stunning past is known?!

*Number in parentheses refers to previous rank.

ONE PIECE POPULARITY POLL

The 6th

#6 (35) ↑	#5 (6) ↑	#4 (2) ↓

JIMBEI	PORTGAZ D. ACE	TRAFALGAR LAW
3,884 votes ◄	4,605 votes ◄	7,997 votes ◄

#10 (10) →	#9 (5) ↓	#8 (8) →	#7 (7) →

BOA HANCOCK	SABO	NAMI	TONY TONY CHOPPER
2,452 votes ◄	2,967 votes ◄	3,269 votes ◄	3,301 votes ◄

#15 (13) ↓	#14 (–) NEW	#13 (27) ↑	#12 (11) ↓	#11 (14) ↑

USOPP	VINSMOKE REIJU	CAVENDISH	NICO ROBIN	SHANKS
1,409 votes ◄	1,665 votes ◄	1,742 votes ◄	1,952 votes ◄	2,010 votes ◄

#21 (12) ↓	#20 (16) ↓	#19 (19) →	#18 (15) ↓	#17 (17) →	#16 (52) ↑

MARCO	FRANKY	BROOK	CROCODILE	DON QUIXOTE DOFLAMINGO	DON QUIXOTE ROCINANTE
861 votes ◄	861 votes ◄	936 votes ◄	1,050 votes ◄	1,125 votes ◄	1,230 votes ◄

Check out the rest of the rankings on the next page!!!

POPULARITY POLL FULL RESULTS

ANNOUNCED AT LAST!!

#22 ~ #138

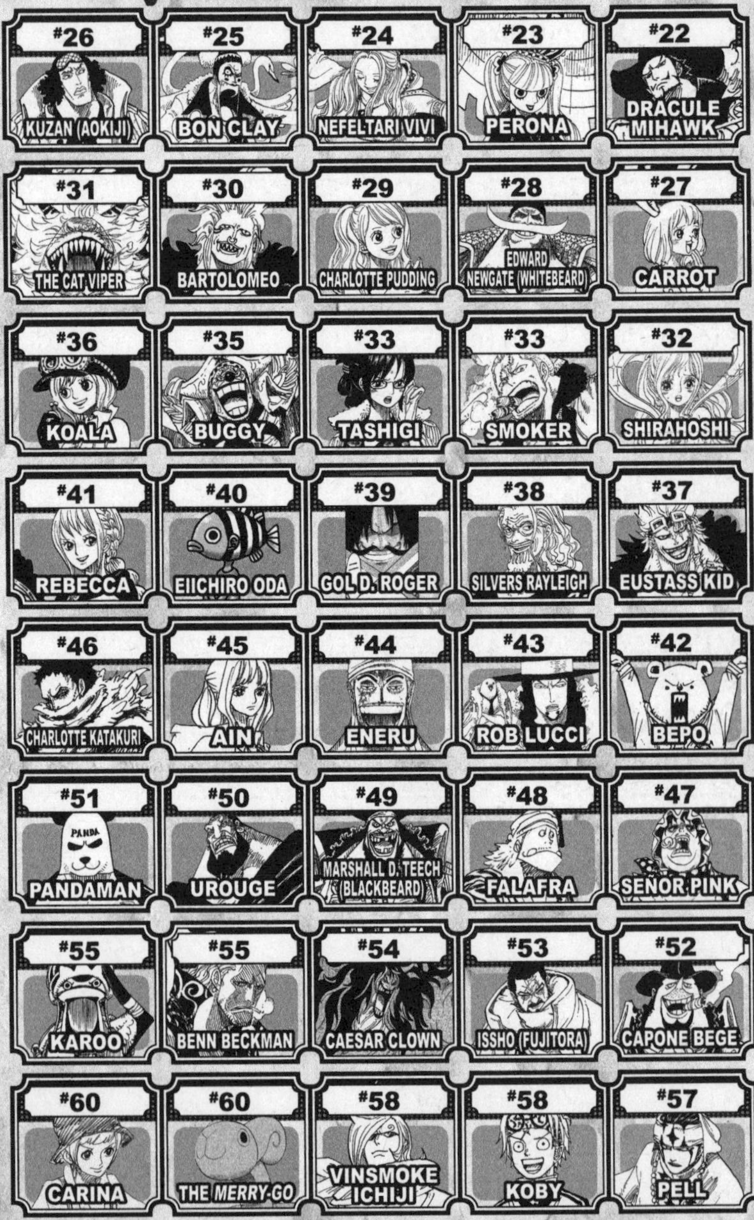

#22
DRACULE MIHAWK
#23
PERONA
#24
NEFELTARI VIVI
#25
BON CLAY
#26
KUZAN (AOKIJI)
#27
CARROT
#28
EDWARD NEWGATE (WHITEBEARD)
#29
CHARLOTTE PUDDING
#30
BARTOLOMEO
#31
THE CAT VIPER
#32
SHIRAHOSHI
#33
SMOKER
#33
TASHIGI
#35
BUGGY
#36
KOALA
#37
EUSTASS KID
#38
SILVERS RAYLEIGH
#39
GOL D. ROGER
#40
EIICHIRO ODA
#41
REBECCA
#42
BEPO
#43
ROB LUCCI
#44
ENERU
#45
AIN
#46
CHARLOTTE KATAKURI
#47
SEÑOR PINK
#48
FALAFRA
#49
MARSHALL D. TEECH (BLACKBEARD)
#50
UROUGE
#51
PANDA
PANDAMAN
#52
CAPONE BEGE
#53
ISSHO (FUJITORA)
#54
CAESAR CLOWN
#55
BENN BECKMAN
#55
KAROO
#57
PELL
#58
KOBY
#58
VINSMOKE ICHIJI
#60
THE MERRY-GO
#60
CARINA

The 6th ONE PIECE CHARACTER

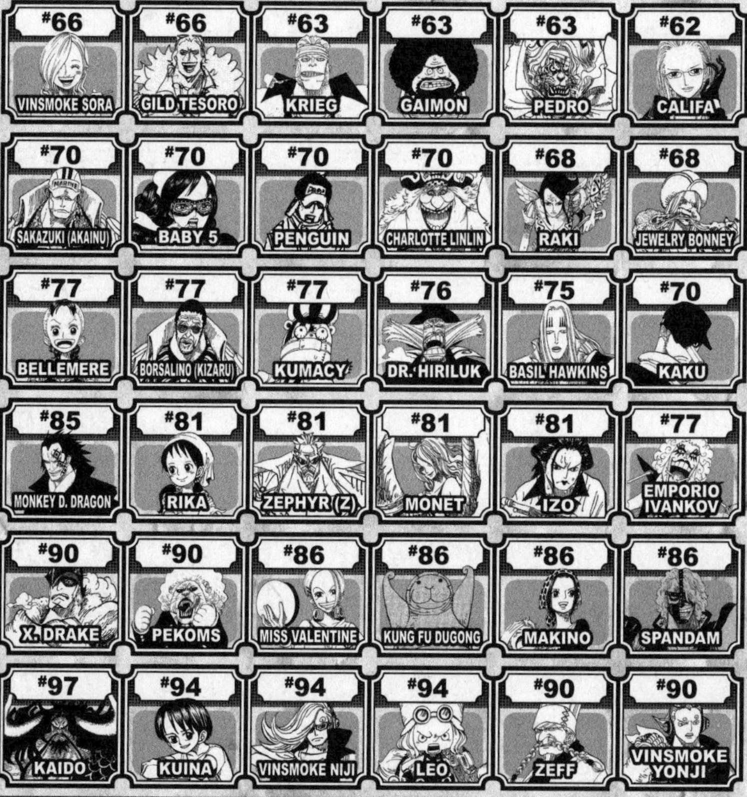
#62 CALIFA
#63 PEDRO
#63 GAIMON
#63 KRIEG
#66 GILD TESORO
#66 VINSMOKE SORA
#68 JEWELRY BONNEY
#68 RAKI
#70 CHARLOTTE LINLIN
#70 PENGUIN
#70 BABY 5
#70 SAKAZUKI (AKAINU)
#70 KAKU
#75 BASIL HAWKINS
#76 DR. HIRILUK
#77 KUMACY
#77 BORSALINO (KIZARU)
#77 BELLEMERE
#77 EMPORIO IVANKOV
#81 IZO
#81 MONET
#81 ZEPHYR (Z)
#81 RIKA
#85 MONKEY D. DRAGON
#86 SPANDAM
#86 MAKINO
#86 KUNG FU DUGONG
#86 MISS VALENTINE
#90 PEKOMS
#90 X. DRAKE
#90 VINSMOKE YONJI
#90 ZEFF
#94 LEO
#94 VINSMOKE NIJI
#94 KUINA
#97 KAIDO

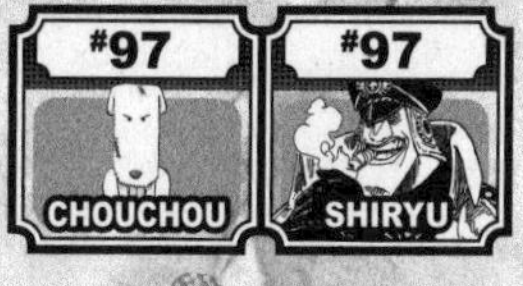
#97 SHIRYU
#97 CHOUCHOU

⬇ Here's everything from #100 on down!!

#100 *Thousand Sunny*, Shachi, Pauly, Laboon
#104 Arlong, Raizo, Mansherry, Marguerite
#108 Helmeppo, Hannyabal, Nico Olvia
#111 Charlotte Cracker, Gecko Moria
#113 Gladius, Kin'emon, Kaya, Camie, Tyrannosaurus, Jaguar D. Saul, Momonosuke, Seira
#121 Lucky Roux, Vergo, Sugar, Gin, Hina, Kalgara, Magellan, Tom
#129 Bartholomew Kuma, Bellamy, Kuro, Killer, Jabra
#134 Sengoku, Wyper, Daz Bonez (Mr. 1), Mother Carmel
#138 Thatch, Yorki, Tanaka, Momonga, Kyros, Viola (Violet), Dr. Kureha

Next up, some side rankings!! What will we learn?!

POPULARITY POLL FULL RESULTS ANNOUNCED!!

Bonus Ranks

Even these obscure characters ranked!!

★ Lion-Pig

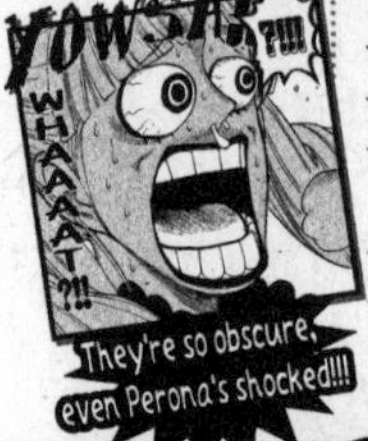
YOWSAS?!!!
WHAAAAAT?!!
They're so obscure, even Perona's shocked!!!

★ Lun the Machete, guard of Structure B
★ Dorry's broken sword
★ Bubbling cauldron♪
★ The syrup stuck to Nami's body
★ Makino's baby
★ The fish in the lunch young Sanji made for his mother

★ #192 Kid wearing a Kuma shirt
★ #218 Minatomo the Carpenter
★ #259 The eggplant guard who slept in Sanji's bed on Whole Cake Island

Beware of Seduction! The Seven Babelords

Can't help but gaze at this bevy of beauties! Which one did you go Love-Love over?♥

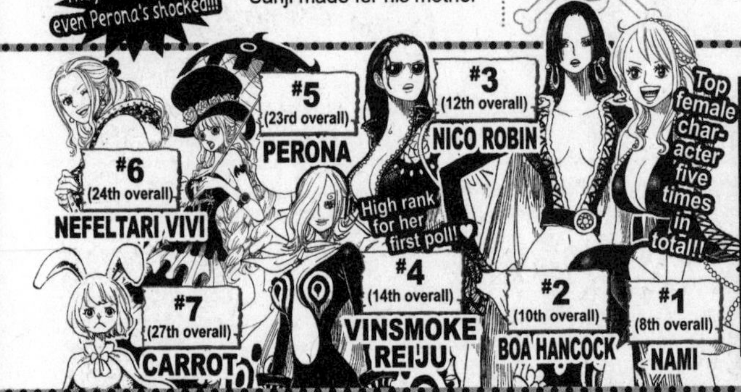
#1 (8th overall) NAMI
#2 (10th overall) BOA HANCOCK
#3 (12th overall) NICO ROBIN
#4 (14th overall) VINSMOKE REIJU
#5 (23rd overall) PERONA
#6 (24th overall) NEFELTARI VIVI
#7 (27th overall) CARROT
Top female character five times in total!!
High rank for her first poll!♥

Don't disrespect their wisdom!! The Seven Haglords

Here's a collection of our seniors, rich in the joys and sorrows of life!!

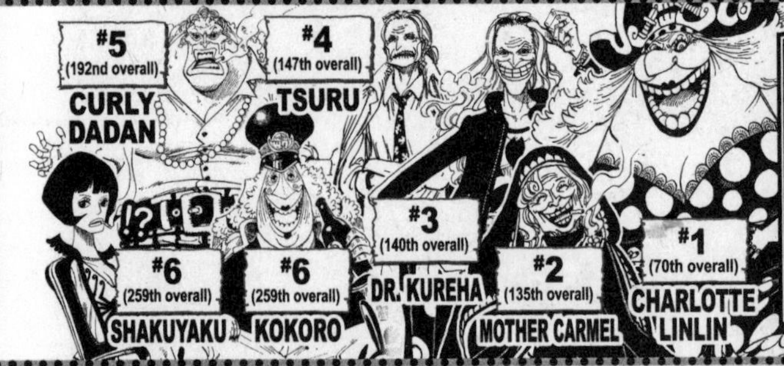
#1 (70th overall) CHARLOTTE LINLIN
#2 (135th overall) MOTHER CARMEL
#3 (140th overall) DR. KUREHA
#4 (147th overall) TSURU
#5 (192nd overall) CURLY DADAN
#6 (259th overall) KOKORO
#6 (259th overall) SHAKUYAKU

20th SPECIAL COLUMN

To celebrate the 20th anniversary, let's look at the historical 20th rankers!!

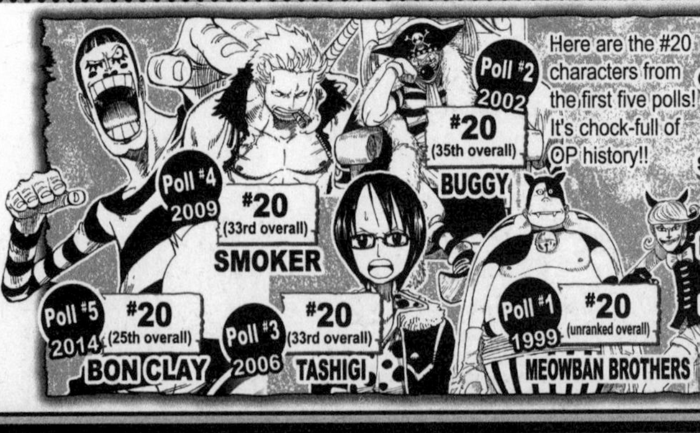
Here are the #20 characters from the first five polls! It's chock-full of OP history!!
Poll #1 1999 #20 (unranked overall) MEOWBAN BROTHERS
Poll #2 2002 #20 (35th overall) BUGGY
Poll #3 2006 #20 (33rd overall) TASHIGI
Poll #4 2009 #20 (33rd overall) SMOKER
Poll #5 2014 #20 (25th overall) BON CLAY

The 6th ONE PIECE CHARACTER

Top 5 Whole Cake Island Ranking

High-impact characters!! They haven't been around long, but they've captured our hearts!!

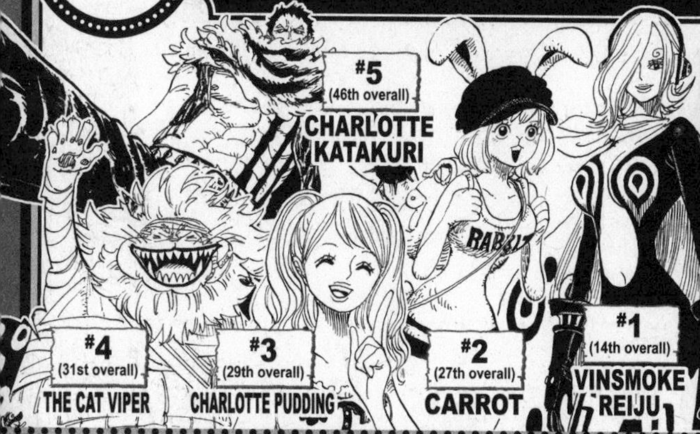

#1 (14th overall) VINSMOKE REIJU
#2 (27th overall) CARROT
#3 (29th overall) CHARLOTTE PUDDING
#4 (31st overall) THE CAT VIPER
#5 (46th overall) CHARLOTTE KATAKURI
RABBIT

Top 5 Straw Hat Fleet Ranking

Even Bartolomeo's stunned by Cavendish's rise!!

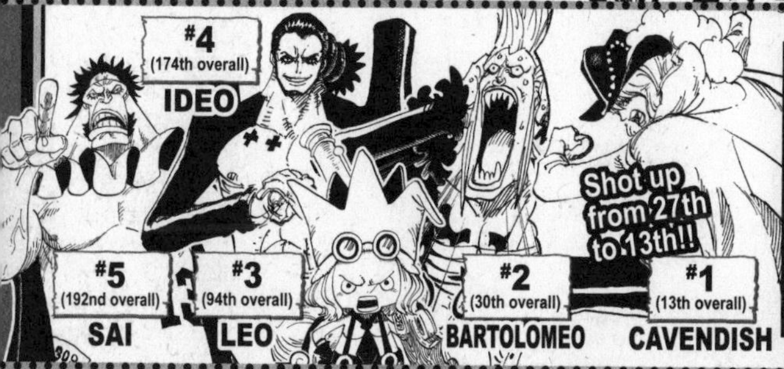

Shot up from 27th to 13th!!
#1 (13th overall) CAVENDISH
#2 (30th overall) BARTOLOMEO
#3 (94th overall) LEO
#4 (174th overall) IDEO
#5 (192nd overall) SAI

Top 5 Charlotte Family Ranking

Sanji's fiancée Pudding muscles Big Mom and the Sweet 3 out of the way!!

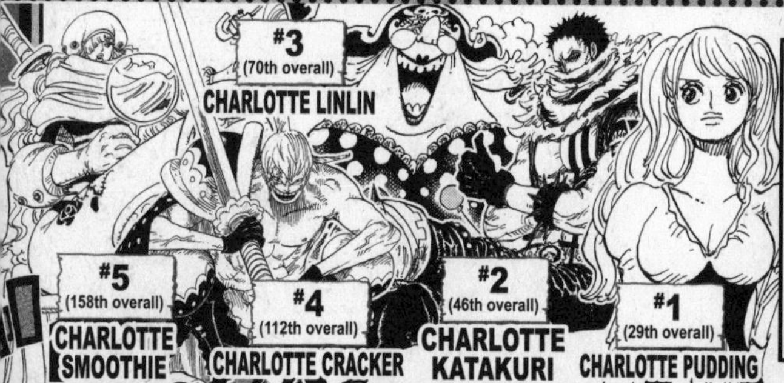

#1 (29th overall) CHARLOTTE PUDDING
#2 (46th overall) CHARLOTTE KATAKURI
#3 (70th overall) CHARLOTTE LINLIN
#4 (112th overall) CHARLOTTE CRACKER
#5 (158th overall) CHARLOTTE SMOOTHIE

One Piece grows along with its readers!! See you in the 7th character poll!!

Thanks to everyone who voted!!

COMING NEXT VOLUME:

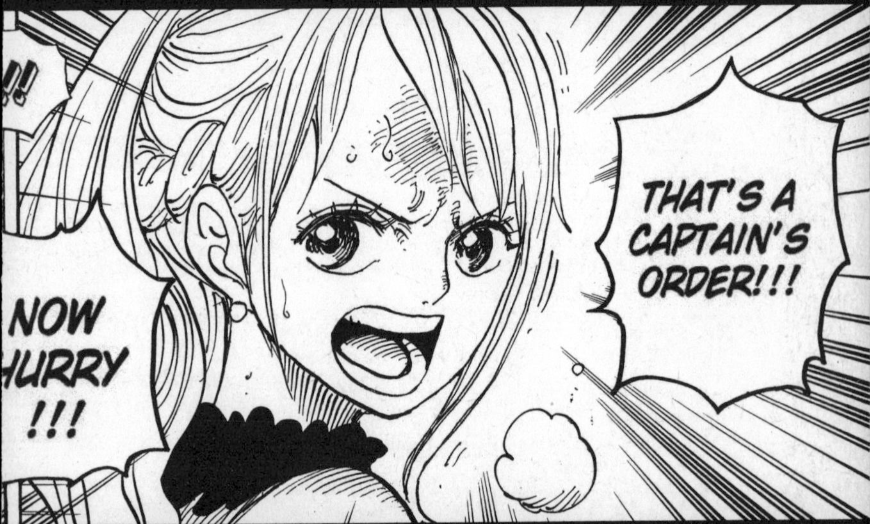
THAT'S A CAPTAIN'S ORDER!!!
NOW HURRY !!!

Luffy finds himself up against his strongest enemy yet in Katakuri. And this foe has very similar powers to Luffy's own. Can rubber beat mochi?! Meanwhile, the other Straw Hats try to escape by sea. But with Big Mom on the chase, things do not look good...

ON SALE NOVEMBER 2018!

ONE PIECE VOL. 87
NEW WORLD PART 27

SHONEN JUMP Manga Edition

STORY AND ART BY EIICHIRO ODA

Translation/Stephen Paul
Touch-up Art & Lettering/Vanessa Satone
Design/Yukiko Whitley
Editor/Alexis Kirsch

Printed in the U.S.A.

Published by VIZ Media, LLC
P.O. Box 77010
San Francisco, CA 94107

10 9 8 7 6 5 4 3 2 1
First printing, August 2018

VIZ MEDIA
viz.com

SHONEN JUMP
shonenjump.com

RATED T TEEN
ratings.viz.com

PARENTAL ADVISORY
ONE PIECE is rated T for Teen and is recommended for ages 13 and up. This volume contains fantasy violence and violence and tabacco usage.

You're Reading in the Wrong Direction!!

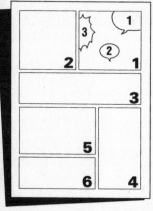

Whoops! Guess what? You're starting at the wrong end of the comic!

...It's true! In keeping with the original Japanese format, **One Piece** is meant to be read from right to left, starting in the upper-right corner.

Unlike English, which is read from left to right, Japanese is read from right to left, meaning that action, sound effects and word-balloon order are completely reversed...something which can make readers unfamiliar with Japanese feel pretty backwards themselves. For this reason, manga or Japanese comics published in the U.S. in English have sometimes been published "flopped"— that is, printed in exact reverse order, as though seen from the other side of a mirror.

By flopping pages, U.S. publishers can avoid confusing readers, but the compromise is not without its downside. For one thing, a character in a flopped manga series who once wore in the original Japanese version a T-shirt emblazoned with "M A Y" (as in "the merry month of") now wears one which reads "Y A M"! Additionally, many manga creators in Japan are themselves unhappy with the process, as some feel the mirror-imaging of their art skews their original intentions.

We are proud to bring you Eiichiro Oda's **One Piece** in the original unflopped format. For now, though, turn to the other side of the book and let the journey begin...!

—Editor